AMERICAN LEADERSHIP
in World Affairs

D1364214

AMERICAN LEADERSHIP
in World Affairs
Vietnam and the breakdown of consensus

Ole R. Holsti and **James N. Rosenau**
Duke University   *University of Southern California*

Boston
ALLEN & UNWIN
London   Sydney

George Allen & Unwin (Publishers) Ltd,
40 Museum Street, London WC1A 1LU, UK

George Allen & Unwin (Publishers) Ltd,
Park Lane, Hemel Hempstead, Herts HP2 4TE, UK

Allen & Unwin, Inc.,
9 Winchester Terrace, Winchester, Mass. 01890, USA

George Allen & Unwin Australia Pty Ltd,
8 Napier Street, North Sydney, NSW 2060, Australia

First published in 1984

Library of Congress Cataloging in Publication Data

Holsti, Ole R.
    American leadership in world affairs.
Includes index.
1. United States—Foreign relations—1969–1974.
2. United States—Foreign relations—1974–1977. 3. United
States—Foreign relations—1977–1981. 4. Vietnamese
Conflict, 1961–1975—Influence. I. Rosenau, James N.
II Title.
E855.H63   1984   327.73   83–22337
ISBN 0-04-355019-3
ISBN 0-04-355020-7 (pbk.)

British Library Cataloguing in Publication Data

Holsti, Ole R.
    American leadership in world affairs.
1. United States—Foreign relations—1945–
I. Title   II. Rosenau, James N.
327.73   E744
ISBN 0-04-355019-3
ISBN 0-04-355020-7 Pbk

Set in 10 on 11 pt Melior by
D. P. Media Limited, Hitchin, Hertfordshire
and printed in the United States of America

For Maija and Heidi, with Love

Contents

List of Tables

Preface

When he replaced Richard Nixon in the White House, Gerald Ford proclaimed the end of the "long national nightmare" of Watergate. Ford expressed similar sentiments some months later when Hanoi's conquest of South Vietnam ended the nightmare of Vietnam for the United States, if not for those that American policy had been intended to protect.

Almost a decade later it seems clear that although the departure of Richard Nixon from the White House and of Americans from Vietnam may have been necessary to repair what was torn asunder by Watergate and Vietnam, they were not sufficient. None of the subsequent administrations has been able to forge an effective foreign policy consensus. The gap between the magnitude of problems and the efficacy of responses stems in part from deep domestic cleavages, not only on what those responses should be, but even on diagnoses of the problems themselves. Divisions reach into the top levels of government. Evidence of confusion in Washington has reached massive proportions. During 1983 three Cabinet officers resigned and the chief of the White House staff called for the departure of another; the Director of the Arms Control Agency and the chief negotiator on Mutual and Balanced Force Reduction talks were fired; State Department and Foreign Service personnel responsible for policy toward El Salvador were purged; the third National Security Adviser in less than three years took office; the dispatch of Marines to Lebanon and Grenada gave rise to disputes about the meaning of the War Powers Act; and the President's closest allies in the Senate used such terms as "frightening" to describe the budgetary consequences of the Administration's two primary programs—lower taxes and higher defense spending. The President offers periodic assurances that only "staying the course" will ensure better days, but America's allies, and perhaps adversaries as well, search for some bedrock of coherence beneath the quicksand of confusion.

But one should be cautious about leaping to the conclusion that these difficulties merely stem from unique deficiencies of the Reagan Administration. The opposition Democrats have demonstrated neither greater unity nor notably creative solutions to these problems. More generally, the sources of difficulties appear to be more fundamental than the leadership abilities of this leader or that party. Indeed, the present study originated in the suspicion that the effects of the Vietnam War would persist well beyond the liquidation of that undertaking. That Americans were divided during the war itself is no secret. That long after its conclusion the war would continue to divide Americans—specifically, because it would serve as the source of quite divergent "lessons" that would be offered as prescriptions to guide the future conduct of the nation's foreign policy—was far from self-evident in 1975. However, it seemed sufficiently plausible that Vietnam would be no less significant than the Munich Conference of 1938 as a source of "lessons" to warrant initiating a long-term project to assess the impact of the war, not only during the immediate aftermath of the conquest of Saigon, but also after other issues, crises, and conflicts had replaced Vietnam on the front pages of newspapers and as lead stories on television news. Evidence presented here offers substantial confirmation that the impact of the war has persisted.

This study explores only one facet of American foreign policy—the manner in which individuals occupying leadership positions in a broad range of public and private institutions perceived and evaluated that policy during two recent Presidential election years, 1976 and 1980. It is, therefore, neither a full-scale examination of foreign policy during the past decade, nor even a comprehensive analysis of its domestic sources. Thus, the reader will not find exhaustive discussions of the pressures and constraints within the international and domestic arenas, nor of all the ways by which these make themselves felt or ignored in the foreign policy process.

The focus here is on how individual leaders perceive and evaluate international relations and American foreign policy. These perceptions and evaluations are part—but only a part—of the dynamics through which the United States formulates a response to the challenges and opportunities that mark contemporary world affairs.[1] Stated differently, the foreign policy perceptions, beliefs systems, and orientations of American leaders are central to the role played by the United States in the world, but the present study does not seek to elaborate how and why this is the case. Discussion of the processes whereby the values and beliefs of leaders are aggregated—through public pressures, lobbying, polls, leadership interactions, policy-making processes and the like—and thereby transformed into the broader patterns and institutions through which foreign policy is framed and executed, is deferred for another time.

Similarly, this study does not trace in detail recent changes and continuities in the international arena that offer challenges and opportunities for American foreign policy. International developments are the raw materials on which foreign policy belief systems are nourished, taking note of them, defining them, assessing their implications, and then processing them so that they take on coherence and meaning. Leaders may see and interpret the same events quite differently, but an understanding of these differences depends on comprehension of external affairs as well as the values and beliefs that leaders bring to bear on them. However, a detailed analysis of the global arena is also beyond the scope of the present study. Suffice it to say that a lengthening list of often seemingly intractable problems both at home and abroad poses important and troubling questions about the nation's capacity to cope with them. The international and domestic arenas are marked by challenges to existing institutions and processes, turmoil, and disarray.[2] The data presented here may raise some sobering questions about whether the United States is capable of reducing, much less managing, global tensions. But it must be repeated that what follows tells only part of the full story—that part where the perceptions, memories, and belief systems of leaders are important.

During the course of this study we have become indebted to many persons and institutions. We wish to express our deep gratitude, while absolving them from responsibility for any shortcomings of the study. Financial support for the 1976 survey was provided by the Duke University Research Council and the Institute for Transnational Studies at the University of Southern California. The 1980 survey received support from the National Science Foundation (Grant No, SOC 79-13977) as well as Duke University and USC. Data analyses were assisted by grants from the Duke University Computer Center. A generous Guggenheim Fellowship and sabbatical leave from Duke University permitted one of the authors to have a full year for writing free from other responsibilities.

Others have helped in many ways. We received helpful comments and suggestions on early drafts of the questionnaire from Andrew Scott, Lancelot Farrar, Hugh Hall, Allan Kornberg, Charles Hermann, Arturo Valenzuela, Lester Salamon, William Mishler, Bruce Russett, Peter Grothe, and Wilburn Blount. Sidney Verba and Donald Ferree helped to coordinate this study with their own elite survey, and Verba made possible co-sponsorship of the project by the Harvard Center for International Affairs. That professional military officers attending military colleges could be included in these surveys was largely due to the invaluable assistance of Professor Edward Laurance, General Robert Gard, and Admiral John C. Barrow.

The great bulk of computer programming assistance was provided by Daniel Harkins, with additional contributions from Tom Johnson and Roy Behr. Others who helped with sampling, coding, and other research tasks are Linda Ram, Joan Campbell, Robert Kolin, Sarah Crenshaw, Antony Burt, Eric Holsti, Cynthia Moore, Jill Chen, Evelyn Davidheiser, Karin Temple, Maija Holsti, Ivy Berg, Alison Bouchard, Robert Buschman, Ellen Hill, Kevin Mallory, Hudson Meadwell, Katherine Peyton, Jennifer Ziska, Edwin McClain, Mark Casciari, Brenda Funches, Raymond Lavine, Hugo Orozco, Elisa Hubbard, Bruce Smith, Cindy Gail Abrams, Jim Wolfe, Gary Gartin, Heidi Rosenau, Lisa Clark, Craig Etcheson, David Marr, Elizabeth Nelson, Julie Thomas, Bob Boydston, Paul Casey, Jeannie Galloway, Tram Hoang, Herbert Krotinger, Timothy O'Brien, William Parker, and Maye Sutherland.

We received useful comments and suggestions on parts or all of an early draft of the manuscript from Alexander L. George, Robert Jervis, Charles Kegley, Bruce Kuniholm and Bruce Russett. Many other colleagues have offered helpful ideas at various conferences and lectures at which some of the ideas and data have been presented during the past few years.

Special mention must be made of the superb secretarial assistance from Alice Dorman, Peggy Alan, Gillian Cockerill, Barbara Wright, Kay Neves, and Carole Gustin. Their skills and diligence have been indispensable to every stage of the project.

At least a small note of thanks should be offered to Apple II+ computer, serial number 036975, in whose chips, circuits, and disks this book took its original form. The apple may be a symbol of man's fall from grace, but any author whose primary tools once included scissors and quarts of rubber cement must be grateful for affordable word processing equipment.

Finally, we are deeply indebted to the thousands of American leaders who took time from their busy schedules to fill out lengthy questionnaires. Without their cooperation this study would not have been possible.

Notes to Preface

1 A focus on leadership beliefs does not imply a dismissal of public opinion as irrelevant to foreign policy. It merely reflects the view that others have adequately traced out and analyzed continuities and changes in public views on foreign affairs, whereas leadership views have received far less systematic attention. In any case, only organizations with resources far in excess of those available to the present authors can hope to undertake reliable sample surveys of the public.

2 Although we are aware of the complex relationships between domestic and foreign policy, the present study focuses solely on the latter. However, a planned extension of this research will involve a leadership survey that touches upon both external and domestic issues.

1
Beneath the Flaps, Flips and Flops of American Foreign Policy

On 25 June 1982, Alexander Haig stunned the nation by announcing his resignation as Secretary of State. Two years earlier, Cyrus Vance had taken the same dramatic step in the wake of the failed mission to rescue American hostages in Iran. Were these merely the actions of principled (or impetuous) officials, the origins and consequences of which are more likely to interest the biographer than the foreign policy analyst? Should one therefore look for explanations in the ambitions, temperaments, and personalities of the central characters? Alternatively, were they perhaps symptoms of broader problems in contemporary American foreign policy—a lack of constancy, coherence, and direction? Might their sudden resignations thus be indicators of more basic difficulties that, in important respects, have led the United States to resemble a ship that has lost not only its rudder but its compass as well?

Recall that between Harry S. Truman's inauguration in 1949 and Richard Nixon's in 1969, only four men served as Secretary of State, and the number would have been three but for the cancer that forced John Foster Dulles's replacement by Christian Herter in 1959. Moreover, although those two decades included both Democratic and Republican administrations, Dean Acheson, Dulles, Herter, and Dean Rusk shared beliefs on most fundamental premises of American foreign policy—what critics sometimes called the "eastern internationalist establishment" viewpoint. Their long tenures in office and the basic continuity of policy were sustained by and reflected a broad foreign policy consensus that had emerged from America's experiences during World War II and the Cold War. That consensus survived until the Vietnam War.

In contrast, when he took the oath of office, George Shultz became the fourth Secretary of State in less than thirty months. It would be understating the case, moreover, to say that Vance, Edmund Muskie, Haig, and Shultz adhered to rather divergent visions of the world and of the appropriate American role in it. More importantly, this rapid turnover in the top echelons of the foreign policy hierarchy appears to be a symptom of a more fundamental problem. Perhaps the only constancy in American foreign policy since the Vietnam War has been the conspicuous lack of constancy in its conduct. Reversals of course, changes in priorities, wavering purposes, major ambassadorships and other important positions that remain unfilled owing to ideological conflicts within the government, overnight shifts of votes in the United Nations, disputes over who speaks for the President, State–Defense rivalries, bruising battles in the Senate over the Panama Canal Treaties and the sale of AWACS aircraft to Saudi Arabia—these have been the norm rather than the exception during the post-Vietnam years.

Why has consistency in foreign affairs eluded Republicans and Democrats alike? Why has a widely recognized need to achieve greater unity of purpose and action not reversed the tendencies toward disunity and disarray? Answers to these questions abound. Some point to a lack of experience or competence among those responsible for the conduct of foreign affairs as the causes of inconsistencies and contradictions. United Nations Ambassador Jeane Kirkpatrick, an articulate neo-conservative, denounced the foreign policy processes within the Reagan Administration in terms that went well beyond what one might expect from an attack by the opposition party on the hustings.[1] Others attribute the lack of effective policy-making to personality conflicts and endemic bureaucratic clashes. Still others contend that deeper cleavages in American society infuse uncertainty and vacillation into its foreign policies.

Each of these lines of reasoning can and has been answered with counter-arguments, and none of them appears to offer a complete explanation for recent difficulties. The lack-of-experience and clash-of-personality theses lose some potency when one recalls many past instances when the nation's foreign policy was effective despite the participation of inexperienced and abrasive officials. Consider the Truman years, a period when both innovation and constancy marked the conduct of external affairs despite the President's lack of foreign policy experience, and even though Dean Acheson and Louis Johnson clashed continuously.

The thesis that more basic cleavages underlie vacillating policies have also elicited rebuttals. Spokesmen for the Ford, Carter, and Reagan administrations have not been reticent about proclaiming the existence of a new foreign policy consensus, whether arising from the American withdrawal from Vietnam, the hostage crisis in Iran, or the 1980 elections. Yet there are also indications that such assertions, as well as pronouncements on the demise of "the Vietnam syndrome," may have been premature. Debates over Angola, SALT II, the Panama Canal, El Salvador, the nuclear freeze, the Siberian gas pipeline, the MX missile, Lebanon and other issues offer little testimony of widespread agreement.

Thus, although a number of factors have no doubt contributed to the persistent lack of coherence and consistency in American foreign policy, the absence of an underlying consensus would appear to be a major source of the problem. This book seeks to describe the ways in which Americans, and especially their leaders, remain profoundly divided in their answers to the fundamental questions that guide the nation's external relations: What is the nature of the international system? What is the proper definition of national security, and whence the primary threats to it? What are desirable and feasible goals of foreign policy? What instruments, strategies, and tactics constitute appropriate means in the pursuit of external goals? The search for answers to these and related questions cannot proceed without taking into account the Vietnam War and its impact on American beliefs about foreign affairs.

The Lessons of Vietnam and the Uses of History

As the South Vietnamese regime was collapsing before a full-scale invasion by North Vietnam in the spring of 1975, Secretary of State Henry Kissinger asserted: "The Vietnam debate has now run its course."[2] A few weeks later, at a news conference, President Gerald Ford was asked about the lessons that Americans should draw from the experience in Vietnam. He replied that there was little point in pursuing the matter in detail because: "The lessons of the past in Vietnam have been learned—learned by Presidents, learned by Congress, learned by the American people." At other times the President stated that the war "is finished as far as America is concerned," and that the final withdrawal from the besieged city of Saigon "closes a chapter in the American experience."[3]

These assertions may have seemed startling in the light of many earlier predictions by the President and Secretary of State that American acquiescence in the conquest of South Vietnam would give rise to disastrous consequences, both abroad, in accordance with predictions of the "domino theory," and at home, in the form of a right-wing backlash against all who were deemed responsible. Also evident in these assertions were some premises about the impact of the past on the present and future; for example, that Americans would feel no compulsion to look back at the Vietnam War—the longest in the nation's history and the most divisive since the Civil War—to ask some basic questions: "How did we become involved?" "Why?" "What went wrong?" "How can we avoid such disasters in the future?" Alternatively, they were assuming that those who could not resist the temptation to conduct post-mortems on the war would find that the answers to such questions were sufficiently self-evident to promote agreement rather than to prolong dissensus. Thus, both Ford and Kissinger seemed to be predicting that, after a decade of deep domestic divisions, a new foreign policy consensus would emerge, either from collective amnesia about the war, or from a broadly shared understanding of the "lessons of Vietnam."

Were these realistic premises? Is it possible to wipe the slate clean on a long and traumatic experience, or is there a powerful tendency to look back at it, sifting through the evidence with a view to averting a repetition of its mistakes? Do complex events so readily yield "lessons" that most reasonable persons will agree on their substance and scope, or is history a grab-bag in which one may readily find evidence to buttress virtually any preferred policy? These are interesting and important questions that have long engaged historians, philosophers, statesmen, and many others. Before assessing further the long-range impact of Vietnam, a brief discussion of more general issues relating to uses of the past is in order.

Whether useful guidelines can be adduced from history has, to understate the point, brought forth diverse responses from those who have pondered the appropriate uses of the past. Santayana's widely cited aphorism, that those who are unable to learn from history are doomed to repeat it, is more quotable than useful. It provides no more direct guidance on the issue than Henry Ford's equally familiar observation that "history is bunk." Nor is it self-evidently more valid than the dictum that "Those who remember the past are condemned to make the opposite mistake."[4] Noted philosophers and historians can be cited in support of virtually any position on this issue.[5]

There has been growing recognition, however, that the familiar query, "What can or should we learn from history?" may not necessarily be the only relevant question. Disagreement among philosophers of history notwithstanding, there is mounting evidence that perceived historical analogies and projections from the past often play an important part in policy decisions.[6] As one observer has put it, "History does not repeat itself in the real world but it does repeat itself in the 'reality world' of the mind."[7]

History may have an impact on policy-making as one of several strategies for coping with such constraints on rational choice as cognitive complexity, pre-decisional stress, and uncertainty. One may use historical models, analogies, and projections, both to diagnose situations and to prescribe policies.[8] There is at least anecdotal evidence that the propensity to seek guidance from the past is rather widespread, involving "lessons" about policy-making processes, diagnoses of the adversary's ambitions and ways of countering them, sequences of events in historical development, and strategies that both succeed and fail. Several familiar episodes illustrate the diverse ways that history has been used, with better or worse consequences, as a guide to the present and the future.

• A vivid example may be found in Harry Truman's diagnosis of the North Korean invasion of South Korea in 1950 as a case of international aggression, essentially similar in its broader global implications to the Japanese, Italian, and Nazi aggressions during the 1930s and 1940s. Truman learned of the North Korean attack while in Independence, Missouri. During the flight back to Washington, he recalled:

In my generation, this was not the first occasion when the strong attacked the weak. I recalled some earlier instances: Manchuria, Ethiopia, Austria. I remembered how each time that the democracies failed to act it encouraged the aggressors to keep going ahead. Communism was acting in Korea just as Hitler, Mussolini, and the Japanese had acted ten, fifteen and twenty years earlier. I felt certain that if South Korea was allowed to fall Communist leaders would be emboldened to override nations closer to our shores. If the Communists were permitted to force their way into the Republic of Korea without opposition from the free world, no small nation would have the courage to resist threats and aggression by stronger Communist neighbors. If this was allowed to go unchallenged it would mean a third world war, just as similar incidents had brought on the second world war.[9]

Truman was convinced that in the study of the past one could discover useful guidelines for improving the present conduct of policy, and the responses of his Administration to the Korean invasion were consistent with lessons that he believed could be drawn from the experiences of the 1930s. As a long-time student of history he was perhaps more likely than most to see parallels between contemporary and past events, but there is substantial evidence that Truman was far from unique in this respect.

• One of Dean Acheson's biographers wrote that the "image of Hitler seared itself on the eyes of all who fought him."[10] Hitler had a deep impact on Anthony Eden, who resigned from the British Cabinet in 1938 to protest British appeasement of Hitler's ally, Mussolini. This decision proved to be a milestone in Eden's career when later events demonstrated that his skeptical views of the Fuehrer's ultimate ambitions were far more accurate than those espoused by the majority of Neville Chamberlain's government. As Prime Minister himself in 1956, Eden diagnosed the policies of Egyptian President Nasser in the light of Hitler and lessons about the futility of appeasing dictators:

It is important to reduce the stature of the megalomaniacal dictator at an early stage. A check to Hitler when he moved to reoccupy the Rhineland would not have destroyed him, but would have made him pause . . . Nowadays it is considered immoral to recognize an enemy. Some say that Nasser is no Hitler or Mussolini. I am not so sure. He has followed Hitler's pattern, even to concentration camps and the propagation of Mein Kampf among his officers. He has understood and used the Goebbels pattern of propaganda in all its lying ruthlessness. Egypt's strategic position increases the threat to others from any aggressive militant dictatorship there.[11]

Eden thus supported the disastrous Suez invasion that was intended to topple Nasser. The aborted invasion in fact had some quite unintended consequences, among them, ironically, the termination of Eden's own political career.

• The impact of Hitler on his opponents was also reflected in important elements of post-war American diplomacy. The United States did not participate in the 1938 Munich Conference that later became the symbol of misguided efforts to avert war by giving in to Hitler's territorial demands, but the experience of having to fight Nazi Germany after the failures of appeasement surely made many Americans more sensitive to the "lessons of Munich" concerning the dangers of permitting aggression by major powers to pass unchallenged. These lessons were deemed to be equally applicable to the problem of Soviet expansion after the war. Hitler and Stalin were both ruthless dictators who adhered to expansionist ideologies, and Nazi Germany and Soviet Russia were both model totalitarian regimes. These similarities seemed to heighten the relevance of the Munich analogy, even for many who had been outspoken isolationists prior to Pearl Harbor.[12]

• A successful example of "learning from history" may be found in the ways that Presidents Woodrow Wilson and Franklin Roosevelt handled the task of bringing the United States into post-war international organizations. Wilson's failure to include influential Republicans on the American delegation to the Paris Peace Conference after World War I was widely regarded as a major political blunder that contributed to ultimate Senate rejection of the Versailles Treaty and, with it, the League of Nations. Roosevelt, who had served in the Wilson Administration, took great care during World War II to solicit the advice and assistance of some leading Republicans in a successful effort to prevent the question of American participation in the United Nations from becoming a partisan issue. Moreover, whereas during the closing days of the 1918 Congressional elections Wilson seemed to link the League of Nations issue to the electoral fortunes of Democratic candidates, Roosevelt joined Thomas Dewey, his Republican opponent in 1944, in an agreement that placed the issue of American participation in the United Nations outside the realm of partisan debate.

• A lesson of history also provides a link between the termination of the two world wars. The armistice that ended World War I came into effect with German armies still deployed on French soil. Some observers believed that this fact enhanced Hitler's ability to make effective political use of the myth that Germany was "stabbed in the back" by Jews and capitalists at home, rather than defeated by Allied armies on the battlefield. In part to avoid the emergence of similar myths within the defeated Axis nations after World War II, the Allied leaders agreed that Germany and Japan would be required to surrender unconditionally.

• In assessing the outlook for the Portuguese regime that emerged after the revolution of 1974, Secretary of State Kissinger apparently concluded that the provisional government in Lisbon would suffer the same fate as the Kerensky government that had succeeded the overthrow of the tsarist regime in Russia. In a conversation with the Portuguese Socialist leader, Mario Soares, he warned: "You [Soares] are a Kerensky . . . I believe your sincerity, but you are naive." To Soares's rejoinder, "I certainly don't want to be a Kerensky," the Secretary of State replied, "Neither did Kerensky."[13] For a period, Kissinger's policy towards the new regime in Portugal was in fact consistent with the pessimistic theory that a Communist dictatorship would ultimately be established in Lisbon, following the same pattern as events in St Petersburg fifty-eight years earlier.

• After faulty advice from the Central Intelligence Agency regarding the feasibility of a successful invasion of Cuba in 1961, President Kennedy was somewhat skeptical about the validity of advice from that source. He let it be known during the following months that he did not welcome certain types of intelligence assessments about Cuba. Because he gave a cold reception to CIA Director John McCone's suspicions about Soviet deployment of offensive missiles in Cuba, that agency was reluctant to distribute further telegrams on the topic from the honeymooning McCone—reports that turned out to be accurate.[14]

• The outbreak of World War I was preceded by arms races involving most of the major European powers, including Great Britain. From this sequence of events some deduced the lesson that arms races cause wars. During the 1930s, it became a virtually unquestioned axiom among members of the British Labour Party that increasing British armaments would be a major step toward another war, even though there was already ample evidence that Nazi Germany was engaged in a full-scale rearmament program. However, others who had lived through the pre-World War I period adduced quite different lessons from the same events, or they looked back to other analogies for policy guidance. Winston Churchill, for example, argued that Hitler should be viewed as another Napoleon, a leader determined to overthrow the existing international order, rather than as just a misguided German nationalist. As a consequence, he favored policies diametrically opposed to those who regarded arms races as the primary threat to European peace.

These illustrations constitute neither a full discussion of, nor systematic evidence on, the uses and misuses of history in policy-making. Although they do not provide an adequate basis for predicting how the Vietnam experience is likely to affect policy choices, they suggest that an understanding of the future course of American foreign policy may require taking into account the impact of the Vietnam War on those who are most likely to have direct or indirect influence on the nation's external relations. Several generalizations relevant to the ensuing analysis may be drawn from the foregoing examples.

The propensity to rely upon the lessons of history as a strategy for coping with the complexities and uncertainties that are often an integral part of foreign affairs is rather widespread. There are, of course, other available strategies, including relying on consensus politics, contingencies plans, and standard operating procedures; avoiding value trade-offs; looking to ideology for guidance; limiting choices to incremental changes from existing policies, and the like. Nevertheless, the practice of looking to history for policy guidance is by no means limited to policy-makers who are also professional students of history (for example, Henry Kissinger), part-time historians (for example, Winston Churchill), or avid readers of history who are convinced that the record of the past contains valuable guidelines for coping with contemporary policy issues (for example, Harry S. Truman). Of special interest for students of foreign policy is the finding that in stressful situations such as crises, one is more likely to rely upon past experience as a guide to policy making.[15]

Some observers have noted that Americans are almost uniquely ahistorical in their approach to international affairs.[16] Others have suggested that an inability to understand the central role of history in Vietnamese life contributed importantly to policies that failed in Southeast Asia.[17] It may be true that Americans tend to have a limited knowledge of, or interest in, the history of others, but it does not therefore follow that elements of historical thinking fail to have a significant impact on the formulation of foreign policy. Indeed, it may be those with an inadequate understanding or appreciation of history in the broadest sense who will, because of their rather limited repertory of historical analogies, be especially prone to using lessons of the past in ways that detract from rather than enhance effective policy analysis.

An inadequate understanding of history can result in costly policy errors, but it does not therefore follow that the introduction of historical thinking into policy deliberations will necessarily improve the quality of either the decision-making process or the resulting choices. De Tocqueville's warning that misapplied lessons from history may be more dangerous than ignorance of the past has not lost its relevance, because policy-makers (and others) often use history less well than they might.[18] A view of history as a readily accessible source of decision rules, unaccompanied by an adequate appreciation of the many reasons that might render invalid parallels between the past and the present, may result in policies that are as inappropriate as decisions based on ignorance of history. Historical analogies may be selected without sufficient awareness that almost certainly one could have found other episodes that would have supported the opposite diagnosis or prescription. Only careful analysis enables one to distinguish genuine historical parallels from false ones, but the analogies may become substitutes for adequate diagnosis, search, and analysis—the very processes that are necessary to appraise the most salient attributes of the situation, to search for alternative historical models, and to analyze the parallels between past experience and the present situation. The choice of a historical analogy often occurs before rather than after the analysis that might reveal its validity, and premature fixation on a particular historical precedent can attenuate, or even eliminate, the search and analysis activities that are necessary to determine which past episodes, if any, might appropriately serve as a model for the present situation.[19] Evidence about the potential dangers of applying the past to present situations is not limited to anecdotes from foreign policy cases. Experimental research has demonstrated that misapplication or overgeneralization of past experience is a primary source of poor-quality decisions.[20]

Some types of historical episodes are especially likely to live on in the "reality world of the mind." Conversely, such episodes may frequently be cited as providing "lessons" because they appear to sustain one's policy predispositions. Such traumatic events as the outbreak of World War I and the failures of British and French efforts during the 1930s to forestall World War II by attempting to satisfy Hitler's demands are among the disasters that continue to be viewed or seized upon as relevant sources of guidance for contemporary international issues. Post-détente debates on Soviet–American relations, for example, have frequently focused on the perceived parallels between the "present danger" and the periods immediately preceding the outbreak of the two world wars. According to some analysts, there are several ominous similarities between 1914 and the present, including uncontrolled arms races, ageing and only modestly competent leaders in major world capitals, and a growing sense of frustration arising from seemingly intractable domestic and international problems; the danger is that the superpowers will stumble blindly into a catastrophic war that, as in 1914, no one really wanted. Another group has identified highly disturbing similarities between the present and 1938–9, including a dramatic arms build-up by a major power determined to transform the fundamental structure of the international system, combined with unwarranted complacency and/or defeatism on the part of the Western democracies. The real danger, according to proponents of this position, is that growing military imbalances may tempt the Soviet Union into adventures that would lead either to Western capitulation (as in 1938) or to another world war (as in 1939). For example, according to Eugene V. Rostow, former director of the Arms Control and Disarmament Agency: "Our posture today is comparable to that of Britain, France and the United States during the 30s. Whether we are at the Rhineland or Munich watershed remains to be seen."[21]

Events that have been experienced first hand, especially during the impressionistic years that one comes to political maturity, may also be prominent candidates from which lessons may be adduced. This implies the hypothesis that one's generation may significantly influence the selection of events from which to draw lessons.[22] The proposition that foreign policy debates in this country reflect differences in the world-views of the "Munich generation" and the "Vietnam generation" has gained some currency in recent years. This thesis is examined in more detail in Chapters 5 and 6.

A particularly dramatic or traumatic event may indeed be the crucial formative episode for those who experience it directly, but it does not therefore follow that all who do so will interpret its significance in an identical manner. This proposition will hardly surprise those who have pondered the cycle of interpretations, revisions, and counter-revisions that follow so many important events. Even the crisis preceding the outbreak of World War I in 1914, an event for which the documentation is almost uniquely rich and complete, continues to yield quite divergent lessons to those who have analysed its records for guidance on crisis management and related topics. One's ideological or other predispositions are likely to affect the interpretation of and selection of "lessons" from particular events.

The Lessons of Vietnam: The Continuing Debate

Whether and to what extent the impact of the Vietnam War has persisted and whether it has also given rise to divergent interpretations and lessons are complex questions. An impressionistic review of debates during the 1970s and 1980s involving American policies in Korea, the Middle East, Angola, and El Salvador, may provide some initial clues to the answers.

Fears that South Korea might again be invaded from the north coincided with the evacuation of Americans from Saigon during the spring of 1975. In the light of the then-recent denouement in Southeast Asia, it is not surprising that speculation about the appropriate American response revealed a striking lack of consensus. Policy recommendations ranged from maintaining the status quo under terms of the security agreement with South Korea, to immediate withdrawal of American forces. Whatever their substance, however, the recommendations often shared one attribute: many participants in the debates on the issue invoked "the lessons of Vietnam" to sustain their policy preferences. Supporters of the American defense commitment to Seoul asserted that the defeat in Vietnam was already threatening to have the outcomes predicted by the "domino theory," as American credibility was declining in Thailand, the Philippines, and elsewhere in Asia. It was, therefore, doubly important not to acquiesce in the defeat of South Korea, an outcome that would have catastrophic consequences in Japan. They argued, moreover, that the war in Vietnam underscored again the lack of patience among the American people for a protracted but limited war; hence, any attack on South Korea should be repelled in short order with whatever force was necessary, rather than by a policy of graduated escalation. Defense Secretary James Schlesinger, for example, asserted that the lesson of the Vietnam conflict was "rather than simply counter[ing] your opponent's thrusts, it is necessary to go for the heart of the opponent's power; destroy his military forces rather than simply being involved endlessly in ancillary military operations."[23]

Advocates of withdrawal from Korea also cited the recent American experience in Southeast Asia as evidence that the United States has no significant national interests on the Asian mainland, certainly none that would justify repeating the experience of Vietnam on the Korean peninsula: "It would be a bitter irony, therefore, if after the defeat of U.S. policy in Indochina, which the President and Kissinger have done so much to publicize, they were now to pursue policies which would entangle them and us in a repeat performance [in Korea] of the Vietnamese tragedy."[24]

Discussions concerning the price and availability of oil from the Middle East also tended to center on the relevance or irrelevance of the lessons of Vietnam. Critics of intervention have found parallels between the Persian Gulf and Vietnam, including distance to the area from the United States, proximity to the Soviet Union, and the dearth of governments enjoying widespread popular support. Their opponents tend to dismiss these parallels, arguing that oil bestows on the area a vital importance to the United States and its allies that never existed in Vietnam. In two widely quoted essays a critic of American involvement in Vietnam advocated the use of force in the Middle East if necessary to ensure the continued flow of oil at an acceptable price. The essays pointed out that the Persian Gulf states lack trees and lush foliage—elements that have been cited as impediments to American military operations in Vietnam—thus negating one of the arguments against attempting to conduct limited military operations in the Middle East. Others, asserting that Vietnam should have taught the United States not to dismiss lightly warnings about the hazards and futility of military interventions in the Third World, have questioned whether the botany of an area is a critical element of comparison, or merely a trivial factor that should affect only marginally appraisals about the utility or limitations on the uses of force in the contemporary international system.[25]

The continuing impact of Vietnam was demonstrated even more clearly during the conflict in Angola that followed liquidation of the Portuguese empire in Africa. If a modern-day Rip Van Winkle had gone to sleep during the height of the Vietnam War and had awakened during the winter of 1975–6, he might have sought out newspapers or television newscasts to learn about changes that had taken place during his hibernation. Reports of Richard Nixon and Gerald Ford eulogizing Chou En-lai in warm phrases usually reserved for the most intimate of political allies would surely have evoked surprise, especially as the political rhetoric from the White House only a few years earlier had repeatedly justified American involvement in Vietnam as an exercise in containing Chinese expansion. He would soon have found himself on much more familiar ground, however, for he would have discovered that Washington was deeply divided by a vigorous foreign policy debate on the appropriate scope of American involvement in a small, war-torn Third World nation in which the USSR and one of its surrogates was playing a significant military role. Assuming that Rip had taken even a casual interest in the often vitriolic disputes about the wisdom and morality of American involvement in Southeast Asia that had divided the country for almost a decade, the reasoning and theories he would have found in speeches, editorials, Congressional debates, news conferences, and press briefings by foreign policy leaders would have had a distinctly familiar ring. Even the key words and phrases might have led him to wonder whether his sleep had indeed been of more than a few hours' duration. "American credibility," "domino theory," "racial war," "the first step into a quagmire," "regional balance of power," "executive secrecy," "covert military operations," "strategic location," "inconsistent with détente," and "danger of World War III," are just a few of the more prominent terms that might have convinced him that the bitter policy battles on American involvement in Vietnam continued to divide the country. And, in a sense, he would have been correct, for the parallels between the substance and terminology of the Vietnam debates and the arguments on an American policy for Angola were no mere coincidence. Near the core of policy differences on Angola were two questions that linked it to the conflict in Southeast Asia: what are the lessons that should have been learned from the long and unsuccessful American involvement in Vietnam? Which, if any, of these lessons are applicable to the conflict in Angola?

The Vietnam experience thus set the terms of the debate. Its impact on diagnoses and prescriptions was evident in the rhetoric of those supporting the Ford Administration's request for authorization to send American supplies to the UNITA and FNLA factions, as well as that of critics who opposed the White House. Amongst arguments adduced by the former were these:

> The Senators opposing aid to the embattled Angolans worry about another Vietnam: if we send some bullets, we will be stepping on a slippery slope and will end up with 500,000 American troops slogging through the jungles of Africa, and this is the last moment we can stop it. Not only is the notion preposterous, it is also not the way Vietnam happened.[26]

> In emphasizing these hard facts, Mr. Sulzberger stands in marked contrast to critics of U.S. involvement in this area . . . who play on fears that Angola will lead on to another Vietnam . . .[27]

> Perhaps learning too well the lesson of Munich led us into Vietnam, and perhaps learning too well the lesson of Vietnam will lead us

into our next tragedy . . . Of course, no one wants to refight the Vietnam war, and Angola may not be the best place to draw the line, any more than Ethiopia [in 1935] would have been.[28]

Vietnam taught us the price of intervention. Angola will teach us the price of non-intervention. And there's something to be learned from both.[29]

The impact of the war in Vietnam was of no less importance in the case of those who opposed President Ford and Secretary of State Kissinger on the issue, as is evident in the following observations:

Under the whole Angolan episode is a series of flawed policy judgments remarkably similar to those once used to rationalize U.S. intervention in Indo-China.[30]

But the point is much larger than the specifics of Angola. Our attitude toward that affair will really indicate whether we have learned from Vietnam and Watergate and the rest how much harm we do to ourselves by secrecy—by letting a handful of officials make policy without public examination of the premises.[31]

America became so heavily involved in Vietnam because the government did not share enough of its decisions with the people . . . To try to play our small part in preventing that mistake this time [CBS News is scheduling a special series on the Angola conflict].[32]

One reads about our new Angola adventure in shame and despair. Our hypocrisy, deviousness and fatal attraction to worthless losers are all again on display, as if the Bay of Pigs and Vietnam and Watergate had never happened.[33]

One might have thought that we would at least have learned something from the disastrous Vietnam war, but apparently we have learned nothing. Already another Vietnam is being prepared for us in Angola.[34]

The point here is not to judge whether proponents or opponents of aid to the UNITA and FNLA factions in Angola were correct. It is, rather, to illustrate how powerfully the Vietnam experience shaped and constrained the debate. Many of those taking part in it were engaged in a rather widespread practice: they were drawing parallels between past events and a contemporary situation, extrapolating from Vietnam both a diagnosis of the situation in Angola and a set of prescriptions that should govern American policy toward the conflict there. More importantly, not only rhetoric was involved. A plausible conclusion is that the policy outcome would have been different had it not been for Vietnam. Congressional action to prohibit further use of American funds in Angola was almost surely influenced by the perceived parallels between the conflict in that African nation and the initial steps leading to military intervention in Vietnam, and the corollary that selected lessons of the latter episode could appropriately be applied to the case of Angola.

The foregoing examples are drawn from a rather brief period of a few months following the defeat in South Vietnam. Perhaps one should therefore not leap to premature conclusions about the persisting effect of Vietnam. Caution in this respect might be especially appropriate in the light of subsequent events in the Middle East and elsewhere that have, in the eyes of some observers, marked the end of the "Vietnam syndrome" in American foreign policy.

The more recent policy debates on an appropriate American stance toward the continuing turmoil in El Salvador offers evidence, however, that the impact of the war in Southeast Asia has persisted into the 1980s. Even a casual perusal of titles appearing on editorials, articles, and essays reveals the widespread tendency to perceive the situation in El Salvador through the lenses of the Vietnam War: "The Old Captured Documents Routine," "Vietnam South of the Border," "Assumptions in El Salvador ... and About Vietnam," "El Salvador—Will it Turn Into Another Vietnam," "Did America Learn Nothing from Vietnam: Salvadoran Quagmire," "The Vietnam Shadow over Policy for El Salvador," "El Salvador: The Next Vietnam?," "El Salvador, Vietnam, and Central American Policy," "It's Not Vietnam, but . . ." and, "El Salvador: It Is Not Vietnam."[35] As was true in the case of Angola and other episodes a half decade earlier, both supporters and opponents of the Reagan Administration's decisions to support the government with military supplies and advisers have debated the relevance of the Vietnam analogy and invoked one or another "lesson" of that war on behalf of a preferred policy toward El Salvador. The ghost of Vietnam has in critical ways defined the central issues and boundaries of the debate on American policy in El Salvador.

Critics of the Reagan Administration's policy argue that even limited assistance to the El Salvador regime will, by placing the United States and its prestige behind a regime that lacks widespread popular support, commit the United States to an unwinnable undertaking which will become increasingly difficult to liquidate. The parallels between the two conflicts are so obvious to some that, in the words of a highly visible critic, "you don't have to be a historian or political scientist to know that El Salvador will become another Vietnam War if we don't act now." For those with a more analytical perspective, the following similarities between Vietnam and El Salvador are sufficient to render the former a valid model for the latter: Washington's ignorance of local history, overly optimistic assessments of government armies, misconceptions of American power and its uses, and the absence of adequate debate on the interests at issue. The critics argue that official portrayals of the conflict in Central America as one which pits Soviet proxies against vital American interests in this hemisphere parallel President Kennedy's flawed assessment of the stakes in Southeast Asia when he sent the first American troops to Vietnam: "Once before, in the early 60s, a President's obsession with guerrilla combat led us into a calamitous war; with another President eager to revive the counterinsurgency establishment, we face the risk of a disastrous encore." Finally, public opinion data reveal that by a margin of 65 to 28 percent people agreed that the war in El Salvador was "much like the war in Vietnam."[36]

To supporters of the Reagan Administration's Latin American policy, such arguments are evidence that many are still mesmerized by the false illusions of the "Vietnam syndrome," rendering them incapable of properly appreciating the substantial geographical, political and military differences between Vietnam and El Salvador. While rejecting the critics' diagnoses and prescriptions. Administration supporters share with them a conviction that there are indeed important lessons to be learned from the Vietnam experience but, of course, their conclusions differ in substance. "The Vietnam parallel is apt," according to an Administration consultant, "although the lesson is the opposite from that commonly drawn"; the real lesson of Vietnam is that intervention should be on a scale sufficient to win. Another common denominator is Soviet complicity in both conflicts. Administration supporters also believe that there are especially salient lessons to be learned about the role of the media. Given the coverage of key event in Vietnam, the public should be highly skeptical of media reports that romanticize the insurgents, emphasize human rights violations by government forces while ignoring those by rebels, and imply that interventions in Third World conflicts are doomed to failure.[37]

Debates over El Salvador thus appear to indicate that, almost a decade after its conclusion, the Vietnam War remains for many a rich lode from which to extract nuggets of wisdom to guide contemporary American foreign policy. But those engaged in the enterprise seem unable to agree on which nuggets are real gold, and which are merely fool's gold.

These examples have only touched upon, rather than exhausted, the voluminous dialogue on the true meaning of the conflict in Southeast Asia. The Vietnam analogy has even been applied to conflicts involving other nations; for example, some have described Afghanistan as "the Russians' Vietnam," and others have suggested that Lebanon is "Israel's Vietnam." Many important international events have given rise to retrospective searches for lessons to guide future policy, but Vietnam may well be unique in the sheer volume of writing and rhetoric it has stimulated. The outpouring of articles, speeches, editorials, and other materials on the topic indicate considerable agreement that Vietnam was a major turning point in American history, but those who have reflected on the meaning of the war have brought forth a wide range of responses about what this nation should learn, not learn, or unlearn from that experience.[38] "No more Vietnams" may be a proposition that evokes little dissent from most

Americans, but it is also so vague that it may well conceal profound differences on more specific aspects of foreign policy. For some, it may mean that the United States must avoid any type of involvement in the Third World that could be one step in a sequence of events ultimately leading to some form of military intervention. For others, it may imply that gradual escalation is a totally ineffective way of coping with limited aggression and, therefore, any future military intervention should proceed according to a greatly foreshortened timetable. Perhaps more importantly, a review of these debates suggests that such divergent responses may well be embedded within broad, internally-consistent interpretations of the entire Vietnam experience.

As a background to subsequent analyses, the summary that follows identifies two quite different interpretations of the war, including the appropriate goals of American policy on Southeast Asia, sources of its failure, consequences of that failure and the lessons to be learned from the war. This does not imply that there are no intermediate positions on the war. Rather, the purpose here is to abstract from the long and often bitter debates two "ideal type" interpretations that differ on most fundamental points. Data analyses in the next chapter will reveal to what extent these two schools of thought actually correspond to the beliefs of American leaders.

The essential elements of one viewpoint include these beliefs:

- The war was a justifiable effort to protect an ally to which the United States had a security commitment, arising from both the Southeast Asia Treaty Organization (SEATO) and the actions of every administration since Eisenhower's.
- The war could have been won had it been conducted properly.
- Unreasonable restraints on the exercise of military power, especially air power, ultimately made victory impossible; the military was asked to conduct a war "with one arm tied behind its back."
- The American military effort was also undermined—and adversaries were concomitantly encouraged to believe that they did not have to negotiate seriously—by several types of domestic activities, including the highly visible protests of dissidents, especially on "elite" university campuses; Congressional interference in and restrictions upon Executive efforts to conduct the war; and biased reporting by media that ultimately turned a substantial part of the American public against the war.
- The North Vietnamese obtained virtually unlimited military assistance from Moscow and Peking, whereas the Western allies were more liberal in offering critical advice than in contributing material support to South Vietnam and the United States.
- As a consequence of the defeat in Southeast Asia, the West has suffered a serious loss, and Communist forces have been encouraged to seek further gains through aggression; other "dominoes" are therefore likely to fall.

- America's credibility and reputation have suffered, as other allies and potential allies will draw appropriate but unfortunate conclusions about the value of Washington's commitments.
- As a result of the war, there is a serious danger that in the future the United States will fail to protect its legitimate international interests rather than risk the trauma of another Vietnam; that is, the United States will be paralyzed by the "Vietnam syndrome" to the detriment of its vital national interests and, ultimately, of a stable world order.

According to the foregoing viewpoint, among the lessons that the United States should learn from the war in Vietnam are these:

- The international system remains essentially bipolar, notwithstanding the rhetoric and optimistic hopes of those advocating a post-Cold War era of détente.
- For the foreseeable future, the primary threats to a just and stable world order continue to derive from the expansionist proclivities of the USSR and its allies.
- In an anarchical international system, military power properly deployed has not lost its utility; there is no effective substitute for the ultimate threat to employ force in defense of vital interests.
- American foreign policy-making processes should be modified in ways that will enable the United States to pursue its external goals, especially in wartime, with greater clarity, unity, and efficiency.

In contrast, the following beliefs represent a very different perspective on the Vietnam experience:

- American intervention in Southeast Asia was unjustified, as it was based on a distorted appraisal of the national interest, unrealistic premises and information about friends and adversaries, and faulty logic.
- The war could not have been won at any price that the American people could reasonably be expected to pay.
- The war was essentially a domestic rather than an international political conflict in which the Saigon factions backed by Washington could never gain sufficient popular support to win; hence, greater or more efficient use of American military power would have been irrelevant and could not have altered the ultimate outcome.
- American ignorance of Vietnam, Southeast Asia, and Third World nationalism contributed significantly to the failure of its policies.
- The major consequences of the war have been domestic, including a damaged American economy, a decline of trust in government and other major institutions, and a distorted set of national priorities.
- The end of American involvement in Southeast Asia will permit

the United States to turn its attention and resources to real rather than phantom threats to national security, including a full agenda of social, economic, environmental, resource, and other problems that are domestic and international in both origin and consequences.

The real lessons of the Vietnam War, according to this viewpoint, are:

- The United States must assess more realistically and with a finer sense of discrimination the scope and substance of its international interests.
- The United States should avoid interventions in Third World conflicts that do not threaten basic national interests—and few of them do.
- Better relations with the USSR, as codified in the policy of détente, are made possible by liquidation of the Vietnam issue, a number of vital common interests, and the growing conservatism of the Soviet leadership; they are made necessary by the unthinkable dangers of a nuclear war between the superpowers.
- The contemporary international system is multipolar rather than bipolar; as a consequence, zero-sum assumptions about international conflict (especially those in the Third World) are anachronisms that can only impede realistic diagnoses of and prescriptions for international issues.
- The United States should strengthen international organizations, notably the United Nations, by using rather than bypassing them to resolve international conflicts.
- Because the sources of contemporary international conflict are rarely military or strategic in origin, the utility of military power in the pursuit of foreign policy goals is limited; such means should be used, if at all, as a last resort rather than in the first instance.

These two viewpoints, summarized in Table 1.1, are composites or "ideal types," representing clusters of ideas that appear to be logically connected. Indeed, they appear to possess sufficient internal consistency that it is appropriate to describe them as *belief systems*: "configuration[s] of ideas and attitudes in which the elements are bound together by some form of constraint or functional interdependence."[39] The two interpretations of the war are also mutually exclusive in many important respects, sharing few if any ideas on the wisdom of the American undertaking in Southeast Asia, the sources of American failure in the conflict, the likely consequences of that failure, and the appropriate lessons of Vietnam. The extent to which such internally-consistent and mutually-exclusive beliefs about the war are found among American leaders will be explored in Chapters 2 and 6.

Table 1.1   *Two Belief Systems Concerning American Participation in the Vietnam War*

	Justified	Unjustified
General assessment of the U.S. effort	To honor a commitment to protect an ally from external aggression	Based on an unrealistic appraisal of the situation and U.S. interests at stake
Could the war have been won?	Yes, if U.S. power had been used properly and more efficiently	No, the conflict was essentially political rather than military
Sources of U.S. failure	Domestic constraints: Congress, the media, dissidents, etc. Soviet and Chinese assistance to North Vietnam Unreasonable restraints on the uses of military power Inadequate assistance from U.S. allies	No reasonable effort could have saved the Saigon regime U.S. goals lacked realism and clarity U.S. ignorance of Vietnam, Southeast Asia, and, more generally, of Third World nationalism
Consequences of the U.S. failure in Vietnam	Primarily international U.S. reputation and credibility have suffered Communist aggression has been encouraged U.S., traumatized by the "Vietnam syndrome," will be unable to protect its vital international interests	Primarily domestic Damage to domestic institutions, both tangible (the economy) and intangible (faith in institutions) End of war may permit the U.S. to turn its attention to genuine rather than phantom threats to national security
Lessons of Vietnam	International system remains bipolar Primary threat is aggression by USSR and its allies Military power remains an indispensable instrument of national policy When military power is employed, it must be with fewer self-imposed restraints Reform foreign policy decision-making to permit greater efficiency and unity of purpose	International system is multipolar Threats arise from multiple sources, not just Soviet aggression Military power is losing its relevance for coping with most international issues Strengthen world order by using international institutions to resolve conflicts Reform foreign policy decision-making to permit greater wisdom in defining national interests Avoid intervention in Third World conflicts

The Vietnam Leadership Surveys

A high-ranking foreign policy official in the Carter Administration wrote, a short time prior to taking office:

> In the final analysis, the lesson of Vietnam will not be forged within the government at all, but in the public, political arena. How the American people assimilate the experience will determine how future bureaucrats, future Presidents—including some who may have participated in antiwar demonstrations in their youth—react the next time they face such a supreme test.[40]

Some students of public opinion and its impact on foreign policy might view this statement as hyperbole, but for at least two reasons it deserves careful assessment rather than casual dismissal. It is at least conceivable that in the post-Vietnam era, public attitudes and beliefs arising from that conflict will have a more significant impact on foreign policy than had been the case in the preceding quarter of a century. Moreover, even if one dismisses mass public attitudes and beliefs as the creation rather than the master of policy-making officials, one might well agree that there are leaders in government, the Foreign Service, and the military—as well as non-governmental ones in the media, labor unions, corporations, universities, churches, and elsewhere—whose beliefs about the international system and the United States's proper role within it are likely to play an important role in shaping and constraining American foreign policy.[41]

Underlying this study is the premise that among such leaders the inclination to adduce lessons from the Vietnam experience may prove especially strong. Certainly there is no compelling reason to believe that the war in Southeast Asia has had less effect on those who experienced it than have other traumatic events. These concerns led to a project to obtain systematic evidence about the reactions of American leaders, both within and outside government, to the Vietnam War, including beliefs about why the war effort failed, the consequences that may flow from the failure, and the lessons to be derived from it. Many former officials of the Kennedy, Johnson, Nixon, and Ford administrations have made their views known on these matters. Others have expressed themselves in articles, speeches, editorials, letters to the editor, and several substantial collections of essays.[42] These materials are useful for gaining insight into the beliefs of some prominent persons about what should be learned from the nation's longest war, but they are not a wholly adequate substitute for more systematic data drawn from a broader spectrum of leaders. Two nationwide surveys of American leaders, conducted in 1976 and 1980, were designed to provide such evidence.[43] Of the 4,290 leaders who received the 1976 questionnaire, 2,282 (53·2 percent) completed and returned it. In 1980, the return rate reached 63·6 percent as there were 2,502 respondents among the 3,936 persons who received the questionnaire. This study neither develops nor depends upon a precise theory of the leadership structure in the United States. In any case, even if the sampling design had reflected such a theory, different return rates among sub-groups would have resulted in deviations from it. The sampling design reflects the premise that leaders in a broad range of institutions—from government to churches, business to universities, labor to the media, and others—have and exercise the opportunity to convey their views and preferences on foreign affairs to significant others. The strategy employed here, in short, is more modest. A large initial sample drawn from multiple listings of leaders, combined with the good fortune of satisfactory return rates, resulted in two groups of respondents that can reasonably be said to include representatives of many, if not all, major components of the nation's leadership structure. There are also enough respondents in most important occupational and other sub-categories to permit reliable comparisons among them. At the same time, the sampling procedures impose some limitations that must be made explicit. The most important of these concern interpretations of aggregate results, which should not be viewed as an exact microcosm of American leadership, comparable to the results of opinion surveys among the population at large. Secondly, comparisons among sub-groups, whether based on occupation, ideology, party, gender, and other leader attributes, are at the core of the analyses that follow. That is, acknowledged uncertainty as to the precise structure of American leadership does not preclude making meaningful comparisons, for example, between military officers and media leaders, men and women, liberals and conservatives, and the like. Nor does it rule out analyses based on more complex combinations of attributes.

Table 1.2 summarizes and compares several background characteristics of the 1976 and 1980 respondents. Subsequent chapters will consider these attributes and their impact on foreign policy beliefs in more detail. It will suffice for the present to describe the two groups of leaders as: occupationally and generationally diverse; more Democrat or independent than Republican; ideologically moderate rather than extremist; mostly male and veterans of military service; and highly educated.

Conclusion

The remainder of this book is organized around three clusters of questions about the foreign policy beliefs of American leaders.

What has been the impact of the Vietnam War on the beliefs of persons holding leadership positions? Has it served as the basis of a new, post-Vietnam foreign policy consensus, as suggested by

Table 1.2 Vietnam Survey Respondents: Selected Background Characteristics of American Leaders

	1976 respondents		1980 respondents	
	n	%	n	%
Occupation				
Business executives	294	12.9	459	18.3
Labor officials	74	3.2	89	3.6
Educators	565	24.8	635	25.4
Clergy	101	4.4	148	5.9
Military officers	500	21.9	177	7.1
Public officials	110	4.8	152	6.1
Foreign Service officers	125	5.5	150	6.0
Media leaders	184	8.1	245	9.8
Lawyers	116	5.1	146	5.8
Health care	*	*	116	4.6
Others and no answer	213	9.3	185	7.4
	2,282	100.0	2,502	100.0

* Included with "Others" in 1976.

Sex				
Men	2,009	88.0	2,173	86.8
Women	224	9.8	289	11.6
No answer	49	2.1	40	1.6
	2,282	99.9	2,502	100.0

Age: Date of birth				
Prior to 1911	40	1.8	28	1.1
1911–15	287	12.6	96	3.8
1916–20	356	15.6	382	15.3
1921–5	332	14.5	400	16.0
1926–30	250	11.0	351	14.0
1931–5	158	6.9	282	11.3
1936–40	173	7.6	242	9.7
1941–5	321	14.1	161	6.4
1946–50	245	10.7	146	5.8
1951 and later	17	0.7	60	2.4
No answer	103	4.5	354	14.1
	2,282	100.0	2,502	99.9

Political party preference				
Republican	590	25.9	728	29.1
Democrat	793	34.8	918	36.7
Independent	763	33.4	764	30.5
Other	15	0.7	13	0.5
No preference	63	2.8	27	1.1
No answer	58	2.5	52	2.1
	2,282	100.1	2,502	100.0

Table 1.2 *Continued:*

	1976 respondents		1980 respondents	
	n	%	n	%
Military service				
Veteran of military service	1,500	65.7	1,513	60.4
No military service	737	32.3	943	37.7
No answer	45	2.0	46	1.8
	2,282	100.0	2,502	99.9
Ideology				
Far left	18	0.8	14	0.6
Very liberal	202	8.9	144	5.8
Somewhat liberal	578	25.3	614	24.5
Moderate	576	25.2	648	25.9
Somewhat conservative	666	29.2	793	31.7
Very conservative	126	5.5	163	6.5
Far right	5	0.2	9	0.3
No answer	111	4.9	117	4.7
	2,282	100.0	2,502	100.0
Highest level of education				
Some high school	7	0.3	7	0.3
High school graduate	32	1.4	38	1.5
Some college	141	6.2	135	5.4
College graduate	221	9.7	290	11.6
Some graduate work	487	21.4	339	13.5
Graduate degree	1,351	59.2	1,646	65.8
No answer	43	1.9	47	1.9
	2,282	100.1	2,502	100.0
Graduate degrees				
MA or MS	366	27.1	382	23.2
Ph.D	572	42.3	666	40.5
MD or DDS	58	4.3	90	5.5
LLB or JD	187	13.9	232	14.1
MBA	49	3.6	107	6.5
Advanced religious degree	68	5.0	55	3.3
No answer	51	3.8	114	6.9
	1,351	100.0	1,646	100.0

President Ford when the last American personnel were being evacuated from Saigon in 1975? If so, in what ways does this consensus differ from the axioms that guided American foreign policy during much of the two decades following the end of World War II?[44] Alternatively, have the domestic divisions that manifested themselves so dramatically during the foreign policy debates of the late 1960s and early 1970s persisted and, perhaps, even hardened? Chapters 2 and 3 address these questions with data from the leadership survey conducted in 1976, within a year of the conquest of South Vietnam.

If the legacy of domestic dissensus has persisted beyond the final disengagement of the United States from Vietnam, what are the main lines of cleavage on the American political landscape? How deep are the chasms, and how systematically do they cut across or between occupational, generational, ideological, and other attributes of American leaders? Chapter 4 assesses some of the main themes of recent foreign policy debates in this country, with a view to identifying several distinct ways of thinking about the main contours of the international system, the primary threats to a just and stable world order, the appropriate American role in the post-Vietnam world, and the means that should be employed in the pursuit of foreign policy goals. Chapter 5 returns to data from the 1976 leadership survey in order to gain a more precise understanding of consensus and dissensus among American leaders.

Have the divisive consequences of the war persisted beyond the months immediately following American disengagement from Vietnam, or have the international events of the years corresponding roughly with the tenure of the Carter Administration, culminating in the invasion of the American Embassy in Iran and the Soviet invasion of Afghanistan during the final weeks of the 1970s, brought an end to the so-called "Vietnam syndrome?" Did the mobs in Teheran and the Soviet invaders in Kabul combine to create what had eluded the architects of détente and of a foreign policy emphasizing human rights—a domestic consensus in the United States? Alternatively, is there evidence that the domestic divisions on international and foreign policy issues persisted and, if so, how did they resemble or differ from the cleavages that existed in 1976? To answer these questions, the analysis in Chapter 6 draws upon responses from the 1980 leadership group, comparing them with figures from the survey undertaken four years earlier. Chapter 7 addresses the issue of consensus from a broader perspective, assessing efforts of the Nixon, Ford, Carter, and Reagan administrations to rebuild a strong base of domestic support for their foreign policies. The final chapter speculates about alternative strategies that might be employed during the 1980s to cope with deep and enduring differences in the United States's external relations.

Notes to Chapter 1

1 *New York Times* (14 May 1982).
2 *New York Times* (18 April 1975; 7 May 1975).
3 *New York Times* (30 April 1975).
4 Robert Jervis, *Perception and Misperception in International Politics* (Princeton, NJ: Princeton University Press, 1976), p. 275.
5 The range of views on this question is illustrated by the following sample of statements:

> Nostalgia is a seductive liar, evoking bowdlerized pictures of times past with all the shadows painted out, thus obscuring or distorting the lessons to be learned. *George Ball*

> The true use of history is not to make men more clever for the next time but to make them wiser forever. *Jacob Burckhardt*

> Histories make men wise; poets, witty; the mathematics, subtle; natural philosophy, deep; moral, grave; logic and rhetoric, able to contend. *Francis Bacon*

> On the breast of the huge Mississippi of falsehood called history, a foam-ball more or less is of no consequence. *Matthew Arnold*

> The only good histories are those that have been written by the persons themselves who commanded in the affairs whereof they write. *Michel de Montaigne*

> Anything but history, for history must be false. *Sir Robert Walpole*

> Peoples and governments have never learned anything from history, or acted on principles deduced from it. *G. W. F. Hegel*

> So difficult a matter it is to trace and find out the truth of anything by history. *Plutarch*

> History offers the lawyer or scholar (or policy-maker) almost any precedent he needs to sustain what he may consider, in a concrete situation, to be wise policy. *Arthur M. Schlesinger, Jr*

> One of the few unequivocally sound lessons of history is that the lessons we should learn are usually learned imperfectly if at all. *Bernard Brodie*

> The lessons of history are never simple. Whoever thinks he sees one should probably go on with his reading. *John K. Fairbank*

> We have need of history in its entirety, not to fall back into it, but to see if we can escape from it. *Ortega y Gasset*

> . . . those who dwell obsessively on the past are prone to poor analysis, divisive debate, unconstructive criticism and bad decisions as they face the future . . . They are doomed to ask the wrong questions, which can only yield the wrong answers. *Strobe Talbott*

> It would be wrong not to lay the lessons of the past before the future . . . It is my earnest hope that pondering upon the past may give guidance in days to come, enable a new generation to repair some of the errors of former years and thus to govern, in accordance with the needs and glory of man, the awful unfolding of the future. *Winston S. Churchill*

6 See, for example, Ernest R. May, *"Lessons" of the Past: The Use and Misuse of History in American Foreign Policy* (New York: Oxford University Press, 1973); and a chapter entitled "How Decision Makers Learn from History" in Jervis, *Perception and Misperception.*
7 Davis Bobrow, "Communist China's conflict system," *Orbis*, 9 (1966), p. 931.
8 For a further discussion, see Alexander L. George, *Presidential Decision-Making*

in *Foreign Policy: The Effective Use of Information and Advice* (Boulder, Colorado: Westview Press, 1980).

9   Harry S. Truman, *Memoirs: Years of Trial and Hope* (Garden City, NY: Doubleday, 1956), pp. 332–3.

10   Gaddis Smith, quoted in May, *Lessons of the Past*, pp. 49–50.

11   Anthony Eden, *Full Circles: The Memoirs of Anthony Eden*, (Boston, Mass.: Houghton-Mifflin, 1960), p. 480.

12   Whether this analogy is valid has been a source of continuing debate. See, for example, Dimitri K. Simes, "Disciplining Soviet power," *Foreign Policy*, no. 43 (Summer 1981), pp. 33–52.

13   Tad Szulc, "Lisbon and Washington: behind Portugal's revolution," *Foreign Policy*, no. 21 (Winter 1975–6), p. 3.

14   Graham T. Allison, "Conceptual models and the Cuban missile crisis," *American Political Science Review*, LXIII (1969), p. 713.

15   Glenn D. Paige, "Comparative Case Analysis of Crisis Decisions: Korea and Cuba," in Charles F. Hermann (ed.), *International Crises: Insights from Behavioral Research* (New York: Free Press, 1972), p. 48; and Thomas W. Milburn, "The Management of Crises," in Hermann, *International Crises*, p. 265.

16   Stanley Hoffmann, *Gulliver's Troubles, or the Setting of American Foreign Policy* (New York: McGraw-Hill, 1968), pp. 109–14.

17   Alexander Woodside, "The Vietnam we refused to know," *Boston Globe* (7 May 1975); and Woodside, "Premeditated amnesia: America's attitudes toward history," *Nation*, 221 (13 December 1975), pp. 614–18.

18   For further evidence on this point, see especially May, *"Lessons" of the Past*, and Jervis, *Perception and Misperception*.

19   Robert Jervis, "Hypotheses on misperception," *World Politics*, 20 (1968), p. 471.

20   N. R. F. Maier, *Problem-Solving Discussions and Conferences* (New York: McGraw-Hill, 1963), p. 221.

21   Eugene Rostow, quoted in Robert Scheer, "Nuclear attack: the unthinkable becomes thinkable," *Sacramento Bee* (4 October 1981), p. A24. For an alternative view see, for example, Miles Kahler, "Rumors of war: The 1914 analogy," *Foreign Affairs*, 58 (Winter 1979/80), pp. 374–96.

22   The link between generation and the impact of history is discussed in more detail in Jervis, *Perception and Misperception*.

23   James R. Schlesinger, "Now—a tougher U.S.," *U.S. News & World Report*, 78 (26 May 1975), p. 25.

24   "The Korean trap," *Nation*, 220 (24 May 1975), pp. 610–11.

25   Robert W. Tucker, "Oil: the issue of intervention," *Commentary*, 59 (January 1975), pp. 21–31; Tucker, "Further reflections on oil and force," *Commentary*, 59 (March 1975), pp. 45–56; "Learning the wrong lessons," *New Republic*, 172 (1 February 1975), pp. 5–7; and Adam Yarmolinsky, "Myths and interests," *New Republic*, 172 (3 May 1975), pp. 14–15.

26   "Dithering over Angola," *Wall Street Journal* (19 December 1975). See also, Bayard Ruskin and Carl Gershman, "Africa, Soviet imperialism, and the retreat of American power," *Commentary*, 64 (October 1977), pp. 33–43.

27   Letter to the *New York Times* (21 December 1975), Section IV, p. 12.

28   "The Neutrality Act of 1975," *Wall Street Journal* (23 December 1975), p. 6.

29   Daniel Patrick Moynihan, quoted in *Newsweek*, 87 (19 January 1976), p. 22.

30   Charles Lipson, "Surrogate targets—Angola and the memory of Vietnam," *Nation*, 222 (17 April 1976), pp. 458–60.

31   Anthony Lewis, "No questions please," *New York Times* (15 December 1975), p. A31.

32   Walter Cronkite, quoted in the *New York Times* (17 December 1975), p. A3.

33   Letter to the *New York Times* (21 December 1975), Section IV, p. 12.

34   Letter to the *New York Times* (21 December 1975), Section IV, p. 12.

35   Mary McGrory, "The old captured documents routine," *Atlanta Constitution* (23 February 1981), p. A4; Hal Gulliver, "Vietnam south of the border," *Atlanta Constitution* (22 February 1981), p. A4; "Assumptions in El Salvador . . . and

about Vietnam," *Chicago Tribune* (13 March 1981), part 3, p. 2; C. J. Migdail, "El Salvador—will it turn into another Vietnam?" *U.S. News & World Report*, 90 (16 March 1981), pp. 28–32; Ronald Steel, "Did America learn nothing from Vietnam: Salvadoran quagmire," *New Republic*, 184 (14 March 1981), pp. 15–17; Sol W. Sanders, "The Vietnam shadow over policy for El Salvador," *Business Week* (16 March 1981), p. 52; Carolyn Forche, "El Salvador: the next Vietnam?," *Progressive*, 45 (February 1981), pp. 27–9; Morton M. Kondracke, "El Salvador, Vietnam, and Central American policy," *Wall Street Journal* (4 March 1982) p. 29; Anthony Lewis, "It's not Vietnam, but . . ." *New York Times* (25 February 1982) p. A31; Strobe Talbott, "El Salvador: it is not Vietnam," *Time*, 119 (22 February 1982), pp. 33–4; and William M. LeoGrande, "Salvador's no domino," *New York Times* (9 March 1983), p. A23.

36 The quotations are from Edward Asner, "We're on the wrong side in El Salvador," *New York Times* (20 February 1982); and Michael T. Klare, "The new counterinsurgency," *Nation*, 232 (14 March 1981), pp. 289, 307–9. See also, Mary McGrory, "Reagan gives El Salvador human rights stamp of approval," *Sacramento Bee* (4 February 1982); John B. Oakes, "Some history for Haig," *New York Times* (6 April 1982) p. A19; and Hodding Carter III, "Mr Reagan's flawed Caribbean thesis," *Wall Street Journal* (25 February 1982), p. 25. The public opinion figures are from William Schneider, "Conservatism, not interventionism," in Kenneth A. Oye, Robert J. Lieber, and Donald Rothchild (eds), *Eagle Defiant* (Boston: Little, Brown, 1983), pp. 33–64.

37 W. Scott Thompson, "Choosing to win," *Foreign Policy*, no. 43 (Summer 1981), pp. 78–83. The reference to the media cites as evidence Peter Braestrup, *Big Story* (Boulder, Colorado: Westview Press, 1977). The role of the press is also debated in "The media's war," *Wall Street Journal* (10 February 1982); David Halberstam, "The press in Vietnam and El Salvador," *Wall Street Journal* (23 February 1982); and Sydney H. Schanberg, "Shoot the messenger," *New York Times* (2 March 1982), p. A23.

38 Among those who have urged caution in adducing lessons from the Vietnam experience are: McGeorge Bundy, "Vietnam," *New York Times* (29 June 1975), and L. H. Gelb, "Today's lessons from the Pentagon Papers," *Life*, 71 (17 September 1971), pp. 34–6.

39 Philip E. Converse, "The Nature of Belief Systems in Mass Publics," in David E. Apter (ed.), *Ideology and Discontent* (New York: Free Press, 1964), p. 207.

40 Richard Holbrooke, "Presidents, Bureaucrats, and Something in-Between," in Anthony Lake, *The Vietnam Legacy: The War, American Society and the Future of American Foreign Policy* (New York: New York University Press, 1976), p. 164.

41 For a critical appraisal of public opinion and its impact on American foreign policy, see Bernard Cohen, *The Public's Impact on Foreign Policy* (Boston, Mass.: Little, Brown, 1973). A formulation that accords a significant role to nongovernmental leaders in the conduct of American foreign policy and seeks to outline the structure and processes through which this role is performed may be found in James N. Rosenau, *National Leadership and Foreign Policy: A Case Study in the Mobilization of Public Support* (Princeton, NJ: Princeton University Press, 1963), pp. 3–41.

42 The collections of essays include Lake, *The Vietnam Legacy*; W. Scott Thompson and Donaldson D. Frizzell (eds), *The Lessons of Vietnam* (New York: Crane, Russak, 1977); "America now: a failure of nerve?," a special issue of *Commentary*, 60 (July 1975); and "The meaning of Vietnam," *New York Review of Books*, 22 (12 June 1975). Book length assessments of the war range from a staunch defense of American purposes and goals in Norman Podhoretz, *Why We Were in Vietnam* (New York: Simon and Schuster, 1982), to a trenchant critique in Paul M. Kattenburg, *The Vietnam Trauma in American Foreign Policy* (New Brunswick, NJ: Transaction Books, 1980). The propensity to examine the war for lessons is pervasive in this literature. Among the most thoughtful is the final chapter of the latter book.

43 Sampling methods are summarized in Appendix A, and both questionnaires are reproduced in Appendix B.

44 Whether or not there was a foreign policy consensus in this country for about two decades after World War II is itself a point on which there is less than full agreement. The desirability of such a consensus has also been debated. These issues are addressed in Chapter 7 below.

2
Vietnam, Consensus, and the Belief Systems of American Leaders, 1976: Beliefs About the War

After the Japanese attack on Pearl Harbor in 1941, Senator Arthur Vandenberg observed, "In my own mind, my convictions regarding international cooperation and collective security for peace took firm form on the afternoon of the Pearl Harbor attack. That day ended isolationism for any realist."[1] The leading opponent of active American involvement in world affairs thus acknowledged that the disaster in Hawaii was of such significance as to reshape his core beliefs about international politics and the proper American response to a rapidly changing world. Whether or not Vandenberg learned and applied the appropriate lessons in subsequent years, the important point is that the impact of Pearl Harbor and the events leading up to it did not end with the destruction of the Pacific fleet—or even with the end of World War II. It lived on in the minds of Vandenberg and many of his colleagues as a symbol of the futility of isolationism and it continued to exercise a powerful grip on the conduct of American diplomacy. Indeed, not until a generation later, with the United States mired in a seemingly endless war in Southeast Asia, did some of the "lessons of Pearl Harbor" and other events leading up to World War II come under serious challenge by informed and thoughtful critics of American foreign policy.

This example highlights the central question to be examined in this chapter: Is the war in Vietnam playing the same role for the present generation of Americans that Pearl Harbor did for Vandenberg and his contemporaries? Has the decade-long war in Southeast Asia also shaped the world-views of American leaders? Does the Vietnam War represent a major turning point in American foreign policy, perhaps analogous to what students of domestic politics have called "critical elections?" It may still be too early to offer definitive answers, and there are not enough data on leadership beliefs during the pre-Vietnam decades to permit comprehensive comparisons, but the discussion in the previous chapter offers both concrete (if anecdotal) indications and theoretical reasons for believing that an affirmative answer is plausible.

; chapter centers on three concepts: *consensus,*
systems. More specifically, analyses are guided
positions. The first two of these are:

sensus among American leaders that marked the
ng World War II has been shattered.
War was a watershed event in the sense that it gave
ty divergent views on the nature of the international
the appropriate international role for the United

Observations of a shattered consensus among American leaders on
foreign policy issues have not been in short supply during recent
years. Even a casual reader of newspaper headlines could hardly miss
some of the more overt symptoms of deep cleavages: for a decade the
Congress and the White House have clashed sharply, not only on a
number of major foreign policy questions, but also on the proper
division of labor between them. Recent electoral campaigns have
revealed clearly that both political parties are split on a broad spectrum of issues, ranging from the Panama Canal Treaties to the sale of
sophisticated military hardware to Saudi Arabia, and from the
appropriate role of arms control in national security policy to the
proper American stance toward key nations, including the Soviet
Union and China; and such concepts as détente or human rights have
failed to generate a broad and enduring consensus in the way that
containment did a generation ago. It has certainly not escaped notice,
moreover, that the American intervention in Vietnam was a divisive
rather than unifying experience.

If all this is the case, why undertake an extensive analysis of American leaders and their foreign policy beliefs merely to document the
obvious? These two propositions go well beyond stating that Americans are divided by proposals to withdraw troops from South Korea or
Europe, the neutron bomb and basing modes for the MX missile, the
Reagan defense budget and nuclear freeze proposals, import quotas
on Japanese automobiles and European steel, or the Siberian gas
pipeline issue. They suggest that the cleavages go far deeper than
disagreements over specific policy issues, reaching into such fundamental questions as the nature of the international system during the
few remaining years of this millenium, the role that the United States
should play within it, and the ends and means that should constitute
the core of the nation's external relations.

Moreover, as suggested by the example of Senator Vandenberg and
Pearl Harbor, the lessons that individuals or whole generations of
leaders may adduce from such episodes as Vietnam can persist far
beyond the temporal boundaries of the event itself. The acknowledgement that during the war Vietnam divided American society
does not exhaust all the significant questions that can be raised about
the impact of that conflict. It is not an answer, for example, to such

questions as these: What do Americans believe they should have learned from the war for the future conduct of foreign policy? Do these lessons continue to reflect deep divisions, or was President Ford correct in asserting in the middle of the last decade that the lessons are obvious, having been learned by all Americans, and that, accordingly, they would serve as the foundations on which to build a new consensus concerning the proper American role in the world?

Finally, if in fact American leaders disagree about the continuing meaning of the Vietnam experience, are the lessons they have adduced reinforced and sustained by clusters of supporting beliefs? Alternatively, are the lessons relatively isolated beliefs and, therefore, probably evanescent ideas in their world-views? The third proposition favors the former rather than the latter interpretation:

- The divergent sets of beliefs about foreign policy are sufficiently coherent to be properly described as competing belief systems.

This proposition extends the first two by predicting not only the existence of deep, Vietnam-related, cleavages among American leaders, but it also suggests that these divisions are rooted in and sustained by internally consistent, reinforcing clusters of foreign policy beliefs. A series of specific hypotheses, involving four clusters of beliefs that may be linked together so as to constitute a belief system, appears below.[2]

If the data fail to sustain these three propositions, one might expect that present and future officials may find the task of reconstructing a workable foreign policy consensus a reasonably manageable one. Should the propositions receive substantial support, on the other hand, one might be far less sanguine about the prospects for consensus-building, at least in the short run.

In order to undertake a plausible test of these propositions, it is necessary to demonstrate not only the existence of cleavages on fundamental foreign policy issues but also the existence of coherent, internally consistent belief systems. It is also necessary to offer evidence that these results are indeed related to the Vietnam issue rather than to other explanations. For example, several students of American foreign policy have commented on the apparently persistent tendency for the nation to swing from periods of isolationism to internationalism and back to isolationism. Theories of generation-long cycles in American orientations toward international affairs thus suggest that by the mid- to late-1960s a mood of retrenchment from expanded global responsibilities would in any case have set in.[3] Although it is virtually impossible to rule out all competing explanations, one way of assessing systematically the impact of Vietnam is to use the respondents' policy preferences on that single issue as the sole criterion for classifying them.

Table 2.1 describes the 1976 respondents' policy preferences during the early and late stages of the Vietnam War. Retrospective statements about positions on controversial issues must be used with some caution; in view of the subsequent failure of the American undertaking in Vietnam, the number of respondents asserting that they had originally favored a complete military victory may be understated. But even disregarding the possible operation of selective memory, a comparison of the two columns in Table 2.1 makes clear that American leaders underwent a dramatic change on this issue, approaching and perhaps even exceeding that experienced by the population as a whole.[4] Indeed, the only comparable change since the advent of regular opinion polling would appear to have taken place in 1945–7, when expectations about Soviet cooperation in the post-war world underwent a precipitous decline.[5]

Table 2.1 *Early and Late Positions on the War in Vietnam (Percentages of 2,282 respondents favoring various policies)*

Some people felt that we should have done everything possible to gain a complete military victory in Vietnam. Others felt that we should have withdrawn as soon as possible. Still others had opinions in between these two. Please indicate which position came closest to your own feelings— both when the war first became an issue and later toward the end of US involvement.

	When the war first became an issue	Towards the end of US involvement
I tended to favor a complete military victory	51	22
I tended to favor a complete withdrawal	22	57
I tended to feel in between these two	22	18
Not sure	5	3
	100	100

These figures do not, however, reveal how many leaders maintained their positions throughout the course of the war and how many altered their views. Moreover, although it is clear that the shifts were predominantly in the direction of favoring withdrawal from Vietnam, the exact patterns of change cannot be determined precisely from the figures. These deficiencies are remedied in Table 2.2, which depicts every combination of policy preferences during the two periods. The distribution of responses reveals that only 869 of the respondents reported having the same policy preference at the beginning and end of the war. Stated differently, three-fifths (62 percent) of the leadership sample perceived themselves as having altered their basic positions in some direction during the course of the war. Of those experiencing a change, 60 percent moved in the direction of favoring a complete American withdrawal from Vietnam.

Table 2.2   *The 2,282 Respondents Classified into Seven Groups by Positions on Vietnam during Early and Late Stages of the War**

Some people felt that we should have done everything possible to gain a complete military victory in Vietnam. Others felt that we should have withdrawn as soon as possible. Still others had opinions in between these two. Please indicate which position came closest to your own feelings—both when the war first became an issue and later towards the end of US involvement.

	Toward the end of US involvement			
When the war first became an issue	I tended to favor a complete military victory	I tended to feel in-between these two	Not sure	I tended to favor a complete withdrawal
I tended to favor a complete military victory	SUPPORTERS (n = 363, 15.9%)	AMBIVALENT SUPPORTERS (n = 346, 15.2%)		CONVERTED CRITICS (n = 867, 38.0%)
I tended to feel in-between these two	CONVERTED SUPPORTERS (n = 128, 5.6%)	AMBIVALENTS (n = 128, 15.6%)		
Not sure				
I tended to favor a complete withdrawal		AMBIVALENT CRITICS (n = 63, 2.8%)		CRITICS (n = 378, 16.6%)

* Nine respondents did not indicate their position on Vietnam in either the early or late stages of the war.

Seven Leadership Groups

Table 2.2 also provides a way of classifying the 2,282 leaders. Although there are sixteen combinations of responses, several that involve change in the same direction are grouped together in order to achieve a more manageable analysis.[6] The resulting seven groups of respondents have been given descriptive labels that were selected to avoid designations that have become burdened with pejorative meanings. Hence the use of such terms as "supporters" and "critics," in preference to some others that often appeared in the Vietnam debates, including "hawks," "doves," "hard-liners," "soft-liners," "cold warriors," "appeasers," and the like.

Of the seven groups that emerge from this classification scheme, three consist of respondents whose views on the appropriate American policy remained consistent throughout the period of the war:

- **Supporters** favored the Johnson Administration's goal of military victory in Vietnam, and continued to do so throughout the war. This group represents just under one-sixth (15·9 percent) of the total.

- **Ambivalents** either sought an outcome between victory and withdrawal, or they were unsure of their policy preferences on the war. Persons in this group—slightly under 6 percent of the respondents—maintained this position during both the early and late stages of the conflict. Or, to put it somewhat differently, at no time did any of them favor either the option of seeking military victory or of withdrawing altogether.
- **Critics** are respondents who consistently favored withdrawal of American forces from Vietnam. This group encompasses approximately one-sixth (16·6 percent) of the 2,282 leaders.

The remaining four groups include respondents whose policy preferences changed during the course of the war.

- **Converted Supporters** are those who favored a policy of seeking complete military victory toward the end of the conflict even though they recalled having taken a different position some years earlier. They include 5·6 percent of the respondents.
- **Ambivalent Supporters** originally favored a military victory, but reported that toward the end of the war they were either unsure of their position or preferred an outcome in between victory and withdrawal.
- **Ambivalent Critics**, the smallest group among those returning the questionnaire (2·8 percent), consist of persons who perceived themselves as having changed their views from favoring withdrawal to an intermediate position between victory and withdrawal.
- **Converted Critics** wanted American forces withdrawn from Vietnam during the later stages of the war even though they remembered having supported a different option some years earlier. This is the largest group of leaders, comprising almost two-fifths (38 percent) of the sample.

The seven groups of respondents may be linked to the two perspectives on the Vietnam War (Table 1.1) to develop hypotheses concerning diagnoses, predictions, and prescriptions relating to that conflict.

Diagnoses of the sources of failure in Vietnam
- Critics are more likely than Supporters to attribute American failure in Vietnam to: the fundamentally unsound nature of the American undertaking in Vietnam (the ends of policy); a lack of knowledge and understanding of the Third World, Southeast Asia and Vietnam; and the opposition of world opinion.
- Supporters are more likely than Critics to attribute American failure in Vietnam to: constraints imposed on the war effort by domestic groups and institutions; self-imposed restraints on the employment of military capabilities (the means of policy); and actions of North Vietnam's allies and of America's partners.

• Respondents in the other five groups will take intermediate positions, arrayed in this order: Converted Supporters, Ambivalent Supporters, Ambivalents, Ambivalent Critics, and Converted Critics.

Predictions of the consequences arising from the Vietnam War
• Critics are more likely than Supporters, in predicting the consequences of the war, to emphasize damage to American society and institutions.
• Supporters are more likely than Critics, in predicting the consequences of the war, to emphasize: adverse effects on structures and processes of the international system; encouragement to America's adversaries; a more limited conception of the nation's national interests; and certain types of future American undertakings.
• Respondents in the other five groups will take intermediate positions in predicting the consequences of the Vietnam conflict.

Prescriptions of the lessons to be learned from Vietnam
• Critics are more likely than Supporters, in prescribing lessons to be learned from the Vietnam War, to give greater emphasis to: reducing the scope of American commitments abroad, limiting the nation's foreign interests, and improving the performance of the government in conducting a sound foreign policy.
• Supporters are more likely than Critics, in prescribing lessons to be learned from the war, to emphasize: bipolarity of the international system; threats from adversaries; the utility of military power; unilateral action to cope with conflict situations; and the negative consequences of domestic constraints on the effective pursuit of foreign policy goals.
• Respondents in the other five groups will take intermediate positions on the lessons of Vietnam.

Uses of the past
• Because there is no reason to believe that either Supporters, Critics or others are more prone to regard Vietnam as a source of lessons, there will be no significant differences among respondents with respect to uses of the past to guide the conduct of foreign policy.

Diagnosis: Sources of Failure in Vietnam

The manner in which a nation's leaders diagnose its foreign policy failures is sometimes tinged with ominous overtones. At various times during the war in Southeast Asia, senior officials in Washington suggested that their policies should be supported to head off a right-wing backlash that would surely follow any withdrawal or defeat in Vietnam. Whether or not these were merely self-serving efforts to garner support for Administration policies, there are historical examples in which diagnoses of past failures have played a significant role in the politics of the post-war era. If they converge around simplistic conclusions that politicians can exploit to advance their own political fortunes, extremists may propel themselves into the mainstream of politics by successfully identifying scapegoats for past defeats. Hitler's effective use of the "stab in the back" myth after World War I was one source of his appeal to Germans. The failure of American policy in China after World War II, followed soon thereafter by the stalemated war in Korea, provided the context for Senator Joseph McCarthy's own version of a "stab in the back" explanation, in which the knives were allegedly wielded by State Department officials ranging from the corps of China experts to Secretaries of State Marshall and Acheson. Although McCarthy's political effectiveness ended soon thereafter, other demagogues, including Richard Nixon, were more successful than McCarthy in advancing their careers through exploitation of such themes.[7]

During the initial post-war debate on Vietnam, few Americans denied that, despite an enormous commitment of manpower and resources, the United States had failed to achieve its goals. But widespread agreement on this conclusion did not imply a broad consensus on the causes of failure. Some considered American goals to be inherently unrealistic and incapable of being realized at virtually any cost; others regarded them as unworthy or unnecessary even if capable of being achieved; and still others viewed them as realistic and worthy, but incapable of being achieved owing to the manner in which Washington conducted the war.[8] Some found the sources of failure in the succession of governments in Saigon, all of which seemed more capable of gaining the trust, respect and support of the White House than of the Vietnamese themselves, whereas others pointed to the actions, or lack thereof, of North Vietnam's allies and those of the United States, or to the anti-war movement at home. Some observers pointed to a White House that often seemed impervious to criticism or incapable of undertaking a sober appraisal of the situation in Vietnam—George Reedy described the Johnson White House as a place "where never was heard a discouraging word," and Cabinet meetings as sessions where no one had the courage to respond to even the most bizarre idea with a resounding "that's stupid"—whereas others found the sources of failure in the actions of Congress, the bureaucracy, or the media.[9] Still others questioned whether American society and institutions are capable of any long-range undertaking that, at best, promises less than total victory in a short period of time. Finally, there were those who located the sources of the failure in strategic and tactical deficiencies. To one group of critics the problem arose from undue restrictions on air power, but they were probably matched in numbers by those who asserted that there was excessive reliance on air power. The merits of more military technology versus less, of the use of draftees versus volunteers, and similar issues were also debated.

In summary, the post-mortems on Vietnam have located the causes of failure in a broad range of factors, most of which fall into one of six groups: the unsound nature of the undertaking; lack of knowledge and understanding about the Third World, Southeast Asia, or Vietnam; the actions of other parties in the conflict; strategic and tactical factors in the conduct of military operations; domestic constraints on the war effort; and the opposition of world opinion. These interpretations are represented in the leadership survey questionnaire by twenty-one summary statements on the sources of failure. Table 2.3 summarizes the results. The left-hand column provides a summary index of responses by the entire leadership sample to each

Table 2.3 Diagnosis: Sources of American Failure in Vietnam (Responses for the entire sample of 2,282 leaders, and analyses of seven groups of respondents classified by their 1976 positions during the early and late stages of the war in Vietnam)

In your judgment, how important were the reasons listed below in America's inability to achieve all of its goals? Please indicate your assessment by checking only one box in each row.	All respondents*	Differences between groups significant?**	Correlation, actual and hypothesized group rankings***
An unsound undertaking			
The regime in Saigon lacked popular support	.77	Yes	.96
America's goals in Vietnam were inherently unrealistic	.75	Yes	.96
The U.S. had no clear goals in the Vietnam undertaking	.72	Yes	.32
Lack of knowledge and understanding			
Americans underestimated the dedication of the North Vietnamese	.80	Yes	.93
The U.S. lacked understanding of nationalism in the Third World	.69	Yes	.96
Americans were ignorant of Vietnamese history, culture, and society	.66	Yes	.96
Intelligence agencies failed to provide adequate information about the situation in Vietnam	.58	No	.07
Actions of others			
The Soviets and Chinese provided aid to North Vietnam and the Vietcong	.78	Yes	.86

Table 2.3   Continued:

In your judgment, how important were the reasons listed below in America's inability to achieve all of its goals? Please indicate your assessment by checking only one box in each row.	All respondents*	Differences between groups significant?**	Correlation, actual and hypothesized group rankings***
North Vietnam violated the 1973 peace agreement	.57	Yes	.93
America's allies failed to support us	.41	Yes	.89
Military factors			
The United States fought with a "no-win" approach	.65	Yes	.89
The use of American air power was restricted	.56	Yes	.96
America relied excessively on air power	.48	Yes	.86
Insufficient attention was paid to advice from the military	.46	Yes	.89
U.S. military assistance to South Vietnam after the 1973 peace agreement was inadequate	.38	Yes	.93
Domestic constraint			
Reporting by the mass media turned the public against the war	.69	Yes	.96
Pressure from domestic dissidents cast doubt on American commitments	.66	Yes	.96
Congressional involvement hampered the executive in the conduct of the war	.50	Yes	1.00
The Watergate scandal paralyzed the American government	.46	Yes	.96
The American people lost the spirit which led to greatness	.40	Yes	.96
World opinion			
Much of world opinion opposed U.S. goals and policies	.62	Yes	.82

* Calculated on a scale of 1.00 (very important) to 0.00 (not at all important).

** Differences between seven groups of respondents, calculated by analysis of variance, at the .001 level of significance.

*** Spearman rank-order correlation between hypotheses and actual rankings of seven groups.

interpretation of American failure. The scale runs from 1.00 (very important) to 0.00 (not at all important). The middle column indicates whether differences among the seven groups of respondents (defined by their policy preferences during the early and late stages of the war) are statistically significant. The correlation coefficients in the right-hand column reveal how closely the responses of Critics, Supporters, and other groups correspond to the hypotheses outlined earlier.

An Unsound Undertaking

Perhaps the most basic question about the failure in Vietnam is this: Could American goals have been achieved under any circumstances? This query implies several further ones about both the realism and clarity of American goals, and the nature of the regime that the United States attempted to protect. The Vietnam debates elicited no shortage of observations that, at best, the intervention was characterized by unrealistic and opaque goals, and by a regime in Saigon that was doomed by several fatal flaws, perhaps the most important being an absence of genuine commitment to its own survival. As one observer put it, "The history of the war could be written in terms of the cowardly performance by South Vietnamese officers—more often than not the very ones American advisers lavishly praised."[10] According to this line of reasoning, "the most disastrous American decision of the century" could be traced back to a situation that offered no realistic prospect of success because "In Vietnam we were trying to reach a deal on a matter that was really none of our business and with a party to whom we had nothing to offer."[11]

The first three items listed in Table 2.3 were designed to permit leaders to assess the thesis that the Vietnam undertaking was fundamentally an unsound one. As a group, they attributed considerable importance to all three propositions concerning the nature of the American undertaking in Vietnam. Nearly half of them indicated that the lack of popular support for the regime in Saigon was a "very important" cause of the failure of the war effort; more than half of the remainder viewed this as a "moderately important" consideration. An almost identical distribution was recorded in response to the proposition that "America's goals in Vietnam were inherently unrealistic," and the statement that the United States lacked clear goals in the Vietnam undertaking was rated as "very" or "moderately important" by almost three respondents in four. Thus, a substantial proportion of the 2,282 leaders diagnosed the situation as basically unpromising, if not completely unwinnable.

These figures fail, however, to reveal the striking differences among the seven groups with respect to most of their assessments of the undertaking in Southeast Asia. The disaggregated data, summarized in the right-hand column of Table 2.3, confirm the expectations that those who supported the goal of military victory in Vietnam would be less likely to attribute importance to the interpretation that

Washington's goals were unrealistic and that the regime in Saigon failed to gain support among the people of South Vietnam, whereas the Critics would diagnose these factors as much more important. Among the latter, 88 percent gave a very important rating to the lack of realistic goals and over 76 percent did so on the question concerning support for the regime in Saigon. The comparable figures for the Supporters were 21 and 26 percent respectively. Differences among the seven groups are significant and in the predicted direction.[12]

The hypothesis that Supporters of the war effort would be more inclined to attribute importance to the absence of clear goals is not verified, however. Differences among the seven groups are statistically significant, but the results do not yield a pattern of increasing or decreasing scores that is consistent with the hypothesis. Although all seven groups tended to attribute moderate importance to the proposition that Washington lacked clear goals, this finding may also conceal a more basic disagreement. For example, both Paul Warnke and Irving Kristol have argued that Washington's goals were poorly articulated. However, the latter argued that the war effort should have been more clearly depicted "as part of a larger war against world communism," whereas the former took the diametrically opposite position that official discussion of American goals in fact suffered from an excess rather than a dearth of emotional content.[13]

Lack of Knowledge and Understanding

A critic of American policy in Southeast Asia once noted that at the start of the involvement in that part of the world, only a single university in the United States offered courses in the Vietnamese language and culture. Other evidence that most Americans knew little of the country into which they poured so much blood and money would not be difficult to find, and for many observers the failure in Vietnam could thus be traced to profound intellectual shortcomings of various kinds. The United States, they believed, misunderstood the situation and, having failed to learn from the previous French experience, it attempted to impose upon Southeast Asia a pattern of containment that was successful in Europe but irrelevant in a different setting. At a more basic level, American ignorance of Vietnamese history and culture contributed to fundamental misunderstandings about both friends and enemies in the conflict.[14] Some of the most critical suggested that the problem was even deeper than the absence of specific knowledge of the area and the people of Vietnam; they argued that the real sources of failure lay in some characteristic American traits, including racism, cultural chauvinism, and a general lack of interest in history.[15] But the fact of ignorance is not the issue here; rather, the question is whether the sample of American leaders attributed importance to a lack of knowledge in their diagnoses of why the war effort failed.

The results summarized in Table 2.3 indicate that a large

proportion—65 percent or more—of the respondents regarded at least three related gaps in knowledge and understanding to be "moderately" or "very" important in explaining the outcome in Vietnam: North Vietnamese dedication was underestimated; the nature of nationalism in the Third World was misinterpreted; and ignorance prevailed with respect to Vietnamese history, culture, and society. However, the proposition that inadequate intelligence contributed to failure in Vietnam elicited only moderate support from the respondents, and a notably high proportion expressed uncertainty. Because the first of these explanations received the highest proportion of "very important" (nearly 56 percent) ratings of the twenty-one items in the diagnosis part of the questionnaire, it is perhaps useful to speculate that the findings may be relevant to the earlier comments about a right-wing backlash. To the extent that diagnoses of failure in Vietnam attribute importance to a lack of knowledge and understanding, they tend to diminish the potential strength of "stab-in-the-back" explanations, because few individuals, groups, or institutions can reasonably claim to have been sufficiently expert on all aspects of Vietnamese society.

As was the case with assessments of the situation in Vietnam, the respondents' relatively high agreement that lack of knowledge and understanding were important sources of failure in Vietnam conceals rather sharp differences among the seven groups. The data indicate strong support for the hypotheses that the Supporters would be much less inclined than the Critics to attribute importance to American ignorance, and that the other five groups would be arrayed between the Supporters and Critics. For the first three items, differences between the seven groups are significant and they trace out a pattern of ascending scores from Supporters to Critics. The hypothesis that the Critics would also attribute greater significance to intelligence failures rested on the same line of reasoning as that concerning the other three propositions. However, the differences between the seven groups were not significant, and no regular pattern emerges from the data.[16]

The Actions of Others

Among the many points of contention in the Vietnam debates were the nature and role of the participants in the conflict. Was the conflict a war of aggression from the north? Of national liberation and unification? For some, the answer to the latter question was clearly affirmative. Others pointed out that, despite communist rhetoric, the conflict was neither a civil war nor a "people's war"—that effort was abandoned after failure of the Tet offensive in 1968—but, rather, a war of aggression, culminating in a massive invasion of South Vietnam by armored units, in gross violation of the 1973 Paris peace agreement.[17] Alternatively, was the conflict primarily a case of Soviet and Chinese expansion, either in concert or in competition with each other? Many analysts asserted that, whatever the military skills of the North Vietnamese leaders, their war effort was only made possible by massive military assistance from the USSR and China. For them, the conflict was a vital effort at containment in which the outcome was important to all Western nations. Those adhering to the latter viewpoint often expressed dissatisfaction with the level of support received from Western allies. Several observers also asserted that an inordinate fear of intervention by Chinese ground troops, following the pattern of Peking's entry into the Korean War in 1950, unduly constrained American military decisions.[18]

The results in Table 2.3 indicate mixed support among the leaders in this survey for interpretations of defeat that emphasize the role of other nations. Many (53 percent) respondents characterized Soviet and Chinese aid to North Vietnam as very important, and virtually none dismissed it as irrelevant to the outcome of the conflict. A substantially smaller number, one-third of the leaders in the sample, viewed North Vietnamese violations of the 1973 Paris peace agreement as a very important factor. Even fewer attributed such significance to the failure of SEATO allies to provide support. Indeed, 29 percent selected the "not at all important" alternative to the proposition that "America's allies failed us;" only two other potential explanations of American failure were dismissed by a larger number of leaders.

When the data are disaggregated into the seven groups, however, they reveal some rather striking differences. All of the groups attributed considerable importance to Soviet and Chinese aid to North Vietnam and the Vietcong, but there was a greater tendency for those toward the Supporter end of the spectrum to do so. This pattern is also evident in the case of the items on North Vietnamese violations of the Paris agreement and the failure of America's allies to provide support. Differences across the groups for all three items are statistically significant and they are generally in the predicted direction.[19] That is, leaders who most consistently supported the goal of military victory in Vietnam were also most likely to attribute importance to the role of other actors in the conflict.

Military Factors

In the debates over the sources of failure in Vietnam, few issues have received more continuing attention than the conduct of military operations. At the heart of the matter lie these key questions: Was the American intervention a doomed undertaking that, by virtue of the very nature of the situation, could not have been won at any reasonable price? Or could the war have been won had military operations been conducted differently? Those who believed that the war was inherently unwinnable are unlikely to endow military factors with great significance, whereas such considerations are more likely to be regarded as crucial by persons who believe that it could have been won.

Leaders who believe that military factors were important in determining the outcome in Vietnam have not exhibited complete agreement on specific strategic deficiencies. Even professional soldiers have been in disagreement on many aspects of the war effort.[20] For example, some analysts asserted that more effective use of air power could have resulted in an early victory at far less cost. They have tended to attribute North Vietnamese willingness to sign the Paris peace agreement in January 1973 to the intense bombing raids conducted by the United States during the previous month. Some of them have further argued that had similar air attacks been undertaken much earlier, the war could have been brought to a successful conclusion. Others have taken the position that the military value of air power has often been overstated, even in conventional wars—for example, in World War II—and that its relevance against guerilla operations is highly dubious, especially in a situation such as the Vietnam conflict. They have been especially emphatic in arguing that air power can never serve as an effective substitute for ground troops.

But disputes over air power merely reflect rather than exhaust debates on military aspects of the conflict. Similar disagreements have marked discussions on the merits of "graduated escalation," and on the limits of risks that could be run without compelling the Chinese to intervene with ground forces, as they did during the Korean War. The proper weight to be attached to political and military considerations in the conduct of war is an issue that recurs after virtually every conflict; given the nature and outcomes of the Korean and Vietnam wars, it is hardly surprising that it received a good deal of critical attention by advocates of several viewpoints on the question.[21]

The results summarized in Table 2.3 indicate substantial significance attributed to the proposition that the United States fought with a "no win" approach. More than two-fifths of the respondents rated this as a "very important" source of failure. Far greater ambivalence is evident on the importance of self-imposed restrictions on air power, excessive reliance on air power, and insufficient attention to advice from military commanders. The proposition that inadequate American military assistance to Saigon after the 1973 Paris peace agreement contributed to the outcome received the least support of any explanation of failure; over one-third of the leaders regarded this explanation as of no importance. During the final weeks before South Vietnam was overrun, President Ford and Secretary of State Kissinger asked the Congress for over one-half billion dollars of additional military assistance for Saigon. This was widely interpreted as an effort by Ford and Kissinger—who knew that the aid would have been too little and too late to save South Vietnam, and certain in any case to be rejected by the Congress—to lay blame for the imminent defeat on the Democrats who controlled both the House and Senate. However, few respondents were inclined to regard this as an important cause of defeat.

Responses of the seven groups yielded widely disparate interpretations. Indeed their views on the role of military factors span virtually
the entire scale. Added perspective on the striking differences can be
gained by examining the proportion of Supporters and Critics who
selected the "very important" and "not at all important" assessments
of the five military factors (Table 2.4). It is hard to imagine more
dramatic evidence of a systematic lack of consensus among the
nation's leaders than these results of their efforts to diagnose why the
longest war in American history ended in failure.

Table 2.4 *Proportions of Supporters and Critics who Characterized
each of Five Military Factors as "Very Important" or "Not at all
Important" Causes of Failure in Vietnam*
(Responses for the entire 1976 sample in percentages)

	Supporters		Critics	
	Very important	Not at all important	Very important	Not at all important
The US fought with a "no win" approach	85	1	13	44
The use of American air power was restricted	69	3	8	50
Insufficient attention was paid to advice from the military	57	4	3	62
US military assistance to South Vietnam after 1973 was inadequate	34	17	3	63
America relied excessively on air power	13	33	27	18

The data also confirm the hypothesis that those who consistently
favored military victory in Vietnam believed that the war could and
should have been won, but was lost because of self-imposed restraints
on military forces. On the other hand, leaders who favored withdrawal from Vietnam not only regarded it as an unwinnable situation
(as noted earlier), but also as one that could not have been salvaged by
a different deployment of military capabilities. The three groups of
Critics were also the most inclined to believe that the United States
relied excessively on air power. Differences among the seven groups
are statistically significant and in the predicted direction.[22]

Domestic Constraints

Whether won or lost, most wars generate extensive post-mortems on
strategy and tactics; Civil War buffs still debate the tactics employed
at Gettysburg. Lost wars, however, are most likely to focus attention

on the home front. Certainly this has been the case almost from the outset of the Vietnam conflict. In seeking explanations for failure, some analysts have pointed to flaws that are said to be deeply etched in the American character; for example, an impatience that operates against success in long-term undertakings, *naïveté* about the realities of power politics, or an alleged tendency to interpret international affairs by means of what Kenneth Boulding has called "cowboy theories," in which the actors all wear white hats or black hats.

An important and venerable school of thought maintains that there are basic incompatibilities between democratic institutions and requirements for success in foreign policy undertakings. Critics of the Wilsonian position that democracy is a necessary and perhaps sufficient condition for successful foreign policy have included a number of articulate observers, from Alexis de Tocqueville to Walter Lippmann. At present this theme is most forcefully and skillfully defended by George F. Kennan. Criticism of Congressional interference in the conduct of American foreign policy and skepticism of public opinion are common themes running throughout his voluminous writings.[23]

Some policy-makers have attempted to blame the Congressional interference for virtually all failings in Vietnam, but conflicts between the Congress and the White House are not the only ones that have received attention. Other analysts have argued that more general domestic divisions ultimately eroded the nation's ability to prosecute the Vietnam War, while at the same time increasing the resolve of adversaries to sustain their military efforts. Still others have pointed to the role of intellectuals. According to one view, they provided the rationale for American intervention; others have charged that intellectuals undermined the war effort.

The relationship between the media and domestic support for the war effort has been an especially contentious point. Views have ranged from the proposition that, in the face of government secrecy and deception, only the media provided the American people with valid information about what was really happening in Vietnam—the media alerted the public to the possibility that the "light at the end of the tunnel" of which so many Administration spokesmen boasted was really light years away. Others attributed American loss of will to media reports that ranged from superficial sensationalism on the evening television news to egregious distortion of key events, notably the Tet offensive of 1968. Calls for censorship, especially of television news, during times of war have been not infrequent. Henry Kissinger has perhaps been the most vocal proponent of the thesis that "The Vietnam defeat was almost entirely a U.S. domestic affair."[24]

Deep divisions over Vietnam in Congress, in the media, on campuses, and in American society in general suggest that a substantial number of leaders would perceive at least some domestic constraints as a major source of failure in Vietnam. The figures in Table 2.3 indicate considerable discrimination in assessing five domestic factors. More than two-thirds of the leaders in this survey attributed at least moderate importance to the role of the mass media and domestic dissidents as a source of failure in Vietnam.[25] At the same time, less than half of them regarded the role of the Congress to be of equal importance, and most respondents were inclined to dismiss as of little or no importance both the Watergate scandal and the diagnosis that "The American people lost the spirit that led to greatness." This source of failure raises the possibility of demagogues asking "Who are the false prophets (or traitors) who led the American people to lose their spirit?"—and then providing their own versions of the answers. That it received so little support may be comforting to those fearing a *post facto* witchhunt.

The data also provide strong support for the hypothesis that persons consistently championing the quest for military victory in Vietnam—the Supporters—would be most inclined to attribute significance to domestic constraints, whereas those favoring withdrawal from Southeast Asia would tend to regard the role of domestic institutions, groups, and events as of less importance. For each of the five items, the highest scores are to be found among the Supporters, whereas those of the Critics are in every case the lowest. Not only do the responses follow a pattern consistent with the hypotheses outlined earlier, but differences among the seven groups are statistically significant.[26] Although one might question whether the absence of the Watergate crimes would have altered the outcome in Vietnam— the Paris peace agreement was signed before the Nixon Administration's cover-up of the Watergate break-in started to come unravelled following the trial and conviction of the burglars—even differences on this item are significant.

World Opinion

The importance to be attributed to world opinion in politics is an issue that Americans have debated virtually every generation during the past two centuries; recall the phrase, "a decent respect for the opinion of mankind" in the Declaration of Independence. The question lies at the heart of the recurrent dialogue between the "realists" and "idealists" on foreign affairs.

Doubts abroad about the wisdom and morality of American intervention in Vietnam were evident in student protests that mirrored those in the United States, and also in a decided lack of enthusiasm among many allied leaders. Acerbic comments by General De Gaulle about American unwillingness to learn from the French experience in Vietnam were not wholly atypical. But the issue here is whether American leaders judged these reflections of "world opinion" to have contributed to the defeat in Vietnam. The last item listed in Table 2.3 permitted respondents to assess the significance of world opinion. More than three-fifths of them attributed at least moderate importance to opposition from many quarters abroad to American goals and policies in Vietnam. The hypothesis that those towards the Critic end of the spectrum would be inclined to give greater weight to world opinion as a source of failure in Vietnam receives some support from the data. Differences among the seven groups of leaders are significant, and there is a general—albeit not perfectly consistent—pattern of descending importance attributed to world opinion across the spectrum from Critics to Supporters.[27]

Sources of Failure: Conclusion

The results reported in Tables 2.3 and 2.4 reveal the manner in which the entire sample of leaders and the seven groups diagnosed the American failure to achieve its goals in Vietnam. The most striking findings to emerge from these data are these: With few exceptions, there are sharp differences over the sources of failure; differences among the seven groups provide strong support for the hypothesis that support and criticism of American policies in Vietnam are systematically linked to different diagnoses; and beliefs about the sources of failure form coherent and internally consistent sets of ideas.

The findings may also be summarized in a somewhat different way. Analyses up to this point have focused on inter-group comparisons, with attention directed at different responses to a single item or to a cluster of related items. Table 2.5, on the other hand, reveals how the leaders in each of the seven groups ranked the most important alternative explanations of failure. Several significant points may be discerned in this table. Notwithstanding a fairly demanding criterion for inclusion in the rankings (at least 0.67 on a scale of 0 to 1), respondents in each group tended to diagnose the failure of American policies in multi-causal terms; with the exception of the Ambivalents, no group had fewer than seven explanations qualifying for inclusion in the table. The results also confirm in a rather striking way the lack of consensus in diagnoses of failure. The ranks assigned to various explanations differ from column to column. Moreover, although the rankings include as many as ten explanations, no one of them appears in all seven columns, and only three—Soviet and Chinese aid, underestimation of North Vietnamese dedication, and lack of clarity in American goals—appear in six of the seven.

Prognosis: The Consequences of Vietnam

Aside from some dissidents who openly rooted for a North Vietnamese victory, relatively few observers have identified many favorable consequences of the American involvement in Southeast Asia.[28] Participants in the Vietnam debates have generally agreed that the United States will continue to pay a heavy price for its efforts to maintain the independence of South Vietnam, but disagreements arise over the precise nature and extent of the costs.

Table 2.5 Ranking of the Most Important Sources of Failure Cited by Each Group*

All Respondents	Supporters	Converted Supporters	Ambivalent Supporters	Ambivalents	Ambivalent Critics	Converted Critics	Critics
N. Vietnamese dedication	American "no win" approach	American "no win" approach	Soviet and Chinese aid	Soviet and Chinese aid	Unrealistic U.S. goals	N. Vietnamese dedication	Unrealistic U.S. goals
Soviet and Chinese aid	Restricted air power	Soviet and Chinese aid	American "no win" approach	N. Vietnamese dedication	Saigon lacked popular support	Saigon lacked popular support	Saigon lacked popular support
Saigon lacked popular support	Soviet and Chinese aid	Restricted air power	N. Vietnamese dedication	Dissidents hurt U.S. credibility	Misunderstood Third World nationalism	Unrealistic U.S. goals	N. Vietnamese dedication
Unrealistic U.S. goals	Media hurt war support in U.S.	U.S. had no clear goals	Media hurt war support in U.S.	Media hurt war support in U.S.	N. Vietnamese dedication	Soviet and Chinese aid	Misunderstood Third World nationalism
U.S. had no clear goals	Military advice unheeded	Media hurt war support in U.S.	Dissidents hurt U.S. credibility	Saigon lacked popular support	U.S. had no clear goals	Misunderstood Third World nationalism	U.S. ignorance of Vietnam
Media hurt war support in U.S.	Dissidents hurt U.S. credibility	Dissidents hurt U.S. credibility	N. Vietnam peace violations	N. Vietnam peace violations	U.S. ignorance of Vietnam	U.S. had no clear goals	U.S. had no clear goals
Misunderstood Third World nationalism	N. Vietnam peace violations	Military advice unheeded	U.S. had no clear goals		Soviet and Chinese aid	U.S. ignorance of Vietnam	Opposition of world opinion
	Congressional interference	N. Vietnam peace violations	Restricted air power		Media hurt war support in U.S.		
	U.S. had no clear goals	N. Vietnamese dedication	Saigon lacked popular support				
		Congressional interference					

* This table lists all the explanations of failure that received an average rating of at least 0.67 (moderately important) on a scale of 1.00 (very important) to 0.00 (not at all important). Explanations are listed in order of decreasing importance for each group.

Discussions of the war in Southeast Asia were rarely limited to the fate of the Saigon regime. Interest in and divergent interpretations of the broader regional and international consequences of success or failure have been no less evident. Terms such as "domino theory," "quagmire," "credibility," "commitment," "lessons of Munich," and many others became central symbols—objects of derision or eternal verities of international life, depending on one's orientation—in the often bitter dialogue about the probable consequences of one course of action or another. At the heart of many debates were to be found such general questions as: Will the consequences of Vietnam be confined to that country, or will they spill over to other nations or regions? Will they significantly affect the balance of power in Asia or, indeed, in the entire international system? What will be the impact of Vietnam on the foreign policy orientation of America's adversaries, allies, and the "non-aligned" nations?

One line of reasoning has emphasized America's reputation as a dependable ally. Other nations will be less willing to align themselves, much less stake their vital security interests, on the basis of commitments from Washington.[29] As a result, the Soviet Union and its allies will be more inclined to become involved in Third World situations that offer gains, knowing both that America's reputation has been damaged and that the United States is likely to avoid future involvement in such conflicts. In short, Vietnam gave rise to a fundamental change in the balance of power between Washington and Moscow. Admiral Elmo Zumwalt's prognosis epitomizes this viewpoint: "This war did more to advance Soviet objectives, long since declared in their annual Party Congresses, than any previous event in the preceding fifty-nine years."[30]

Not all predictions are quite so apocalyptic, however. To some, the most pessimistic scenarios are basically invalid for several reasons: the outcome in Vietnam has not affected in any fundamental way the balance of power in the global system; the Vietnam experience was unique and, therefore, it will not be repeated in other regions; and it may well ensure that the United States will not again squander its resources in such futile undertakings.[31] The more serious problem, according to some, is that the Vietnam experience, rather than giving rise to a more careful and sophisticated assessment of vital national interests, will result instead in an undiscriminating isolationism, resurrecting and reinforcing traditional American fears of international involvement, distaste for bargaining, and the like.[32] As one observer has put it, "The most lasting international consequence of Vietnam—and not only for Americans—may well be on Americans' perceptions of themselves, of the world, and of the proper role of the United States in it."[33]

Discussions of the consequences arising from the Vietnam experience have not been limited to its impact on foreign policy and international relations. They have also included further controversial questions about domestic effects. To what extent and in what ways has the American economy suffered lasting damage as a result of the war? More generally, has the war left permanent scars on American society and, perhaps even more importantly, on public trust in the efficacy and probity of the government, the media, and other important institutions? Conversely, have reactions to the war and to the related Watergate crimes resulted in even more serious damage than the abuses they were intended to correct? Have they, for example, crippled the ability of the President or of the Central Intelligence Agency to conduct properly the nation's foreign relations? Finally, in what ways, if any, will the bitter memories of Vietnam act as a domestic constraint—for better or worse—on the future conduct of the nation's foreign policy?

This section explores concern over the future repercussions of Vietnam by examining responses of the leadership sample to thirteen possible consequences of Vietnam. In addition to reporting results for the entire leadership group, data for the seven groups will permit a test of the hypotheses outlined earlier. To recapitulate briefly, these predicted that the Supporters would, in assessing the consequences of the war, emphasize: adverse effects on the international system; encouragement of expansionist tendencies on the part of adversaries; and constraints on future American foreign policies, including restrictions on military actions, even when vital interests are at stake. On the other hand, Critics would be likely to stress the adverse consequences of the Vietnam experience on American society and institutions, and the other five groups would respond in ways that fall between the Supporters and Critics.

Impact on the International System

Much of the debate during and since the conclusion of the Vietnam War centered on predicted international consequences. At issue were questions about the impact of various outcomes in Vietnam on the structure of the international system, America's leadership role in that system, the credibility of American defense commitments, and the future international conduct of both allies and adversary nations, especially the Soviet Union and China.

The first three items in Table 2.6 reveal substantial ambivalence among the leadership sample about the impact of the Vietnam experience on the international system. Nearly three-fourths agreed that the credibility of American defense commitments had been seriously eroded as a consequence of the war. However, slight majorities disagreed with the general proposition that the structure of the international system was fundamentally altered by the outcome in Vietnam, and the more specific thesis that a swing toward the ascendancy of communist influence in world affairs emerged from the conflict. In short, these leaders as a group assessed the systemic consequences of the war in ways that fell roughly in between the most optimistic and most pessimistic positions.

Table 2.6 Prognosis: *Consequences of the Vietnam War*
(Responses for the entire sample of 2,282 leaders, and analyses of
seven groups of respondents classified by their 1976 positions during
the early and late stages of the war in Vietnam)

There has been quite a bit of discussion about the consequences of the Vietnam episode. Some of these are listed below. Please indicate your assessment of each statement by checking only one box for each item.	*All respondents**	*Differences between groups significant?***	*Correlation, actual and hypothesized group rankings****
Impact on the international system			
The Vietnam episode has raised profound doubts about American credibility in the minds of our allies	.38	Yes	.96
The shape of the international system we have known since World War II has been irrevocably altered by America's inability to prevent collapse of the Thieu regime in 1975	−.12	Yes	1.00
The tide of influence in world affairs has swung toward communism as a result of the Vietnam War	−.16	Yes	1.00
Adversaries encouraged			
Communist nations have been encouraged to seek triumphs elsewhere as a result of Vietnam	.32	Yes	1.00
The major assumptions of détente have been proven false by the events in Vietnam	−.13	Yes	.89
Constraints on future U.S. policy			
The U.S. is likely to operate with a more limited conception of the national interest as a result of the outcome in Vietnam	.43	No	.24
The memory of Vietnam will prevent the U.S. from using force even when vital American interests abroad are threatened	−.05	Yes	.95

Table 2.6   Continued:

There has been quite a bit of discussion about the consequences of the Vietnam episode. Some of these are listed below. Please indicate your assessment of each statement by checking only one box for each item.	All respondents*	Differences between groups significant?**	Correlation, actual and hypothesized group rankings***
Types of future U.S. undertakings As a result of the Vietnam experience, the U.S. is likely to keep military assistance to anti-Soviet factions in Angola to a minimum	.76	Yes	.74
As a result of events in Vietnam, the U.S. is likely to engage in high risk ventures in order to re-establish its credibility	−.64	Yes	.63
As a consequence of the Vietnam episode, American policies toward the "Third World" will emphasize humanitarian rather than military aid	.09	Yes	.93
Damage to American society The real long-term threats to national security—energy shortages, the environment, etc.—have been neglected as a result of our preoccupation with Vietnam	.36	Yes	.86
The American people have lost faith in the honesty of their government as a result of the Vietnam War	.33	Yes	.71
The foundations of the American economy were seriously damaged by our involvement in Vietnam	.22	Yes	.75

* Calculated on a scale of 1.00 (Agree strongly) to −1.00 (Disagree strongly).
** Differences between seven groups of respondents, calculated by analysis of variance, at the .001 level of significance.
*** Spearman rank-order correlation between hypotheses and actual rankings of seven groups.

The hypotheses introduced earlier predicted that leaders toward the Supporter end of the spectrum would be more inclined to predict negative international consequences fostered by the war, and those toward the Critic end would be likely to focus on the domestic consequences of the conflict. The data provide strong support for this line of reasoning. For the two items on the shape of the international system and the tide of influence in world affairs, there is a consistent pattern of agreement as one moves from the Critics toward the Supporters. With but a single exception, the same pattern is evident on the issue of declining American credibility. For all three items the differences across the seven groups are also statistically significant.[34]

Impact on Adversaries

Spokesmen for the Kennedy, Johnson, Nixon, and Ford administrations often claimed that the primary rationale for American involvement in Vietnam was to ensure that aggression would not pay. Unless it were clearly demonstrated that so-called "wars of national liberation" could not succeed in the face of American commitments to defend all of its allies, the Soviet Union, China, and their proxies would be encouraged to undertake similar adventures elsewhere. Ambassador Frederick Nolting summarized this fear: "If we recoil in horror from helping a friendly country maintain its independence against this kind of subversion, and if the other side judges that we are going to recoil in horror because of the Vietnam experience, undoubtedly there will be other cases in many parts of the world."[35] Those opposing the war effort usually questioned such arguments, often focusing their critical attention on the "domino" metaphor that seemed to lie at the center of Administration reasoning and rhetoric.

Whatever the merits of the much-debated and often-derided "domino theory," two-thirds of the responding leaders predicted that the outcome of the war in Vietnam would in fact encourage communist nations to seek other triumphs. The evidence summarized in Table 2.6 also reveals that, while many respondents believed that the American defeat in Vietnam would provide an impetus for communist expansion, they were unwilling to regard détente as a policy based on false premises. Because responses to the items are highly correlated ($r=.46$), perhaps it is useful to speculate on why this is so. Several possible explanations may be offered. There may have been a good deal of variation, if not confusion, in understandings of the term "détente." The fact that an unusually high proportion—11 percent—of the respondents selected the "no opinion" alternative on this item may be an indication of uncertainty about its meaning. Perhaps some respondents understood the first item to refer primarily to competition in the Third World, and the second to Soviet–American relations only. A third explanation is closely related: during the Nixon–Ford–Kissinger era, administration spokesmen frequently warned about domino effects arising from certain outcomes in Southeast Asia, while at the same time soliciting active support for a policy of détente with the USSR.

When the data are disaggregated, substantial support is uncovered for the hypothesis that the Supporters would be most likely to predict threatening actions by adversaries in the aftermath of Vietnam. The range of group scores for both items is exceptionally wide, differences among the groups are statistically significant, and there is a consistent, if not perfect decline in scores from the groups on the Supporter end of the spectrum to those on the Critic end of the scale.[36]

Constraints on Future American Foreign Policy

"No more Vietnams" may be merely a slogan that summarizes the frustrations of many Americans who opposed American involvement in Southeast Asia, as well as of many others who, while not opposed to the undertaking itself, were critical of the manner in which the war was conducted. But the Nixon Doctrine signalled to the entire world that, at the very least, the United States would in the future be highly selective in deciding whom it would defend and the terms for doing so; in essence, it reduced almost to vanishing point the probabilities that American ground troops would be introduced into conflicts in peripheral areas. The era that began with the Truman Doctrine and that reached a peak, at least at the rhetorical level, in John F. Kennedy's Inaugural Address—it offered to "bear any burden or pay any price" in support of freedom—had come to an end. As a consequence of the Vietnam conflict, debate focused less on the issue of whether there were limits on America's vital interests abroad, emphasizing instead the questions of where those limits were located and whether future administrations would go to excessive lengths, even to the neglect of the national interest, to avoid "another Vietnam,"[37]

The data reflect some ambivalence on these issues. Almost four-fifths of the leaders agreed that in the future the United States would be likely to conduct its foreign relations with a narrower conception of the national interest. (It is worth noting, however, that a much smaller proportion of the respondents (56 percent) believed that the United States should operate with a scaled-down conception of its leadership role; see Table 2.8 below.) At the same time, they were almost evenly divided over the proposition that the memory of Vietnam would serve as a constraint against the use of force even when vital American interests were in jeopardy.

The prediction that leaders who supported the war effort would be more inclined to perceive the Vietnam experience as constraining the future conduct of American foreign policy is only partially sustained by the data. All seven groups are clustered in a very narrow range, with each having recorded agreement with the prediction that the Vietnam experience will result in a more limited conception of the national interest. On the other hand, data on the proposition relating to future use of force to protect vital interests support the hypothesis at a significant level.[38]

Types of Future American Undertakings

Up to this point attention has been directed at predictions about the international system, the conduct of adversaries, and the general American orientation towards international affairs. This section examines the likely consequences of the Vietnam War on specific types of future foreign policy undertakings. The questionnaire included three items relevant to this issue: likely responses to the Ford Administration's call for material assistance to anti-Soviet factions in Angola; and two more general questions about the types of activities that the United States might undertake in the future— humanitarian rather than military assistance, and high-risk ventures aimed at restoring American credibility in the wake of the losing war effort.

The respondents agreed almost unanimously that there would be a minimal American role in Angola despite manifest Soviet and Cuban intervention in that country. This response is not surprising. The issue was still to be settled when the questionnaire was printed, but the leaders received it just after the debate in Washington had resolved that the United States would not play an active role in the conflict. On 26 January, 1976, 200 members of the House of Representatives signed a resolution opposing American aid to Angola, and on 18 February, the Senate passed by a margin of 60–30 a foreign aid bill that included a prohibition on covert military aid to any forces in Angola. The questionnaires were distributed during the first week of February. Far less agreement is evident on the prediction that foreign aid would be redirected from military to humanitarian programs, and the respondents rejected by an overwhelming margin the prognosis that the United States would seek to re-establish its lost credibility by engaging in high-risk adventures abroad.

The line of reasoning developed earlier suggested that the more respondents supported the American effort in Vietnam, the more they would be inclined to predict (but not applaud) the war as giving rise to a weakened and constrained United States with a reduced ability to play a significant role in international affairs. Differences among the seven groups are statistically significant, with a tendency toward support of the hypotheses.[39] That is, fewer Supporters than Critics were inclined to believe that the United States would play an active role in Angola, or to re-establish its credibility, and more of them predicted a shift away from military aid to Third World countries. However, the pattern across groups is mixed and somewhat inconclusive.

Impact on American Society

Vietnam has been linked to everything from the sexual revolution to the drug culture. Whether it will ultimately become the political equivalent of sunspots—cited as the cause of virtually everything that goes wrong in American society—remains to be seen, but clearly the idea that the war had important domestic effects has come to be widely shared. Among the consequences to which it has been linked are economic dislocations, loss of confidence in institutions from the press to the Presidency, and a general decline of faith, spirit, and optimism.[40]

Three questionnaire items focused on the impact of the war on American society and institutions. The results, presented at the end of Table 2.6, reveal support for the propositions that the war effort resulted in a neglect of more serious, non-military threats to national security; in a loss of faith in the honesty of the government; and in structural damage to the economy. More than 70 percent of the respondents expressed some degree of agreement with the first two propositions, and more than three-fifths agreed with the third item.

According to the hypotheses introduced earlier, those who consistently favored withdrawal from Vietnam would be more inclined to focus on the negative domestic consequences of the war than would leaders who supported the search for a military victory. The results support the hypothesis. All three items yielded a wide range of responses. Differences among the groups are statistically significant and they are generally in the predicted direction.[41]

Consequences of Vietnam: Conclusion

The findings have revealed sharp differences among the seven groups. Some emphasized the negative consequences of the war on the nation's position in the world, whereas others stressed its impact on domestic institutions. Most of the differences are in the predicted direction.

The data may also be summarized in a somewhat different way by ranking the predicted consequences of the war within each group (Table 2.7). This procedure highlights several points. The three groups on the Supporter end of the scale all cited international consequences as the most important legacies of Vietnam. Indeed, the rankings for these three groups are identical (although the underlying scores on which they are based are not). The Ambivalents cited the same international consequences, although in a different order. Among the Critics groups the most important results of the war are almost wholly different than those cited by the Supporters; the consequences they assessed as the most important are oriented toward domestic rather than international ones. Lack of consensus among the groups is underscored by the fact that only a single item—"The United States is likely to operate with a more limited conception of

Table 2.7 Ranking of the Consequences of Vietnam Receiving Highest Agreement from Each Group*

	All Respondents	Supporters	Converted Supporters	Ambivalent Supporters	Ambivalents	Ambivalent Critics	Converted Critics	Critics
1	U.S. will limit conception of national interest	Communists will seek other triumphs	Communists will seek other triumphs	Communists will seek other triumphs	U.S. will limit conception of national interest	U.S. economy damaged	Long-term threats neglected	Long-term threats neglected
2	American credibility damaged	American credibility damaged	American credibility damaged	American credibility damaged	Communists will seek other triumphs	Long-term threats neglected	U.S. will limit conception of national interest	Lost faith in U.S. government
3	Long-term threats neglected	U.S. will limit conception of national interest	U.S. will limit conception of national interest	U.S. will limit conception of national interest	American credibility damaged	Lost faith in U.S. government	Lost faith in U.S. government	U.S. economy damaged
4	Lost faith in U.S. government					American credibility damaged		U.S. will limit conception of national interest
5	Communists will seek other triumphs					U.S. will limit conception of national interest		

*This table lists all the "consequences of Vietnam" that received at least an average rating of 0.03 on a scale of 1.00 (agree strongly) to −1.00 (disagree strongly). Consequences are listed in order of decreasing importance for each group. This table does not include data for the item stating: "As a result of the Vietnam experience, the USA is likely to keep military assistance to anti-Soviet factions in Angola to a minimum." Congressional action had settled that issue before respondents returned their questionnaires.

the national interest as a result of the outcome in Vietnam"— appears in all seven columns, and none of the other items appear in six columns.

Prescription: The Lessons of Vietnam

The Vietnam War is not the first event to inspire post-mortems aimed at adducing lessons for the future conduct of foreign policy. But it is doubtful that any previous episode in American history has given rise to such an extensive and conscious effort to learn from the past, so as not to be "doomed to repeat it." As soon as American intervention in Southeast Asia had become controversial during the mid-1960s, and long before the conflict had been resolved by the conquest of South Vietnam, politicians, soldiers, pundits, editorial writers, and many others began offering a continuing stream of advice about what Americans should and should not learn from the Vietnam experience. Thirty-four questionnaire items represent a sample of these lessons; Table 2.8 summarizes the responses of the 2,282 leaders who participated in this survey. These data also provide the basis for testing a series of hypotheses about the pattern of responses among the seven groups. Summarized very briefly, the Supporters were expected to emphasize: bipolarity of the international system, threats from communist adversaries, the utility of military power, unilateral actions to cope with conflicts, and the adverse effects of domestic constraints on foreign policy. On the other hand, the Critics were expected to stress reduced American involvement abroad and governmental ineffectiveness in formulating foreign policy.

The International System

A variety of interpretations that were central to the debates during and since the Vietnam War revolved around some questions pertaining to the structure of the international system: Is the system essentially bipolar in nature—as during the height of the Cold War—or have its structure and characteristic patterns of interaction changed in ways that challenge the premises of bipolarity? This broad question implies several further ones about the degree of cohesion among communist nations and the locus of control of various revolutionary groups. At least three viewpoints emerged from the Vietnam debates: unity of the communist movement; fragmentation among communist nations, but continued hostility of the parts toward the United States; and such permanent cleavages that "The communist world will never be able to function as a single force."[42] Concern with structure was not merely a semantic debate. Those perceiving a bipolar system regarded the effects of a defeat, as in Vietnam, as far more serious than persons who believed that the fragmentation and diffusion of effective power had created a multi-polar system. The latter were therefore

Table 2.8   Prescription: The Lessons of Vietnam
(Responses for the entire sample of 2,282 leaders, and analyses of
seven groups of respondents classified by their 1976 positions during
the early and late stages of the war in Vietnam)

This question asks you to indicate your position on certain foreign policy issues. Indicate how strongly you agree or disagree with each statement	All respondents*	Differences between groups significant?**	Correlation, actual and hypothesized group rankings***
The international system			
A nation will pay a heavy price if it honors its alliance commitments only selectively	.49	Yes	.96
There is considerable validity in the "domino theory" that when one nation falls to communism, others nearby will soon follow a similar path	.24	Yes	.93
Revolutionary forces in "Third World" countries are usually nationalistic rather than controlled by the USSR or China	.19	Yes	.93
Any communist victory is a defeat for America's national interest	−.14	Yes	.93
American foreign policy should be based on the premise that the Communist "bloc" is irreparably fragmented	−.25	Yes	.96
Threats from adversaries			
The Soviet Union is generally expansionist rather than defensive in its foreign policy goals	.59	Yes	.96
Détente permits the USSR to pursue policies that promote rather than restrain conflict	.15	Yes	.94
China is generally expansionist rather than defensive in its foreign policy goals	−.27	Yes	.96

Table 2.8   Continued:

This question asks you to indicate your position on certain foreign policy issues. Indicate how strongly you agree or disagree with each statement	All respondents*	Differences between groups significant?**	Correlation, actual and hypothesized group rankings***
Utility of military power			
If foreign interventions are undertaken, the necessary force should be applied in a short period of time rather than through a policy of graduated escalation	.55	Yes	.88
The efficiency of military power in foreign affairs is declining	.17	No	.82
The U.S. should never try to get by with half measures; we should apply necessary power if we have it	.07	Yes	.99
Rather than simply countering our opponent's thrusts, it is necessary to strike at the heart of the opponent's power	.01	Yes	.89
Limited wars should be fought primarily with air power so as to avoid introducing American ground troops	−.17	No	.25
When force is used, military rather than political goals should determine its application	−.21	Yes	.89
Reducing U.S. involvement abroad			
The best way to encourage democratic development in the "Third World" is for the U.S. to solve its own problems	.27	Yes	.25
Stationing American troops in other countries encourages them to let us do their fighting for those countries	.15	Yes	.71
Weak allies excessively influence U.S. foreign policy	.04	No	−.03
America's conception of its leadership in the world must be scaled down	.04	Yes	.95
Military aid programs will eventually draw the United States into unnecessary wars	−.11	Yes	.71

Table 2.8   Continued:

This question asks you to indicate your position on certain foreign policy issues. Indicate how strongly you agree or disagree with each statement	All respondents*	Differences between groups significant?**	Correlation, actual and hypothesized group rankings***
Vital interests of the U.S. are largely confined to Western Europe, Japan, and the Americas	−.19	Yes	.47
It was a serious mistake to agree to locate American technicians in the Sinai	−.47	Yes	.51
Coping with conflict unilaterally			
The U.S. should avoid any involvement in the Angolan civil war	.49	Yes	.86
It is vital to enlist the cooperation of the U.N. in settling international disputes	.20	Yes	.96
The U.S. should undertake military intervention in the Middle East in case of another oil embargo	−.50	Yes	.96
Performance of the U.S. government			
Americans have relied too much on Presidents to define the national interest	.22	Yes	.86
The press is more likely than the government to report the truth about the conduct of foreign policy	.15	Yes	.93
The conduct of American foreign affairs relies excessively on military advice	.02	Yes	.96
Domestic constraints on foreign policy			
An effective foreign policy is impossible when the Executive and Congress are unable to cooperate	.47	Yes	.93
The American people lack the patience for foreign policy undertakings that offer little prospect for success in the short run	.39	Yes	.86

Table 2.8   Continued:

This question asks you to indicate your position on certain foreign policy issues. Indicate how strongly you agree or disagree with each statement	All respondents*	Differences between groups significant?**	Correlation, actual and hypothesized group rankings***
Americans lack an understanding of the role that power plays in world politics	.36	Yes	.96
Limited war cannot be conducted successfully because of constraints imposed by the American political system	.23	Yes	.88
The freedom to dissent at home inhibits the effective conduct of American foreign policy	−.43	Yes	.96
Uses of the past			
If officials would treat each new crisis on its own merits, rather than relying on past experience, they would usually make better foreign policy decisions	−.06	Yes	.57
It is best to forget the foreign policy mistakes of the past as quickly as possible	−.57	Yes	.88

  * Calculated on a scale of 1.00 (Agree strongly) to −1.00 (Disagree strongly).
 ** Differences between seven groups of respondents, calculated by analysis of variance, at the .001 level of significance.
*** Spearman rank-order correlation between hypotheses and actual rankings of seven groups.

less persuaded by premises of the domino theory or of a zero-sum (your gain is my loss) relationship between the United States and its adversaries.

The first five items listed in Table 2.8 focus on several facets of these issues. The aggregate responses revealed substantial ambivalence. On the one hand, they indicated very strong support—agreement by more than two-thirds of the respondents—for the validity of the "domino theory," and for the proposition that failure to honor alliance commitments will result in heavy costs. Moreover, they were decidedly skeptical about the permanence of divisions among communist states, a central tenet of those who assert that the Cold War has indeed passed into history. On the other hand, substantial if not overwhelming majorities questioned some core premises of the Cold War period. Almost 60 percent of the leaders disagreed with the proposition that "any communist victory is a defeat for America's national interest," and a like proportion agreed that revolutionary forces in the Third World are more likely to reflect nationalist aspirations than those of Moscow or Peking.[43]

The results for the entire sample of 2,282 leaders reflect perceptions of the international system that conform consistently to the views of neither the staunch advocates of bipolarity nor of multi-polarity, but when disaggregated into the seven groups, a much clearer pattern of responses emerges. Leaders who persisted in favoring military victory in Vietnam offered strong support for lesson that the international system maintains its essentially bipolar structure; that is, they expressed strong agreement with the first, second and fourth items in Table 2.8. Conversely, they were least supportive of the items on Third World revolutionary forces and cleavages within the communist block, both of which are more consistent with a definition of the international system as multi-polar rather than bipolar. Differences among the seven groups are statistically significant, and they form a consistent, if not perfect, pattern corresponding to the hypothesis.[44]

Adversaries

The war in Vietnam coincided with some highly visible changes in relations between Washington and its most powerful adversaries—at least at the symbolic level. President Nixon's visit to China in 1972, and the exchange of visits between Nixon and Chairman Brezhnev seemed to indicate that, despite conflicting interests in Southeast Asia, the hostile relationships of the Cold War period were undergoing some fundamental transformations; but the nature of the changes are hardly free from controversy. Some believed that détente both reflected and reinforced a transformation of Soviet leaders into "pragmatic managers far more interested in securing national borders, developing its own consumer economy, and controlling its own population than in making revolution anywhere."[45] Others were far less optimistic about either the sources or consequences of détente, which "in no way affects the long-term objectives of the Communist movement."[46]

Beliefs about the international system are closely related to images of adversaries and their intentions. The previous section noted a tendency among leaders to accept some of the general axioms that are often associated with bipolarity—for example, the "domino theory"—while rejecting some others. The second cluster of items in Table 2.8 also reveals some ambivalence about adversaries and their foreign policy goals. The most interesting finding is the sharply divergent interpretations of Soviet and Chinese goals. During the height of the Cold War, assessments of these communist nations typically took one of two forms: they are indistinguishable with respect to powerful expansionist motivations, or the older Soviet regime has come to play a relatively conservative role in world affairs, whereas that in Beijing is not only inherently expansionist, but it is also recklessly and irrationally so. Thus, American involvement in Vietnam was often described and justified as an exercise in containing Chinese expansion, and the rhetoric of senior officials in Washington rarely failed to portray the leadership in Beijing as aggressive and not altogether predictable with respect to foreign affairs.[47] Yet less than 30 percent of the respondents agreed with the proposition that China is expansionist in its foreign policy goals, and only 7 percent expressed strong agreement with that interpretation.

Perhaps one explanation for the radical shift in leadership views of China is the venerable political adage that, "My enemy's enemy is my friend." Certainly an overwhelming majority (83 percent) of the leaders regarded the Soviet Union as an expansionist rather than defensive power. This view of Soviet foreign policy motives is also evident in the decidedly skeptical assessment of détente; a clear majority (56 percent) of the respondents expressed some degree of agreement with the lesson that the USSR is using détente to promote rather than to limit conflict.

The hypothesis that the Supporters would be more inclined than the Critics to regard Cold War adversaries as expansionist and threatening is strongly supported when the data are disaggregated. Differences between the groups are statistically significant and they are in the predicted direction for all three items.[48] All the groups were inclined to agree that the Soviet Union is expansionist and that China is not, but the degree to which they did so varies rather widely. Even less consensus is evident on the proposition that the Soviet Union abuses détente to promote conflict; the Supporters agreed, and the Critics disagreed. These results appear to indicate that the former were more consistent than the latter in appraising Soviet goals and uses of détente. As noted earlier, however, this may be the result of ambiguities about the precise meaning of détente.

The Utility of Military Power

That the failure of a military effort costing some 50,000 lives and $150 billion should give rise to sober second thoughts about the role of military power in contemporary foreign affairs is scarcely surprising. In the search through the Vietnam experience for usable lessons, few topics have generated more attention—and controversy—than those concerning the utility and proper deployment of military capabilities in the contemporary international system. Many observers have noted an American tendency to place strong, and perhaps inordinate, faith in the deployment of advanced military technology. If World War II seemed to provide the ultimate confirmation of the belief that technology will be decisive in determining the victor, the Vietnam experience has at least stimulated some serious reconsideration about its applicability to certain types of contemporary conflicts. Out of this assessment of the war has come an outpouring of proposed lessons on the proper relationship of military power to national security and foreign policy goals.. Whether, and under what circumstances, military power can serve as an effective instrument of policy are questions that have brought further varied responses. More specific issues focused upon the most effective timetable for the application of force, with special attention to the merits and demerits of "graduated escalation." But even critics of American strategy could not agree on the proper prescription. For some, the appropriate lesson is that, to be effective, "Escalation must be massive and sudden"; others argued that more rather than less patience would have enhanced the efficacy of American military strategy.[49]

Responses to six items centering on the utility of military power are summarized in Table 2.8. Of the thirty-four items appearing on this part of the questionnaire, the lesson that received the strongest support from the entire sample of leaders was that in any future foreign intervention, force should be applied quickly rather than through a policy of graduated escalation. Although almost 10 percent of the respondents expressed "no opinion" on this lesson of the war, more than three-fourths of them agreed with it, and most did so strongly. The overwhelmingly favorable reaction to this proposition perhaps confirms, in part, another of the lessons (discussed below): "The American people lack the patience for foreign policy undertakings that offer little prospect for success in the short run."

Results for the next five items, however, reflect at least some ambivalence about the role of military power in contemporary world affairs. Sixty percent of the leaders agreed that the efficiency of military power as an instrument of policy is declining. Moreover, items on avoiding half measures and striking at "the heart of the opponent's power" elicited only slightly more agreement than disagreement, with a high level of "no opinions" on the latter issue. The proposal to reduce the costs of limited wars by heavier reliance on air power received only modest (32 percent) support. The final item addresses a question that recurs during every war: Should military operations be conducted to maximize military or political goals? By a margin of almost two to one, the respondents favored the primacy of political goals.

When the data are disaggregated the results reveal a striking range of views among the seven groups. They provide consistent and substantial support for the hypothesis that the military lessons drawn from the Vietnam War would be systematically related to positions on the proper course of American policy in that conflict. Leaders at or near the Supporter end of the spectrum tended to believe that military power should be used more quickly, with fewer self-imposed restraints, and with greater efficiency, whereas those with diametrically opposed policy preferences on Vietnam were less inclined to accept these lessons. Differences among the seven groups are generally in the predicted direction, and they are statistically significant for four of the six items; the exceptions are the propositions on the declining efficiency of military power, and the substitution of air power for ground forces.[50]

American Involvement Abroad

In the wake of the Vietnam War, many questions were asked about if, when, where, and how the United States should attempt to regulate, if not control, its international environment. How active a role should the United States play in international affairs—and for what ends? What is the nature of the national interest, and to what extent is it engaged by foreign conflicts, especially by those in Third World areas? What lessons, if any, can be learned from Vietnam about the proper scope and exercise of a leadership position in the world—or at least in its non-communist sector? What values, opportunities and constraints define the desirable and the possible in external relations? Those who sought answers to such questions in the Vietnam experience offered lessons that covered virtually the entire spectrum of possibilities, from the prescription that extended international responsibilities are inescapable for the "rich and powerful," to the conclusion that the United States "must abandon the illusion that we can purchase safety or advantage by regulating and controlling our political environment."[51]

Seven questionnaire items provided leaders in the sample an opportunity to address such questions. Their responses, summarized in Table 2.8, reveal a general lack of consensus on appropriate international roles for the United States, although there is some tendency toward preference for a somewhat reduced American involvement in world affairs. A slight majority of the respondents agreed that the United States should scale down its international leadership role, and a somewhat larger proportion (64 percent) was in accord with the proposition that America's ability to influence the course of events in the Third World may be limited to power of example, by demonstrating a capability for solving its own problems. Although this pattern of responses suggests a yearning for fewer global responsibilities, other items indicate no great groundswell of support for a post-Vietnam return to traditional isolationism. By a margin of more than three to two the leaders in this survey rejected the proposition that American vital interests are confined to the industrial democracies in Europe, Japan, and the Americas.

Three additional items are of special interest in the light of suggestions that America's military commitments abroad should be curtailed. Evidence of such sentiments may be found in: the Nixon Doctrine; former President Carter's campaign promise to withdraw American troops from South Korea; and support in the Congress, revealed in the close vote on the Mansfield Amendment and the 1982 vote of 12–1 in the Senate Foreign Relations Committee, for reducing the American military presence in Western Europe. By a margin of approximately three to two, respondents agreed that stationing troops abroad encourages the host country to let the United States do their fighting for them. But by a roughly comparable proportion they rejected the proposition that military assistance programs will draw the United States into unnecessary wars, and only a small plurality agreed that weak allies have excessive influence on American foreign policy. Finally, only 17 percent of the leaders agreed that deployment of American technicians in the Sinai Desert was a mistake. Although great caution must be exercised in generalizing from responses to a single item, the latter finding may provide some comfort to those who feared that a "Vietnam syndrome" would result in indiscriminate rejection of even the most benign types of American interventions abroad.

The hypothesis that leaders toward the Supporter end of the spectrum would adduce lessons from Vietnam that recommended a more active American role in the world, whereas those on the Critics side would draw the opposite conclusion, received mixed support. The data summarized in Table 2.8 reveal that responses to propositions on conceptions of America's leadership role and on military aid programs are strongly in accord with the hypothesis. Differences among the seven groups are statistically significant and they are generally in the predicted direction.[52] Although differences among groups for four of the other five items concerning American involvement abroad are also significant (the exception is the proposition on the influence of weak allies), the distribution of scores across groups follows a less regular and pronounced pattern.

These findings generally reveal that Critics are more prone than Supporters to cut back on American involvement abroad; but there are sufficient deviations in the pattern of responses to warrant some further thought. The results may indicate the existence of a second element of thinking about international affairs—an internationalism–isolationism dimension—that is not completely reflected in a classification scheme based on Vietnam policy preferences. This speculation receives some support from the rather similar prescriptions of observers who differed on virtually every aspect of the Vietnam War. According to Senator Edward Kennedy, "The lesson is that we must throw off the cumbersome mantle of world policeman and limit our readiness to intervene to areas where our interests are truly endangered."[53] John Frisbee arrived at a similar conclusion about reducing commitments abroad, for quite different reasons:

> Our contest with the amoeba-like force (international communism) is open-ended. There can be no effective opposition to it without U.S. participation or support. And since the U.S. has neither the means nor the will (nor now, perhaps, the credibility) to counter aggression everywhere, our truly vital national interests must be redefined.[54]

But such anecdotal evidence is suggestive rather than conclusive. The question of an internationalist–isolationist dimension in foreign policy beliefs is examined in more detail in Chapters 4 and 5.

Coping with Conflict

In addition to eliciting views on the appropriate global role for the United States, the questionnaire also included three items on conflict situations abroad and, more specifically, on ways of dealing with such situations. Two of the items focused on issues of current interest at the time the questionnaire was mailed—the appropriate American role in the Angola conflict, and the advisability of intervening militarily in the Middle East in case of another oil embargo. The third item concerns the extent to which the United Nations should be used to cope with international conflicts.

The results reveal some predisposition against unilateral actions to deal with conflict issues. Solid majorities indicated a preference against involvement in Angola, and for enlisting the cooperation of the United Nations in settling international disputes. Three-quarters of the respondents rejected the proposition that military intervention would be an appropriate response to any future oil embargo, as had been proposed by a number of prominent academic observers.[55] In short, although these three items do not represent the full range of potential problems that the United States may face in the years ahead—it is therefore necessary to be wary of generalizations based on these data—the findings appear to reflect at least a mood of caution and skepticism about unilateral action to cope with international conflict issues.

The disaggregated data reveal a strong and consistent relationship between positions on American policy in Vietnam and how best to cope with other conflicts. Differences among the seven groups are significant and they are in the predicted direction.[56] None of the groups, on balance, favored intervention in the Middle East in the event of another oil embargo; the Critics were overwhelmingly opposed to such action, whereas the Supporters were almost evenly divided on the issue, and the other five groups were arrayed between them. Responses to the other two lessons also reveal a wide range of differences across the seven groups. Four of them favored total abstention from the conflict in Angola, and the other three took the opposite position, albeit by a rather narrow margin in two cases. The range between the Supporters and Critics on the question of Angola is especially large—more than one full point on a two-point scale. An almost equal lack of consensus marks responses of the groups on the appropriate role of the United Nations in settling international disputes.

Making Foreign Policy

The post-Vietnam debate on American foreign policy has not been limited to the substance or content of diplomacy. Observers at various points on the political spectrum have alleged that there are serious flaws, identified and magnified during the war in Southeast Asia, in the foreign policy process. In its reactions to the war and the related Watergate crimes, the public has also been repeatedly found in polls to share a widespread skepticism, if not cynicism, about the performance of the government in Washington. In response, advocates of reform have proposed giving the Congress a more meaningful role in foreign policy, replacing an "imperial presidency" with Cabinet government, strengthening the State Department, relying more on outside expertise, making bureaucratic changes, increasing or decreasing the role of the military in policy-making, facilitating the flow of information in to and out of the government, decentralizing intelligence functions, as well as a host of other suggestions aimed at ensuring against future Vietnams.[57] Defenders of the status quo argued that impairing the executive role in policy-making would damage the nation's ability to conduct a credible foreign policy in the future.[58] They might also have pointed out that many advocates of reform, for example, those who proposed a greater Congressional role in foreign policy, were rather recent converts to that position; not a few of them had vigorously opposed the Bricker Amendment during the 1950s, citing the need for strong Presidential leadership in foreign affairs.

Three items in the questionnaire focused on governmental performance in foreign affairs. The results reveal that leaders in this study are rather critical of the government. More than 60 percent of them agreed that in defining the national interest there had been excessive reliance on the President. Although many leaders felt that the press had helped to undermine the American war effort in Vietnam, as noted earlier, a clear majority of them also supported the proposition that the press is more likely than the government to report the truth about the conduct of foreign affairs. The most controversial item concerned the existence of excessive military advice in the conduct of American foreign policy; responses were divided evenly, with 49 percent in agreement and 48 percent in opposition.

These overall indicators of dissatisfaction with the performance of the government do not begin to hint at the strong and systematic differences of viewpoint that emerge when the data are disaggregated. There is overwhelming support for the hypothesis that persons who most consistently supported the goal of military victory in Vietnam would be least critical of the government, whereas those favoring withdrawal of American forces from Southeast Asia would be the most prone to finding fault with the policy-making process. The range of mean scores is high for all three items, especially on the issue of excessive military advice in the conduct of foreign affairs. Differences among the groups are statistically significant and, with a few exceptions among the middle groups, they follow a general pattern of an increasingly critical stance toward Washington as one moves from the Supporters to the Critics.[59]

Domestic Constraints

Vietnam has been called the most unpopular war in American history. Although draft riots, dissident movements, and jailing of protesters have accompanied virtually every previous conflict, none was accompanied by such widespread disaffection with government policies and the conduct of military operations. Although protests on the campuses of elite universities may have been the most visible signs of discontent, before the end of the war even such establishment newspapers as the *Wall Street Journal* carried full-page ads, signed by prominent business leaders, advocating withdrawal from Southeast Asia. Congressional actions, poll data, and other indicators showed that domestic support for the war effort had declined precipitously. In the light of American failures in the war, what lessons do its leaders believe should be learned about the impact of domestic constraints on the conduct of external relations?

Table 2.8 reveals rather consistent support for a series of propositions focused on the deleterious effects of various domestic constraints on the quality of foreign policy. The striking exception to this generalization is overwhelming disagreement (70 percent) with the proposition that freedom to dissent inhibits the effective conduct of foreign policy; whether or not respondents agreed with the policies of dissidents—recall that two-thirds of them had agreed that the protesters had been a "very" or "moderately important" cause of failure in Vietnam (Table 2.3)—they seemed unprepared to restrict the right to disagree publicly. However, substantial majorities, ranging from over 60 percent to nearly 80 percent, agreed that lack of cooperation between the White House and Congress negates the possibility of an effective foreign policy; that the American political system is poorly suited to conduct a limited war; and that the American people are lacking in two important requisites for a sound foreign policy—patience, and an understanding of the role that power plays in world affairs.

The absence of an even division on any of these issues does not, however, reflect a consensus among the seven groups of leaders. The hypothesis that Supporters would be more likely than Critics to find in the Vietnam experience a set of lessons about the damaging impact of domestic constraints is strongly sustained (Table 2.8). On balance, all seven groups agreed with the propositions on executive–legislative cooperation, the lack of patience, and appreciation of power realities among Americans, but the strength of agreement varies widely and in the predicted direction. All but the Critics agreed that the American political system is poorly suited to conduct a limited war, and all groups rejected the lesson that freedom to dissent is incompatible with a sound foreign policy. The range of mean scores is highest for the latter two items, and for all five items the differences are statistically significant.[60]

The Uses of History

Not long after the evacuation of the last Americans from Saigon, McGeorge Bundy, a key foreign policy adviser in the Kennedy and Johnson administrations, warned against efforts to find policy guidance in the recently concluded conflict: "There is one great lesson about Vietnam which deserves to be learned and understood by all of us just as soon as possible: it is that the case of Vietnam is unique."[61] While Bundy was not alone in cautioning against adducing lessons from Vietnam, his position was clearly in the minority. Most Americans would probably have agreed with the plea that "Vietnam was a tragic lesson, and it is essential that we learn from it, and that our leaders in the future may be men who see the errors of the past."[62]

Without taking sides on the relative merits of these viewpoints, this inquiry is largely founded on the premise that the propensity to look to history for guidance and decision rules is widespread, not only among policy-makers, but also among a broader group of the society's leadership. Some leaders may be more likely than others to seek guidance from specific historical episodes; for example, Supporters of the war effort in Vietnam would be more likely than Critics to look to the 1938 Munich Conference for decision rules on how to cope with aggression. However, there seemed to be no reason to believe that persons in any group would be more or less inclined to accept the general proposition that one may profitably look to the past for policy guidance. Hence the hypothesis that there would be no significant differences among the Supporters, Critics, and the other five subgroups on the uses of history.

Results for the two items relating to uses of the past are summarized at the end of Table 2.8. There is moderate support for the premise of a widespread belief that the past may usefully inform the present. The respondents rejected overwhelmingly (80 percent) the proposition that it is best to forget foreign policy mistakes of the past, but their reactions were much more evenly divided on the wisdom of treating each crisis "on its own merits" rather than "relying on past experience." Contrary to the hypothesis, however, the seven groups do in fact differ in their propensities to look to the past.[63] Critics were the least inclined to "forget the foreign policy mistakes of the past as quickly as possible." Although any explanation must be speculative, it is perhaps the case that those who most opposed intervention in Vietnam are the most fearful that Americans will soon forget the experience and, more specifically, the lessons that the Critics believe should be learned from it.

Table 2.9 Ranking of the "Lessons of Vietnam" Receiving Highest Agreement from each Group*

All Respondents	Supporters	Converted Supporters	Ambivalent Supporters	Ambivalents	Ambivalent Critics	Converted Critics	Critics
USSR is expansionist	Avoid graduated escalation	USSR is expansionist	Avoid graduated escalation	USSR is expansionist	Avoid Angola involvement	Avoid graduated escalation	Avoid Angola involvement
Avoid graduated escalation	USSR is expansionist	Avoid graduated escalation	USSR is expansionist	Must honor alliance commitments	Third World revolutionaries nationalistic	USSR is expansionist	Press more likely to tell truth on foreign policy
Must honor alliance commitments	Must honor alliance commitments	Must honor alliance commitments	Domino theory is valid	Executive–Congress cooperation is vital	Executive–Congress cooperation is vital	Avoid Angola involvement	Excessive reliance on military advice
Executive–Congress cooperation is vital	Domino theory is valid	Executive–Congress cooperation is vital	Must honor alliance commitments	Avoid graduated escalation	Americans lack patience	Executive–Congress cooperation is vital	Rely too much on President for national interest
	Avoid half measures militarily	Americans don't understand role of power	Executive–Congress cooperation is vital	Americans lack patience	Rely too much on President for national interest	Must honor alliance commitments	Third World revolutionaries nationalistic
	Executive–Congress cooperation is vital	Domino theory is valid	Americans lack patience		USSR is expansionist		Scale down U.S. international role
	Americans don't understand role of power	Americans lack patience	Americans don't understand role of power		U.S. should solve own problems		Enlist U.N. cooperation

Soviets abuse détente	Avoid half measures militarily	Americans can't fight limited war	Press more likely to tell truth on foreign policy
Americans lack patience	Americans can't fight limited war		
Americans can't fight limited war			
Strike at heart of enemy power			
Communist victory antithesis of U.S. interest			

This table lists all ''Lessons of Vietnam'' that received at least an average rating of 0.40 on a scale of 1.00 (agree strongly) to −1.00 (disagree strongly). Lessons are listed in order of decreasing importance for each group.

Lessons of Vietnam: Conclusion

Assessments of thirty-four items that have been proposed as lessons of Vietnam by 2,282 American leaders suggest two conclusions. The first is a pattern of deep and profound divisions among the respondents. Although there is widespread agreement that Americans should learn from past mistakes, this consensus breaks down once attention is directed to specific matters of substance. Disagreement pervades virtually all levels of thinking about how the lessons of Vietnam should guide the future conduct of American foreign policy, from the broadest questions of the true nature of the international system and of America's proper role within it, to narrower ones about the most appropriate instruments and tactics to be used in the pursuit of foreign policy goals. Secondly, with only a few exceptions, the pattern of responses corresponds rather closely to that predicted by the hypotheses outlined earlier.

A somewhat different perspective on the data may be achieved by ranking, for each of the seven groups, the lessons that received the strongest support. Table 2.9 provides added evidence for the conclusion that there is a notable absence of consensus among groups defined by Vietnam policy preferences. Although the criteria of inclusion are only moderately stringent (an average rating of 0.40 on a scale of 1.00 to −1.00), not one of the thirty-four lessons appears on all seven lists. Only two appear in six columns; these are items on Soviet expansionist tendencies and executive–congressional disagreements. Only three additional items appear on five of the seven lists. Another reflection of disagreement is the fact that only four of them gained sufficient support among the entire sample of leaders to be included in the left-hand column. If the actual rankings of each lesson within columns were taken into account, the lack of consensus would be even greater. One final observation further illustrates the sharp cleavages. For the Supporters, twelve lessons met the criteria for inclusion in Table 2.9; the comparable figure for the Critics is seven. Yet not one lesson appears on both lists!

Conclusion

This chapter has centered on three propositions: the post-World War II consensus on foreign policy has been shattered; the Vietnam experience has been a critical causal factor; and the resulting views on foreign policy can appropriately be designated as competing belief systems. To what extent do the findings support these propositions?

Surely they uphold the first proposition. The existence of deep cleavages among the seven groups of respondents has been confirmed repeatedly, and these differences extend across a broad spectrum of questions, ranging from beliefs about the international system to issues of strategy and tactics. Tables 2.3, 2.6 and 2.8 summarize the absence of consensus, but they do not fully reveal the significance of the results. Table 2.10 lists a series of axioms of "widely shared images" that "a majority of American officials (as well as the American public)" held during much of the post-war period.[64] They are paired with the more or less corresponding lessons of Vietnam, along with the level of agreement for each item. Of the thirteen lessons, all but the second, third, fourth and seventh represent the antithesis of the post-war axioms. Even a cursory glance at the results confirms widespread erosion of support for most of the axioms, as well as a general absence of consensus on many of them. To be sure, an overwhelming majority of the respondents continued to regard the Soviet Union as an expansionist power, and two-thirds of them considered the "domino theory" to be valid. But beyond that, change and disagreement are much more evident than continuity and consensus. In short, propositions about world politics and foreign policy that were usually taken for granted rather than widely debated during much of the post-war period no longer appear to be unquestioned verities among American leaders.

In order to test the second proposition—that Vietnam was a watershed experience with respect to American beliefs about international politics and foreign policy—respondents were divided into seven groups solely on the basis of their policy preferences during the early and late stages of the war. Admittedly this is a rather simple classification scheme, but it serves present purposes well because it isolates views on the war from other variables that might be associated with views about world affairs.[65] Indeed, it is precisely because the classification scheme described in Table 2.2 is simple and based purely on the Vietnam issue that the results are so striking.

The third proposition postulated that responses to four clusters of issues—policy preferences on Vietnam, diagnoses of the sources of failure, prognoses of the consequences of the war, and prescriptions about the lessons of Vietnam—would form coherent and internally consistent belief systems. The hypotheses that guided the foregoing analysis represented a conception of beliefs that seemed logically to form a coherent system of thought. The data yielded strong support for this line of reasoning.

But is the finding that Critics and Supporters hold sharply divergent views on the Vietnam War sufficient evidence from which to draw broad conclusions about a breakdown in the foreign policy consensus? Even the bipartisan, center-of-the-road coalition that supported the main outlines of American foreign policy from the late 1940s through the mid-1960s did not lack critics on either end of the political spectrum. Does an emphasis on Supporters and Critics overlook the possibility of a broad consensus within the area bounded by those who consistently favored military victory in Vietnam and those who were just as undeviating in their demands for a complete withdrawal? The point is well taken, but further examination of the data

Table 2.10   *Comparison of Axioms of the Post-war Era with Data on the Lessons of Vietnam Provided by 2,282 American Leaders:* Responses of the 2,282 leaders with respect to the lessons of Vietnam (in percentages)

Axioms of the post-war era*	Lessons of Vietnam	Agree**	Disagree**
The preeminent feature of international politics is conflict between Communism and the Free World	American foreign policy should be based on the premise that the Communist "bloc" is irreparably fragmented	32	60
Every nation that falls to Communism increases the power of the Communist "bloc" in its struggle with the Free World Peace is indivisible . . . Thus any expansion of Communist influence must be resisted The surest simple guide to U.S. interests in foreign policy is opposition to Communism	Any Communist victory is a defeat for America's national interest	39	59
Russian intentions toward Western Europe are essentially expansionist. So, too, are Chinese intentions in Asia	The Soviet Union is generally expansionist rather than defensive in its foreign policy goals	83	14
	China is generally expansionist rather than defensive in its foreign policy goals	30	61
The main source of unrest, disorder, subversion, and civil war in underdeveloped areas is Communist influence and support	Revolutionary forces in "Third World" countries are usually nationalistic rather than controlled by the USSR or China	60	33
The United States—and only the United States—has the power, ability, responsibility, and right to defend the Free World and maintain international order	America's conception of its leadership role in the world must be scaled down	56	42

Table 2.10 *Continued:*

Axioms of the post-war era*	Lessons of Vietnam	Agree**	Disagree**
Concessions made under pressure constitute appeasement which only whets the appetite of aggressors	There is considerable validity in the "domino theory" that when one nation falls to communism, others nearby will soon follow a similar path	67	32
The Third World really matters, because (a) it is the battleground between Communism and the Free World; (b) Western capital will generate economic development and political stability with a minimum of violence; and (c) instability is the great threat to progress in the Third World	The best way to encourage democratic development in the "Third World" is for the U.S. to solve its own problems	65	29
	Vital interests of the U.S. are largely confined to Western Europe, Japan, and the Americas	38	58
	The efficiency of military power in foreign affairs is declining	60	31
	The conduct of American foreign affairs relies excessively on military advice	48	47
Military strength is the primary route to national security	Stationing American troops in other countries encourages them to let us do their fighting for those countries	59	36
	Military aid programs will eventually draw the United States into unnecessary wars	41	55

* *Source:* Morton Halperin, *Bureaucratic Politics and Foreign Policy* (Washington: Brookings Institution, 1974), pp. 11–12.

** "Agree" combines the "agree strongly" and "agree somewhat" responses. "Disagree" combines the "disagree strongly" and "disagree somewhat" responses. The rows do not total 100 percent because the "no opinion" responses have been omitted from this table.

does not reveal the existence of a previously overlooked consensus. In the first place, the Supporters and Critics are not merely insignificant fringe groups; between them, they constitute about one-third of the entire leadership sample. Moreover, divisions also exist among the middle groups. For example, both Converted Supporters and Converted Critics differed significantly from an adjacent group on more than three-fourths of the items, and the data reveal substantial disagreements between many of the other groups. In short, the analysis indicates that Vietnam policy positions tend to define a scale, but it is a scale that is both wide in scope and lacking a solid core of agreement on many key issues, either at one of the end points or in the middle.

Although these findings seem consistent with the three core propositions on Vietnam, consensus, and belief systems, it is important not to overstate the conclusions. An obvious limitation of the analysis up to this point is that each of the questions discussed in this chapter was focused on some aspect of the American experience in Vietnam. One might grant that the Vietnam War created deep divisions on foreign policy, and yet also question whether those cleavages carry over to other foreign policy issues that do not bear on the conflict in Southeast Asia. Chapter 3 addresses this question by examining the manner in which the 2,282 American leaders responded to several clusters of questions unrelated to Vietnam.

Notes to Chapter 2

1 Arthur H. Vandenberg, Jr (ed.), *The Private Papers of Senator Vandenberg* (Boston, Mass.: Houghton Mifflin, 1952), p. 1.

2 As indicated in Chapter 1, the working definition of a belief system is derived from Philip E. Converse, "The Nature of Belief Systems in Mass Publics," in David E. Apter (ed.), *Ideology and Discontent* (New York: Free Press, 1964), p. 207.

3 See, for example, Frank L. Klingberg, "The historical alternation of moods in American foreign policy," *World Politics*, IV (January 1952), pp. 239–73; Frank L. Klingberg, "Cyclical Trends in American Foreign Policy Moods and Their Policy Implications," in Charles W. Kegley, Jr, and Patrick J. McGowan (eds), *Challenges to America: United States Foreign Policy in the 1980s* (Beverly Hills, Calif.: Sage International Yearbook of Foreign Policy Studies, IV, 1979); and Arthur M. Schlesinger, *Paths to the Present* (New York: Macmillan, 1949).

4 Data in John E. Mueller, *War, Presidents and Public Opinion* (New York: Wiley, 1973), indicate that the proportion of Americans supporting the war effort fell from approximately 60 percent in 1965 to 30 percent in 1971.

5 See, for example, the results of a Roper survey published in *Fortune* in 1945, which revealed substantial optimism about the future of Soviet–American relations; 42·4 percent of respondents expected future relations to improve, 23·5 percent predicted that they would remain about the same, and only 19·1 percent felt that relations with Moscow would deteriorate. "U.S. Opinion on Russia," *Fortune*, 32 (September 1945), pp. 233–43.

6 Although this procedure yielded seven groups of uneven size, all of them are large enough to permit statistical analysis; none has less than sixty-three respondents, and six of the seven include well over 100 leaders.

7 Although McCarthy gave his name to this sorry period in American history, Nixon was in fact four years ahead of the Senator from Wisconsin in making wild and unproven charges of communism and treason against his electoral opponents. For

a brilliant and detailed analysis, see Fawn M. Brodie, *Richard Nixon: The Shaping of His Character* (New York: Norton, 1981).

8 These arguments are further developed in Earl C. Ravenal, "Was Vietnam a 'mistake?'", *Asian Survey*, XIV (July 1974), pp. 589–607. See also the fuller discussion in his *Never Again: Learning from America's Foreign Policy Failures* (Philadelphia: Temple University Press, 1978).

9 George Reedy, "Divided We Stand," NBC News Special, 10 May 1970. This point is developed further in Reedy's *The Twilight of the Presidency* (New York: World Publishing, 1970). For a somewhat more benign view of Johnson by a critic of his policies in Vietnam, see George W. Ball, *The Past Has Another Pattern* (New York: Norton, 1982).

10 Donald Kirk, "The final tragedy of Vietnam," *New Leader*, 58 (28 April 1975), p. 12.

11 Robert Shaplen, "Southeast Asia—before and after," *Foreign Affairs*, 53 (April 1975), p. 540; and Paul Warnke, "The Search for Peace—Vietnam Negotiations," in Anthony Lake (ed.), *The Vietnam Legacy: The War, American Society and the Future of American Foreign Policy* (New York: New York University Press, 1976). p. 328.

12 Analyses of variance (ANOVA) were used to assess the significance of differences among groups. F ratios of 90.7, 57.1, and 4.7 for the first three items in Table 2.2 are significant at beyond the .001 level.

13 Warnke, in Lake, *The Vietnam Legacy*, p. 314; Irving Kristol, "Consensus and Dissent in U.S. Foreign Policy," in Lake, *op. cit.*, p. 90; and Comments by Sir Robert Thompson in W. Scott Thompson and Donaldson D. Frizzell (eds), *The Lessons of Vietnam* (New York: Crane, Russak, 1977), p. 119.

14 Stanley Hoffmann, "The sulking giant," *New Republic*, 172 (3 May 1975), p. 16; V. J. Croizat, *Lessons of the War in Vietnam*, cited in Thomas C. Thayer, "Quantitative Analysis of a War Without Fronts," in Thompson and Frizzell, *The Lessons of Vietnam*, p. 36; Donaldson D. Frizzell, "The Strategy of Attrition," in Thompson and Frizzell, *op. cit.*, p. 75; Hubert H. Humphrey, "Building on the Past: Lessons for a Future Foreign Policy," in Lake, *The Vietnam Legacy*, p. 358; and Donaldson D. Frizzell and W. Scott Thompson, "The Lessons of Vietnam," in Thompson and Frizzell, *op. cit.*, p. iv.

15 Andrew Kopkind, "The press at war," *Ramparts*, 13 (August–September 1975), p. 38; Alexander Woodside, "The Vietnam we refused to know," *Boston Globe*, (7 May 1975); and David S. Sullivan, "Introduction," in Sullivan and Martin J. Sattler (eds), *Revolutionary War: Western Response* (New York: Columbia University Press, 1971), p. ix.

16 F ratios of 36.9, 48.0, and 22.4 for the first three items are significant at the .001 level; the figure of 3.5 for the fourth is not.

17 For compelling evidence on changes in North Vietnamese military practice, including abandonment of the concept "people war," see the prize-winning dissertation study by Timothy Lomperis, published as *The War Everyone Lost—and Won* (Baton Rouge: Louisiana State University Press, 1983).

18 Michel Tatu, "Moscow, Peking, and the Conflict in Vietnam," in Lake, *The Vietnam Legacy*, p. 20; and Comments by Uri Ra'anan, in Thompson and Frizzell, *The Lessons of Vietnam*, p. 12.

19 F ratios of 20.0, 62.6, and 25.1 for these three items are significant.

20 See, for example, Douglas Kinnard, *The War Managers* (Hanover, NH: University Press of New England, 1977); James M. Gavin, "A communication on Vietnam," *Harper's Magazine*, 232 (February 1966), pp. 16–21; William Westmoreland, *A Soldier Reports* (Garden City, NY: Doubleday, 1976); and the observations of several military officers in Lake, *The Vietnam Legacy*, and Thompson and Frizzell, *The Lessons of Vietnam*. Subjects of the Kinnard study are general officers who served in Vietnam.

21 The diversity of viewpoints on the military aspects of the war can be seen in, among others, William Safire, "What went wrong?" *New York Times* (24 April 1975), p. A.35; Comments by George Keegan, in Thompson and Frizzell, *The*

Lessons of Vietnam; Thomas C. Thayer, "The Impact of the Air Effort Probably Outweighed Many of Its Benefits," in Thompson and Frizzell, *op. cit.*, p. 149; Comments by Francis West, in Thompson and Frizzell, *op. cit.*, p. 83; and Comments by Donaldson D. Frizzell, in Thompson and Frizzell, *op. cit.*, p. 136. See also the works cited in the previous note.

22   All five F ratios (109.6, 109.7, 10.4, 123.2, and 63.8) are significant at the .001 level.

23   Alexis de Tocqueville, *Democracy in America* (ed. Phillips Bradley), Vol. I (New York: Knopf, 1945); Walter Lippmann, *Essays in the Public Philosophy* (Boston, Mass.: Little, Brown, 1955); and the entire body of Kennan's writings on American foreign affairs, beginning with *American Diplomacy, 1900–1950* (Chicago: University of Chicago Press, 1951), and running through *The Cloud of Danger* (Boston: Atlantic–Little, Brown, 1977).

24   Henry A. Kissinger and Arnaud de Borchgrave, "Straight talk from Kissinger," *Current*, 210 (February 1979). pp. 51–8. Kissinger's memoirs attribute virtually all foreign policy difficulties to the Congress and the Watergate revelations, both of which eroded executive freedom of action in foreign affairs. H. Kissinger, *Years of Upheaval* (Boston: Little, Brown, 1982). On the putative role of intellectuals, see essays by Ronald Steel, Peter L. Berger, Seymour M. Lipset, Herman Kahn, and Edward N. Luttwak in "America now: a failure of nerve?" *Commentary*, 60 (July 1975). On inadequate press coverage of the Tet Offensive, in which a military disaster was turned into a political victory for the North Vietnamese, see Peter Braestrup, *Big Story: How the American Press and Television Reported and Interpreted the Crisis of Tet 1968 in Vietnam and Washington* (Boulder, Colorado: Westview Press, 1977); Norman Hannah, "Vietnam: now we know," *National Review*, 28 (11 June 1976), pp. 612–16; and Peter C. Rollins, "TV's Battle of the Khe Sauh: Selective Images of Defeat," in William C. Adams (ed.), *Television Coverage of International Affairs* (Norwood, NJ: Ablex, 1982) pp. 203–16. Among those calling for media censorship is General William Westmoreland, *Sacramento Bee* (19 March, 1982). Other critical appraisals of domestic constraints may be found in: Irving Kristol, "Consensus and Dissent in U.S. Foreign Policy," in Lake, *The Vietnam Legacy*, p. 90; William Westmoreland, quoted in "After the fall: reactions and rationales," *Time*, 105 (12 May 1975), p. 20; Henry A. Kissinger, "U.S. foreign policy: finding strength through adversity," *Department of State Bulletin* (5 May 1975), p. 559; Paul H. Nitze, 'The Evolution of National Security Policy and the Vietnam War," in Thompson and Frizzell, *The Lessons of Vietnam*, p. 6; William C. Westmoreland, "A Military War of Attrition," in Thompson and Frizzell, *op. cit.*, pp. 60–1; and Lawrence J. O'Brien, Jr, "The final conquest of Vietnam: a look back," *Wall Street Journal* (25 January 1983). p. 32.

25   Note, however, that in response to other questions, a majority (58 percent) of the leaders believed that the press was more truthful than the government about foreign affairs, and very few (28 percent) of them wished to restrict the right to dissent on the conduct of foreign relations. See Table 2.8 below.

26   F ratios of 26.6, 21.8, 74.4, 12.8, and 51.0 exceed the requirements for the ·001 level of significance.

27   Differences among groups resulted in a significant F ratio of 4.5.

28   An exception may be found in William P. Bundy, "New tides in Southeast Asia," *Foreign Affairs*, 49 (January 1971), pp. 187–200. Bundy asserts that the governments of Malaysia, Indonesia, Thailand, and Singapore were able to save themselves as a result of the time won by the American intervention in Vietnam. Others who see at least some positive results from the outcome in Vietnam are Edwin O. Reischauer, "Reaping the benefits of defeat," *Saturday Review*, 55 (18 November 1972), pp. 33–7; and Ernest R. May, "American Security Interests After Vietnam," in Lake, *The Vietnam Legacy*, pp. 278–91.

29   Maxwell D. Taylor, "The 'Vietnam Disaster' and U.S. security," *New York Times* (9 May 1975), p. A35; Vermont Royster, "Thinking things over," *Wall Street Journal* (16 April 1975).

30   Comments by Elmo Zumwalt, in Thompson and Frizzell, *The Lessons of Vietnam*, p. 202.

31 Reischauer, "Reaping the benefits"; Richard Barnet, "Lessons Learned and Unlearned," in Lake, *The Vietnam Legacy*, p. 336; and Norman Mailer, "The meaning of Vietnam," *New York Review of Books*, 12 (12 June 1975), pp. 26–27.

32 Warnke, in Lake, *The Vietnam Legacy*; Larry Elowitz and John W. Spanier "Korea and Vietnam: limited war and the American political system," *Orbis*, 28 (Summer 1974), p. 512; and Anthony Lake, "Introduction," in Lake, *The Vietnam Legacy*.

33 Alastair Buchan, "The Indochina War and world politics," *Foreign Affairs*, 53 (July 1975), p. 649.

34 The three F ratios of 23.8, 12.2, and 31.7 are significant.

35 Frederick E. Nolting, Jr, quoted in James C. Hasdorff, "Vietnam in retrospect: interview with Ambassador Frederick E. Nolting, Jr," *Air University Review*, 25 (January–February 1974), p. 9. See also Zumwalt, in Thompson and Frizzell, *The Lessons of Vietnam*, p. 202; and Alvin J. Cottrell, quoted in "Europe: fears," *Newsweek*, 85 (12 May 1975), p. 51. For different views, see John G. Tower, "Foreign Policy for the Seventies," in Lake, *The Vietnam Legacy*, p. 249; Reischauer, "Reaping the benefits," p. 36; and Arthur Schlesinger, Jr, "Vietnam and the end of the age of superpowers," *Harper's Magazine*, 238 (March 1969), pp. 41–9.

36 Analyses of variance yielded F ratios of 83.9 and 45.4, both of which exceed the requirements of the .001 level of significance.

37 Frizzell and Thompson, "The Lessons of Vietnam," in Thompson and Frizzell, *The Lessons of Vietnam*, p. iv; Robert Thompson, "Retreat," *New York Times* (3 April 1975), p. A37; Elowitz and Spanier, "Korea and Vietnam,"p. 512; and Edward N. Luttwak, "American has lost the will to win a war," *Los Angeles Times* (23 January 1983), p. iv–1, 3.

38 Of the two F ratios of 2.1 and 14.3, only the latter is significant.

39 The F ratios are 6.4, 9.7, and 7.1 for these three items; all are significant.

40 Thomas C. Thayer, "The American Style of War Made it Costly," in Thompson and Frizzell, *The Lessons of Vietnam*, p. 209; Philip Geyelin, "Vietnam and the Press: Limited War and an Open Society," in Lake, *The Vietnam Legacy*, p. 193; Anthony Lake, "The War and American Society," in Lake, *op. cit.*, p. 38; and Lucian Pye, "Foreign Aid and American Involvement in the Developing World," in Lake, *op. cit.*, p. 386.

41 All three of the F ratios (51.5, 25.9, and 27.9) are significant at the .001 level.

42 Mailer, "The Meaning of Vietnam."

43 This item was one of several that has also appeared in other recent surveys of American leaders. Russett and Hanson found that 84 percent of military officers and 74 percent of business executives agreed that "Revolutionary forces in the Third World are usually nationalist rather than controlled by the USSR and China." In Barton's study, the comparable figures were: business leaders 70 percent, Republican politicians 77 percent, Democratic politicians 72 percent, labor leaders 60 percent, civil servants 84 percent, volunteer organizations 83 percent, and media persons 91 percent. Bruce M. Russett and Elizabeth Hanson, *Interest and Ideology* (San Francisco, Calif.: W. H. Freeman, 1975); and Allen H. Barton, "Consensus and conflict among American leaders," *Public Opinion Quarterly*, 38 (Winter 1974–5), pp. 507–30.

44 The five F ratios of 41.6, 135.6, 55.9, 86.1, and 29.1 are significant.

45 Richard Barnet, "Lessons Learned and Unlearned," in Lake, *The Vietnam Legacy*, p. 335.

46 John L. Frisbee, "Vietnam—some policy implications," *Air Force Magazine*, 58 (May 1975), p. 6.

47 Recall, for example, arguments by President Johnson and Secretary of State Dean Rusk about the imperatives of confronting Chinese expansion in Vietnam in order to avoid having to do so later in Honolulu or San Francisco, or by Secretary of Defense McNamara on the role of a limited anti-ballistic missile system. The latter is reported in *New York Times* (19 September 1967), pp. 18–19.

48 The F ratios of 29.3, 46.6, and 20.6 are significant at the .001 level.

49 Morton H. Halperin, "The Lessons Nixon Learned," in Lake, *The Vietnam Legacy*,

p. 412; and Neil Howe, "Special report from Vietnam," *The Alternative* 8 (March 1975), p. 8.

50   The F ratios are 47.0, 2.5, 100.6, 56.1, 3.0, and 52.4; all but the second and fifth are significant.

51   Earl C. Ravenal, "The Strategic Lessons of Vietnam," in Lake, *The Vietnam Legacy*, p. 272.

52   Of the seven F ratios—4.2, 9.0, 2.5, 49.5, 48.5, 3.6, and 8.6—all but the third are significant.

53   Edward Kennedy, quoted in "The lessons of Vietnam: toward a post-Vietnam foreign policy," *The Defense Monitor*, 4 (September 1975), p. 5.

54   Frisbee, "Vietnam – some policy implications," p. 6.

55   At the time that the questionnaire was sent out, the issue of military intervention to counter another oil embargo was quite salient. Secretary of State Kissinger had hinted that such a course of action could not be ruled out, and a number of prominent academic observers had proposed that intervention would be both feasible and necessary to avoid the costs of any future oil embargo. See Robert W. Tucker, "Oil: the issue of American intervention," *Commentary*, 59 (January 1975), pp. 21–31; Tucker, "Further reflections on oil and force," *Commentary*, 59 (March 1975), pp. 45–56; Tucker, "Oil and American power: three years later," *Commentary*, 63 (January 1977), pp. 29–36; and Edward Friedland, Paul Seabury, and Aaron Wildavsky, *The Great Détente Disaster: Oil and the Decline of American Foreign Policy* (New York: Basic Books, 1975).

56   All three F ratios of 103.4, 19.6, and 43.3 exceed the requirements for the .001 level of significance.

57   Stuart Hampshire, "The meaning of Vietnam," *New York Review of Books*, 12 (12 June 1975), pp. 28–30; Anthony Lewis, "Condemned to repeat it," *New York Times* (8 May 1975), p. 39; James Reston, "The end of the tunnel," *New York Times* (30 April 1975), p. 41; Committee on Foreign Relations, United States Senate, *Vietnam Commitments, 1961: A Staff Study Based on the Pentagon Papers* (20 March 1972), p. 7; and David M. Abshire, "Lessons of Vietnam: Proportionality and Credibility," in Lake, *The Vietnam Legacy*, p. 396.

58   Abshire, "Lessons of Vietnam," pp. 406, 409.

59   The three F ratios of 34.5, 68.9 and 91.3 are statistically significant.

60   The requirements for the .001 significance level were exceeded by each of the five F ratios of 12.7, 13.4, 22.8, 29.4, and 32.3.

61   McGeorge Bundy, "Vietnam," *New York Times* (29 June 1975).

62   "After Vietnam," *Commonweal*, 102 (23 May 1975), pp. 131–2.

63   Both F ratios (6.4 and 4.3) indicate significant differences between the groups.

64   Morton H. Halperin, *Bureaucratic Politics and Foreign Policy* (Washington, Brookings Institution, 1974), pp. 11–12.

65   For a discussion of other attributes that may be related to foreign policy beliefs, see Chapters 5 and 6 below.

3
Vietnam, Consensus, and the Belief Systems of American Leaders, 1976: Post-Vietnam Foreign Policy Issues

The previous chapter offered substantial evidence that the post-World War II consensus on foreign policy has broken down, at least with respect to assessments and interpretations of the Vietnam issue. But it is quite appropriate to ask whether these results are confined to the Vietnam experience, thereby merely confirming once again the rather obvious point that it was indeed a traumatic and divisive episode in American history. Alternatively, have the consequences of that conflict spilled over into a much broader range of foreign policy and international issues? Should the former interpretation be valid, it would be reasonable to conclude that, divisive as Vietnam had been, its effects are of far greater historical interest than they are of contemporary policy relevance. This is, of course, the hope and expectation of those who have proclaimed that the nation has by now transcended the "Vietnam syndrome," permitting it to pursue its external interests without excessive and obsessive fears of repeating the experience in Southeast Asia.

The question of a "Vietnam syndrome" actually encompasses two dimensions: the range of issues affected by the Vietnam conflict, and the persistence of Vietnam effects with the passage of time. The present chapter considers the first of these (the second is examined in Chapter 6), extending the analysis of the previous one by analyzing the responses of American leaders to a number of issues unrelated to Vietnam: the proper goals of American foreign policy, aspects of the nation's international role, and the types of objective that the United States should pursue in its relations with the less developed nations. The methods of analysis and presentation will follow as closely as possible those employed in Chapter 2. Leaders taking part in the 1976 survey are again classified into seven groups (Supporters, Converted Supporters, Ambivalent Supporters, Ambivalents, Ambivalent Critics, Converted Critics, and Critics), based on their preferences for American policy during the early and late stages of the Vietnam War—that is, the classification scheme summarized in Table 2.2 above.

The expectation that the beliefs of leaders form internally-consistent belief systems gives rise to several hypotheses that will guide data analyses in this chapter.

Goals for American foreign policy

- In assessing the importance of various foreign policy goals, Supporters will attach greater importance than Critics to American responsibilities for global security, and to promoting American interests and institutions abroad.
- Compared to Supporters, Critics will attach greater importance to promoting international cooperation on both security and non-security issues.
- Respondents in the other five groups (Converted Supporters, Ambivalent Supporters, Ambivalents, Ambivalent Critics, and Converted Critics) will take intermediate positions; more precisely, the responses of these five groups will be arrayed in the order given.

America's role in the world

- The Supporters, in defining an appropriate international role for the United States, will place greater emphasis than the Critics on the responsibilities of the United States as leader of the Free World.
- Compared to Supporters, the Critics will attach greater importance to the United States as a source of economic assistance, while at the same time favoring a generally reduced international involvement for this country.
- Leaders in the other five groups will take intermediate positions in defining an appropriate international role for the United States.

Policy objectives in less developed countries

- Compared to Critics, Supporters will, in defining goals for American foreign policy in less developed nations, attach greater importance to governments that are capable of maintaining internal order, neutral or pro-American in foreign policy, retain the free enterprise system, and permit broad opportunities for American business investment.
- Compared to Supporters, Critics will give greater emphasis to working for governments in less developed nations that achieve rapid economic development, maintain civil liberties, and abstain from unprovoked aggression against other nations.
- Respondents in the other five groups will take intermediate positions in defining goals for American foreign policy in underdeveloped nations.

Foreign Policy Goals

Responsibilities for Global Security

The essential premise of the "revolution in American foreign policy" after World War II was the proposition that only if the United States took an active part in world affairs would it be possible to avoid another major war. Franklin D. Roosevelt's "Grand Design" for a post-war international order included American membership in the United Nations, and cooperation among the "Four Policemen"—the United States, Great Britain, Soviet Union, and China—to ensure peace. The optimistic belief that wartime collaboration between members of the alliance against the Axis nations had laid solid foundations for continued agreement among the major powers did not survive to the end of the decade. Disagreements about the future of Eastern Europe—notably Poland—and crises in the "northern tier" (Iran, Greece, and Turkey) rapidly drained the reservoir of good will between the United States and Great Britain, on the one hand, and the Soviet Union on the other. In those circumstances, an active American role in world affairs came to include a policy of containing Soviet expansion, the first peacetime alliance in American history, and economic and military assistance to allies in Europe and elsewhere. For at least two decades thereafter, the premises of the Truman Doctrine, Marshall Plan, and NATO served as the foundations of American external relations.[1] Equally important, they were sustained by broad domestic support; for example, each of the post-war presidential elections until 1964 found the two major parties led by candidates who espoused these premises in principle, if not in all details of actual policy execution and management. Indeed, the foreign policy debates in most of these campaigns revolved around competing claims about who could better implement policies based on these premises, rather than on the assumptions themselves.

The first five items listed in Table 3.1 asked leaders to rate the importance of several types of global responsibilities encompassed in American foreign policy after World War II.[2] The most striking result is that not one of these goals was rated as "very important" by as many as 50 percent of the respondents. Somewhat over a third of them did indicate that containing communism, defending allies, and maintaining a balance of power were very important goals, but there was significantly less urgency attached to strengthening friendly nations abroad and protecting weaker ones from aggression. Perhaps one explanation is that many leaders attributed importance to certain broad global responsibilities (containment, balance of power), but were much less disposed toward commitments that bear a close resemblance to those undertaken in Vietnam (strengthening friends, protecting weaker nations).

When the results are disaggregated into the seven groups defined

Table 3.1   *Foreign Policy Goals*
(Responses for the entire sample of 2,282 leaders, and analyses of seven groups of respondents classified by their 1976 positions during the early and late stages of the war in Vietnam)

Here is a list of possible foreign policy goals that the United States might have. Please indicate how much importance should be attached to each goal.	*All respondents**	*Differences between groups significant?***	*Correlation actual and hypothesized group rankings****
Responsibilities for global security			
Maintaining a balance of power among nations	.69	Yes	.83
Defending our allies' security	.67	Yes	.82
Containing communism	.63	Yes	.93
Strengthening countries who are friendly towards us	.57	Yes	.86
Protecting weaker nations against foreign aggression	.53	Yes	.82
Promoting American interests and institutions			
Promoting and defending our own security	.92	Yes	.86
Securing adequate supplies of energy	.85	Yes	.68
Protecting the jobs of American workers	.59	No	.93
Protecting the interests of American business abroad	.44	Yes	.67
Helping to bring a democratic form of government to other nations	.33	No	.38
Promoting the development of capitalism abroad	.24	Yes	.90
International cooperation: non-military issues			
Fostering international cooperation to solve common problems, such as food, inflation, and energy	.84	Yes	.96
Combatting world hunger	.72	Yes	.86
Helping to solve world inflation	.73	Yes	.92
Helping to improve the standard of living in less developed countries	.65	Yes	.88
Strengthening the United Nations	.47	Yes	.89

Table 3.1   Foreign Policy Goals Cont.

Here is a list of possible foreign policy goals that the United States might have. Please indicate how much importance should be attached to each goal.	All respondents*	Differences between groups significant?**	Correlation actual and hypothesized group rankings***
International cooperation: security issues			
Keeping peace in the world	.85	No	.54
Worldwide arms control	.82	Yes	.96

* Calculated on a scale of 1.00 (very important) to 0.00 (not important at all).
** Differences between seven groups of respondents, calculated by analysis of variance, at the .001 level of significance.
*** Spearman rank-order correlation between hypotheses and actual rankings of seven groups.

by policy preferences during the early and late stages of the war in Vietnam, they reveal striking and consistent differences among them.[3] The range of responses is especially noteworthy on the issue of containing communism: 77 percent of the Supporters rated that foreign policy goal as very important, whereas only 7 percent of the Critics did so. Wide differences also characterize the proportions of those who replied that containment was not at all important: 2 percent and 39 percent respectively. The range of group responses on the other four items is somewhat smaller, but in all cases the differences among them are significant and, more importantly, they are generally in the predicted direction.

Promoting American Interests and Institutions

At a news conference soon after being appointed National Security Adviser, Henry Kissinger wryly listed among his qualifications for the position a complete ignorance of international economics. Events of the intervening years make it quite unlikely that, even in jest, an important American foreign policy official would today make a similar confession. Since at least 1971, when President Nixon attempted to deal with a burgeoning balance of payments problem and a quickening drain of American gold reserves by devaluing the dollar and rendering it no longer convertible into gold, the economic component of America's relations with the rest of the world has become increasingly visible. The oil embargo, a twenty-fold increase in the price of that important commodity, dubious payoffs abroad by several major corporations, and growing protectionist pressures against imports, ranging from Japanese auto and electronics, to textiles from Korea, steel from Europe, and shoes from Italy, have given international economic issues an unprecedented public prominence. Economic concerns have thus achieved a visibility that is perhaps comparable to some more traditional foreign policy goals, including protection of the nation's security.

More controversy surrounds the desirability and feasibility of promoting American values and institutions abroad. From the earliest days of the Republic through contemporary controversies over the wisdom of a human rights emphasis in diplomacy, Americans have debated the wisdom and prudence of a foreign policy that actively promotes political and economic freedom elsewhere. The issue first arose in connection with nationalist revolutions of the late eighteenth and nineteenth centuries, and in various guises, it has re-emerged periodically as a significant element in debates pitting idealists versus realists and pragmatists versus absolutists.

Six questionnaire items provided the leaders with an opportunity to assess the importance of promoting various American interests and institutions. The results reveal a dramatic range of responses. Not surprisingly, they ascribed great importance to protecting the security of the nation; only 3 percent failed to rate this as of at least moderate importance. Whereas comparable results could have been expected in virtually any period, the high value attributed to secure energy supplies appears to reflect the oil embargo and the dramatic price increases that had taken place during the several years immediately preceding this survey. That the adequacy of energy supplies received nearly twice as many "very important" ratings as either containment of communism or defense of allies represents a startling shift of priorities. Recall that only two decades earlier the Eisenhower Administration placed restrictions on oil imports to protect the prices received by domestic petroleum producers, and as late as 1970 the Nixon Administration reduced quotas for oil imports from Canada in what many Canadians believed was punishment for according diplomatic recognition to the Peking regime in China.

Despite an increasingly competitive trade environment and almost routine expropriations of American firms abroad, relatively few leaders ascribed great importance to protecting jobs of American workers, and even fewer—less than one in seven—rated the protection of business interests abroad as very important foreign policy goals. Indeed, on the latter issue, fully a quarter of the respondents checked off the "not important at all" option.

Even more striking is the evident lack of interest in promoting either democratic governments or capitalism in other nations. The absence of any substantial enthusiasm for remaking the world in the American image is amply reflected in the responses summarized in Table 3.1. Lacking a baseline of comparable data from earlier periods—for example, the mid-1950s—it is impossible to determine precisely how much change is reflected in these figures. However, it is at least a plausible guess that, in the wake of the Vietnam experience, there has been a marked decline of support for efforts to promote American values and institutions abroad.[4]

The expectation that the Supporters would be more inclined than Critics to attribute significance to promotion of American interests and institutions is generally borne out by the data. Differences among the seven groups are significant, save on the issues of protecting jobs and helping to establish democratic governments abroad, and the pattern of responses is quite consistently as predicted, with Supporters at the high end of the scale and the Critics at or near the bottom.[5] The range of views is widest on the question of protecting business interests abroad, with Supporters attributing substantially greater significance than did the Critics.

International Cooperation on Non-Military Issues

During and immediately after World War II, the United States played a leading role in establishing a number of international institutions to cope with problems that seemed beyond the reach of effective unilateral action. The next two decades witnessed a general economic recovery from wartime devastation, and a broad expansion of international trade. Although America's pre-eminent international role inevitably declined in relative terms as Japan, West Germany, and other nations recovered and then surpassed their pre-war economic capacities, the period was also one of unprecedented American economic prosperity.

By the 1970s, however, some of these favorable conditions had been eroded. American drivers in German and Japanese cars, waiting in long lines at service stations to buy gasoline made scarce by an OPEC oil embargo, symbolized some dramatic changes. Even the world's most powerful economy was not invulnerable. The "Keynesian revolution" in economics no longer appeared to provide permanent answers to problems of inflation and unemployment. These problems among industrial nations coincided with growing demands from less developed nations for a "new international economic order." Added to this agenda of non-strategic problems was a series of additional ones, ranging from control of sea beds to refugees, and from growing demands for protection of the environment to increasing threats of major famines.

It would be impossible to encompass the entire range of such issues in a single survey, but five items touch upon some facets of international non-military issues. Seventy percent of the leaders rated international cooperation on economic issues such as food, inflation, and energy as a very significant foreign policy goal, and another quarter of them felt that this was somewhat important. These ratings are almost identical to those accorded the security of energy sources, and place this goal as the fourth from the top among the eighteen listed in Table 3.1. Coping with world hunger and inflation also received significant support, as approximately half of the respondents checked off the "very important" option in connection with these goals. The other two issues—raising the standard of living in less developed countries and strengthening the United Nations—were assigned a somewhat lower priority. Indeed, whereas one-quarter of the leaders considered the latter goal to be very important, 30 percent of them rated it as of no real significance.

When the data are disaggregated into the seven groups defined by Vietnam policy preferences, they bear out the expectation that the Critics would ascribe substantially greater importance to this type of international cooperation than would the Supporters. For each of the items the highest scores among the seven groups are those of the Critics and, with a single exception, those of the Supporters are the lowest. Differences among the groups are statistically significant for all five issues.[6] Divisions on the importance of strengthening the United Nations are especially notable. Whereas nearly half of the Critics regarded that as an important foreign policy goal, less that 10 percent of the Supporters did so, and over half of the latter believed that this objective was of no importance.

International Cooperation on Security Issues

The 1976 survey took place during the waning months of the Nixon–Ford–Kissinger period of American foreign policy. Détente, the SALT I Treaty, and an interim agreement signed in Vladivostok for a SALT II Treaty were among the important foreign policy undertakings of the period. Yet at about that time there were growing political challenges to those policies; for example, during the 1976 primary elections Ronald Reagan mounted a strident attack against Ford and Kissinger, with sufficient success to miss by only the narrowest of margins wresting the presidential nomination from an incumbent of his own political party.

The final two items in Table 3.1 asked respondents to rate the urgency of keeping peace and worldwide arms control. Both of these goals were regarded as very important by sizeable majorities of two-thirds or more. The expected differences among the seven groups of respondents materialized only on the question of arms control, with substantially greater importance accorded to the issue by the Critics than by any of the others. Scores for the other six groups are arrayed in the predicted pattern with but a single exception, and the differences between them are statistically significant.[7]

Conclusion

Data on eighteen foreign policy goals for the United States generally support the proposition that cleavages related to the Vietnam War also extend into other aspects of American foreign policy. Differences among the seven groups defined by their policy positions on the war are significant and in the predicted direction for all save three foreign policy goals: peace (highly important to all groups), protection for jobs of American workers (moderately important), and promotion of democratic institutions in other nations (of little importance).

Table 3.2 Most Important U.S. Foreign Policy Goals as Ranked by 2,282 American Leaders Classified into Seven Groups According to Vietnam Policy Preferences*

All Respondents	Supporters	Converted Supporters	Ambivalent Supporters	Ambivalents	Ambivalent Critics	Converted Critics	Critics
Own security	Own security	Own security	Own security	Own security	International economic cooperation	Own security	International economic cooperation
Energy supplies**	Energy supplies	Energy supplies	Energy supplies	Peace	Energy supplies	International economic cooperation	Arms control
Peace**	Containing communism	Peace	Peace	International economic cooperation	Arms control**	Peace**	Peace
International economic cooperation	Peace	International economic cooperation	International economic cooperation	Energy supplies**	Own security**	Energy supplies**	World hunger
Arms control	Defending allies	Containing communism	Containing communism	World hunger**	Peace	Arms control	Own security
		Arms control	Arms control	Arms control		World hunger	World inflation
				Defending allies			LDC standard of living
							Energy supplies

* This table includes all items that received a rating of at least 0.75 on a scale of 1.00 (very important) to 0.00 (not important at all).
** Tied ranks

Another perspective on the data may be achieved by comparing the rankings accorded by respondents in each group to the entire set of eighteen foreign policy goals (Table 3.2). Differences among them emerge clearly once again. In some cases goals that were appraised as very important by groups at one end of the scale—for example, containing communism or coping with world hunger—received very low ratings at the other end. Indeed, despite the presence of such seemingly uncontroversial issues as peace and American security among the eighteen goals, it is striking that not one of them was ranked among the four most important by leaders in all seven groups!

Rating Foreign Policy Performance

Additional insight into cleavages may be gained by examining the ways in which American leaders rated the nation's foreign policy performance. For each of eighteen goals respondents were asked to "rate the job the United States is doing" as excellent, pretty good, fair or poor.[8]

The results reported in Table 3.3 reveal an almost pervasive dissatisfaction. On sixteen of eighteen goals fewer than 10 percent appraised Washington's efforts as excellent. Only with respect to "promoting and defending our own security" were there more excellent than poor ratings, and just two other goals—defending our allies and maintaining a balance of power—also found more than 50 percent of the respondents satisfied. These results suggest that the respondents were a bit less critical of Washington's success in pursuing the more traditional Cold War goals. But even this conclusion must be tempered somewhat because less than one leader in five rated the record in containing communism as either excellent or pretty good.

Over 20 percent of the respondents judged American performance as poor on the last nine goals and, significantly, these included a broad spectrum of issues, ranging from containment to energy, and from protecting weaker nations to arms control. In short, virtually any reading of these results leads to the conclusion that during the early months of 1976, American leaders were broadly and deeply dissatisfied with the conduct of the nation's foreign policy.

Is it possible, however, that these results overstate the level of dissatisfaction? That would be the case if respondents gave the highest performance ratings for goals they deemed to be the most important, and the lowest ones for what they judged to be peripheral goals. Conversely, if the relationship between importance and performance ratings were negative, the index would be understating the level of dissatisfaction.

Analysis of the data in fact reveals that the latter interpretation is valid, as there is a tendency for leaders to give higher performance ratings to goals they judge as less important, and to be more critical of

Table 3.3   *Performance of the United States on Foreign Policy Goals* (Responses for the entire sample of 2,282 leaders, and analyses of seven groups of respondents classified by their 1976 positions during the early and late stages of the war in Vietnam)

Here is a list of possible foreign policy goals that the United States might have. Now indicate how you rate the job the U.S. is doing with respect to each goal.	All respondents*	Differences between groups significant?**	Correlation: group ratings of goal importance and goal performance***
Promoting and defending our security	.23	Yes	−.82
Maintaining balance of power among nations	.02	Yes	.04
Defending our allies' security	.01	Yes	−.50
Protecting the interests of American business abroad	.00	Yes	−.96
Strengthening countries who are friendly to us	−.05	Yes	−.36
Keeping peace in the world	−.10	Yes	.21
Protecting the jobs of American workers	−.11	No	.10
Promoting the development of capitalism abroad	−.18	Yes	−.97
Fostering international cooperation to solve common problems, such as food, inflation, and energy	−.23	Yes	−.93
Combatting world hunger	−.25	Yes	−.71
Helping to improve the standard of living in less developed countries	−.31	Yes	−.76
Worldwide arms control	−.39	No	−.64
Strengthening the United Nations	−.45	Yes	−.82
Securing adequate supplies of energy	−.45	No	−.54
Helping solve world inflation	−.48	Yes	−.72
Protecting weaker nations against foreign aggression	−.49	Yes	−.86
Containing communism	−.49	Yes	−.39
Helping to bring a democratic form of government to other nations	−.70	Yes	.13

* Calculated on a scale of 1.00 (excellent) to −1.00 (poor).
** Differences between seven groups of respondents, calculated by analysis of variance, at the .001 level of significance.
*** Spearman rank-order correlation between ratings of goal importance and goal performance by the seven groups.

performance on the more important undertakings. This pattern is evident in the predominance of negative correlations between ratings of importance and performance. The goals deemed most important by the Supporters, for example, (US security, energy supplies, containment), also received the lowest performance ratings by members of that group. Conversely, the Critics rated such goals as international economic cooperation, arms control, peace, and world hunger as important, but they were among the least satisfied with American policy on those issues. Few groups gave high marks to American policy on any issue. The Critics were on balance satisfied on six issues, but generally on goals they regarded as unimportant (protecting business and promoting capitalism abroad, etc.). On the other hand, the Supporters were satisfied with respect to none of the goals, not even on protection of American security.

In summary, these results would seem to indicate that the dismal performance ratings in Table 3.3 actually understate the degree of unhappiness with American foreign policy. These findings are also relevant to the central concern of this chapter. Not only did the seven Vietnam-related groups disagree on the nation's foreign policy goals (as revealed in the previous section); they didn't even agree on how well the United States is doing in the pursuit of these goals.[9] More ominously, they were least inclined to credit Washington with doing well on those goals they believed to be most important.

America's Role in the World

Several questionnaire items on the American role touch upon three facets of the issue: the United States as a free world leader, as a source of economic assistance, and, most fundamentally, on the relative priority of domestic and international concerns.[10]

Free World Leader

On any list of international roles assumed by the United States during the post-war decades, that of the global leader of free world forces has been at or close to the top.[11] The internationalist foreign policies of the Roosevelt and Truman administrations were not without domestic critics, but by the early 1950s there was strong bipartisan agreement that only the United States had the resources to assume a position of leadership in opposition to communist expansion. Senator Robert Taft's failure to win the Republican Presidential nomination in 1952 and Dwight Eisenhower's assumption of Republican leadership ensured that the internationalist Roosevelt–Truman premises would survive even after the Democrats lost control of the White House. The 1950s witnessed the proliferation of American security commitments, massive economic and military assistance programs, covert intervention by the Central Intelligence Agency in

Iran and Guatemala, as well as dramatic economic recovery and trade expansion within the context of an international economic system in which the United States played a leading role. In addition to alliance relationships with over forty nations, the United States also had less formal commitments to the security of others, including Israel. Before Vietnam ignited a firestorm of acrimonious debate on American foreign policy, there was only limited debate, even within the Congress, about whether these activities and commitments represented a sound and necessary exercise of leadership within the free world, or a dangerous over-extension of the nation's economic, military, political, and other resources.

A thorough exploration of America's leadership clearly cannot be undertaken with a very limited number of questions, but the first four propositions listed in Table 3.4 probe some aspects of the nation's proper international role. Over two-thirds of the leaders in this survey agreed that the United States has a moral obligation to prevent destruction of Israel, and less than 30 percent disagreed. When strength of agreement is taken into account, this proposition is the only one among those listed in Table 3.4 that received favorable treatment.

The 1976 survey was undertaken at a time when the conduct of the Central Intelligence Agency, both abroad and at home, was the focus of several major investigations. The controversies aroused by these inquiries were reflected in the responses of American leaders. They were almost evenly divided between those who expressed approval and disapproval of using the CIA to destabilize hostile governments, and a notably high proportion of them indicated strong views on the issue.

At the same time, public attention was also focused on the state of Soviet–American relations, as major figures in both political parties—for example, Republican Ronald Reagan and Democrat Henry Jackson—were calling attention to what they believed were the poisoned fruits of détente: Soviet adventures in Angola and elsewhere, dramatically accelerated defense expenditures by the USSR, and the like. However, approximately two-thirds of the respondents rejected two propositions that lay at the core of the attack on détente: American credibility depends on a willingness to use force, if necessary, to contain Soviet expansion; and, détente serves the national interest poorly because it is a one-sided bargain. Indeed, less than 30 percent of them expressed agreement with the latter item.

The aggregate responses to these four items conceal some rather dramatic differences among the seven groups of respondents. For three of the four items, the data provide very strong support for the expectation that those at the Supporters' end of the scale would provide stronger endorsement of an international leadership role for the United States. Differences among the groups are exceptionally large and in the predicted direction.[12] Whereas 45 percent of the Supporters agreed strongly that there is nothing wrong with using the CIA to undermine hostile governments, only 5 percent of the Critics

Table 3.4   America's Role in the World
(Responses for the entire sample of 2,282 leaders, and analyses of seven groups of respondents classified by their 1976 positions during the early and late stages of the war in Vietnam)

Please indicate how strongly you agree or disagree with each of the following statements concerning America's role in the world.	All respondents*	Differences between groups significant?**	Correlation, actual and hypothesized group rankings***
Free world leader			
The U.S. has a moral obligation to prevent destruction of the State of Israel	.31	No	−.04
There is nothing wrong with using the CIA to try to undermine hostile governments	−.02	Yes	.93
The U.S. should take all steps including the use of force to prevent the spread of Communism	−.29	Yes	.96
It is not in our interest to have better relations with the Soviet Union because we are getting less than we are giving to them	−.33	Yes	.89
Providing economic assistance			
The U.S. should give economic assistance even if it means higher prices at home	−.05	Yes	.89
Even though it probably means higher food prices here at home, it is worth selling grain to the Soviet Union since it may improve out relations with Russia	−.23	Yes	.85
Isolationism			
We shouldn't think so much in international terms but concentrate more on our own national problems	−.24	No	.42

* Calculated on a scale of 1.00 (agree strongly) to −1.00 (disagree strongly).
** Differences between seven groups of respondents, calculated by analysis of variance, at the .001 level of significance.
*** Spearman rank-order correlation between hypotheses and actual rankings of seven groups.

did so. The comparable figures on the question of using all means to contain communism are 32 and 1 percent. On the latter issue, over two-thirds of Critics expressed strong disagreement, compared to only 8 percent of the Supporters who did so. The value of better relations with the Soviet Union gave rise to a somewhat narrower range of responses, but the differences among the groups are substantial and in the predicted direction.

The notable exception to this pattern concerns the survival of Israel. Not only did a strong majority approve of an American commitment to this end, but the pattern of agreement and disagreement bears no relationship to that uncovered on other foreign policy questions. Stated somewhat differently, the issue of Israel appears to cut across rather than along the same lines of cleavage that have emerged repeatedly in this and the previous chapters.

Economic Assistance

Winston Churchill may have been engaging in hyperbole when he characterized the Marshall Plan as "the most unsordid act in history," but by virtually any standards it was one of the notable successes of post-war American diplomacy. It may also have been the high-water mark of domestic support for foreign assistance programs. Growing economic difficulties at home and suspicions that foreign aid, whether economic or military, does not always improve the lot of the average citizen in recipient countries, have tended to erode public support for such undertakings. Despite eloquent pleas for greater generosity by former World Bank President Robert McNamara and others, opinion surveys usually reveal that foreign aid appears high on any list of government programs which should be reduced rather than expanded.

Two items in the leadership survey asked respondents to assess American policies in the context of a trade-off between foreign assistance and domestic inflation. The question of economic aid to poorer countries resulted in an almost even division, a figure that reveals greater support for foreign aid among leaders than among the public at large.[13] Grain sales to the USSR that might result in higher food prices at home received less support, as almost three-fifths of the respondents expressed opposition to such exports. No doubt the Nixon Administration's grain sales of 1972—soon thereafter dubbed by many as the "great grain robbery"—were an important contributing factor. Perhaps another is that the sample of leaders in the present survey includes few members of the occupational group that has always been most supportive of agricultural exports—farmers.

The hypothesis that the Critics would be more inclined than Supporters to agree with economic assistance programs receives support when the results are tabulated according to the seven groups defined by Vietnam policy preferences. Differences among the groups are statistically significant on both issues, and they are in the predicted direction.[14] But whereas four groups supported economic aid to poorer countries, none of them was, on balance, in favor of grain exports to the Soviet Union if higher prices at home were the result; differences among them consist essentially of varying degrees of opposition to such sales.

Isolationism

For many Americans, Pearl Harbor represented the bankruptcy of isolationism. By the mid-1970s, however, the context seemed the most propitious since World War II for a serious reconsideration of the nation's internationalist foreign policy stance; the loss in Vietnam, the Watergate crimes, inflation, and a general loss of public confidence in virtually all major institutions led a number of thoughtful observers to call for a new agenda of national priorities in which domestic issues would return to their traditional, pre-World War II position of primacy. Others characterized such thinking as an egregious exercise in nostalgia, unworthy of a great power and, in any case, no more realistic than a return to the horse and buggy as the basic mode of transportation.

The final item in Table 3.4 addresses this issue. The fears of some, and hopes of others, that disillusionment with the outcome in Vietnam would lead to a dramatic revival of isolationism appear to have been exaggerated or premature. A solid majority disagreed with the proposition that "We shouldn't think so much in international terms but concentrate more on our own national problems," and among respondents expressing strong opinions on the matter, those taking an internationalist stance on the issue outnumbered leaders favoring the primacy of domestic problems by a margin of three to one.

The expectation that the Critics would record significantly greater opposition to external commitments was not borne out by the data, however, as the respondents in the seven groups did not differ significantly on the proposal for a less internationalist orientation by the United States.[15] This finding provides further impetus to the suspicion raised in the previous chapter that there is an internationalist–isolationist dimension among respondents to this survey that cuts across the Vietnam-related cleavages.

Conclusion

Table 3.5 reveals how respondents in each of the seven groups ranked the propositions relating to the nation's proper international role. It provides further testimony to some striking differences in perspective. Beyond a degree of similarity in their concerns for the survival of Israel, there are few shared priorities among the groups. For example, sanctioning CIA activities against hostile governments and preventing the spread of communism received the highest priority among the three groups at the Supporter end of the scale, but these ranked as the

Table 3.5 America's Role in the World as Ranked by 2,282 American Leaders Classified into Seven Groups According to Vietnam Policy Preferences*

All Respondents	Supporters	Converted Supporters	Ambivalent Supporters	Ambivalents	Ambivalent Critics	Converted Critics	Critics
Israel's security	Using the CIA	Using the CIA	Using the CIA	Israel's security	Israel's security	Israel's security	Israel's security
	Prevent spread of communism	Israel's security	Israel's security	Aid to poor countries	Aid to poor countries	Aid to poor countries	Aid to poor countries
	Israel's security	Prevent spread of communism		Using the CIA			
	Oppose better relations with USSR						

* This table includes all items that received a rating of at least 0.01 on a scale of 1.00 (agree strongly) to −1.00 (disagree strongly).

two least worthy undertakings for the Critics. A similar lack of consensus exists with respect to other roles as well. As a consequence, only the proposition relating to Israel evoked more agreement than disagreement within the entire leadership sample.

American Policy Objectives in Underdeveloped Countries

Few foreign policy issues have created more controversy and less consistency of policy than the goals that the United States should pursue in its relations with less developed countries. The ideal is not hard to define. The United States should encourage development of stable democratic governments that: respect basic human rights; provide real economic growth; live at peace with their neighbors; and, if not avowedly pro-American in foreign policy orientations, are at least not reflexively anti-American. The problem, of course, is that the real world offers few such models; the Ugandas, Cubas, Libyas, and Pakistans far outnumber the Costa Ricas, Ivory Coasts, and Singapores. Thus, trade-offs are necessary, and the choices are often between the least-of-evils. As one foreign policy official put it, referring to a less than model democracy, "Sure they're bastards, but at least they're our bastards."

Preferences among trade-offs have varied from administration to administration. John Foster Dulles's pronouncement that "neutralism is immoral" represented a rhetorical position, not always followed in practice, that gave high priority to Cold War considerations. The policies of the Kennedy Administration placed more emphasis on political and economic development, and the Carter Administration attempted to give greater attention to human rights criteria. The Reagan government has followed the lead of its United Nations Ambassador in drawing a distinction between "authoritarian" and "totalitarian" governments in the Third World.[16] Although that distinction is not especially original and it is not without merit, at least a few observers have suggested that for the Reagan Administration, "authoritarian" is a code word for "our bastards," whereas "totalitarians" are "their bastards."

A cluster of questions borrowed from a study of business executives and military officers asked the leaders in this survey to rank in order of importance a series of possible objectives for the United States to pursue in its relations with less developed nations.[17] Responses for the entire sample of 2,282 leaders are described in Table 3.6. The results reveal a strong preference for policies that encourage politically effective and responsible government in the Third World—that is, governments able to maintain internal order while preserving civil liberties. Somewhat lower priority is attached to the foreign policy orientation of the less developed nations; there is a strong preference for regimes that will leave their neighbors in peace, but much less concern for governments that pursue pro-American or neutral

Table 3.6 *U.S. Foreign Policy Objectives in Underdeveloped Countries*
(Responses for the entire sample of 2,282 leaders, and analyses of seven groups of respondents classified by their 1976 positions during the early and late stages in the war in Vietnam)

Please indicate the relative importance you believe the U.S. should attach, in general, to the following policy objectives in its involvement with underdeveloped countries. If a choice must be made, which ones should be considered most important?	*All respondents**	*Differences between groups significant?***	*Correlation, actual and hypothesized group rankings****
A stable government capable of preserving internal order	2.55	Yes	.75
A government which maintains civil liberties	2.83	Yes	.93
A government which will not engage in unprovoked aggression against other nations	2.95	Yes	.57
A government which is neutral or pro-American in its foreign policy	3.72	Yes	.90
Rapid economic development	4.38	Yes	.89
A government which retains the free enterprise system	4.81	Yes	.96
A government which allows broad opportunities for American business investment	5.90	No	.79

* Calculated on a scale of 1.00 (most important) to 7.00 (least important.)
** Differences between seven groups of respondents, calculated by analysis of variance, at the .001 level of significance.
*** Spearman rank-order correlation between hypotheses and actual rankings of seven groups.

external policies. Thus, the Dullesian dictum that those who are not with us are deemed to be against us receives little support.

Perhaps the most striking finding is the consistently low rating accorded to economic objectives. Rapid economic development and retention of the free enterprise system—characteristics that have marked the most successful developing nations—ranked far below any of the political objectives. The priority attached to the goal of a congenial environment for American business investments in the Third World gained little or no support; almost one half of the respondents rated this as the least important American objective among the less developed nations, and only one-sixth placed it among the top four.

As can also be seen in Table 3.6, a description of responses for the entire sample once again masks considerable differences among leaders when they are classified into seven groups according to Vietnam policy preferences. Without exception, all groups rated opportunities for American business investment as the least important policy objective. Beyond this shared view, significantly different priorities with respect to the other goals were evident, and in all cases they were in the predicted direction.[18] Supporters ascribed greater importance to achievement of stable governments adhering to neutral or pro-American policies and preserving free enterprise, whereas the Critics emphasized the importance of rapid economic development, maintenance of civil liberties, and governments that refrain from external aggression. Differences among the groups were especially pronounced on questions of foreign policy orientation, economic development, civil liberties, and free enterprise.

Conclusion

The analysis in Chapter 2, focusing on the sources of failure, consequences, and lessons of Vietnam, uncovered strong support for three propositions about the breakdown of leadership consensus on foreign policy, the catalytic role of the Vietnam War in that process, and the existence of competing belief systems. Evidence in this chapter extends these findings to a broader spectrum of issues, ranging from the proper international role of the United States and the goals that should guide its external relations, to some issues of strategies and tactics. As in the previous chapter, the 2,282 American leaders were classified into seven groups defined solely by their policy preferences during the early and late stages of the Vietnam War.

The results summarized in Tables 3.1–3.6 offer further support for the propositions on consensus, Vietnam, and foreign policy belief systems. There are deep cleavages among American leaders on a wide range of issues, and these are in virtually all cases systematically related to Vietnam policy positions. Moreover, out of the data have emerged two quite different ways of thinking, not only about the conflict in Southeast Asia, but also more broadly about foreign policy and international relations.

One of the belief systems is embedded in the responses of the Supporters. Leaders in this group tend to attribute failure in Vietnam to the manner in which the war was conducted (means) rather than to the nature of the undertaking itself (ends). They believe that the conflict should have resulted in victory, and it could have except for self-imposed restraints. In explaining the defeat in Southeast Asia, they point not only to Soviet and Chinese assistance to North Vietnam, but also to the actions of domestic dissidents, reporting by the mass media, Congressional interference in policy-making, insufficient attention to military advice, restrictions on employment of air power, and a pervasive "no win" approach to the war. They would, on the whole, agree with former President Ford's diagnosis: "I thought our motives were right. Our tactics were not the best tactics that could have been used."[19] Further, they believe that the price of failure will be paid in the international arena; the consequences of the war will be a world that is far less congenial to American interests and aspirations. Defeat in Vietnam will give rise to adverse structural changes in the international system, encouragement for communist adversaries to pursue more aggressive expansionist policies, erosion of American credibility, and serious constraints on America's ability to pursue its goal of a just and stable world order. Supporters also tend to adduce lessons from the Vietnam experience that are consistent with their diagnoses of failure and predictions about the consequences of Vietnam. Emphasis on the bipolar structure of the international system, credibility, and the domino theory; doubts about the permanent fragmentation of the communist bloc; and skepticism about the value of détente characterize some of the more important lessons about world politics that many Supporters perceive as confirmed by the Vietnam experience. Although they appear to question whether the United States can have much influence in Third World development, they are ambivalent about the suggestion that the United States should scale down its leadership role. And when it comes to the means by which the United States can best pursue its foreign policy goals, they place considerable emphasis on the more effective management of military power, including fewer restraints on the magnitude and timetable governing the employment of force.

Tables 3.1–3.6 reveal that respondents in the Supporter group also appear to maintain a consistent world-view on issues other than those concerned directly with Vietnam, emphasizing international security/military issues and such concepts as balance of power and containment. With respect to the instruments of foreign policy, they generally subscribe to a *realpolitik* position. Although they expressed doubts about American uses of military power in Vietnam and almost 60 percent agreed that, "the efficiency of military power in foreign affairs is declining" (Table 2.8), they are nevertheless more prone than other groups of leaders to regard force and subversion as means that have not lost their utility in contemporary world affairs. These beliefs are also consistent with the objectives in the Third World that receive high priority among the Supporters: stable governments that will subscribe to pro-American, or at least neutral, foreign policies.

In contrast, leaders in the Critics group have a very different interpretation of the Vietnam experience. Regarding the undertaking as an unwinnable one, they trace the defeat to unrealistic goals; to a lack of knowledge, especially of Third World nationalism, the history and culture of the region, and the motivations of both friends and adversaries in Vietnam; and to shortcomings of the regime in Saigon.

Unlike the Supporters, they tend to view the consequences of the war in terms of domestic costs: inflation, loss of faith in American institutions, and neglect of more important issues. Critics also derive lessons from the war that appear consistent with their diagnoses of failure and assessments of consequences. They regard the international system as a multi-polar one in which revolutionary forces in the Third World are often motivated by factors other than Soviet and Chinese foreign policy goals, and in which the communist nations are fundamentally, if not irreconcilably, at odds with each other. Within such a system they tend to prescribe a reduced role for the United States (especially in undertakings that involve, or might ultimately lead to, military intervention), and they are skeptical about the utility of military power in the conduct of foreign relations. And, most emphatically, Critics find in the Vietnam experience ample evidence pointing to the need for changes in the formulation and execution of foreign policy. By giving overwhelming support to three propositions—foreign policy has suffered from an excess of military advice and an "imperial presidency," as well as a shortage of candor with the American people—the Critics are arguing that greater decentralization, democratization, and demilitarization of American diplomacy are among the primary lessons of the Vietnam War.

The Critics' assessment of the Vietnam experience thus appears to form a coherent and mutually-supporting cluster of beliefs. This consistency also extends to issues other than Vietnam. Unlike their counterparts among the Supporters, the Critics rate international cooperation on such issues as arms control, inflation, hunger, use of resources, and living standards in less developed countries as the most important goals for American foreign policy, and they assign significantly lower priority to such objectives as containment of communism and maintenance of a global balance of power. The Critics tend to be highly skeptical about the efficacy of force in international affairs, emphasizing such instruments as foreign economic assistance. The goals that they would pursue in relations with less developed nations also seem consistent with their other views. Compared to leaders in the Supporters group, the Critics place a greater value on efforts to establish or support governments that protect civil liberties of their citizens, that live at peace with their neighbors, and that are capable of achieving rapid economic growth.

At least two questions might be raised about the findings summarized above, however. How can one be certain that the differences in foreign policy beliefs did not pre-date rather than arise in the wake of the Vietnam War? In the absence of directly comparable evidence on leadership beliefs from the 1950s and early 1960s it is, of course, impossible to answer that query with total certainty. However, the fact that well over one-half of the leaders in this survey admitted to a change in policy preferences (see Tables 2.1 and 2.2 above) on an issue that had achieved as much visibility, and had generated such widespread and intense debate, as the Vietnam War would seem to weigh rather heavily against the thesis that foreign policy dissensus preceded rather than followed American involvement in Vietnam. It seems unlikely that changes on Vietnam could be isolated from other beliefs about the nature of the international system, America's global role, and its foreign policy goals, strategies and tactics. If it could be demonstrated that Vietnam were a rather minor and peripheral issue for the leaders, or that they were generally unconcerned with foreign affairs, one might plausibly argue that changes in Vietnam policy preferences could be undertaken without significant impact on other beliefs. Neither of these conditions can be demonstrated, however. The very fact of participation in a survey that required several hours to complete a questionnaire suggests that the 2,282 respondents whose views have been summarized here have substantially greater than average interest in foreign affairs. Moreover, when asked to assess the personal impact of Vietnam, their answers indicated that the war was by no means of merely marginal interest. Well over half of the leaders stated that it was both "one of my major worries and concerns at the time" (toward the end of the war), and a "profoundly important experience" (Table 3.7).

One might also object that the classification scheme based on Vietnam policy preferences may in fact be a surrogate for other, more basic, respondent attributes—for example, occupation, generation, ideology, political party preference, or other background characteristics. Stated differently, has the analysis to this point centered on a spurious rather than genuine explanation of foreign policy cleavages? A fuller exploration of this issue is deferred until Chapter 5. For the moment, suffice it to say that every effort to undermine the power of the Vietnam-based classification scheme, through multi-variate analyses involving a wide range of social background attributes, failed. Thus, the impact of Vietnam appears to be independent of other background characteristics that are often associated with political beliefs.

The data have generally sustained the thesis that the Vietnam War eroded the post-World War II foreign policy consensus, giving rise to competing belief systems. However, it is worth recalling that questions bearing most directly on the proper extent of American involvement in the world fit less well into the overall pattern of responses. For example, no significant differences among groups were found on the proposition that "We shouldn't think so much in international terms but concentrate more on our own national problems." Respondents in all groups tended, on balance, to be slightly opposed, but their responses suggest a further examination of leadership beliefs that includes the possible emergence of an internationalist-isolationist dimension. The next two chapters address this question. Chapter 4 examines recent foreign policy debates in the United States, as reflected in newspaper editorials, magazines of opinion, and the like, with a view to identifying several fundamentally different ways of thinking about foreign affairs.

Table 3.7   *Importance of Vietnam Issue*
(Distribution of responses of 2,282 American Leaders)

Which of the following statements describes what your feelings were about the war in Vietnam?

	When the war first became an issue		Towards the end of US involvement	
	N	%	N	%
The war in Vietnam was one of my major worries and concerns at that time	628	28	1,287	56
I was concerned about the war, but it was not one of my major causes of worry	1,244	55	863	38
I was not very concerned about the war	372	16	53	2
Not sure	17	1	4	0
Uncodable and no answer	21	1	75	3
	2,282	101*	2,282	99*

In retrospect, how would you assess the meaning of the Vietnam War for you personally?

	N	%
It was a profoundly important experience that is likely to influence my outlook for a long time	1,192	52
It had an important influence on me at the time, but this influence has now waned	676	30
It had no more influence on me than any other foreign policy issue	308	13
It did not influence my outlook in any significant way	82	4
Uncodable and no answer	24	1
	2,282	100

* Percentage totals more or less than 100 owing to rounding error.

Chapter 5 returns to the 1976 leadership survey to assess with systematic evidence some of the ideas developed in Chapter 4.

Notes to Chapter 3

1   The premises of these policies are summarized in Table 2.10 and they are discussed in somewhat greater detail in Chapter 7. The best assessment of the impact of the crises in Iran, Greece, and Turkey in 1946–7 is in the prize-winning study by Bruce R. Kuniholm, *The Origins of the Cold War in the Near East: Great Power*

Conflict and Diplomacy in Iran, Turkey and Greece (Princeton, NJ: Princeton University Press, 1980).

2 This cluster of items on American foreign policy goals was drawn from a survey conducted for the Chicago Council on Foreign Relations by the Harris Organization. Its results are summarized in John E. Rielly, *American Public Opinion and U.S. and Foreign Policy* (Chicago: Chicago Council on Foreign Relations, 1975).

3 F ratios of 11.5, 28.8, 101.5, 22.1, and 21.5 are all significant at the ·001 level.

4 Lack of data on leadership beliefs from earlier periods makes it difficult to assess the extent to which the 1976 data represents a significant change. For a further discussion, see Chapter 7.

5 F ratios for these six items are 31.6, 8.9, 1.9, 27.4, 2.4, and 26.3. All but the third and fifth are significant.

6 The F ratios for these items—18.4, 25.3, 5.1, 24.9, and 30.5—are all significant.

7 F ratios are 2.4 and 18.4. Only the latter is significant.

8 Non-responses to these questions were higher than for any of the other items in the questionnaire, probably because respondents failed to read instructions that appeared at the bottom of the page. The questionnaire is reproduced in Appendix B.

9 Differences in performance ratings among respondents in the seven groups were significant on all except three goals: protecting the jobs of American workers, worldwide arms control, and energy supplies. The F ratios for the eighteen items are: 20.2, 10.1, 11.4, 28.2, 5.6, 7.0, 12.8, 0.7, 13.9, 10.7, 14.6, 6.5, 12.1, 2.2, 4.3, 8.4, 6.0, and 2.6.

10 This set of questions on America's role in the world was drawn from the Harvard–*Washington Post* leadership survey, conducted under the leadership of Professor Sidney Verba. Its findings are summarized in Barry Sussman, *Elites in America* (Washington, DC: *The Washington Post*, 1976).

11 For systematic evidence on national role conceptions, including those of the United States, see K. J. Holsti, "National role conceptions in the study of foreign policy," *International Studies Quarterly*, 14 (September 1970), pp. 233–309.

12 The F ratios are 2.4, 84.3, 123.8, and 36.6. The last three are significant at the .001 level.

13 For evidence on this point see, for example, Rielly, *American Public Opinion*, as well as numerous opinion surveys that reveal a low level of public support for foreign aid programs.

14 F ratios of 27.7 and 7.6 for these items are significant.

15 The F ratio of 4.7 is not significant.

16 See Jeane Kirkpatrick, "Dictatorships and double standards," *Commentary* 68 (November 1979), pp. 34–45. This article reportedly drew President Reagan's attention to Mrs Kirkpatrick, and ultimately led to her appointment as American Ambassador to the United Nations.

17 This cluster of questions was drawn from Bruce M. Russett and Elizabeth Hanson, *Interest and Ideology* (San Francisco, Calif.: W. H. Freeman, 1975).

18 The F ratios for these items are 4.4, 18.4, 6.8, 12.8, 15.6, 15.2, and 4.1. All except the last one are significant.

19 *New York Times* (8 February 1977), p. 61:1.

4

The Three-Headed Eagle: Three Perspectives on Foreign Affairs

The previous two chapters offered evidence that the post-World War II foreign policy consensus had broken down. They also suggested the existence of some views concerning the proper scope of America's global interests and responsibilities that do not fit well along a single dimension defined by Vietnam policy preferences. Moreover, public opinion data lead to much the same conclusion. For example, a secondary analysis of the 1975 Chicago Council of Foreign Relations survey revealed the existence of three quite distinct ways of thinking about foreign affairs—conservative internationalism, liberal internationalism, and non-internationalism—of which the latter is quite similar to traditional isolationism.[1] This chapter describes three similar schools of thought, first drawing upon an impressionistic survey of recent foreign policy debates in this country, and then through a more systematic examination of some data from the 1976 leadership survey. The analysis necessarily deals with central tendencies and common denominators, at the expense of subtle nuances and precise details that may characterize the foreign policy beliefs held by the most articulate spokesmen for the three viewpoints. A more detailed analysis or a more extensive survey would no doubt reveal that a three-way classification scheme fails to highlight some differences, especially subtle ones, within each group, as well as the existence of foreign affairs analysts or policy-makers whose views do not fit comfortably within the classification scheme. Nevertheless, in order to provide a context for the data presented later in this chapter and in Chapter 5, there is some value in identifying the central ideas that distinguish what are certainly three of the more important contemporary schools of thought on international relations and foreign policy.

Cold War Internationalism

The Committee on the Present Danger was formed in 1976 by a number of prominent officials, defense intellectuals, and others who shared a profound malaise about and a pessimistic appraisal of basic trends in American foreign and defense policies.[2] The CPD and its members, many of whom serve in the Reagan Administration, is but one of many organizations and individuals who represent the Cold War Internationalist outlook.[3]

The Cold War Internationalist viewpoint revolves around a gloomy appraisal of "the present danger" and what ought to be done to overcome it. It can be summarized by several clusters of propositions that center on the state of the contemporary international system, the nature of the Soviet Union and its foreign policy, and the sources of recent American failures in the international arena. There is also a substantial consensus among adherents of this viewpoint on what needs to be done to set things right.[4]

The belief system of the Cold War Internationalists is organized around the state of relations between East and West, locating along that axis the most fundamental challenges to a just and stable international order. Without denying that some changes have marked the international system since the 1950s, they see a fundamental continuity in its structure, the sources of threats to peace and stability, the appropriate American role in the world, and the most effective instruments of external policy. They perceive a conflict-ridden world in which the primary cleavages are those dividing the United States and its allies from the Soviet empire and in which most, if not all, of the most salient issues and conflicts are closely linked to each other and to that fault line.

A quintessential statement of this outlook on world affairs may be found in Ronald Reagan's assertion, "Let's not delude ourselves. The Soviet Union underlies all the unrest that is going on. If they weren't engaged in this game of dominoes, there wouldn't be any hot spots in the world."[5] In a system thus structured, disturbances in one region will reverberate throughout the international arena, and the consequences of failures in one area are accurately predicted by the domino theory. With respect to security, in short, interdependence is a fact of international life. Within such an international system the United States faces an ambitious, often aggressive, and always patient coalition of adversaries led by Moscow. Cold War Internationalists perceive the Soviet Union as an expansionist power that, under the guise of "peaceful coexistence" or détente, is lulling and gulling the United States into policies that bear a disturbing resemblance to those of Britain and France during the 1930s. The analogy between the ill-fated policies of the Western democracies, culminating in the Munich Conference of 1938, and those pursued by Washington during the 1970s is invoked repeatedly, not only for diagnostic purposes, but also as a source of lessons of the futility and dangers of appeasement. As Paul Nitze, an articulate spokesman for this line of reasoning, has put it, "to make accommodation [with the USSR] the touchstone of our policy is, as Peking never ceases to remind us, the road to appeasement."[6]

According to Cold War Internationalists, détente is merely a contemporary version of appeasement that has permitted the Soviet Union to pursue a relentless Cold War against the West. In that conflict the Soviet arsenal of methods ranges from terrorism and subversion to Third World interventions by Cuban proxies. Proponents of détente are charged with misunderstanding the Soviet Union and its external goals, with erroneously believing that Moscow seeks only parity with the United States (and acknowledgement of that status), and with wrongly viewing the USSR as a conservative, status quo force in world affairs. In reality, according to the Cold War Internationalists, the Soviet Union is not merely another great power whose goals and methods may at times bring it into conflict with its lesser neighbors or with other major powers. Moscow harbors revolutionary global aspirations, never having abandoned its commitment "not to preserve but to destroy the state system that was organized under the Charter of the United Nations in 1945, and to replace it with an imperial system dominated by its will."[7]

Thus, only the most superficial or naive appraisal of the contemporary world situation would lead to the conclusion that the nature of international relations has fundamentally changed since the death of Stalin. President Carter's Notre Dame speech, in which he proclaimed that "We are now free of that inordinate fear of Communism which once led us to embrace any dictator who joined us in our fear," is often cited by Cold War Internationalists as a notorious example of such naiveté. The overarching reality of the global system remains the continuing conflict between an expansionist Soviet Union and its allies on the one hand, and the non-communist nations on the other. With respect to this fundamental fact of international life, changes during the past two decades are the occasion for neither congratulations nor complacency.

Even if one applies a generous discount to statements made during the course of presidential campaigns, the Cold War Internationalist assessment of contemporary international affairs is gloomy, bordering on the apocalyptic, with suggestions that the very existence of the United States, if not Western civilization, is in jeopardy. According to Eugene V. Rostow, for example, "We are living in a prewar and not a postwar world."[8] Citing trends in Soviet defense spending during the past decade and a half, as well as recent adventures in Angola, Ethiopia, Yemen, Afghanistan, Somalia, Vietnam, and elsewhere, the Cold War Internationalists argue that the balance of power—what Soviet theoreticians call "the correlation of forces"—has swung so far in favor of the USSR that at best the international system is unstable, and at worst it may be headed for war. According to the Committee on the Present Danger, "The size, sophistication and rate of growth of Soviet military power far exceeds Soviet requirements for defense. The Soviet military buildup reflects the offensive nature of the Soviet political and military challenge and the Soviet belief that the use of force remains a viable instrument of foreign policy." Moreover, the question "Has America become number two?" calls forth a disturbing reply: "The answer is unequivocally yes."[9] The consequence of American and Western failure to keep pace with Soviet defense spending is a dangerous transformation of power relationships. The Kremlin may thus be encouraged to embark upon international adventures that will ultimately lead to war with the United States.[10]

The dangerous military asymmetry between the two superpowers is not limited to the imbalance of strategic and conventional forces. It also encompasses a sharp divergence in American and Soviet thought about the role of force. Whereas Washington is concerned with containment and deterrence, leaders in the Kremlin are also thinking about the political implications of strategic forces and with winning a war should it break out. As a consequence, the Cold War Internationalists fear that the Soviets may gain their expansionist goals through nuclear coercion and blackmail. A frequently-cited scenario portrays the USSR as exploiting a "window of vulnerability" during the mid-to-late 1980s to launch a "limited" strike that destroys American land-based missiles. The Kremlin would simultaneously warn that any American retaliation would bring forth a devastating Soviet counter-response against population and industrial centers. Because retaliation in such circumstances is tantamount to national suicide, the American president is unlikely to strike back.[11] To avoid being faced with a "surrender or suicide" choice, the United States must immediately come to grips with the gaps both in strategic hardware and in realistic thinking about how to win a nuclear war as well as how to deter one. While nuclear war would bring severe losses, Cold War Internationalists reject as defeatist the argument that such a conflict would mark the end of viable societies in the United States and USSR. Eugene Rostow claimed, in response to a question in a Senate hearing, "There would be 10 million [dead] on one side and 100 million on the other, but that is not the whole population."[12]

The basic problem for the United States is therefore to maintain the territorial and political integrity of the non-communist parts of the world in the face of a highly-armed, expansionist power that continues to seek global hegemony. Some Cold War Internationalists accept the proposition that the contemporary international system is more complex than that facing Metternich or Bismarck, but they deny that the prudent, time-tested axioms of international intercourse—the *realpolitik* "rules of the game"—have been rendered obsolete. The idea that there is an alternative to *realpolitik* is one of the central myths of liberal thought on American foreign policy.[13] Some may agree that the game is more complex than dominoes, but few are prepared to dismiss the metaphor of the chessboard, a game with a well-defined hierarchy based on power in which position is a critical factor, and which is basically zero-sum (your gain is my loss, and vice versa) in nature. Proposals that contemporary American foreign policy should be guided by "new realities" rather than by "old myths" elicit the response that, rather than invalidating old truths about international relations, the Vietnam War confirmed the importance of power, reputation, and fidelity to commitments: "image counts, power counts, dominoes live, and freedom counts."[14]

The prescription is thus clear and unequivocal: the United States must accept the responsibilities and burdens of its leadership position within the non-communist sector and, at minimum, it must restore a balance of power sufficient to convince the Soviet leadership that aggrandizement will not pay. To charges that such policies will merely revive the Cold War, Cold War Internationalists usually reply that it never ended. Détente and arms control were merely ploys by which the Soviets continued the conflict, while the United States slept. Moreover, they dismiss the argument, often used by defenders of détente, that hypervigilance and American rearmament will strengthen the hands of the "hawks" in Moscow, while undercutting the position of the "moderates." Because aggressive Soviet policies are inherent in the Soviet system—a totalitarian state cannot relax tensions or abandon the expansionist ideology that legitimates the repressive dictatorship—they are sensitive neither to personnel changes in the Kremlin nor to American policies. Soviet leaders honor Lenin's dictum, "If you strike mush, advance; if you strike steel, retreat." Thus, only a firm demonstration of American resolve is likely to moderate Soviet policies.[15]

Cold War Internationalists are not blind to obvious Soviet weaknesses, notably in the economic realm. Indeed, *Wall Street Journal* editorialists have written of "the collapse of the Communist economic system . . . Poland is first but the rest, including the Soviet Union, are not far behind."[16] But from this prediction they draw two conclusions: such weakness may make the USSR more rather than less reckless in foreign affairs; and/or it gives the Soviets a clear incentive to avoid an arms race that they cannot win. In either case, the prescription for the United States is to press on with rearmament.

Expressions of deep concern about recent trends in American foreign and defense policies abound among Cold War Internationalists. As a source of danger to national survival, running a close second behind self-generated delusions about détente, is Washington's obsession with arms control, and especially with what they perceived as its most notorious product—the SALT II Treaty. To those who warn of an uncontrolled arms race in a SALT-free world, they reply that the United States long ago opted out of the competition, leaving the USSR as the lone entrant in the race. Eugene Rostow, former Arms Control Director in the Reagan Administration, charged that the policies of his predecessors were nothing short of "unilateral disarmament."[17] Thus, to the question posed by Drew Middleton's book, *Can America Win the Next War?*, the optimists among Cold War Internationalists answer, "Maybe—but not for long," whereas the pessimists' answer is unequivocally negative.

Thus, although Cold War Internationalists may disagree among themselves on the fine details of how to cope with the "present danger," two shared themes unite them. First, the United States must undertake substantial increases in military spending. The 1980 campaign saw talk of spending a trillion dollars during a single four-year period for defense, a proposal that, ironically, may have first been suggested by a former Arms Control Director.[18] Present Reagan Administration defense plans call for spending $1.6 trillion in five years. However, it is becoming increasingly clear that many Cold War Internationalists within and outside the Administration believe that even this figure would be totally inadequate, and that far greater defense outlays are necessary to restore American credibility and the genuine war-fighting capability that they believe to be the only effective deterrent to the Soviet challenge. They tend to support the Administration's effort to preserve the TRIAD concept through deployment of the MX land-based missile system, acceleration of the Trident II sub-launched ballistic missile program, and revival of the B–1 bomber, and this is by no means a complete shopping list, for it touches only upon strategic forces.[19] Thus, more than a few of them have been extremely critical of the Reagan Administration decision to abandon the Carter version of the MX deployment (200 missiles moving among 4,600 firing points) in favor of a reduced, fixed-site system of 100 missiles.

The deterrence doctrine of "mutual assured destruction" (MAD), according to which the threat of nuclear destruction deters both of the superpowers, finds few supporters among the Cold War Internationalists, most of whom prefer a "damage limitation" strategy, along with the programs that may be required to implement it: highly accurate missiles with "hard target" capabilities; anti-ballistic missiles, although (or perhaps because) that would require abrogating the SALT I Treaty; civil defense; and the like. Even economists who have been notably restrained in their applause for free-wheeling government spending have advocated removing virtually all of the traditional political and administrative constraints on the defense budget; that there may be limits on what the nation can afford for defense is dismissed as "hokum."[20] Indeed, the Reagan Administration has come under attack by some for being excessively concerned with balanced budgets, although that goal seems likely to be missed by hundreds of billions of dollars: "I'm not happy with the pattern that seems to be emerging . . . Whenever there is a conflict between the domestic economy and the interests of foreign policy, the Administration seems to favor the domestic economy. I find that troublesome. The priority ought to be rebuilding American defenses and trying to get ground forces in the Persian Gulf."[21]

But perhaps even more than imbalances in military capabilities, the Cold War Internationalists are concerned about what they diagnose as an imbalance in resolution and willingness to use power, if necessary, to preserve vital national interests. Some of them have already written off Western Europe as hopelessly caught in a web of neutralism, pacifism, and defeatism—they view the Siberian gas pipeline deal as latter-day confirmation of Lenin's prediction that capitalists would sell the rope that will be used to hang them—and they regard the United States as only a few steps behind in the process. A typical diagnosis is that there has been a "collapse of Western will," the origins of which are to be found in a war—Vietnam—that could have been won, but was lost owing to unreasonable restraints on the military; opposition at home by the media, the Congress, and dissidents; and a general failure of nerve. It has since been sustained by the "Vietnam syndrome," a deleterious mixture of unwarranted guilt feelings, neo-isolationism, and, above all, a profound misreading of "the lessons of Vietnam."[22] According to Irving Kristol,

> We have for too long lived with the illusion that the prime purpose of our foreign policy should be to restrict and eventually eliminate the use (and abuse) of power in international affairs. The moral intention is splendid—but utopian, since much of the world does not share it. We know that power may indeed corrupt. We are now learning that, in the world as it exists, powerlessness can be even more corrupting and demoralizing.[23]

To charges that they are excessively concerned with the use of force, the Cold War Internationalists reply, "Some things are worth fighting for," a statement that only committed pacifists would reject. However, as will be evident later, theirs is a broader definition of "some things" than, for example, that of either the Semi-Isolationists or the Post-Cold War Internationalists. Finally, to accusations that they are taking a simplistic view of contemporary international affairs, they reply that there are some simple truths, for example, about the Soviet threat or the proper means of dealing with it. Moreover, in order to gain public support and a foreign policy consensus, it is necessary to emphasize these truths.

Analyses to be undertaken in Chapter 5 will seek to uncover some of the characteristics of leaders who are associated with Cold War Internationalism and other perspectives on foreign affairs. Responses to several questions will be used to construct an index for each of the viewpoints. Sixteen items in the 1976 leadership survey questionnaire represent several of the more salient aspects of Cold War Internationalism, as described in the preceding paragraphs (Table 4.1). Four items emphasize the expansionist nature of Soviet foreign policy and the importance of containment (4.1:A, 4.1:C, 4.1:G), especially after the American failure in Vietnam encouraged communists to undertake international adventures (4.1:L).[24] Two others focus on important aspects of a tight bipolar system, defining conflict between the United States and communist nations as zero-sum in nature (4.1:F), and likely to follow the pattern of further losses predicted by the domino theory (4.1:E). The skeptical stance of Cold War Internationalists toward détente or other forms of accommodation with the USSR is captured in two items (4.1:I, 4.1:M). Also central to this outlook is the belief that, however much one may regret it, the use of

Table 4.1 *Questionnaire Items from the 1976 Leadership Survey Comprising the Cold War Internationalism Index**

A Containing communism (as an important U.S. foreign policy goal).
B There is nothing wrong with using the C.I.A. to try to undermine hostile governments.
C It is not in our interest to have better relations with the Soviet Union because we are getting less than we are giving to them.
D The U.S. should take all steps including the use of force to prevent the spread of Communism.
E There is considerable validity in the "domino theory" that when one nation falls to communism, others nearby will soon follow a similar path.
F Any communist victory is a defeat for America's national interest.
G The Soviet Union is generally expansionist rather than defensive in its foreign policy goals.
H The U.S. should never try to get by with half measures; we should apply necessary power if we have it.
I Détente permits the USSR to pursue policies that promote rather than restrain conflict.
J Rather than simply countering our opponent's thrusts, it is necessary to strike at the heart of the opponent's power.
K When force is used, military rather than political goals should determine its application.
L Communist nations have been encouraged to seek triumphs elsewhere as a result of Vietnam.
M The major assumptions of détente have been proven false by the events in Vietnam.
N The United States fought with a "no win" approach (as a cause of U.S. failure in Vietnam).
O The use of American air power was restricted (as a cause of U.S. failure in Vietnam).
P Insufficient attention was paid to advice from the military (as a cause of U.S. failure in Vietnam).

* For responses to these items by the sample of 2,282 American leaders, see Tables 2.2, 2.5, 2.7, 2.10 and 3.3 in Chapters 2 and 3. Positive responses to these items are assumed to be consistent with the Cold War Internationalist belief system.

force continues to be a fact of international life, especially in the light of the dramatic Soviet arms build-up. Four items address several facets of the issue: the use of force to stop the spread of communism (4.1:D); the utility of self-imposed restraints on the use of force (4.1:H); the weight to be attached to military and political considerations in decisions involving the use of force (4.1:K); and a question that recalls the debates on "massive retaliation" during the mid-1950s, on the relative merits of local deterrence versus "striking at the heart of the opponent's power" (4.1:J). The latter item was drawn directly from an assertion by former Secretary of Defense James Schlesinger. Related and more specific propositions concern various types of self-imposed restraints on the use of force that, according to some, lay behind the American failure in Vietnam: a "no-win" approach to the conflict

(4.1:N), restrictions on air power (4.1:O), and insufficient attention to military advice on the proper conduct of the war (4.1:P). Finally, one item addresses the view that the Central Intelligence Agency, the effectiveness of which was allegedly destroyed in the aftermath of the Vietnam War, must be revived and permitted to play a more significant role in American foreign relations (4.1:B).

Post-Cold War Internationalism

Post-Cold War Internationalists are not unaware of East–West tensions, if only out of recognition that therein lies the major danger of nuclear holocaust, but their conceptual map is more strongly oriented toward issues that tend to divide the world along a North–South line. At the center of their world-view is a series of closely related propositions concerning the international system, key actors, and America's proper role within it.[25]

The growing list of serious threats to a stable and just world order has created an international system of such complexity and interdependence as to render totally obsolete the premises that informed American foreign policy during the two decades following the end of World War II. Hence, whereas the Cold War Internationalists perceive an essentially bipolar structure that dominates most critical issues, the Post-Cold War Internationalists see a far richer and more varied menu of both threats to and opportunities for creation of a viable world order. Dangers arising from strategic/military issues remain real, but the roots of future international conflict are to be located not merely in military imbalances—real, perceived, or fabricated—but also in problems arising from poverty, inequitable distribution of resources, unfulfilled demands for self-determination, regional antagonisms, population pressures, technology that outpaces the political means for controlling its consequences, and the like.[26] Thus, "it is here, in our relationships with the developing nations, that the future of the world may be decided . . . Above all, there is the overwhelming problem of the rich and the poor, which cannot simply be equated with technical competence versus non-competence, industrialized countries versus underdeveloped countries."[27] Cold War Internationalists maintain that the chessboard remains a valid metaphor of the global system, while the Post-Cold War Internationalists perceive a multi-dimensional game in which the logic of the situation will ultimately reward cooperation more handsomely, and in which outcomes are more often than not non-zero sum.

The age of bipolarity is thus seen to have passed (if, indeed, it ever existed), and, according to Post-Cold War Internationalists, it is both futile and dangerous to believe that it may be replaced by resurrecting a classical balance-of-power system or, worse, by returning to the Cold War. Unprecedented changes relating to actors, objectives, values and, indeed, the very nature of power itself, have rendered the balance of power a wholly inadequate model for world order. The primary task, then, is to create, nurture, and sustain new structures and processes for dealing effectively and equitably with a range of issues that goes well beyond traditionally-defined security concerns. At the core of this belief system is the premise that one cannot effectively cope with problems and opportunities arising from "complex interdependence" save by means of international cooperation on an unprecedented scale. A crucial lesson of Vietnam is that no nation, not even one as powerful as the United States, can alone shape a world order.

The image of the Soviet Union shared by Post-Cold War Internationalists varies sharply from that of the Cold War Internationalists. Whereas the latter emphasizes that the monolithic nature of the Soviet system gives rise to a uniformity of foreign policy goals, the former places stress on the complexity of both Soviet structures and external motivations: typically, they regard the USSR as a traditional great power rather than as a revolutionary, inherently expansionist one. Soviet foreign policy motivations can thus be understood as a mixture of security concerns and aspirations for recognition as the equal of the United States. Not infrequently, the USSR is compared to Wilhelminian Germany prior to World War I.[28] In their searches for what they perceived to be their proper places in the sun, both nations may have been less than punctilious in adhering to all of the niceties, but it does not therefore follow that their goals were nothing less than global hegemony. Pursuing the parallel further, many Post-Cold War Internationalists believe that just as blustering German behavior, misinterpreted elsewhere in Europe, set the stage for the crisis leading up to World War I, so there is a danger that American misunderstanding of Soviet behavior materially increases the risks of World War III.

Thus, in contrast to the Cold War Internationalist interpretation of Soviet actions in Afghanistan and elsewhere as part of a master plan to gain control of strategic areas—for example, as stepping stones toward control of the Persian Gulf oil fields—the Post-Cold War Internationalists usually interpret such actions as motivated by local conditions, defensive considerations, temptations to take advantage of low-risk gains that few major powers could resist, or as efforts to score points in the continuing conflict with China. Consequently, although they do not applaud such actions as the invasion of Afghanistan, they are likely to be at least as critical of American "overreactions" to these episodes as the Cold War Internationalists are to condemn Washington's complacency. Stated differently, whereas the former tended to see few, if any, vital American interests at stake in the nature of the government in Kabul, the latter argued that the implications of the episode were much broader and more serious for both a just and stable world order and American interests, properly understood.

Because the Post-Cold War Internationalists are less than awed by the Soviet Union, they are prepared to explore various forms of accommodation with Moscow, and they assert that success will require flexibility by both of the superpowers.[29] Former Senator John Sparkman, voicing a view not uniquely his, described the USSR as militarily strong, but otherwise it "exhibits many of the characteristics of a developing country." Guided by this perception, he suggested that in the future, American presidents should be as ready to "sit down with the Russians as they have been to stand up to them."[30] Similarly, the *New York Times* editorialized that "Like the United States, the Soviet Union is becoming a mostly conservative force in world affairs, restrained by the fear of nuclear war and burdened with defense of far-flung political and economic interests." As a consequence, "The central axiom of Soviet–American relations today is that the interests of the two nations will periodically coincide and produce collaboration to try to preserve stability in unstable lands and so to avert a superpower conflict."[31]

From the perspective of Post-Cold War Internationalists, the clearest conjunction of Soviet and American interests lies in the area of arms control. Unlike the Cold War Internationalist insistence upon establishing and maintaining tight linkages between SALT (now START) and other issues, Post-Cold War Internationalists are skeptical of efforts to render arms control hostage to the whole panoply of questions that divide the superpowers. The former tend to define interdependence broadly to include security issues; hence the importance of linkages. The latter, on the other hand, typically conceive of interdependence in narrower, economic terms, and they believe that efforts to link activities across issues areas are counterproductive. They are especially critical of tying arms control negotiations to satisfactory Soviet–American relations on such issues as Third World conflicts. Only by decoupling Soviet–American relations into their component parts is there any real prospect of achieving progress on any of them.

Cold War Internationalists regard both the rate of growth in Soviet defense spending and external adventures in Africa and the Middle East, as well as terms of the agreement itself, as ample reasons for rejecting the SALT II Treaty and for intense skepticism about the entire arms control process. In contrast, Post-Cold War Internationalists—many of whom have questioned whether the Soviet Union has even matched, much less surpassed, American force levels—almost uniformly support the treaty as inherently equitable, as a barrier against even greater Soviet military spending, and as the centerpiece of any effort to stabilize relations between the superpowers. Indeed, some of them argue that American failure to ratify the treaty promptly encouraged the Soviet invasion of Afghanistan; that is, once Moscow perceived SALT II as a dying or dead undertaking, they felt that there was little to lose by unleashing the invasion. Many Post-Cold War Internationalists find an instructive historical parallel between the alarmist claims of Soviet military superiority by the

Committee on the Present Danger, the Reagan Administration, and others, and uninformed cries about a "missile gap" during the closing months of the Eisenhower Administration. When confronted with statistics that would appear to challenge the theory that the Soviets seek only parity in military capabilities, they respond that even if the claims of Soviet military superiority were valid, such capabilities cannot be translated into political advantage, owing to defense needs arising from the Sino–Soviet dispute, the probable unreliability of its Eastern European allies, and other difficulties.[32]

Consistent with these interpretations, the Post-Cold War Internationalists believe that an active American role in creating an equitable and stable world order is indispensable because mankind is denied the luxury of procrastination in dealing with many world order issues. This is not to say that they are uncritical of American policies or institutions. Indeed, some of them hold views—for example, "The disposition toward repression in American foreign policy is mainly a matter of structure, not will"[33]—that are strikingly similar to the Cold War Internationalists' Manichean image of the USSR. Nevertheless, the United States has both the obligation, especially in relations with the less developed nations, and the capabilities to contribute toward creation of the institutions and processes necessary to deal effectively and in a timely fashion with the broad agenda of critical international issues that is by no means limited to purely geopolitical and strategic ones. Withdrawal from an active international role, as suggested by the Semi-Isolationists (see below), is neither morally acceptable nor, in any case, a realistic option for the United States.[34] Indeed, failure to act in the face of such compelling needs abroad will ultimately poison the quality of life in this country: "Callousness toward misery abroad will eventually affect the way we lead our lives and deal with one another at home."[35]

As a result, some of the notable differences between the Cold War Internationalists and Post-Cold War Internationalists revolve around their conceptions of the Third World. The former view the less developed nations largely in strategic terms, as one of several sites of the ongoing East–West conflict. Few of them would adhere to the Dullesian doctrine that "neutralism is immoral," but some question the sincerity of a neutralism that embraces a highly skewed double standard in assessing Soviet and American policies in the United Nations and elsewhere; for example, condemning American actions in Vietnam while remaining silent about the invasion of Afghanistan or the Soviet–Cuban interventions in Angola and Ethiopia. Thus, they are much quicker to condemn repressive practices in Third World governments run by "their bastards" than in those run by "our bastards."

In contrast, the Post-Cold War Internationalists tend to view the Third World as the hapless victims of nature (the uneven distribution of such vital resources as oil or arable land, or unfavorable climatic conditions), or of their colonial heritages. Post-liberation exploitation by the rich industrial nations of the West and, above all, by the multi-national corporations, are an added burden. These conditions are regarded as necessary, and usually sufficient, to explain everything from populations that grow faster than gross national products to highly repressive regimes. It follows that there are both prudential and moral reasons for the industrial democracies to undertake massive programs of resource transfers as part of a "New International Economic Order:" prudential because only such undertakings can promote international stability and ultimately avert a North–South conflict; moral because justice and retribution for past sins require a more equitable distribution of the globe's goods and services. If the Cold War Internationalists rarely exhibit excessive sensitivity to repressive governments of the right, most Post-Cold War Internationalists are equally tolerant of the most authoritarian left-wing governments, for whose excesses blame can usually be assigned elsewhere. Genocide in Cambodia, racial persecution in Vietnam, or mass executions by zealots in Iran are often traced to American support for the pre-revolutionary regimes. Critiques of elections in El Salvador are in plentiful supply, but the failure to hold elections at all in Nicaragua is rarely subject to adverse comment. As one observer has put it:

> This school insists on seeing everyone from the Sandinistas in Nicaragua to the mullahs and Mujahedin in Iran to the Khmer Rouge and Viet Cong of another day as your basic Eleanor Roosevelt in national dress, nice but exasperated liberals driven to do, perhaps, some desperate and violent things, but wouldn't you be, too? . . . When the peerless general, prince, or civilian strongman gets chased out of his palace, or maybe strung up in it, and the forces of "light" take over and turn out to be vicious repressive butchers themselves, what is to be said by their erstwhile champions? Not that they turned out to be a rotten lot, but rather that our earlier support of their oppressors made them that way.[36]

Like the Cold War Internationalists, but for very different reasons, the Post-Cold War Internationalists see the need for a dramatic reorientation of America's international role. Stanley Hoffmann poses the alternatives in the title of his book: *Primacy or World Order*.[37] To opt for primacy means a continuation of excessive concern for military/strategic concerns; interventions to support unworthy regimes in areas where vital interests are, at best, marginally at stake; and neglect of global problems that ultimately offer a far greater threat to American security than many of those that have recently obsessed Washington. That choice assures for the United States, and the global community as well, a future of confrontation, conflict, crises, and chaos—and the certainty of ultimate failure to achieve either primacy or world order. To choose the course of world order, on the other hand, requires a significant re-examination of some deeply ingrained

American pretentions, premises, patterns of thought, and policies. At minimum, the politics of negotiation, compromise, and cooperation—what Hoffmann calls "moderation plus"—must replace the politics of confrontation and crisis.

Finally, the Post-Cold War Internationalists share an ambivalence about the processes by which American foreign policy is made. Although staunchly pro-détente, they are generally restrained in their praise for the secrecy and executive dominance that characterized policy-making during the Nixon–Kissinger period. But it would be an error to assume that they therefore welcome reassertion of a significant Congressional role in foreign policy or the rapid growth of information—"instant history"—to the public about external relations. More than a few Post-Cold War Internationalists have expressed dismay at the increasing role of the Congress in general and, more specifically, at its role in wrecking expansion of Soviet–American trade through the Jackson–Vanik Amendment, in almost defeating the Panama Canal Treaties, and in delaying ratification of the SALT II Treaty. Some are equally distressed about the role of the media (especially television) in sustaining the growth of populism, the impact of presidential elections on foreign policy, or even such basic constitutional provisions as the separation of powers.[38] Thus, on the recurring issue of executive–legislative relations in foreign policy-making, neither of the two groups of internationalists has a very consistent position. Both prefer a strong executive—when one of their own occupies the White House. Cold War Internationalists were vocal supporters of executive leadership on the conduct of the Vietnam War, but they argued vehemently for Congressional action to scuttle the Panama Canal and SALT II Treaties, and they opposed President Carter's decision to open full diplomatic relations with Peking without Senatorial approval for ending the security treaty with Taiwan. The positions of the Post-Cold War Internationalists were exactly reversed; indeed, some of them proposed that President Carter define the SALT II Treaty as an executive agreement in order to bypass the constitutional requirement of approval by a two-thirds of the Senate. In short, both groups are constitutional pragmatists on foreign policy-making, preferring an arrangement that will facilitate policies of their choice.

Eight questionnaire items drawn from the 1976 leadership survey, reflecting some salient features of the Post-Cold War Internationalist world-view, are used to construct an index of that perspective (Table 4.2). They emphasize several international issues other than military–strategic ones, including the standard of living in less developed nations (4.2:A), global hunger (4.2:C), and food, inflation, and energy (4.2:E), while also ascribing great importance to worldwide arms control as a foreign policy goal (4.2:B). Post-Cold War Internationalists are also skeptical of the view that Third World revolutionary leaders, rather than reacting to local conditions and grievances, usually take their marching orders from Moscow or

Peking (4.2:H). Finally, in contrast to the Cold War Internationalists, they support using means other than military ones in the pursuit of foreign policy objectives; for example, economic assistance (4.2:F), and greater reliance upon such international institutions as the United Nations (4.2:D, 4.2:G).

Table 4.2   *Questionnaire Items from the 1976 Leadership Survey Comprising the Post-Cold War Internationalism Index**

A   Helping to improve the standard of living in less developed countries (as an important U.S. foreign policy goal).
B   Worldwide arms control (as an important U.S. foreign policy goal).
C   Combatting world hunger (as an important U.S. foreign policy goal).
D   Strengthening the United Nations (as an important U.S. foreign policy goal).
E   Fostering international cooperation to solve common problems, such as food, inflation and energy (as an important U.S. foreign policy goal).
F   The U.S. should give economic aid to poorer countries even if it means higher prices at home.
G   It is vital to enlist the cooperation of the U.N. in settling international disputes.
H   Revolutionary forces in "Third World" countries are usually nationalistic rather than controlled by the USSR or China.

---

* For responses to these items by the sample of 2,282 American leaders, see Tables 2.8, 3.1 and 3.4. Positive responses to these items are assumed to be consistent with the Post-Cold War Internationalist belief system.

Semi-Isolationism

Until World War II, George Washington's injunction against "permanent entangling alliances" that might draw the United States into recurring European wars represented axiomatic truth for many Americans. World War II and the Cold War so undermined faith in isolationism that by 1950 Senator Robert Taft, a leading opponent of the Roosevelt–Truman foreign policies, complained, "I don't know what they mean by isolationism, nobody is an isolationist today."[39] But during and after the Vietnam War, the broad conception of American security needs and obligations, outlined in the Truman Doctrine and expanded in President Kennedy's inaugural address, came under serious scrutiny and attack. That such "establishment internationalists" as George Kennan, George Meany, J. William Fulbright, and Mike Mansfield were calling for a sharply reduced conception of the American role in the world perhaps symbolized the fact that, by the 1970s, many traditional isolationist themes were no longer confined to the outer fringes of the nation's political landscape. They had re-emerged as an important part of discourse on foreign affairs.

Unlike the two internationalist schools of thought on contemporary international affairs, the Semi-Isolationists are concerned primarily with domestic problems, the sources of which can be located at least partly in excessive, if not obsessive, concern with both East–West and North–South issues. Much of their criticism of recent diplomacy is directed at premises that an activist foreign policy can create, either through balance-of-power manipulations or through pursuit of utopian schemes, a world order that is more congenial to American security and interests.[40] Viewing the international environment as fundamentally intractable, if not inherently anarchic, they regard the premise that this nation can create a just or stable world order as an ill-conceived, but typically American, exercise in hubris. At worst it leads to dangerous and futile crusades to "make the world safe for democracy" or some other equally elusive goal; at best it can only lead to cynicism and despair when, as is inevitable, the utopian plans are not fulfilled.

For the Semi-Isolationists, the cardinal rules that should guide America's concerns are "Know thy limits" and "Heal thyself first." George McGovern's plea, "Come home, America," although clearly not a formula upon which to ride into the White House in 1972, nevertheless strikes a responsive chord among a not insignificant element in the United States. George Kennan's assertion, "I think I am a semi-isolationist," George Meany's proclamation that "Free trade is a sham," Senator Fulbright's complaints against "the arrogance of power," and the appeal of "project independence" to many once confirmed internationalists indicate that isolationist ideas have achieved a degree of respectability and support unknown since before Pearl Harbor.[41] For some persons the appeal of the Libertarian Party may reflect the fact that, unlike many of the "small government" advocates among the Cold War Internationalists, the Libertarians also apply that viewpoint to defense budgets and other by-products of internationalism.

Semi-Isolationists share with the Post-Cold War Internationalists several key propositions about contemporary international relations. They agree that the era of bipolarity has passed, in large part because the Soviet Union has been transformed from an aggressive revolutionary state into a conservative great power, governed by an ageing leadership whose memories of the destruction wrought by World War II far outstrip their zeal for high-risk international adventures. Thus, what the Cold War Internationalists perceive as a military superpower, confident that a dramatic change in the "correlation of forces" is opening up an era of unprecedented opportunities for Soviet expansion, the Semi-Isolationists diagnose as a great power beset with intractable domestic problems: economic stagnation, rampant alcoholism, an inefficient agricultural sector, uncertainties of leadership succession, and potential ethnic conflicts as the proportion of Russians in the USSR continues to decline. Additionally, the Kremlin has a full agenda of international difficulties including, but not confined to, the China problem and resurgence of nationalism within its Eastern European empire. And whereas the Cold War Internationalists see in the fast-rising Soviet arms budget a clear index of ultimate Soviet intentions—an unprecedented threat to Western civilization—the Semi-Isolationists are inclined to attribute the Soviet side of the arms race to a mixture of genuine fears of a two-front war, bureaucratic momentum, and strategic irrationalities that are not the monopoly of the leadership in the Kremlin. Moreover, the record of Soviet efforts must not be exaggerated by alarmists. Abysmal failures in China, Yugoslavia, Egypt, Sudan, and elsewhere far outstrip the few successes in such lesser countries as Yemen, Angola, Ethiopia, and Vietnam.

In some respects the Semi-Isolationist diagnosis of Soviet–American relations goes further. With its emphasis on the fact that the real problems and threats faced by both of the superpowers are domestic in origin, the Semi-Isolationists are inclined to deny that there are any genuine conflicts of interest between them. The danger, then, is not so much that either poses a mortal threat to the vital interests of the other but, rather, that fear, miscalculation, and misperception will drive them into a conflict that can only result in their mutual destruction, if not that of all mankind. By denying both sides the resources that could be used to deal with vital domestic issues, the arms race plays a central role in this dangerous situation. More dangerously, the propensity to adduce aggressive foreign policy motivations from arms budgets and deployments drives the arms race in an action–reaction cycle that must lead to disaster.

But the Semi-Isolationists are not inclined to give much greater credence to either the direst fears or the fondest hopes of the Post-Cold War Internationalists. For starters, they tend to regard the term "complex interdependence" as descriptively inaccurate and a fact to be deplored rather than celebrated where in fact it does exist. As Kennan has put it, "To what extent this interdependence really exists and constitutes a commanding reality of our time, I cannot say. I will only say that however much there is of it, as a feature of the situation of the United States, I wish there were less."[42] Hopes and expectations that interdependence provides both imperatives and opportunities for long-overdue structural changes in the international system are dismissed as chimeral and utopian. The progeny of interdependence are more likely to be intervention and conflict than cooperation and progress. While they would no doubt express themselves more elegantly, many Semi-Isolationists would generally agree with the assertion by a committed Cold War Internationalist that "global institution building is, unfortunately, nothing more than 'globaloney.'"[43]

The Semi-Isolationist diagnosis of the contemporary international situation thus differs radically from that of the two internationalist viewpoints described earlier. It may be summarized with a set of three propositions.

• The USSR does indeed possess the capabilities to rain great destruction on the United States and the other Western democracies, but it lacks the slightest intention of doing so. The danger of war is not rooted in an expansionist Soviet master plan, but in the possibility that the two superpowers, misunderstanding their real national interests and the motivations of the other, will stumble into an unwanted war.

• Many Third World nations envy and oppose the industrial democracies, often successfully exploiting wholly irrational guilt complexes in the West, but save for a few isolated instances they lack the capabilities for threatening the vital interests of the United States. There are thus few if any compelling reasons for taking seriously some of the more strident demands from the Third World for "reparations" or other types of massive resource transfers. Where the power to threaten such national interests in fact exists, notably with respect to oil, it is largely the consequence of a short-sighted, mad rush to place America's head in the noose by failing to exercise sufficient discipline in the use of resources to avoid becoming the eager hostages of OPEC:

> If the Persian Gulf is really vital to our security, it is surely we who, by our unrestrained greed for oil, have made it so. Would it not be better to set about to eliminate, by a really serious and determined effort, a dependence that ought never to have been allowed to arise, than to try to shore up by military means, in a highly unfavorable region, the unsound position into which the dependence has led us? Military force might conceivably become necessary as a supplement to such an effort; it could never be an adequate substitute for it.[44]

There are also stark differences between the Post-Cold War Internationalists and the Semi-Isolationists on the Third World. The former are often inclined to insist that the United States cannot, either morally or practically, be indifferent to the claims of the Third World; in the words of one critic of the Semi-Isolationist view, "morally wrong" American policies toward the less developed nations have created compelling obligations and, in any case, "Our engagement with the world is so multidimensional and so complex that we will never be able to play the circumscribed role that Kennan urges upon us."[45] Isolationists reject the moral argument and assert that economic and political development can only arise from self-reliance; they cannot be imposed or implemented from abroad, and the effort to do so may in fact hinder rather than assist the development process.[46]

• The real threats to a just and humane social order in the United States are largely to be found within its own borders rather than abroad. Decaying cities, inflation, unemployment, cultural decadence, illiteracy, crime, unresolved racial issues, environmental depredation, and other familiar problems pose, according to the Semi-Isolationists, a far greater threat to the quality of American institutions and lives than do the ambitions of the men in the Kremlin or the strident and generally unjustified demands of Third World leaders for a new international order. Many Semi-Isolationists share with their intellectual forefathers a conviction that an activist foreign policy is incompatible with a stable and progressive domestic order. Some assert that it may not even be compatible with the maintenance of democratic institutions. The Semi-Isolationist argument is thus sustained not only by a pessimistic estimate of Washington's ability to solve pressing international problems. It is perhaps even more fundamentally grounded in a fear that the United States will lose its soul by excessive international involvement, whether by playing the *realpolitik* game prescribed by the Cold War Internationalists, or the "complex interdependence" game favored by the Post-Cold War Internationalists. "*The inescapable lesson common to both Vietnam and Watergate is that the ultimate trade-off is between internationalist foreign policies and the integrity of our constitution. We cannot maintain both.*"[47] This thesis has venerable roots in American thought, having been expressed by some of the Founding Fathers over two centuries ago, as well as by the isolationists of the interwar period and many others.

Consistent with these diagnoses, the Semi-Isolationist "grand design" for American foreign policy differs sharply from those of both internationalist belief systems. It recognizes the existence of conflicts along both North–South and East–West axes, but it tends to dismiss as a dangerous delusion the notion, widely accepted in the United States during the decades following the end of World War II, that there is any compelling practical or ethical imperative for the United States to be centrally involved in ameliorating the world's ills. Especially discriminating selectivity should be exercised in limiting defense commitments to the indispensable minimum. Most importantly, there must be an awareness that just as every international problem cannot claim American paternity, so it does not necessarily have a unique or effective American solution.

But the Semi-Isolationists are not without specific foreign policy prescriptions. The United States should place high priority on negotiating outstanding differences with the Soviet Union, with the minimal goal of slowing down or reversing the arms race and thereby reducing the threat of unintended or unwanted conflict.[48] As for appropriate policies toward the Third World, Semi-Isolationists reject both the Cold War Internationalist conception of the less developed nations as a crucial battleground between the two major blocs, and the Post-Cold War Internationalist view that the LDCs are the victim of neglect, if not exploitation, by the rich nations. They deny the first because it can only lead to endless American interventions in volatile areas that do not threaten or even seriously engage vital American interests, and the second because it fails to recognize that self-reliance rather than external assistance offers the only effective path to development. Hence the prescription that the United States should deal with Third World nations only on the basis of genuinely shared interests—these are likely to be quite limited in scope—rather than on the basis of guilt for conditions not of America's making, or of romantic visions about what those interests might be. The United States should be guided by the dictum that "The first requirement of getting on with most foreign people is to demonstrate that you are quite capable of getting on without them. An overeagerness to please suggests just the opposite."[49] For the Semi-Isolationists, the central lesson of Vietnam is that the United States cannot provide security for those who are incapable or unwilling to make the necessary sacrifices; nor can it provide the means of material, political, or spiritual improvement for those who are indifferent to such problems. In any case, they are likely to be marching to a different drummer. Thus, the United States must shed the illusion that it either can or should export democratic institutions or economic development into areas that possess neither the wish nor the self-discipline necessary to create such conditions for themselves.

With respect to linkages, the Semi-Isolationists believe that the United States should not only seek to decouple issues and reduce interdependencies as much as possible, but that it should also initiate a process of disengagement from external alliances and military commitments that will not end until the security perimeter has reached a clearly defensible position. Some would define such a position as including Western Europe, Japan, and Israel; others would support an even more circumscribed defense perimeter for the United States.[50] Even should the Soviets or Chinese choose to take advantage of such a situation by embarking upon external adventures in the Third World, vital American interests would rarely if ever be engaged, thus ruling out any imperatives for intervention by the United States.[51]

Finally, if the United States is to have a salutary influence on the rest of the world, it will come about largely through a demonstrated ability to solve its own pressing domestic problems. A nation unable to cope effectively with domestic issues cannot be an inspiring model to others.[52] In a large sense, then, America's ability to contribute to a solution of many global issues—be they human rights or democratic development—is limited to the power of example. It therefore behooves the United States to achieve a satisfactory resolution of these problems at home before turning its attention and energies to preaching at or materially helping others.

Table 4.3 includes eight items from the 1976 leadership survey questionnaire that reflect core Semi-Isolationist beliefs. The central proposition of that belief system is that the United States should redefine its international role in more modest terms (4.3:A), especially with respect to any temptation to intervene in such Third World conflicts as Angola (4.3:B). Semi-Isolationists are also critical of military assistance programs (4.3:D) and stationing American military personnel abroad (4.3:F), as both might draw the United States into conflicts that do not involve defense of basic national interests. Part of the problem, they believe, is that those interests have been badly defined owing to the excessive role of the President (4.3:C) and the military (4.3:E) in the formulation and conduct of American foreign relations. Finally, most Semi-Isolationists believe that undue attention to international undertakings will have negative domestic consequences (4.3:G), or at least will result in neglect of more pressing problems at home (4.3:H).

Table 4.3   *Questionnaire Items from the 1976 Leadership Survey Comprising the Semi-Isolationism Index**

A   America's conception of its leadership role in the world must be scaled down.
B   The U.S. should avoid any involvement in the Angolan civil war.
C   Americans have relied too much on Presidents to define the national interest.
D   Military aid programs will eventually draw the United States into unnecessary wars.
E   The conduct of American foreign affairs relies excessively on military advice.
F   Stationing American troops in other countries encourages them to let us do their fighting for those countries.
G   The foundations of the American economy were seriously damaged by our involvement in Vietnam.
H   The real long-term threats to national security—energy shortages, the environment, etc.—have been neglected as a result of our preoccupation with Vietnam.

---

* For responses to these items by the sample of 2,282 American leaders, see Tables 2.6 and 2.8. Positive responses to these items are assumed to be consistent with the Semi-Isolationist belief system.

Conclusion

Table 4.4 summarizes a few of the more salient beliefs that characterize the three schools of thought on international relations and foreign policy. It is worth recalling once more that such brief summaries must necessarily deal with central tendencies rather than fine details and subtle distinctions that might characterize the beliefs of any single person.

Although the items in Tables 4.1–4.3 appear to reflect some important elements of the three ways of thinking about foreign affairs, it remains to be demonstrated that, among the leaders in this survey, they in fact represent three distinct systems of beliefs. If they do, responses to the sixteen items in Table 4.1 should be positively correlated with each other; that is, leaders who respond favorably to one of the items should also tend to do so with the others, whereas those expressing disapproval of one should be inclined to disagree with the others as well. Similarly, correlations among the items in Table 4.2 should be positive, as should those for Table 4.3. Such results would indicate the existence of three belief systems about international affairs, but they would not necessarily be sufficient to establish that the three are distinct from one another.[53] To meet that requirement, correlations among the items in the different tables (4.1 and 4.2, 4.1 and 4.3, 4.2 and 4.3) should either be negative or so low as to indicate that they are in fact independent.

The patterns of responses to the questionnaire items used to construct indices of the three belief systems tend to confirm the existence of three distinct belief systems. The sixteen Cold War Internationalist items in Table 4.1 yield a total of 120 correlation coefficients. All 120 of them are positive, the mean coefficient is .40, and fourteen of them exceed .50. Results for the Post-Cold War Internationalist and Semi-Isolationist items indicate that they also form clusters of related ideas. All of the correlations for items in Table 4.2 are positive, as are those for Table 4.3, and the mean figure in each case is a coefficient of .30. These results indicate that there is a moderately high degree of internal consistency within each of the three belief systems, and that this is most notably true in the case of the Cold War Internationalist beliefs.

This analysis also reveals the items which are most important and distinctive to each of the three belief systems. For the Cold War Internationalist, central beliefs concern stopping the spread of communism, validity of the domino theory, and the importance of military advice in the conduct of war. Improving the standard of living in less developed countries, combatting world hunger, and strengthening the United Nations are comparably important for the Post-Cold War Internationalists, and the Semi-Isolationist belief system emphasizes a concern for an excessive military role in American foreign affairs, avoiding involvement in Angola, and scaling down the nation's leadership role in the world.

Correlations between the items constituting different belief systems also indicate that they do in fact describe distinctive ways of thinking about foreign policy and international relations. There is a consistent pattern of negative correlations between responses to the Cold War and Post-Cold War Internationalist items; all 128 correlation coefficients are negative, and their mean is −.23. With the exception of a single item, the pattern of responses to the Cold War Internationalist and Semi-Isolationist items is very similar, with a mean correlation of −.19. The exception is that several positive but very low correlations appear in connection with the proposition that "Stationing American troops in other countries encourages them to let us do their fighting for those countries." Finally, the results indicate a pattern of largely independent relationships (very low correlation

Table 4.4   Three Foreign Policy Belief Systems

	Cold War Internationalism	Post-Cold War Internationalism	Semi-Isolationism
Nature of the international system			
Structure	Bipolar (and likely to remain so)	Complex and interdependent (and becoming more so)	Multipolar (and becoming more so)
	Tight links between issues and conflicts	Moderate links between issues and conflicts	Weak links between issues and conflicts
World order priorities	A world safe from aggression and terrorism is a necessary pre-condition for dealing with other issues	International regimes for coping with a broad range of issues, with high priority on North–South ones	It is utopian to think in such terms; top priority should be to reduce linkages, dependencies, and interdependencies
Conception of interdependence	Encompasses security issues ("domino theory")	Encompasses economic/social issues	Exaggerated by internationalists
Primary threats to the United States	Soviet and Soviet-sponsored aggression and terrorism; Military imbalance favoring the USSR; Soviet ability to engage in political coercion based on nuclear blackmail	North–South issues (e.g. rich–poor gap) which threaten any prospects for world order; International environmental problems; Danger of nuclear war	Danger of war by miscalculation; Domestic problems (inflation, unemployment, energy, crime, drugs, illiteracy, racial conflict, etc.); Arms trade
The Soviet Union			
Nature of the system	A model totalitarian state	A great power	A great power with manifest domestic problems
Driving force of foreign policy	Aggressive expansionism inherent in the Soviet system	Seeks parity with U.S.; Defensiveness (exaggerated view of defense needs may create further tensions)	Fear

	Highly successful	Moderately unsuccessful	Generally unsuccessful [but this is largely irrelevant as USSR poses little threat to United States]
Appraisal of recent foreign policies			
Soviet–American relations *Nature of the conflict*	Conflicts of interest are genuine Largely zero-sum	Some real conflicts of interest, but these are exaggerated by hard-liners on both sides Largely non-zero-sum	Few if any genuine conflicts of interest [mostly arise from failure to see that real threats are unresolved domestic issues] Largely non-zero-sum
Appraisal of détente *Appraisal of SALT process*	A dangerous delusion Skeptical; dangerous as conducted in the past	Some useful first steps Some useful first steps	Some useful first steps Some useful first steps, but need to go much further
Primary dangers of war	Military imbalance will lead Soviets to threaten vital U.S. and western interests Recent successes will make Soviets more aggressive, perhaps recklessly so.	Uncontrolled arms race Both sides equally likely to misperceive other's actions, leading to unwanted war	Misperception, miscalculation of true national interests and threats to them U.S. and Soviet meddling in volatile Third World areas Uncontrolled arms race
Linkages	Vital to link issues	Decouple issues	Decouple issues
The Third World *Role in present international system*	Primary target of Soviet and Soviet-inspired subversion and aggression	Primary source of unresolved social/economic problems that must be resolved to create a viable world order	With a few exceptions, largely peripheral and irrelevant, especially to U.S. interests

Table 4.4 cont.

	Cold War Internationalism	Post-Cold War Internationalism	Semi-Isolationism
Primary source of Third World problems	Subversion and aggression by USSR and its proxies (Cuba, Libya, etc.) Left-wing authoritarian governments	Legacies of western colonialism and imperialism Right-wing authoritarian governments Structural flaws in the international system	Largely of their own making [lack of self-discipline, corruption, etc.]
Primary U.S. obligations	Help provide security from aggression and terrorism, but on a selective basis [to strategically important ones, oil producers, etc.]	Economic and other forms of non-military assistance Play a leading role in structural systemic changes [N.I.E.O., etc.]	Few, if any, obligations for either security or economic development
Prescription for American foreign policy	Rebuild military strength to regain a position of parity with the USSR Rebuild collective security system	Stabilize relations with USSR, in order to free energy and resources for dealing with North–South and other high priority issues	Stabilize relations with USSR and reduce commitments and dependencies abroad, in order to free energy and resources for dealing with domestic issues
	Active U.S. role in the world is a necessary but not sufficient condition to create a stable and just world order	Active U.S. role in the world is a necessary but not sufficient condition to create a stable and just world order	American retrenchment is a necessary, but not sufficient, condition to ensure that U.S. democracy will survive; the power of example is the best U.S. contribution to the welfare of other nations Dramatic efforts to control arms race

coefficients with a mean of .13) between the Post-Cold War Internationalist and Semi-Isolationist items. At the same time, there also appears to be a moderate propensity for them to agree on questions that reflect an anti-military, anti-interventionist, and pro-United Nations viewpoint. Thus, while the differences between Cold War Internationalism and the other two viewpoints are the most pronounced, there are sufficient distinctions between all three of them to warrant treating them as distinct.

Empirical support for the existence of three belief systems leaves unanswered a number of important questions, however. Who are adherents of the three viewpoints? Are they generally to be found in certain occupational, generational, or other groups, or are they essentially similar with respect to background characteristics? The analysis in Chapter 5 will address these and related questions. The purpose of doing so is not merely to satisfy curiosity. The answers may also provide some clues about the strength of factors that may sustain or erode leadership cleavages on foreign affairs.

Notes to Chapter 4

1   Michael Mandelbaum and William Schneider, "The New Internationalisms: Public Opinion and American Foreign Policy," in Kenneth Oye, Donald Rothchild, and Robert Lieber (eds), *Eagle Entangled: U.S. Foreign Policy in a Complex World* (New York: Longman, 1979).

2   The goals and policies of the CPD are described in: CPD, "How the Committee on the Present Danger Will Operate—What It Will Do, and What It Will Not Do" (Washington, 11 November 1976); CPD, "Common Sense and the Common Danger" (Washington, n.d.); CPD, "What Is The Soviet Union Up To?" (Washington, 4 April 1977); and CPD, "Countering the Soviet Threat" (Washington, 9 May 1980).

3   David Shribman, "Group goes from exile to influence," *New York Times* (23 November 1981); and CPD, "The Fifth Year . . . and the New Administration" (Washington, 11 November 1981).

4   A representative sample of the enormous literature of this genre includes Robert Conquest et. al., *Defending America* (New York: Basic Books, 1977); Daniel Patrick Moynihan, *A Dangerous Place* (Boston: Little , Brown, 1978); Norman Podhoretz, *The Present Danger* (New York: Simon and Schuster, 1980); Podhoretz, *Why We Were in Vietnam* (New York: Simon and Schuster, 1982); Edward Friedland, Paul Seabury, and Aaron Wildavsky, *The Great Détente Disaster* (New York: Basic Books, 1975); most foreign policy articles in *Commentary* and *National Review*; editorials in *The Wall Street Journal*; columns by George Will, Irving Kristol, Roland Evans and Robert Novak; the writings of Paul Nitze and others associated with the Committee on the Present Danger; and analyses prepared under the auspices of the National Strategy Information Center, the Heritage Foundation, the Ethics and Public Policy Center at Georgetown University, and The Committee for the Free World.

5   Karen Elliott House, "Reagan's world: Republican's policies stress arms buildup, a firm line to Soviet," *The Wall Street Journal* (3 June 1980). p. 1.

6   Paul Nitze, "A Plea for Action," *New York Times Magazine* (7 May, 1978). p. 120. See also Norman Podhoretz, "The culture of appeasement," *Harper's*, 255 (October 1977), pp. 25–32; Walter Laqueur, "America and the world: the next four years—confronting the problems," *Commentary*, 63 (March 1977), pp. 33–41; Edward N. Luttwak, "Churchill and us," *Commentary*, 63 (June 1977), pp. 44–9;

Ben J. Wattenberg, "It's time to stop America's retreat," *New York Times Magazine* (22 July 1979), pp. 14–16, 68–9; Walter Laqueur, "Taking stock of the Soviets," *New Republic*, 182 (1 March 1980), pp. 13–15; Thomas Powers, "This time it is Munich," *Commonweal*, 107 (15 February 1980), pp. 73–4; Carl Gershman, "The rise and fall of the new foreign-policy establishment," *Commentary*, 70 (July 1980), pp. 13–24; Michael Novak, "America and crisis," *Commonweal*, 102 (May 1975), pp. 104ff.; Vermont Royster, "Lessons from Mein Kampf," *Wall Street Journal* (4 June 1980); Drew Middleton, "Does it seem like 1914? 1939? or just jittery 1980?," *New York Times* (6 May 1980); Walter Laqueur, "The West in retreat," *Commentary*, 60 (August 1975), pp. 44–52; "Selling security," *Wall Street Journal* (2 October 1981). p. 26; "On superiority," *Wall Street Journal* (7 April 1982) p. 32; and Daniel Patrick Moynihan, "A new American foreign policy," *New Republic* p. 182 (9 February 1980), pp. 17–21.

7   Eugene V. Rostow, "Rearming America," *Foreign Policy*, no. 39 (Summer 1980), p. 8. See also, Novak, "America and crisis"; Norman Podhoretz, "Making the world safe for communism," *Commentary*, 61 (April 1976), pp. 31–41; Sol W. Sanders, "The faulty assumption that Ivan is like Uncle Sam," *Business Week* (24 September 1979), p. 80; and Richard Pipes, *U.S.–Soviet Relations in the Era of Détente* (Boulder, Colorado: Westview Press, 1981).

8   Eugene V. Rostow, quoted in Robert Scheer, "Nuclear attack: the unthinkable becomes thinkable," *Sacramento Bee* (4 October 1981), p. A1; Podhoretz, *The Present Danger*; W. W. Rostow, "The Soviet misunderstanding of U.S. policy," *Wall Street Journal* (8 May 1980), p. 26; and a number of public statements by former Secretary of State Alexander Haig.

9   Quoted in Kenneth H. Bacon, "The coming debate on SALT," *Wall Street Journal* (12 December 1978), p. 26. For opposing views on Soviet defense spending, see Les Aspin, "How to look at the Soviet–American balance," *Foreign Policy*, no. 22 (Spring 1976), pp. 96–106; and Amos A. Jordan, "Soviet strength, U.S. purpose," *Foreign Policy*, no. 23 (Summer 1976), pp. 32–40.

10 Fred Iklé, quoted in Drew Middleton, "Defense specialists worried by trend of Russian efforts," *New York Times* (17 July 1978), p. A10. See also, Iklé, "What it means to be number two," *Fortune*, 98 (20 November 1978), pp. 73–4, 78–83; and "A reply by Mr Iklé," *Fortune*, 99 (26 February 1979), p. 53.

11 Simon Ramo, "National will and nuclear war," *Wall Street Journal* (2 October 1981). Ramo fears that even if the United States retaliated, "Then they [Soviets] could accept our weak retort, one harming their nation no more than they were hurt in World War II." That, presumably, is not viewed as a sufficient deterrent!

12 Eugene V. Rostow, quoted in Scheer, "Nuclear attack," p. A24.

13 Colin S. Gray, "There is no choice," *Foreign Policy*, no. 24 (Fall 1976), pp. 114–27. See also, Daniel O Graham, "Détente adieu," *National Review*, 28 (3 September 1976), 946–50.

14 Wattenberg, "It's time to stop America's retreat."

15 Stephen Sternheimer, "Letter to the Editor," *New York Times* (11 July 1978), p. A16.

16 "The Kremlin bailout," *Wall Street Journal* (16 November 1981). Elsewhere the same editorialists asserted, "history suggests that heavily armed expansionist nations become more, not less, dangerous during periods of domestic economic adversity." "Selling security," *Wall Street Journal* (2 October 1981). See also, John M. Maury, "The Kremlin's unchanged objectives," *New York Times* (5 September 1980), p. A22; "Soviet weakness," *Wall Street Journal* (19 November 1981), p. 26; and Drew Middleton, "Rearming U.S.: will Soviets decide to revise their strategy as a result?," *New York Times* (2 November 1981), p. A6.

17 Eugene V. Rostow, quoted in Robert Scheer, "Military balance," *Sacramento Bee* (11 October 1981). See also, Colin S. Gray and Keith Payne, "Victory is possible," *Foreign Policy*, no. 39 (Summer 1980), pp. 14–27; Albert Wohlstetter, "Is there a strategic arms race?," *Foreign Policy*, no. 15 (Summer 1974), pp. 3–20; Wohlstetter, "Rivals, but no race," *Foreign Policy*, no. 16 (Fall 1974), pp. 48–81; Edward N. Luttwak, "America and the world: the next four years—defense reconsidered,"

Commentary, 63 (March 1977), pp. 51–8; Luttwak, "Why arms control failed," *Commentary*, 65 (January 1978), pp. 19–28; Paul H. Nitze, "Deterring our deterrent," *Foreign Policy*, no. 25 (Winter 1976–7), pp. 195–210; Nitze, "The strategic balance between hope and skepticism," *Foreign Policy*, no. 17 (Winter 1974–5), pp. 136–56; Nitze, James E. Daugherty, and Francis X. Kane, *The Fateful Ends and Shades of SALT* (New York: Crane, Russak, 1979); Nitze, "Strategy in the decade of the 1980s," *Foreign Affairs*, 59 (Fall 1980), pp. 82–101; E. L. Rowny, "The errors of abiding by SALT's terms," *Wall Street Journal* (21 March 1980), p. 24; Nitze, "Is SALT II a Fair Deal for the United States?," (CPD: Washington, 16 May 1979); Richard Pipes, "Why the Soviet Union Wants SALT II," (CPD: Washington, 17 September 1979); CPD, "Has America Become Number Two?," (29 June 1982); and the views of Fred C. Iklé, as cited in note 10 above. Given their key foreign policy and arms control positions in the Reagan Administration, the views of Nitze, Rowny, Pipes, Iklé, and Eugene Rostow (notes 7, 8, and 12) are of more than passing significance.

18   Fred Charles Iklé, "Defense: $1 trillion," *New York Times* (5 February 1980), p. A23.

19   See, for example, Paul H. Nitze, "Assuring strategic stability in the era of détente," *Foreign Affairs*, 54 (January 1976), pp. 207–32; and Colin S. Gray, "The strategic forces triad: end of the road?," *Foreign Affairs*, 56 (July 1978), pp. 771–89.

20   "It is an ugly fact but a fact nonetheless that America's defense spending must be determined by the Kremlin, not by the poor condition of our cities . . . The idea that we cannot afford a given amount of defense to meet Soviet activity is, simply, hokum." Wattenberg, "It's time to stop America's retreat." See also, Herbert Stein, "The undelivered basic speech," *Wall Street Journal* (28 May 1980), p. 24; Stein, "Thinking about the defense budget," *Wall Street Journal* (15 January 1981), p. 22; Stein, "Why spending for defense is different," *Wall Street Journal* (29 October 1981), p. 30; Stein, "How World War III was lost," *Wall Street Journal* (3 December 1982), p. 30; and Stein, "Why disarm unilaterally?," *Wall Street Journal* (11 February 1983), p. 20. Typical assessments of mutual assured destruction are G. E. Synhorst, "M.A.D. is mad, mad!," *Saturday Evening Post*, 251 (July/August 1979), pp. 54–5, 79; and Kenneth Adelman, "Beyond MAD-ness," *Policy Review*, 17 (Summer 1981), pp. 77–85.

21   Norman Podhoretz, quoted in David Shribman, "Neoconservative role uncertain in Reagan camp," *New York Times* (28 September 1981). According to the Committee on the Present Danger, "The [Reagan] Administration's defense program is a minimal one. It will not halt the unfavorable trends in the U.S.–Soviet military balance, let alone reverse them." CPD, "Is the Reagan Defense Program Adequate?," (Washington, 17 March 1982), p. 34.

22   W. Scott Thompson, "The Projection of Soviet Power," in Conquest et al., *Defending America*, p. 35. This phrase, or its equivalent, appears in much of the Cold War Internationalist writing on foreign affairs.

23   Irving Kristol, "Foreign policy: end of an era," *Wall Street Journal* (18 January 1979), p. 16. Eugene Rostow makes the point even more strongly: "The answer is: fear. The American political class is afraid of living with the evidence of reality, because if you accept that the Russians are embarked on an imperialist course, then you have to do something about it." Quoted in George Will, "Fear of facing the truth," *Newsweek*, 93 (22 January 1979), p. 88. See also the rejoinder to Kristol's article, Arthur Schlesinger, Jr, "Whose foreign policy is bankrupt?," *Current*, 212 (May 1979), pp. 44–7.

24   Numbers and letters in parentheses refer to the table and item. Thus, (4.1:A) signifies Table 4.1, item A.

25   This view point is effectively represented by Stanley Hoffmann, *Primacy or World Order* (New York: McGraw-Hill, 1978); Robert Keohane and Joseph Nye, *Power and Interdependence*, (Boston: Little, Brown, 1976); and Seyom Brown, *New Forces in World Politics* (Washington: Brookings Institution, 1974), as well as in several subsequent essays, some of which are cited below; articles in *The Nation* and *Progressive* magazines; columns by Arthur Schlesinger, Tom Wicker and

Anthony Lewis; and editorials in the *New York Times* and *Washington Post*. Also of interest, owing to the political prominence of the authors and the roles that they may play in the 1984 or later elections are: Edward M. Kennedy, "Beyond détente," *Foreign Policy*, no. 16 (Fall 1974), pp. 3–29; and Walter F. Mondale, "Beyond détente: toward international economic security," *Foreign Affairs*, 53 (October 1974), pp. 1–23.

26 The literature developing these points is enormous. In addition to the sources cited in the previous note, see Hans J. Morgenthau, "Old superstitions, new realities," *New Republic*, 176 (22 January 1977), pp. 50–5; Sanford Gottlieb, "The irrelevance of force," *New York Times* (19 April 1980), p. A23; George McGovern, "On the military budget, " *New York Times* (10 June 1980); James Chace, "The Kissinger years," *New Republic*, 171 (9 November 1974), pp. 30–3; Benjamin R. Barber, "America cannot survive alone any longer," *U.S. News & World Report*, 79 (7 July 1975), pp. 45–6; Harlan Cleveland, "Our coming foreign policy crisis," *Saturday Review*, 2 (6 September 1975), pp. 10ff.; President Carter's address to the American Society of Newspaper Editors on 10 April 1980; and Elliott L. Richardson, " 'Fortress America' is out of date," *Wall Street Journal* (10 July 1980). The latter is a critique of both Cold War Internationalist and Isolationist premises.

27 Jean Meyer, "Foreign-policy needs," *New York Times* (19 October 1981).

28 "Given our longstanding obsession with the 1930s, a return of our gaze to the war that emerged suddenly from Europe's last untroubled summer may at least introduce a healthy element of doubt." Miles Kahler, "Rumors of war: the 1914 analogy," *Foreign Affairs*, 58 (Winter 1979/80), pp. 374–96.

29 See, for example, Richard Rosecrance, "Détente or entente?," *Foreign Affairs*, 53 (April 1975), pp. 464–81; Daniel Yergin, "Politics and Soviet–American trade: the three questions," *Foreign Affairs*, 55 (April 1977), pp. 517–38; Robert Legvold, "The super rivals: conflict in the Third World," *Foreign Affairs*, 57 (Spring 1979), pp. 755–78; and Richard J. Barnet, "U.S.–Soviet relations: the need for a comprehensive approach," *Foreign Affairs*, 57 (Spring 1979), pp. 779–95.

30 In the introduction to a book published by the Senate Foreign Relations Committee, *Perceptions: Relations Between the United States and the Soviet Union* (Washington: USGPO, 1978), p. viii.

31 "A Rhomboid of rhetoric," *New York Times* (11 January 1979), p. A20. See also, Seyom Brown, "A cooling-off period for U.S.–Soviet relations," *Foreign Policy*, no. 28 (Fall 1977), pp. 3–21; Brown, "An end to grand strategy," *Foreign Policy*, no. 32 (Fall 1978), pp. 22–46; Stanley Hoffmann, 'No choice, no illusions," *Foreign Policy*, no. 25 (Winter 1976–7), pp. 97–140; and Hoffmann, "Muscle and brains," *Foreign Policy*, no. 37 (Winter 1979–80), pp. 3–27.

32 See, for example, Paul C. Warnke, "Apes on a treadmill," *Foreign Policy*, no. 18 (Spring 1975), pp. 12–39; Stephen A. Garrett, "Détente and the military balance," *Bulletin of Atomic Scientists*, 33 (April 1977), pp. 10–20; Les Aspin, "What are the Russians up to?," *International Security*, 3 (Summer 1978), pp. 30–54; Morton Kondracke, "Is there a present danger?," *New Republic*, 176 (29 January 1977), pp. 18–20; Jan M. Lodal, "Assuring strategic stability: an alternate view," *Foreign Affairs*, 54 (April 1976), pp. 462–81; Lodal, "SALT II and American security," *Foreign Affairs*, 57 (Winter 1978–9), pp. 245–68; Michael T. Klare, "The power projection gap," *Nation*, 228 (9 June 1979), pp. 671–6; Marshall D. Shulman, "An overview of U.S.–Soviet relations," *U.S. State Department Bulletin*, 79 (December 1979), pp. 40–5; Clayton Fritchey, "The fall and rise of Andy Young," *Nation*, 229 (15 September 1979), pp. 201–4; and Adam Yarmolinsky, "The military balance: about equal," *New York Times* (4 February 1980), p. A19.

33 Richard A. Falk, "Beyond internationalism," *Foreign Policy*, no. 24 (Fall 1976), p. 99. See also Falk, "Exporting counterrevolution," *Nation*, 228 (9 June 1979), pp. 659–62; Falk, "America now: a failure of nerve," *Commentary*, 60 (July 1975), pp. 33–5; Walter LaFeber, "Empire begins at home," *Nation*, 228 (9 June 1979), pp. 656–9; and Andrew Kopkind, "Cold War II," *New York Times*, 11 (30 October 1978), pp. 28–41.

34 The following represent some of the ethical and practical arguments adduced by the Post-Cold War Internationalists against the isolationist prescription:

Just as a pinch of salt in the hands of an able chef is often essential to a successful dish, so an occasional small dose of American independence may be an essential ingredient of leadership for interdependence. But if we swallow too much of the neoisolationists' offering now, our children will be choking well before the end of the third century [of the nation's existence]. Joseph S. Nye, Jr, "Independence and interdependence," *Foreign Policy*, no. 22 (Spring 1976), p. 161.

There can be no "fortress America" in today's interdependent world economy. C. Fred Bergsten, "The response to the Third World," *Foreign Policy*, no. 17 (Winter 1974–5), p. 34.

It [the administration] must be able to show how deep involvement that will continue to be required of us, and the retreats we may have to accept in certain realms, will contribute to the emergence of a world in which our main interests and our security will be assured. Stanley Hoffmann, "The conduct of American foreign policy—a view from at home: the perils of incoherence," *Foreign Affairs*, 57 (1979), pp. 463–91.

See also, Barnet, "U.S.–Soviet relations"; Roger D. Hansen, "North–South policy—what is the problem?," *Foreign Affairs*, 58 (Summer 1980), pp. 1104–28; and William P. Bundy, "Who lost Patagonia?: foreign policy in the 1980 campaign," *Foreign Affairs*, 58 (Fall 1979), pp. 1–27.

35 Richard H. Ullman, "Washington versus Wilson," *Foreign Policy*, no. 21 (Winter 1975–6), p. 118.

36 Meg Greenfield, "An American disease," *Newsweek* (2 November 1981), p. 120. Italics in the original.

37 Stanley Hoffmann, *Primacy or World Order* (New York: McGraw Hill, 1978). See also, Hoffmann, "Toward world order," *New Republic*, 176 (19 March 1977), pp. 10–12; and Hoffmann, "Carter's Soviet problem," *New Republic*, 179 (29 July 1979), pp. 20–3.

38 See, for example, Thomas L. Hughes, "Foreign policy: men or measures?," *Atlantic Monthly*, 234 (October 1974), pp. 48–60; Charles William Maynes and Richard H. Ullman, "Ten years of foreign policy," *Foreign Policy*, no. 40 (Fall 1980), pp. 3–17; Thomas L. Hughes, "The crack-up," *Foreign Policy*, no. 40 (Fall 1980), pp. 33–60; Laurence Radway, "The curse of free elections," *Foreign policy*, no. 40 (Fall 1980), pp. 61–73; and Lloyd N. Cutler, "To form a government," *Foreign Affairs*, 59 (Fall 1980), pp. 126–43.

39 The Taft quotation is from Cecil V. Crabb, *Policy Makers and Critics: Conflicting Theories of American Foreign Policy* (New York: Praeger, 1976), p. 4.
Other terms might have been used to describe the beliefs of this group; for example, quasi-isolationism, neo-isolationism, non-internationalism, or non-interventionism, all of which have been used to describe critics of globalist American foreign policies. "Semi-isolationist" appears to have two advantages: it indicates that most of these critics are prepared to accept some international responsibilities beyond those of pre-World War II isolationists, which typically encompassed only hemispheric ones (e.g. the Monroe Doctrine); and it is the term used by one of the most articulate proponents of this viewpoint, George Kennan (cited in note 41 below). Whatever the merits of the various terms that might be used to describe this belief system, it is important to keep in mind some major similarities between contemporary critics of internationalism and those of the pre-Pearl Harbor era, notably the thesis that an internationalist foreign policy is incompatible with stable and progressive democracy at home.
That there has been an increasing acceptance of a more isolationist role for the United States is reflected in virtually all public opinion polls. See, for example, John E. Rielly, "The American mood: a foreign policy of self-interest," *Foreign Policy*, no. 34 (Spring 1979), pp. 74–86, and Rielly, "American opinion: continuity, not Reaganism," *Foreign Policy*, no. 50 (Spring 1983), pp. 86–104, as well as the same author's reports on the Chicago Council of Foreign Relations surveys: *American Public Opinion and Foreign Policy 1975*, and *American Public Opinion and Foreign Policy 1979*, both published by the Chicago Council.

40　"A thorough set of strategic lessons would require us to abandon the illusion that we can purchase safety or advantage by regulating and controlling our political environment—that is, dominating the will or orchestrating the behavior of other nations, whether through the pursuit of a balance of power, or the construction of an international organization." Earl C. Ravenal, "The Strategic Lessons of Vietnam," in Anthony Lake (ed.), *The Vietnam Legacy: The War, American Society and the Future of American Foreign Policy* (New York: New York University Press, 1976), p. 272.

　　Among the most articulate proponents of isolationism are George F. Kennan and Earl C. Ravenal. See, for example, Kennan, *The Cloud of Danger* (Boston: Little, Brown, 1977); Kennan, "On turning to global problems," *Current*, 174 (July/August 1975), pp. 49–50; Kennan, "Is détente worth saving?," *Saturday Review*, 3 (6 March 1976), pp. 12–14; Kennan, "The Soviet threat: how real?," *Inquiry* (17 March 1980), pp. 15–18; Kennan, "Two views of the Soviet problem," *New Yorker* (2 November, 1981), pp. 54–6, 61–2; Kennan, *The Nuclear Delusion* (New York: Pantheon, 1982); Ravenal, *Never Again: Learning From America's Foreign Policy Failures* (Philadelphia: Temple University Press, 1978); Ravenal, "The case for strategic disengagement," *Foreign Affairs*, 51 (April 1973), pp. 505–21; Ravenal, "Consequences of the end game in Vietnam," *Foreign Affairs*, 53 (Spring 1975), pp. 651–67; Ravenal, "Who needs it?," *Foreign Policy*, no. 18 (Spring 1975), pp. 80–91; Ravenal, "Walking on water," *Foreign Policy*, no. 33 (Winter 1978–9), pp. 151–60; Ravenal, "Toward Disengagement and Adjustment," in Robert A. Bauer, (ed.), *The United States in World Affairs* (Charlottesville: University Press of Virginia, 1975); Ravenal, "Reagan's 1983, Defense Budget: An Analysis and an Alternative" (Washington: Cato Institute, 30 April 1982); and Ravenal, "Doing nothing," *Foreign Policy*, no. 39 (Summer 1980), pp. 28–39. See also, Arlen J. Large, "A cheer for prudent isolationism," *Wall Street Journal* (30 April 1971): Samuel H. Day, Jr, "The bursting of the bubbles: no cause for lament," *Bulletin of Atomic Scientists*, 31 (June 1975), pp. 6–7; and Sam Cohen, "A plea for nuclear isolation," *Newsweek*, 99 (26 April 1982), p. 13.

41　George F. Kennan, "An appeal for thought," *New York Times Magazine* (7 May 1978), p. 125; J. William Fulbright, *The Arrogance of Power* (New York: Random House, 1967); and Fulbright, *The Crippled Giant* (New York: Random House, 1972).

42　Kennan, *Cloud of Danger*, p. 50.

43　Colin S. Gray, "There is no choice."

44　George F. Kennan, "Washington's reaction to the Afghan crisis: 'Was this really mature statesmanship?'," *New York Times* (1 February 1980), p. A27.

45　Richard H. Ullman, "The 'realities' of George F. Kennan," *Foreign Policy*, no. 28 (Fall 1977), pp. 139–55. See also, John Taft, "A diplomat for the eighties," *New Republic*, 180 (17 March 1979), pp. 19–21; and Theodore A. Couloumbis, "George F. Kennan and the self-containment of democracy," *U.S.A. Today*, 107 (July 1978), pp. 13–14. Kennan has also been equally harshly attacked by Cold War Internationalists. Rejecting Kennan's isolationist analysis and prescription, Edward N. Luttwak wrote, "Unfortunately, it is the modern predicament of America itself that the only practical strategy is one of involvement. The security of America itself must derive from a tolerable balance of power with its potential adversaries, and a balance of power is more easily maintained with allies than without." Luttwak, "The strange case of George F. Kennan: from containment to isolationism," *Commentary*, 64 (November 1977), pp. 30–5; and Henry Fairlie, 'Mr. X2; the special senility of the diplomat," *New Republic*, 177 (24 & 31 December 1977), pp. 9–11.

46　"There is no survival without self-reliance, which cannot be donated from the outside. Self-reliance must be generated inside each nation by the people themselves. There is no other way." Garrett Hardin, "The toughlove solution," *Newsweek*, 98 (26 October 1981), p. 45.

47　Ravenal, "Who needs it?," p. 91. Italics in the original. See also, Arlen J. Large, "A cheer for prudent isolationism," *Wall Street Journal* (30 April 1971), p. 6.

48　See, for example, George F. Kennan, "Cease this madness: our collision course with the USSR," *Atlantic*, 244 (January 1981), pp.25–8; and Kennan, *The Nuclear Delusion* (New York: Pantheon, 1982).

49   Kennan, *Cloud of Danger*, p. 70.
50   *ibid.*; and Ravenal, "Doing nothing," p. 36.
51   Kennan, *Cloud of Danger*, p. 96.
52   Kennan, *Cloud of Danger* p. 25. "The critical question for America is then not our-role-in-the-world but the nature of the democracy we can or cannot create here. Even if three-quarters of the world turns communist, our interest, even our most conservative interest, will not be endangered. The communist world will never be able to function as a single force." Norman Mailer, "The meaning of Vietnam," *New York Review of Books*, 22 (12 June 1975), p. 27.
53   This is consistent with the Converse definition of a belief system as "a configuration of ideas and attitudes in which elements are bound together by some form of constraint or functional interdependence." Philip Converse, "The Nature of Belief Systems in Mass Publics," in David Apter (ed.), *Ideology and Discontent* (New York: Free Press, 1964), p. 207

5

A Leadership Divided: Who Are the Cold War Internationalists, Post-Cold War Internationalists, and Semi-Isolationists?

Chapter 4 revealed the existence of three rather distinct ways of thinking about foreign affairs. This is not to imply that all persons can be fitted neatly into three impermeable categories, that the intensity of commitment is uniform within each, or that there are no issues that tend to cut across the three perspectives. The American commitment to Israel's security, for example, appears to have widespread support and, to the extent that it divides Americans, it does so in ways that do not conform precisely to the tripartite division described in the previous chapter. These caveats notwithstanding, the evidence of at least three major belief systems on foreign affairs seems persuasive, especially in as much as comparable findings have emerged independently from analyses of public opinion polls.[1]

Chapter 4 cited some individuals, organizations and publications that have served as prominent spokesmen or sponsors of each foreign policy perspective, but such anecdotal evidence does not provide a sufficient basis for identifying the attributes that are most closely associated with the three sets of beliefs. Conventional wisdom and "common sense" have offered some answers: military officers, business executives, labor leaders, and veterans are "hardliners" on foreign policy issues, as are the older generation of leaders; women and the younger generation prefer idealism and reduced security commitment abroad to *realpolitik*; and the politically apathetic are isolationists, whereas Foreign Service officers are not. Analyses to be undertaken in this chapter assess the validity of these and other propositions linking foreign policy beliefs to respondent attributes. These include many conventional background characteristics (occupation, age, party, gender, ideology, military service, and the like), as well as one that emerged in Chapters 2 and 3 as an important predictor of foreign policy beliefs—Vietnam policy preferences.

Responses to the items listed in Tables 4.1–4.3 permitted all leaders taking part in this survey to be assigned a score on each of the three scales. For example, a person expressing strong agreement with each of the sixteen Cold War Internationalist items in Table 4.1 would have received a summary score of 1.00, whereas one indicating strong disagreement with each item would have been assigned a score of −1.00. Of course, few respondents were that consistent and thus most of them received scores somewhere between the extreme points on the scale. Similar procedures were used for the other two belief systems, reflecting their responses to the items in Tables 4.2 and 4.3. For purposes of reporting the results, leaders were ranked from 1 to 2,282 and then grouped into quintiles on scales representing each of the three belief systems.[2]

Vietnam Policy Position

Analyses reported in previous chapters revealed that a classification scheme based on leaders' policy positions during the early and late stages of the Vietnam War proved to be a potent predictor of foreign policy beliefs. That was true not only with respect to a number of questions related to the war itself (Chapter 2), but also on a much broader range of contemporary foreign policy issues (Chapter 3).

The results summarized in Table 5.1 reveal a clear and uniformly strong relationship between the seven groups based on Vietnam policy preferences during the early and late stages of the war, on the one hand, and the three foreign policy belief systems on the other. Leaders who consistently favored efforts to achieve a victory in Vietnam—the Supporters—ranked very high on the Cold War Internationalism index; indeed, more than 60 percent of them are within the highest quintile on that scale, and not a single one is to be found in the lowest one. The Supporters are also the least enthusiastic group with respect to the other two perspectives.

Conversely, leaders at the Critics end of the scale—those who favored a complete American withdrawal from Vietnam in both the early and late stages of the war—are overwhelmingly (53 percent) in the lowest quintile on Cold War Internationalism, and less than 1 percent of them appear in the highest one. Responses of leaders in the other five groups follow a quite regular pattern, and the close relationship between that belief system and groups formed by Vietnam policy preferences is confirmed by the high (C=.58) correlation between them.[3] Results for Post-Cold War Internationalists are almost the reverse, although the relationship is not quite as strong (C=.40) because six of the seven groups are, on balance, favorably disposed toward items constituting that belief system; the Supporters constitute the only exception. The distribution of respondents on Semi-Isolationism is virtually the mirror image of the Cold War Internationalist scale, with a wide range of group scores and a high correlation (C=.51). There is some similarity in responses to Post-Cold War Internationalism and Semi-Isolationism, as the three groups of critics agree with both, but among the other four groups there is a divergence in support for the two belief systems. In summary, leaders at the

Table 5.1   Three Foreign Policy Belief Systems and Vietnam Policy Position Among 2,282 American Leaders: 1976 Survey

Vietnam policy position	n	Cold War Internationalism			Post-Cold War Internationalism			Semi-Internationalism		
			% of group in extreme quintiles			% of group in extreme quintiles			% of group in extreme quintiles	
		Index[a]	Highest	Lowest	Index[a]	Highest	Lowest	Index[a]	Highest	Lowest
Supporters	363	.56	61	0	−.06	3	39	−.27	4	48
Converted Supporters	128	.37	33	3	.06	9	31	−.01	13	23
Ambivalent Supporters	346	.29	23	2	.16	11	22	−.11	5	29
Ambivalents	128	−.04	3	13	.34	19	9	−.12	4	28
Ambivalent Critics	63	−.23	6	37	.36	30	14	.43	48	6
Converted Critics	867	−.08	10	23	.31	23	14	.23	23	10
Critics	378	−.40	1	53	.55	47	4	.52	55	2
All respondents	2,273[b]	.04	19[c]	20[c]	.26	21[c]	18[c]	.12	21[c]	19[c]
Correlation [C coefficient]		[.58]			[.40]			[.51]		

[a] Scales range from 1.00 (all responses most Cold War Internationalist, Post-Cold War Internationalist, Semi-Isolationist) to −1.00 (all responses least Cold War Internationalist, etc.). For items that constitute the three scales, see Tables 4.1–4.3.
[b] Nine respondents did not indicate their positions on Vietnam in either the early or late stages of the war.
[c] Owing to many tied scores on each of the three scales, divisions into quintiles did not yield groups of exactly 20 percent.

Supporter end of the scale tend to be Internationalists, with a decided preference for the Cold War rather than Post-Cold War version. In contrast, the three groups of Critics share support for Post-Cold War Internationalism and Semi-Isolationism, as well as a skeptical view of Cold War Internationalism.

It remains to be demonstrated, however, that the strong relationship between Vietnam policy positions and the three foreign policy belief systems is not an artifact of other attributes. Multivariate analyses were undertaken for each of the thirty-two items that constitute the three belief systems, combining Vietnam policy with other respondent attributes described in this chapter: ideology, occupation, party, age, military service, and gender.[4] The results are striking and unambiguous: each of the 192 separate analyses revealed that differences among the seven Vietnam policy position groups are significant, exceeding rather demanding statistical criteria. Thus, every effort to undermine the impact of the Vietnam policy position variable by holding constant such factors as ideology, occupation, and others, failed. This is not to say that these attributes are independent of each other. On the contrary, there is a discernible link between ideology, for example, and Vietnam preferences; almost one third (31 percent) of the self-described liberal leaders were also Critics, whereas a comparable proportion (29 percent) of the conservatives were also Supporters. In those cases the conjunction of two attributes tended to reinforce their responses to items representing the three foreign policy belief systems.

However, there were also some leaders who did not fit this pattern; for example, liberals whose Vietnam policies placed them in one of the Supporter groups (N=112) or conservatives who were also among the three groups at the Critic end of the scale (N=286). Responses of these "cross-pressured" leaders generally reflected views that had more in common with those of like Vietnam preferences rather than of similar ideological orientations. For example, liberal and moderate Supporters as a group agreed with the domino theory, viewed any communist victory as a defeat for the United States, judged Soviet foreign policy to be expansionist rather than defensive, and approved of force as a means of containing communism; they also disagreed with the propositions that Third World revolutionary forces are essentially nationalists, and that the communist bloc is irreparably fragmented. Their views were thus rather closely oriented toward Cold War Internationalism. Conversely, conservative and moderate Critics tended to hold views that were typically much less congenial to that foreign policy belief system.

A more detailed examination of eight key propositions that seem to reflect different world-views reveals more clearly the relative impact of ideology and Vietnam policy positions. The first six items in Table 5.2 depict a bipolar world in which the United States has primary responsibilities for coping with a variety of threats from implacable enemies. The remaining two propositions depict a very different view

Table 5.2 Strongest and Weakest Support for Selected Foreign Policy Beliefs Among 2,282 Leaders Classified According to Vietnam Policy Positions and Ideology

	Sub-groups with strongest Cold War positions		Sub-groups with weakest Cold War positions	
	Vietnam Policy position	Ideology	Vietnam policy position	Ideology
There is considerable validity in the "domino theory" that when one nation falls to Communism, others nearby will follow a similar path	Supporters	Conservative	Critics	Liberal
	Ambivalent Supporters	Conservative	Ambivalent Critics	Liberal
	Supporters	Moderate	Critics	Moderate
	Converted Supporters	Conservative	Converted Critics	Liberal
	Converted Supporters	Moderate	Ambivalent Critics	Moderate
Any communist victory is a defeat for America's national interest	Supporters	Conservative	Ambivalent Critics	Liberal
	Supporters	Moderate	Critics	Liberal
	Ambivalents	Conservative	Critics	Moderate
	Ambivalent Supporters	Conservative	Converted Critics	Liberal
	Converted Supporters	Liberal	Ambivalent Critics	Moderate
The Soviet Union is generally expansionist rather than defensive in its foreign policy goals	Supporters	Conservative	Critics	Liberal
	Converted Supporters	Conservative	Ambivalent Critics	Liberal
	Converted Critics	Conservative	Converted Critics	Liberal
	Ambivalent Supporters	Conservative	Ambivalent Critics	Moderate
	Converted Supporters	Moderate	Critics	Conservative
Détente permits the USSR to pursue policies that promote rather than restrain conflict	Supporters	Conservative	Critics	Liberal
	Supporters	Moderate	Ambivalent Critics	Liberal
	Supporters	Liberal	Converted Critics	Liberal
	Converted Supporters	Conservative	Critics	Moderate
	Converted Supporters	Liberal	Ambivalent	Liberal

The U.S. should take all steps including the use of force to prevent the spread of Communism	Supporters Supporters Supporters Ambivalents Ambivalent Supporters* Converted Supporters*	Conservative Moderate Liberal Conservative Conservative* Liberal*	Critics Ambivalent Critics Critics Converted Critics Critics	Liberal Liberal Moderate Liberal Conservative
The U.S. should undertake military intervention in the Middle East in case of another oil embargo	Supporters Supporters Supporters Converted Supporters Ambivalent Critics	Liberal Moderate Conservative Conservative Conservative	Critics Ambivalent Critics Ambivalents Critics Converted Critics	Liberal Liberal Liberal Moderate Liberal
Revolutionary forces in Third World countries are usually nationalistic rather than controlled by the USSR or China	Supporters Supporters Supporters Ambivalent Supporters Ambivalent Supporters	Conservative Liberal Moderate Conservative Moderate	Ambivalent Critics Critics Converted Critics Ambivalent Critics Critics	Liberal Liberal Liberal Moderate Moderate
America's conception of its leadership role in the world must be scaled down	Supporters Ambivalents Supporters Supporters Converted Supporters	Conservative Conservative Liberal Moderate Moderate	Critics Ambivalent Critics Ambivalent Critics Critics Critics	Liberal Moderate Conservative Moderate Conservative

* Tied Ranks

Table 5.2 cont.

	Summary: number of appearances in each column	Sub-groups with strongest Cold War positions	Sub-groups with weakest Cold War positions
Vietnam policy positions:			
	20	Supporters	0
	10	Converted Supporters	0
	6	Ambivalent Supporters	0
	3	Ambivalents	2
	1	Ambivalent Critics	13
	1	Converted Critics	7
	0	Critics	18
Ideology:			
	22	Conservative	4
	11	Moderate	12
	8	Liberal	24

of the world and America's proper role in it. When leaders are classified into twenty-one groups (ideologies aggregated into conservatives, moderates and liberals × 7 Vietnam policy positions), the results reveal that, although both factors are important, the latter tends to be the more potent. Various Supporters groups dominate the left-hand column, indicating higher agreement with Cold War positions; conversely, the Critics groups dominate the entries in the right-hand column, revealing lower agreement with Cold War beliefs. Although conservatives and liberals tend to dominate the right- and left-hand columns, respectively, these patterns are less clear cut, as cross pressures, the latter usually emerge as the more potent predictor of foreign policy beliefs.

Multivariate analyses of a broader range of 111 foreign policy issues provide further sustenance for the conclusion that Vietnam policy preferences are not merely a reflection of ideological predispositions. The two attributes often reinforce each other, but in cases of possible cross pressures, the latter usually emerge as the more potent predictor of foreign policy beliefs.

Ideology

A substantial majority of those taking part in the foreign policy leadership survey described themselves as in the center of an ideological scale ranging from "far left" to "far right." Almost four-fifths regarded themselves as "somewhat liberal," "moderate," or "somewhat conservative." Because there are so few leaders in the "far left" (N=18) and "far right" (N=5) groups, in the analyses that follow they are combined with the "very liberal" and "very conservative" groups, respectively. Thus, a seven-point scale has been collapsed to one of five categories.

The data summarized in Table 5.3 reveal a strong relationship between ideology and foreign policy beliefs. The most conservative respondents are overwhelmingly (60 percent) among the staunchest adherents to Cold War Internationalism and, as a group, they are the weakest advocates of the other two foreign policy belief systems. The pattern among liberal respondents is precisely the reverse, as a majority of the most liberal leaders appear within the highest quintile of both the Post-Cold War Internationalist (60 percent) and Semi-Isolationist (55 percent) scales. The systematic nature of the relationship between ideology and the three perspectives on foreign policy is reflected in the correlations of .55, .46, and .42. Responses by leaders in the five ideological groups are spread across a broad range, and they follow a regular pattern, with the most liberal and most conservative at the end points to each scale.

A series of multivariate analyses failed to undermine the conclusion that there is a strong relationship between ideology and foreign policy beliefs. Although most respondents placed themselves in or

Table 5.3 Three Foreign Policy Belief Systems and Ideology Among 2,282 American Leaders: 1976 Survey

Ideology	n	Cold War Internationalism			Post-Cold War Internationalism			Semi-Isolationism		
		Index[a]	% of group in extreme quintiles Highest	Lowest	Index[a]	% in group in extreme quintiles Highest	Lowest	Index[a]	% of group in extreme quintiles Highest	Lowest
Far left and very liberal	220	-.47	3	62	.63	60	4	.51	55	3
Somewhat liberal	578	-.22	5	35	.44	32	8	.30	31	9
Moderate	576	.07	15	14	.27	17	15	.12	16	16
Somewhat conservative	666	.34	33	2	.06	7	28	-.09	9	32
Far right & very conservative	131	.55	60	1	-.17	1	50	-.18	8	43
Other	111	.03	18	18	.23	20	21	.14	23	14
All respondents	2,282	.04	19[b]	20[b]	.26	21[b]	18[b]	.12	21[b]	19[b]
Correlation [C coefficient]			[.55]			[.46]			[.42]	

[a] Scales range from 1.00 (all responses most Cold War Internationalist, Post-Cold War Internationalist, Semi-Isolationist) to −1.00 (all responses least Cold War Internationalists, etc.) For items that constitute the three scales, see Tables 4.1–4.3.
[b] Owing to many tied scores on each of the three scales, divisions into quintiles did not yield groups of exactly 20 percent.

close to the center of the ideological spectrum, even moderate ideological differences are systematically associated with significantly different foreign policy beliefs. That conclusion remains valid even after holding constant the effects of occupation, gender, party, and other respondent attributes. At the same time, the results also indicate that ideology is not merely a surrogate for the Vietnam policy preferences.

Occupation

Leaders taking part in this survey were classified into ten occupational groups: military officers (N=500), business executives (294), lawyers (116), clergy (101), Foreign Service officers (125), labor leaders (74), public officials (110), educators (565), and chief editorial writers of major daily newspapers and other media leaders (184). The remaining 213 respondents, including the self-employed, physicians, artists, architects, engineers, entertainers, and those who did not identify their occupations, are grouped together in the "others" category.[5]

The findings summarized in Table 5.4 reveal a moderately strong relationship between occupation and foreign policy beliefs. Military officers and business executives are ranked high on Cold War Internationalism, and very low on the other two scales. Indeed, on fifteen of the sixteen items comprising that scale (Table 4.1), those two groups occupied the first and second positions. Conversely, educators and media leaders were among the most enthusiastic advocates of the other two foreign policy perspectives and they were, by a substantial margin, at the low end of the Cold War Internationalist index. As indicated earlier, the media have in recent years attracted charges of systematic bias from both the political right and left, notably on such issues as American policy in Vietnam and El Salvador. The present findings certainly are not sufficient to assess the merits of these accusations, but they do appear to cast some doubt on the thesis that "conservatives" dominate the media and that "progressives do not command significant resources with which to influence these main arenas of [foreign policy] decision."[6]

Of the remaining occupational groups, labor leaders and the clergy provided more complex patterns of responses. Leaders in these two groups were, on balance, moderately supportive of Cold War Internationalism, ranking third and fourth behind military officers and business executives. At the same time, labor leaders were by far the most isolationist among the ten groups of leaders. The persistence of that isolationism is reflected in the fact that their responses to six of the eight items listed in Table 4.3 were more favorable than those of any other occupational group. This finding indicates a substantial change in labor views. During much of the post-World War II period, labor leaders were counted among those most staunchly supporting

Table 5.4   Three Foreign Policy Belief Systems and Occupation Among 2,282 American Leaders: 1976 Survey

Occupation	n	Cold War Internationalism			Post-Cold War Internationalism			Semi-Isolationism		
		Index[a]	% of group in extreme quintiles Highest	Lowest	Index[a]	% of group in extreme quintiles Highest	Lowest	Index[a]	% of group in extreme quintiles Highest	Lowest
Military officers	500	.40	37	1	.02	4	31	-.22	3	40
Business executives	294	.24	27	5	.07	9	30	.09	15	18
Clergy	101	.14	19	6	.53	44	4	.18	20	13
Labor leaders	74	.05	24	24	.37	27	10	.38	43	12
Lawyers	116	.02	16	18	.22	15	21	.15	22	17
Foreign Service officers	125	-.03	15	23	.32	19	13	.06	18	24
Public officials	110	-.07	18	28	.30	26	17	.15	24	18
Educators	565	-.22	8	37	.40	32	11	.29	31	9
Media leaders	184	-.22	8	36	.40	30	9	.31	32	8
Others	213	-.07	12	24	.37	31	13	.26	33	11
All respondents	2,282	.04	19[b]	20[b]	.26	21[b]	18[b]	.12	21[b]	19[b]
Correlation [C coefficient]		[.45]			[.37]			[.40]		

[a] Scales range from 1.00 (all responses most Cold War Internationalist, Post-Cold War Internationalist, Semi-Isolationist) to −1.00 (all responses least Cold War Internationalist, etc.). For items that constitute the three scales, see Tables 4.1–4.3.

[b] Owing to many tied scores on each of the three scales, divisions into quintiles did not yield groups of exactly 20 percent.

virtually all facets of a broadly internationalist American approach to foreign affairs.

The clergy, on the other hand, were moderately high on the Cold War Internationalist scale; for example, they were the only occupational group that rated Chinese foreign policy goals as expansionist rather than defensive. At the same time, however, they also expressed by far the strongest support for the Post-Cold War Internationalist perspective. By a substantial margin they agreed most strongly that the United Nations has a vital international role, and they attributed the greatest importance to strengthening it. Moreover, the clergy were most inclined to support such foreign policy goals as combatting world hunger, improving the standard of living in less developed countries, and fostering international cooperation on common economic problems. On five of the eight items listed in Table 4.2, the clergy ranked as the group with the highest score.

These data also reveal once again that the broadest range of responses occurs on the Cold War Internationalist scale, whereas all occupational groups—including business executives and military officers—were at least moderately supportive of Post-Cold War Internationalism. Only military officers were, on balance, unfavorably disposed toward the Semi-Isolationist perspective on foreign affairs.

The occupational groups described here are clearly not homogeneous with respect to age, gender, ideology, and other attributes. The suspicion thus arises that it may be these differences, reflecting varying patterns of recruitment, socialization, and professional norms, rather than occupation per se, which account for the results summarized in the preceding paragraphs. Multivariate analyses fail, however, to confirm that conjecture. Even when the other background attributes are held constant, differences among occupational groups with respect to foreign policy beliefs remain. Stated differently, such analyses do not alter either the conclusions about the consistent views of military officers, business executives, educators, and media leaders, or those concerning the more varied responses of labor leaders and the clergy. Nor, finally, do multivariate analyses bring forth results that would mandate a reassessment of the factors discussed in the previous sections: Vietnam policy position and ideology.[7]

Political Party

Two generalizations about American politics, if valid, would lead to the expectation that party affiliation is at best weakly linked to foreign policy beliefs. The first is that the two major parties are broad coalitions that cut across rather than between ideological orientations. The second stipulates that, however divided Americans may be on domestic questions, bipartisanship rather than partisanship is the rule on foreign policy issues: "politics stops at the water's edge" has been a favorite slogan of countless orators on the hustings.

Table 5.5 Three Foreign Policy Belief Systems and Political Party Preference Among 2,282 American Leaders: 1976 Survey

Political party	n	Cold War Internationalism			Post-Cold War Internationalism			Semi-Isolationism		
			% of group in extreme quintiles			% of group in extreme quintiles			% of group in extreme quintiles	
		Index[a]	Highest	Lowest	Index[a]	Highest	Lowest	Index[a]	Highest	Lowest
Republican	590	.32	32	4	.08	8	28	-.08	9	30
Democrat	793	-.21	9	37	.42	32	9	.31	34	8
Independent	763	.09	20	16	.23	21	20	.09	19	21
Other	136	.10	18	12	.22	16	18	.03	18	22
All respondents	2,282	.04	19[b]	20[b]	.26	21[b]	18[b]	.12	21[b]	19[b]
Correlation [C coefficient]			[.39]			[.29]			[.31]	

[a] Scales range from 1.00 (all responses most Cold War Internationalist, Post-Cold War Internationalist, Semi-Isolationist) to -1.00 (all responses least Cold War Internationalist, etc.). For items that constitute the three scales, see Tables 4.1–4.3.

[b] Owing to many tied scores on each of the three scales, divisions into quintiles did not yield groups of exactly 20 percent.

Whether these generalizations were ever an even modestly accurate depiction of the foreign policy process is open to question. In recent years bipartisanship has lost its status as a sacrosanct symbol; by 1979 a leading Republican Senator called for its termination and a return to a frankly partisan foreign policy stance. Moreover, although American parties may be less ideological than many in Europe, there is at least a moderate relationship between party and ideology among the leaders taking part in this survey; 71 percent of the Republicans described themselves as conservative to some degree, whereas 66 percent of the Democrats placed themselves somewhere on the liberal end of the scale.

The sample of leaders participating in this survey differs substantially from the general population with respect to most attributes. This is notably the case for age, occupation, gender, military service and education. However, the distribution of political party preferences among the respondents—about one third each Democrat (37 percent) and independent (34 percent), and about one-quarter Republican (27 percent)—is roughly parallel to that among the entire American population at the time of this survey, and it reflects the widely-noted erosion of loyalty to the two major political parties.[8]

Analyses of party preference and foreign policy beliefs reveal that Republicans tend to be Cold War Internationalists, Democrats tend to favor Post-Cold War Internationalism and Semi-Isolationism, and independents are evenly arrayed across quintiles on all three belief systems (Table 5.5). However, those relationships are only moderately strong—as reflected in correlations of .39, .29, and .31—and on scales summarizing the positions of Republicans, Democrats and independents, the differences among them are less than dramatic, especially on Post-Cold War Internationalism and Semi-Isolationism.

When political party is paired with other leader attributes in multivariate analyses, a rather striking pattern emerges. In all but a single analysis party preferences are associated with differing patterns of response to the items constituting the three belief systems. However, when party is paired with ideology in further analyses, the effects of the former virtually disappear, especially in connection with Post-Cold War Internationalism. Thus, the independent contribution of party affiliation is even more limited than suggested by an initial examination of the data. Liberal Republicans are more likely to respond as liberals than as members of the GOP, and the foreign policy beliefs of conservative Democrats are also more likely to reflect their ideological inclinations than their party affiliations, as the results summarized in Table 5.6 make strikingly evident.

Generation

Some years ago, Karl Mannheim suggested that generation is one of the more important factors shaping social beliefs and action:

The fact of belonging to the same class, and that of belonging to the same generation or age group, have this in common, that both endow the individual with a common location in the social and historical process, and thereby limit them to a specific range of experience, predisposing them for a certain characteristic mode of thought and experience, and a characteristic type of historically relevant action.[9]

His thesis is especially germane for this study because it posits such explicit linkages between age and "lessons of history." Mannheim's injunction has not gone unheeded. In recent years the concept of generation has played a central role in analyses ranging from the political right in inter-war Finland to a proposed new paradigm for the entire course of American history, and from the Sino–Soviet conflict to the political views of American students.[10] Even the recent turmoil in Poland has been explained by reference to generational differences.[11] And, as befits its growing prominence in social research, the concept has also spawned a critical literature and several controversies.[12]

American involvement in Vietnam and its attending domestic conflict have generated a good deal of speculation about generational differences and, more specifically, about the divergent lessons that Americans of different ages have drawn from the most salient foreign policy episodes they have experienced. "Generation gap" has thus joined those other famous gaps—bomber, missile and credibility—in the vocabulary of many foreign policy analysts. The most visible lines of cleavage have quite often been described as falling between persons whose views were shaped by events leading up to World War II, on the one hand, and, on the other, those whose outlook has been molded by the war in Southeast Asia.[13] The interpretation that links contemporary dissensus on matters of foreign policy to the lessons that each generation has adduced from dramatic and traumatic episodes has been summarized by a former White House National Security Adviser:

There is a tendency in America to be traumatized by international difficulties. The generation of the Nineteen-forties was always thinking about the failure of the League of Nations. I'm talking about leadership groups now. The leadership of the sixties was always thinking about Munich. Now there is a generation worried by Vietnam, with consequences of self-imposed paralysis, which is likely to be costlier in the long run.[14]

To be more specific, the "Munich generation versus Vietnam generation" thesis usually takes some variant of the following line of reasoning. Those who experienced the bitter fruits of appeasement and American isolationism during the 1930s tended to identify the 1938 Munich Conference as the paradigmatic example of how not to

Table 5.6   *Strongest and Weakest Support for Selected Foreign Policy Beliefs Among 2,282 Leaders Classified According to Political Party and Ideology*

	Sub-groups with strongest Cold War positions		Sub-groups with weakest Cold War positions	
	Party	Ideology	Party	Ideology
There is considerable validity in the "domino theory" that when one nation falls to communism, others nearby will follow a similar path	Democrat Republican Independent	Conservative Conservative Conservative	Democrat Independent Democrat	Liberal Liberal Moderate
Any communist victory is a defeat for America's national interest	Republican Independent Democrat	Conservative Conservative Conservative	Democrat Independent Democrat	Liberal Liberal Moderate
The Soviet Union is generally expansionist rather than defensive in its foreign policy goals	Republican Independent Democrat	Conservative Conservative Conservative	Democrat Independent Democrat	Liberal Liberal Moderate
Détente permits the USSR to pursue policies that promote rather than restrain conflict	Democrat Republican Independent	Conservative Conservative Conservative	Independent Democrat Republican	Liberal Liberal Liberal
The U.S. should take all steps including the use of force to prevent the spread of Communism	Republican Independent Democrat	Conservative Conservative Conservative	Democrat Independent Democrat	Liberal Liberal Moderate
The U.S. should undertake military intervention in the Middle East in case of another oil embargo	Independent Democrat Republican	Conservative Conservative Conservative	Democrat Independent Republican	Liberal Liberal Liberal
Revolutionary forces in Third World countries are usually nationalistic rather than controlled by the USSR or China	Republican Independent Democrat	Conservative Conservative Conservative	Democrat Independent Republican	Liberal Liberal Liberal
America's conception of its leadership role in the world must be scaled down	Democrat Republican Independent	Conservative Conservative Conservative	Democrat Independent Republican	Liberal Liberal Liberal

Summary: *number of appearances in each column*

Party:				
	8	Republican	4	
	8	Democrat	12	
	8	Independent	8	
Ideology:	24	Conservative	0	
	0	Moderate	4	
	0	Liberal	20	

deal with expansionist totalitarian regimes. When faced after World War II with the Soviet occupation of Eastern Europe, the absence of any liberalization within the USSR, as well as periodic crises in Berlin and elsewhere, persons of this generation were prepared to support an active American foreign policy to meet challenges from the Soviet Union and its satellites.

In contrast, according to this thesis, persons of a more recent generation—for whom World War II and its genesis, as well as the origins of the Cold War, are merely distant historical events rather than episodes experienced at first hand—are more likely to look to the war in Southeast Asia as a source of guidance on the proper and improper conduct of foreign relations. According to this description of contemporary American society, then, what the parents regard as indispensable commitments to maintain a viable world order their offspring view as indiscriminate (if not incriminating) undertakings against ill-defined, often phantom threats that have no intimate connection to legitimate American interests, let alone the propagation or preservation of democratic values and institutions abroad.[15] Unencumbered by the memories and ideological baggage accumulated during World War II and the Cold War, the new generation is sometimes described as concerned with not only the physical safety of the nation, but also of this fragile spaceship earth; as ready to give up the hidebound political shibboleths of their elders in favor of a more enlightened world-view; as eager to renounce a materialistic life-style that eats up a disproportionate share of the world's resources in favor of simpler pleasures; and as inclined to respond to the sound of falling dominoes with a bored, "so what?" To some, this is a harbinger of better days to come, and to others it is no doubt a profoundly threatening one. This is, of course, a vastly oversimplified summary of a rather complex line of reasoning. Nevertheless, even if it is something of a caricature, it does capture some central elements of the thesis that in important respects the cleavages on foreign policy issues in this country represent a confrontation of two distinct world-views, each rooted in and sustained by the experiences of different generations.

The generational thesis, if valid, has some important implications for the future conduct of American foreign policy because it suggests that members of the "Vietnam generation," as they achieve positions of leadership and influence during the next several decades, will bring to their roles an intellectual baggage radically different from that of the leaders they are replacing. Under these circumstances, moreover, the prognosis is that as the next generation of leaders replaces those currently in positions of influence, a new consensus reflecting the sensibilities of the younger group will emerge in the not-too-distant future.[16] Recall that persons who had reached voting age at the time of the Munich Conference will reach retirement age during the 1980s.

However plausible the generational interpretation of foreign policy differences may be, it is not universally accepted. Both survey and voting data suggest that, at least within the public at large, cleavages do not fall quite so neatly along age lines. Thus, the image of a "dovish" or neo-isolationist generation of students demonstrating on campuses to protest the excessive foreign policy commitments of their elders provides, according to some observers, a skewed, if not inaccurate, picture of contemporary American society. For example, analyses of the Chicago Council on Foreign Relations poll failed to reveal striking differences among age groups. Of those under the age of 30, 30 percent were classified as "liberal internationalists," 32 percent as "conservative internationalists," and 38 percent as "non-internationalists." Indeed, compared to the 30–64 and over 64 age groups, those of the youngest generation were the most evenly distributed among these three categories.[17]

Even the more specific proposition that ties generational conflict to the war in Vietnam receives little support from polls conducted during the decade prior to the 1973 Paris agreement that was to have ended the war. Indeed, these surveys revealed that, compared to their elders, the younger respondents were usually more inclined to support American policy in Southeast Asia, as well as to oppose withdrawal.[18] However, at least some advocates of the generational thesis suggest that, whatever may be true of the public at large, it describes accurately the cleavages among elites, actual and emerging.[19]

To assess the effects of age on foreign policy beliefs, the entire sample of leaders was divided into four groups based on year of birth. In the absence of any standard guidelines for identifying generations, the designation of cutting points is an arbitrary decision, based on two premises. The three wars in which the United States has been involved since 1941 were assumed to provide significant benchmarks. The "Munich generation versus Vietnam generation" thesis also identifies two of these wars as watershed points in American thinking about external affairs. The second premise is that late adolescence and young adulthood may have special signficance. Because that period encompasses for many the beginning of eligibility for military service, consciousness of and interest in foreign affairs may be enhanced when prospects for personal involvement hinge upon the outcome of foreign policy undertakings. More generally, those years in the life cycle have often been identified as especially crucial in the formation and development of political beliefs.[20]

Following this reasoning, three cutting points, 1923–4, 1932–3, and 1940–1, divided the respondents into four groups. Even the youngest of the World War II generation—those born in 1923—had reached at least the age of 18 when the attack on Pearl Harbor brought the United States into World War II. By the end of that war they would have been likely, if otherwise eligible, to have experienced military service. But even those who were not on active military duty could scarcely have lived through the war without having taken cognizance of it. Leaders born between 1924 and 1932 would at least have reached the age of 21 during some part of the Korean War. The older among them would also have been young adults during World War II, but for this group the Korean War would presumably have been an especially salient experience. Persons born between 1933 and 1940 would, if inducted into the armed forces, most likely have served during the period following the Korean armistice of 1953 and before the rapid escalation in 1965 of the Vietnam conflict. Hence this group is labeled the "interim generation." Finally, those born after 1940 have been designated as the "Vietnam generation." Even the oldest persons in the group would have been only 13 years old when the fighting in Korea ended. For them "the war" almost certainly refers to the conflict in Southeast Asia. The "World War II generation" constitutes the largest group (39 percent of all leaders), followed by the "Vietnam generation" (26 percent), the "Korea generation" (19 percent), and the "interim generation" (11 percent). The remaining 5 percent did not reveal their year of birth.

The data in Table 5.7 offer rather limited support for the thesis that cleavages on foreign policy issues in the United States are essentially generational in origin. Responses to items comprising the three foreign policy belief systems reveal only modest differences, a conclusion also reflected in the correlations of .21, .20, and .22. More importantly, there is little evidence of a consistent pattern of cleavages that arrays the youngest group of leaders against their elders.[21]

However, owing to some variations in the attributes of leaders in the four age groups, these results do not constitute a definitive test of the generational thesis. In order to assess conclusively the impact of age on foreign policy beliefs, each of the groups should be as similar as possible with respect to other characteristics that might serve as competing explanations—for example, occupation. For several reasons this is not the case with the present sample. Return rates were not uniform across all groups; they ranged from a low of 39 percent for labor leaders to figures approaching 60 percent for chief editorial writers, military officers, and educators. Some of the directories used to compile the mailing lists did not provide birth dates, ruling out efforts at the sampling stage to ensure an even distribution across generations. Moreover, the sociology of occupations is such that prominence or leadership positions tend to come earlier in some professions than in others. For example, business executives typically do not reach the top levels of management before an age (mid to late 50s) at which most senior military officers have already retired. Finally, access to and a very high return rate from one of the middle level service schools resulted in a high proportion of military officers among the "Vietnam generation."

As a consequence of such wide disparities among the four age groups, direct comparisons may not be sufficient to support the conclusion that generational differences are somewhat less pronounced than is implied in some current commentary on the state of American attitudes on foreign policy. That conclusion is sustained by multivariate analyses, however, from which emerged two main findings:

Table 5.7 Three Foreign Policy Belief Systems and Generation Among 2,282 American Leaders: 1976 Survey

Generation	n	Cold War Internationalism			Post-Cold War Internationalism			Semi-Isolationism		
		Index[a]	% of group in extreme quintiles Highest	Lowest	Index[a]	% of group in extreme quintiles Highest	Lowest	Index[a]	% of group in extreme quintiles Highest	Lowest
Vietnam War generation (born since 1940)	583	.21	28	11	.12	12	25	−.05	12	28
Interim generation (born 1933–40)	256	−.01	17	25	.23	19	20	.12	21	20
Korean War generation (born 1924–32)	442	−.07	14	25	.29	23	18	.21	26	14
World War II generation (born before 1924)	898	.01	18	22	.20	27	15	.19	26	16
Age not stated	103	.02	17	17	.31	20	11	.12	17	12
All respondents	2,282	.04	19[b]	20[b]	.26	21[b]	18[b]	.12	21[b]	19[b]
Correlation [C coefficient]			[.21]			[.20]			[.22]	

[a] Scales range from 1.00 (all responses most Cold War Internationalist, Post-Cold War Internationalist, Semi-Isolationalist, etc.) to −1.00 (all responses least Cold War Internationalist). For items that constitute the three scales, see Tables 4.1–4.3.

[b] Owing to many tied scores on each of the three scales, divisions into quintiles did not yield groups of exactly 20 percent.

differences across generations arise much less frequently than in the case when respondents are classified according to Vietnam policy position, occupation, ideology, and political party; and, when generational differences do occur, they do not consistently conform to a pattern of "hawkish" (Cold War Internationalist) older leaders versus "dovish" (the other belief systems) younger ones.

These conclusions may be illustrated by analyses comparing the effects of generation and occupation on foreign policy beliefs. Multivariate analyses for the thirty-two items selected to represent the three belief systems indicate that the explanatory potency of occupation far exceeds that of generation.

Because the generational thesis has been so widely accepted, however, it is also worth broadening the analysis to encompass a wider range of 111 foreign policy issues concerning: the goals of American foreign policy (18 items), lessons of Vietnam (34), sources of failure in Vietnam (21), consequences of the war (13), the appropriate international role for the United States (7), and appraisals of current foreign policy performance (18). The results further sustain the finding that foreign policy beliefs tend to cut between occupations and across generations. Moreover, generational differences do not by any means always conform to the pattern of a "hard line" older group versus a "dovish–isolationist" younger cohort. For example, in eight of ten occupational groups, the youngest respondents were least inclined to attribute importance to the containment of communism (exceptions: public officials, others), but in only four of the ten groups did those of the Vietnam generation register the lowest rating on the somewhat related goal of maintaining a global balance of power. On the goal of "fostering international cooperation to solve common problems," the youngest respondents provided the highest importance rating in some occupations (clergy, military, media, lawyers), and the lowest in others (Foreign Service, business executives, others). Questions concerning the nature of the contemporary international system revealed that respondents of the Vietnam generation were, within their occupations, often among the most inclined to cast doubts on the Cold War premises of a tight bipolar system. But other questions gave rise to much less clear-cut results. The issue of involving the United Nations in the resolution of international disputes found members of the youngest generation in strongest agreement within three occupations (labor leaders, educators, clergy), and those of the older age group in greatest agreement in six others (Foreign Service, business, military, public officials, lawyers, and others). The proposition that American influence in the Third World could best be exercised by solving its own problems yielded equally mixed results. Among media leaders and military officers, the youngest respondents were most fully in agreement, but they were also the most opposed in three other occupations (business, labor, and clergy).

A more detailed examination of eight propositions that touch upon beliefs often ascribed to the older and younger generations reveals most clearly the influence of generation. When respondents are classified into forty groups (4 generations × 10 occupations), some generational differences do emerge. For example, the World War II generation appears eleven times in the left-hand columns of Table 5.8 (strongest Cold War positions), but it is also found three times in the right-hand column. Conversely, the Vietnam generation appears six times in the left-hand column and nineteen in the right. Compared to this moderate support for the generational thesis, a much more consistent pattern emerges from the data on occupational status of the strongest and weakest supporters of the Cold War positions. Military officers and business executives, and not only those of the older generation, provide the strongest support for Cold War positions— together they account for thirty-four of the forty-two entries in the

Table 5.8 *Strongest and Weakest Support for Selected Foreign Policy Beliefs Among 2,282 Leaders Classified According to Generation and Occupation*

	Sub-groups with strongest Cold War positions		Sub-groups with weakest Cold War positions	
	Occupation	Generation	Occupation	Generation
There is a considerable validity in the "domino theory" that when one nation falls to communism, others nearby will follow a similar path	Military	WW II	Media	Vietnam
	Military	Korea	Media	Korea
	Military	Interim	Foreign Service	Vietnam
	Military	Vietnam	Clergy	Vietnam
	Business*	WW II*	Media	Interim
	Business*	Interim*		
Any communist victory is a defeat for America's national interest	Military	WW II	Media	Vietnam
	Military	Korea	Media	Interim
	Military	Interim	Media	Korea
	Clergy	WW II	Educators	Vietnam
	Business	Interim	Educators	Korea
The Soviet Union is generally expansionist rather than defensive in its foreign policy goals	Military	Korea	Educators	Vietnam
	Military	Interim	Clergy	Vietnam
	Business	Interim	Labor	Interim
	Clergy	WW II	Clergy	Interim
	Military	Vietnam	Media	Vietnam
Détente permits the USSR to pursue policies that promote rather than restrain conflict	Military	WW II	Public officials	Interim
	Military	Interim	Foreign Service	Vietnam
	Military	Vietnam	Clergy	Vietnam
	Clergy	WW II	Lawyers	Interim
	Military	Korea	Educators	Vietnam

Table 5.8 cont.

	Sub-groups with strongest Cold War positions		Sub-groups with weakest Cold War positions	
	Occupation	Generation	Occupation	Generation
The U.S. should take	Military	Interim	Media	Korea
all steps including	Military	WW II	Media	Vietnam
the use of force to	Military	Korea	Educators	Vietnam
prevent the spread	Military	Vietnam	Educators	WW II
of Communism	Clergy	Interim	Foreign Service	Vietnam
The U.S. should	Business	Vietnam	Media	Korea
undertake	Business	Interim	Foreign Service	Interim
military	Clergy	Interim	Media	Vietnam
intervention in	Military	Interim	Media	WW II
the Middle East in	Military	Korea	Media	Interim
case of another oil embargo				
Revolutionary	Military	WW II	Public officials	Interim
forces in Third	Clergy	WW II	Educators	Vietnam
World countries	Business	Korea	Foreign Service	Vietnam
are usually	Military	Interim	Educators	Interim
nationalistic	Clergy	Korea	Media	Korea
rather than controlled by the USSR or China				
America's	Military	Vietnam	Labor	Korea
conception of its	Military	Korea	Educators	Korea
leadership role in	Military	WW II	Media	Vietnam
the world must be	Military	Interim	Educators	Vietnam
scaled down	Business*	Interim*	Educators	WW II
	Labor*	Interim*		

	Sub-groups with strongest Cold War positions		Sub-groups with weakest Cold War positions	
Summary: number of appearances in each column				
Occupation:	26	Military officers	0	
	8	Business executives	0	
	7	Clergy	4	
	1	Labor leaders	2	
	0	Lawyers	1	
	0	Public officials	2	
	0	Foreign Service	5	
	0	Educators	11	
	0	Media leaders	15	
Generation:	11	World War II	3	
	9	Korea	8	
	16	Interim	10	
	6	Vietnam	19	

* Tied Ranks

left-hand column—whereas media leaders and educators are almost as consistent in their skepticism, appearing twenty-six times in the summary for the right-hand column.

Military Service

A substantial proportion of the leadership sample has served in the military. Among the entire group, two-thirds have done so, and even when professional military officers are excluded from consideration, veterans constitute well over one-half (58 percent) of the sample. Over 10 percent of the women leaders had also served in the armed forces.

Military service is often thought to have a significant impact on political attitudes. More than in most organizations, socialization in the military emphasizes national security and the role of the armed forces in its maintenance, both historically and at present. Hence the often asserted thesis that those with military experience will tend to take a "harder line" on questions of foreign and defense policy, a viewpoint that is more likely to resemble the Cold War Internationalist belief system than the other two. Helping to sustain this image is the fact that organizations claiming to represent veterans, notably the American Legion, have usually adopted predictable positions, not only on veterans' benefits and related concerns, but also on such issues as the proper level of the defense budget, conscription, containment, and the like. Evidence on the impact of military service is rather mixed, however. Most studies have focused on the professional military, and those comparing veterans and non-veterans among the general public have yielded somewhat contradictory findings.[22]

The data summarized in Table 5.9 reveal that veterans are somewhat more inclined toward Cold War Internationalism, whereas non-veterans tend to support Post-Cold War Internationalism and Semi-Isolationism. Differences between the two groups are not especially striking, however, and correlations between military service and the three perspectives on foreign affairs reach only modest levels (.20, .18, and .23). More importantly, these results appear to overstate the importance of military service. The earlier finding of a strong relationship between occupation and foreign policy beliefs, especially for military officers, suggests the need for analyses that assess the impact of military service after controlling for occupation. Do the differences found in Table 5.9 arise generally from the fact of service in the armed forces, or are they more narrowly attributable to those who are pursuing military careers?

Multivariate analyses for each of the thirty-two items constituting the three belief systems provide a rather conclusive answer: differences between veterans and non-veterans are significant for only three items, whereas those among the various occupations remain strong for all but one of them. Stated somewhat differently, these results indicate that a distinction between the impact of a military

Table 5.9 Three Foreign Policy Belief Systems and Military Service Among 2,282 American Leaders: 1976 Survey

Military experience	n	Cold War Internationalism			Post-Cold War Internationalism			Semi-Isolationism		
		Index[a]	% of group in extreme quintiles		Index[a]	% of group in extreme quintiles		Index[a]	% of group in extreme quintiles	
			Highest	Lowest		Highest	Lowest		Highest	Lowest
Veteran	1,500	.11	23	17	.20	17	21	.05	17	23
Non-veteran	737	−.10	12	27	.37	29	13	.28	30	11
No response on military service	45	.10	20	7	.34	22	11	−.09	22	16
All respondents	2,282	.04	19[b]	20[b]	.26	21[b]	18[b]	.12	21[b]	19[b]
Correlation [C coefficient]			[.20]			[.18]			[.23]	

[a] Scales range from 1.00 (all responses most Cold War Internationalist, Post-Cold War Internationalist, Semi-Isolationist, etc.) to −1.00 (all responses least Cold War Internationalist, etc.). For items that constitute the three scales, see Tables 4.1–4.3.
[b] Owing to many tied scores on each of the three scales, divisions into quintiles did not yield groups of exactly 20 percent.

career, on the one hand, and temporary service in the armed forces, on the other, is in order. As a group, the professional military officers in the sample hold foreign policy beliefs that differ from those in most other occupations. Among the remaining groups, however, veterans and non-veterans are virtually indistinguishable with respect to the three foreign policy belief systems.

Gender

Few predictions about social change seem as safe as the proposition that women will play an increasingly important role in leadership positions. However, one may judge the pace of change in this respect, there can be little disagreement about the trend.[23] If that premise is valid, how will this development affect politics? Will it bring a higher standard of probity to the political process? A more humane set of concerns into the formulation of political agendas? In the realm of external affairs, will it give rise to a more serious concern and a higher priority for undertakings that often fall outside the purview of those espousing or practicing *realpolitik* diplomacy? These questions imply that women may bring to the political process a set of beliefs or world-views that differ systematically from those of their male counterparts.

These are interesting and important questions for which the evidence is both sparse and inconclusive. Although the literature on women in politics is not insubstantial and has grown dramatically in recent years, much of it is concentrated in several areas, including background attributes and political participation, socialization, voting behavior, and the like.[24] Other questions, including foreign policy beliefs of women in leadership positions, have received much less attention.[25] For example, foreign policy surveys undertaken by the Chicago Council on Foreign Relations in 1975 and 1979 included both leaders and members of the public at large. Summaries of the findings do not even report the results for men and women separately, much less analyze the similarities and differences between them.[26] The available information is not only scanty; it has also yielded rather contradictory conclusions. Almond's classic but now dated study of *The American People and Foreign Policy* found that "more women than men seem to be ignorant of or apathetic to foreign policy issues," a conclusion that received no support in an investigation of women at the leadership level.[27]

It is possible to develop at least two different lines of reasoning concerning the foreign policy beliefs of American women in leadership positions. According to one, their beliefs will differ significantly from those of their male counterparts. More specifically, women will tend to have more benign and optimistic views of the international system, to give priority to social–economic–humanitarian issues rather than to political–strategic concerns, and to be less inclined toward the use of military capabilities and force as means of dealing with global issues. This viewpoint conforms to a long tradition, going as far back as Lysistrata and earlier, which depicts women as the less belligerent half of the species. It also finds some sustenance in more recent evidence. For example, a summary of polls on the Vietnam War found that women consistently provided less support for the American war effort, and they were stronger advocates of withdrawal from Southeast Asia.[28] Another review of Gallup and Harris surveys revealed that these results were not confined to the Vietnam issue; women were generally found to be less inclined to seek military solutions to international problems.[29] It is important to recall, however, that these findings are derived from sample surveys of the entire public rather than of persons in leadership positions. The premise is that sex-role experiences constitute such a potent force that their effects persist throughout the population, including those who have achieved positions of leadership in various institutions. That is, sex-role factors outweigh those linked to occupation and other roles in shaping foreign policy beliefs.

According to an alternative line of reasoning, the foreign policy beliefs of women leaders do not differ significantly from those of men in comparable roles. Whatever the differences among women and men in the entire population, their views converge at the leadership level. According to this thesis, then, leaders have more in common with each other than they have with members of their own gender in the public at large. This line of reasoning is also supported by some evidence. However, as indicated earlier, empirical studies of gender differences among leaders are quite scarce. A survey of leaders attending a 1958 conference on national security revealed that any differences among men and women disappeared after controlling for occupation and party preference.[30]

The findings reported in Table 5.10 indicate that the primary cleavages on foreign policy issues do not originate in gender. With the possible exception of the Semi-Isolationist scale, these results suggest that similarities between male and female leaders are more striking than the differences.[31] More specifically, among the sixteen Cold War Internationalist items there are significant differences between the male and female leaders on only four. Women tended to be somewhat more optimistic about the international goals of communist nations, including the Soviet Union.[32] Most strikingly, women were more opposed than men to using the CIA to undermine hostile governments. But these exceptions notwithstanding, the most impressive finding is that on most questions differences between women and men are negligible, whether the issue is the containment of communism, the validity of the domino theory, or the value of better Soviet–American relations. Even on six of seven questions relating to the use of force in foreign policy, women expressed views that differed little from those of their male counterparts. In short, these results provide only the most modest sustenance for the theory that "dovishness" is a feminine attribute, whereas "hawkishness" is a masculine one.

Table 5.10 Three Foreign Policy Belief Systems and Gender Among 2,282 American Leaders: 1976 Survey

Gender	n	Cold War Internationalism			Post-Cold War Internationalism			Semi-Isolationism		
		Index[a]	% of group in extreme quintiles Highest	Lowest	Index[a]	% of group in extreme quintiles Highest	Lowest	Index[a]	% of group in extreme quintiles Highest	Lowest
Men	2,009	.06	20	19	.25	21	19	−.01	20	20
Women	224	−.07	16	26	.35	25	13	.34	34	9
Gender not stated	49	.07	10	8	.33	20	10	−.01	12	27
All respondents	2,282	.04	19[b]	20[b]	.26	21[b]	18[b]	.12	21[b]	19[b]
Correlation [C coefficient]			[.12]			[.08]			[.16]	

[a] Scales range from 1.00 (all responses most Cold War Internationalist, Post-Cold War Internationalist, Semi-Isolationist, etc.) to −1.00 (all responses least Cold War Internationalist). For items that constitute the three scales, see Tables 4.1–4.3.

[b] Owing to many tied scores on each of the three scales, divisions into quintiles did not yield groups of exactly 20 percent.

Moreover, the evidence reveals that gender-based differences are not substantial on Post-Cold War Internationalist propositions; they are, in fact limited to the items concerning the United Nations, with greater support for that organization among women. Notably absent is any compelling evidence of stronger concern by female leaders for such international undertakings as improving the standard of living in less-developed countries, combatting world hunger, economic aid, and international cooperation on a broad range of non-security issues. Moreover, women were less inclined than men—although not significantly so—to accept a central proposition in the Post-Cold War Internationalist belief system: that revolutionary movements in the Third World are nationalistic rather than controlled by Moscow or Beijing.

In contrast to the findings on the two internationalist belief systems, a somewhat different pattern emerges in connection with isolationism. On six of the eight items, women in the leadership sample responded in a significantly more isolationist manner. Moreover, even in the other two cases women tended to favor a more restricted international role for the United States.

But it is appropriate to inquire whether these largely negative findings may be an artifact of other differences in the two subsamples. It may therefore be useful to describe some of the more salient similarities and differences between the 224 female and 2,009 male leaders, and then to undertake multivariate analyses that assess more precisely the independent contribution of gender in explaining foreign policy beliefs.[33]

- A substantial number of the women are clustered in two occupations (27 percent of the women are educators; 15 percent of them are media leaders), whose members are most likely to take a "dovish" position on international issues, whereas a high proportion of the male leaders are to be found in the more "hawkish" occupations (military officers, 24 percent; business executives, 13 percent).
- Leaders taking part in this survey are highly educated. Among both women (53 percent) and men (61 percent) the modal respondent holds some type of post-graduate degree, and overall educational differences are only moderate.
- The female leaders are, on balance, younger than their male counterparts. One-third of the women and one-fifth of the men were born since 1940.
- Although both groups of respondents include more Democrats than Republicans, the margin favoring the former among women is more than two-to-one, whereas among men it is about four-to-three.
- The female respondents are more liberal than the males; one-half of the former describe themselves as being on the "liberal" end of the scale, compared to one-third of the latter who do so.

- Not surprisingly, the most striking gender difference concerns military service; 73 percent of the men and 11 percent of the women have served in the armed forces.
- The two groups of leaders expressed equal interest in politics, but men were somewhat more interested than women in those at the international level, whereas this situation was reversed with respect to local politics.[34]
- Male leaders engaged more frequently in consulting and travel, but there were no differences between the sexes in other types of political activity: writing or talking to a Congressman, Senator, or local official; making speeches at public meetings; appearing on radio or television; and contributing articles to a newspaper or magazine.[35]

These differences are of sufficient magnitude to warrant further analyses that go beyond direct comparison of men and women, and that control for occupational, generational, political, and other differences between them. Multivariate analyses involving gender and other attributes failed to overturn the main finding of marginal differences between men and women.[36] Comparing the impact of occupation and gender will illustrate the point. The results of multivariate analyses for the thirty-two items that comprise the three belief systems tend to confirm the conclusion that differences among women and men in leadership positions are of rather modest proportions, with the exception of the Semi-Isolationist items. Although some gender-based differences survive when occupation is controlled, the dominant lines of cleavage among this sample of leaders are those defined by occupation.

One might inquire, however, whether the results for these thirty-two items are representative of the main tendencies within the much larger set of foreign policy issues, including those discussed in earlier chapters. The results of multivariate analyses pairing occupation and gender for a larger set of 111 foreign policy items support those reported above, as significant effects of the former occurred on 103 items, compared to only twenty-three for the latter. It should be reiterated, moreover, that even when gender differences yielded significant results, the underlying scores did not uniformly fit the pattern of "hawkish" men versus "dovish" women.

Analyses of the same eight propositions examined earlier reveal more clearly the effects of gender and occupation. When leaders are classified into twenty groups (2 sexes × 10 occupations), evidence of differences between men and women is quite weak, save on the issue of cutting back America's leadership role in the world (Table 5.11). Women are found with almost equal frequency among both the strongest and weakest supporters of the Cold War positions. A much more consistent pattern emerges from the data on occupation. Military officers and business executives, including both men and women, provided the strongest support for Cold War views—together

Table 5.11   *Strongest and Weakest Support for Selected Foreign Policy Beliefs Among 2,282 Leaders Classified According to Gender and Occupation*

| | Sub-groups with strongest Cold War positions | | Sub-groups with weakest Cold War positions | |
	Occupation	Gender	Occupation	Gender
There is considerable validity in the "domino theory" that when one nation falls to communism, others nearby will follow a similar path	Labor Military Public officials Business Business	Women Men Women Men Women	Media Media Educators Educators Lawyers	Women Men Men Women Women
Any communist victory is a defeat for America's national interest	Public officials Military Business Military Business	Women Women Women Men Men	Media Media Educatiors Labor Educators	Men Women Men Women Women
The Soviet Union is generally expansionist rather than defensive in its foreign policy goals	Milita Military Business Lawyers Foreign Service	Women Men Men Women Women	Educators Media Educators Labor Business	Women Women Men Women Women
Détente permits the USSR to pursue policies that promote rather than restrain conflict	Military Public officials Military Clergy Labor	Men Women Women Men Men	Labor Lawyers Media Foreign Service Educators	Women Women Women Men Men
The U.S. should take all steps including the use of force to prevent the spread of Communism	Military Military Public officials Business Business	Women Men Women Women Men	Media Media Educators Educators Lawyers	Women Men Women Men Women
The U.S. should undertake military intervention in the Middle East in case of another oil embargo	Military Public officials Business Business Military	Women Women Women Men Men	Labor Media Foreign Service Media Educators	Women Women Women Men Men
Revolutionary forces in Third World countries are usually nationalistic rather than controlled by the USSR or China	Business Public officials Clergy Military Business	Women Women Men Men Men	Lawyers Media Public officials Educators Foreign Service	Women Men Men Men Men

Table 5.11 cont.

	Sub-groups with strongest Cold War positions		Sub-groups with weakest Cold War positions	
	Occupation	Gender	Occupation	Gender
America's conception	Military	Men	Educators	Women
of its leadership	Military	Women	Educators	Men
role in the world	Public officials	Men	Business	Women
must be scaled	Foreign Service	Men	Foreign Service	Women
down	Clergy	Men	Lawyers	Women

Summary: number of appearances in
each column

Occupation:			
	14	Military officers	0
	11	Business executives	2
	7	Public officials	1
	3	Clergy	0
	2	Foreign Service	4
	2	Labor leaders	4
	1	Lawyers	5
	0	Media leaders	11
	0	Educators	13
Gender:	20	Women	24
	20	Men	16

they account for twenty-five of the forty entries in the left-hand column—whereas media leaders and educators were almost equally pronounced in their skepticism, accounting for twenty-four of the forty groups in the right-hand column. Stated somewhat differently, cases in which cross-pressures may be at work—for example, male media leaders or female business executives—the impact of occupation clearly tends to override that of gender.

Level of Political Interest

Isolationism is sometimes said to appeal mostly to persons with a limited interest in foreign affairs. Do the present data support this proposition? More generally, is there a relationship between support for the three foreign policy belief systems and levels of political interest? Affirmative answers to these and related questions would offer some clues about the potential impact that advocates of the three viewpoints may have on American foreign policy.

Leaders were asked to "describe your interest in international, national, and local politics" on a seven-point scale, the end points of which were labelled as "It is one of my major concerns," and "I pay little attention." Responses to three items were combined to form a single scale for classifying the entire group of leaders. Not

Table 5.12   Three Foreign Policy Belief Systems and Level of Political Interest Among 2,282 American Leaders: 1976 Survey

Level of Political interest	n	Cold War Internationalism			Post-Cold War Internationalism			Semi-Isolationism		
			% of group in extreme quintiles			% of group in extreme quintiles			% of group in extreme quintiles	
		Index[a]	Highest	Lowest	Index[a]	Highest	Lowest	Index[a]	Highest	Lowest
Very high	797	.00	21	25	.32	26	16	.09	23	22
High	500	.09	21	16	.21	21	23	.10	19	22
Somewhat high	433	.03	17	20	.28	19	16	.14	21	17
Moderate	370	.07	17	16	.25	17	17	.20	25	15
Somewhat low	105	.02	12	16	.20	18	22	.18	20	11
Low and none	47	.29	30	2	-.01	6	34	.13	15	17
No response on political interest	30	.03	17	17	.09	30	13	.05	17	17
All respondents	2,282	.04	19[b]	20[b]	.26	21[b]	18[b]	.12	21[b]	17
Correlation [C coefficient]			[.18]			[.16]			[.14]	

[a] Scales range from 1.00 (all responses most Cold War Internationalist, Post-Cold War Internationalist, Semi-Isolationist, etc.) to −1.00 (all responses least Cold War Internationalist, etc.). For items that constitute the three scales, see Tables 4.1–4.3.
[b] Owing to many tied scores on each of the three scales, divisions into quintiles did not yield groups of exactly 20 percent.

surprisingly, the reported level of political interest among the leaders is rather high, with more than a third of the respondents in the "very high" category (defined as a mean score of at least 5.6 on a scale of 1 to 7), but there is sufficient variation to permit meaningful analyses. There is little evidence of a systematic relationship between levels of political interest and foreign policy beliefs (Table 5.12). Perhaps the exception to this conclusion is the tendency of respondents with the least interest in politics to rank high on the Cold War Internationalism scale and low on Post-Cold War Internationalism. Beyond that, the correlations of .18, .16, and .14 reflect only modest linkages between levels of political interest and foreign policy beliefs.

Conclusion

Analyses in this chapter have explored some correlates of foreign policy cleavages among American leaders. The results sustain some popular notions about the location of post-Vietnam fault lines on the American political landscape, and challenge several others. The findings may also throw some light on the likely durability of the cleavages. They indicate that Vietnam policy position, ideology, and occupation are most strongly associated with the three foreign policy belief systems, whereas divisions corresponding to gender, generation, and military service are much weaker.

This outcome appears to cast some doubt on the thesis that the passage of time—which will certainly bring into positions of leadership a new generation that is almost sure to include substantially more women and fewer veterans—is sufficient by itself to forge a new consensus. Because divergent and internally consistent belief systems are also sustained and reinforced by ideological and institutional cleavages, as these data would appear to indicate, expectations of a new foreign policy consensus sooner rather than later may err on the side of optimism.

However, dramatic events may forge agreement out of disunity, as demonstrated most strikingly by the Japanese attack on Pearl Harbor. Some commentators have suggested that this is precisely what happened during the closing weeks of the 1970s as a consequence of developments in Iran and Afghanistan. Chapter 6 considers the thesis that a new foreign policy consensus emerged from those episodes in Southwest Asia.

Notes to Chapter 5

1 For example, Michael Mandelbaum and William Schneider, "The New Internationalisms: Public Opinion and American Foreign Policy," in Kenneth Oye. Donald Rothchild, and Robert Lieber (eds), *Eagle Entangled: U.S. Foreign Policy in a Complex World* (New York; Longman, 1979). A slightly different, four-fold classification is developed in Michael Maggiotto and Eugene Wittkopf, "American

attitudes toward foreign policy," *International Studies Quarterly*, 25 (December 1981), pp. 601–31.

2   Because there were many tied scores at most points on each of the three scales, it was not always possible to divide them precisely at the 20th, 40th, 60th and 80th percentiles. As a consequence, the quintiles do not include exactly 20 percent of the leaders; for example, the highest quintiles on the three scales actually include 19 percent, 21 percent, and 21 percent of the respondents, whereas the lowest ones consist of 20 percent, 18 percent, and 19 percent.

3   The C coefficient is a measure of correlation for categorical data. Its interpretation is approximately the same as that for the more familiar product–moment correlation coefficient. One drawback of C is that its maximum score, designating a perfect relationship, is not only less than 1.00, but its maximum value also varies according to the size of the table; for example, for a 2 × 2 table, the maximum score for C is .707. A coefficient of .00 indicates complete independence of two variables.

4   Multivariate analyses in this chapter are two-way analyses of variance (ANOVA). In order to avoid undue proliferation of tables, only the more interesting results are reported in that format. Differences among groups are reported as significant only if they exceed the requirements for the .001 level.

5   Occupational groups clearly vary considerably in size. However, all of them are sufficiently large to permit comparisons between them. Figures in Table 5.4 and the multivariate analyses described in the text factor out the effects of differences in the size of occupational groups.

6   Richard A. Falk, "Beyond internationalism," *Foreign Policy*, no. 24 (Fall 1976), p. 93. Of course, the validity of this statement depends on how one defines "progressive." Just as some conservatives regard anyone to the left of Louis XIV as a radical liberal, some liberals tend to dismiss all American leaders and institutions as hopelessly conservative, if not reactionary. For an almost conspiratorial view of the American media, see Noam Chomsky, *Towards A New Cold War: Essays on the Current Crisis and How We Got There* (New York: Pantheon, 1982).

   A careful analysis of public opinion data that attributes a significant role to the media is Bruce Russett and Donald R. DeLuca, " 'Don't tread on me': public opinion and foreign policy in the eighties," *Political Science Quarterly*, 96 (Fall 1981), pp. 381–99. See also, David Paletz and Robert Entman, *Media Power Politics* (New York: Free Press, 1981); and the sources cited in Chapter 1, n. 37.

7   These findings are quite similar to those emerging from a survey of American values, including those of leadership groups similar to those in this study. According to that study, military officers and business executives were strongest proponents of conscription and an American military second to none, media leaders ranked in the middle on these issues, and educators were the least enthusiastic. On a question about American involvement in the Vietnam War, media leaders ranked at the top in judging that effort to be unjust, educators and business executives were in the middle, and military officers were the lowest-ranking occupational group. Research and Forecasts, Inc., *The Connecticut Mutual Life Report on American Values in the '80s* (Hartford, Conn., 1981).

   For more detailed analyses involving occupation, see Ole R. Holsti and James N. Rosenau, "Cold War Axioms in the Post-Vietnam Era," in Ole R. Holsti, Randolph M. Siverson, and Alexander L. George (eds), *Change in the International System* (Boulder, Colorado: Westview Press, 1980).

8   According to the University of Michigan Survey Research Center, by the 1972 election Democrats had declined to about 40 percent of the electorate, Republicans to about 24 percent and independents constituted about 33 percent. Figures cited in William Schneider, "Public opinion: the beginnings of ideology?," *Foreign Policy*, no. 17 (Winter 1974–5), p. 93.

9   Karl Mannheim, *Essays in the Sociology of Knowledge*, ed. Paul Kecskmeti (London: Routledge and Kegan Paul, 1952), p. 291. For a more detailed analysis of generational differences, see Ole R. Holsti and James N. Rosenau, "Does where you stand depend on when you were born? The impact of generation on post-Vietnam foreign policy beliefs," *Public Opinion Quarterly*, 44 (Spring 1980), pp. 1–22.

   The generational hypothesis seems so firmly rooted in discussions of contemporary American foreign policy that it warrants a more extensive discussion here than some of the other leaders' attributes. The same is true of gender as a correlate of foreign policy beliefs.

10 Marvin Rintala, *Three Generations: The Extreme Right Wing in Finnish Politics* (Bloomington, Ind.: Indiana University Publications, 1962); Samuel P. Huntington, "Paradigms of American politics: beyond the one, the two, and the many," *Political Science Quarterly*, 89 (1974), pp. 1–26; Stan A. Taylor and Robert S. Wood, "Image and Generation: A Social–Psychological Analysis of the Sino–Soviet Dispute," *Brigham Young University Studies*, 7 (1966), pp. 143–57; and Seymour Martin Lipset and Everett Carll Ladd, Jr, "College generations: from the 1930s to the 1960s," *Public Interest*, 25 (1971), pp. 99–113.

11 Jonathan Spivak, "Generation gap: Polish crisis is a clash of old and entrenched with impatient youth," *Wall Street Journal*, (11 February 1981), pp. 1, 20; and Spivak, "Changes in Poland's Communist Party show switch to a younger generation," *Wall Street Journal* (3 September 1981), p. 26.

12 See especially, Alan B. Spitzer, "The historical problem of generations," *American Historical Review*, 78 (1973), pp. 1353–85.

13 On generational cleavages, see Graham T. Allison, "Cool it: the foreign policy of young America," *Foreign Policy*, no. 1 (Winter 1970–1), pp. 144–60; Michael Roskin, "From Pearl Harbor to Vietnam: shifting generational paradigms and foreign policy," *Political Science Quarterly*, 89 (1974), pp. 563–88; Roger B. Handberg, Jr, "The 'Vietnam analogy': student attitudes on war," *Public Opinion Quarterly*, 36 (1972–3), pp. 612–15; Thomas J. Knight, "The passing of the Cold War generation," *Intellect*, 105 (February 1977), pp. 236–41; and Steven J. Kelman, "Youth and foreign policy," *Foreign Affairs*, 48 (April 1970), pp. 414–26. Also useful on the effects of generation are Bruce M. Russett, "The Americans' retreat from world power," *Political Science Quarterly*, 90 (1975), pp. 1–21; Kenneth J. Gergen and Kurt W. Back, "Aging, time perspective, and preferred solutions to international conflicts," *Journal of Conflict Resolution*, 9 (June 1965), pp. 177–86; Davis Bobrow, and Neal E. Cutler, "Time-oriented explanations of national security beliefs: cohort, life state and situation," *Peace Research Society (International) Papers*, 8 (1967), pp. 31–7; and Neal E. Cutler, "Generational succession as a source of foreign policy attitudes," *Journal of Peace Research*, 7 (1970), pp. 33–47.

14 Elizabeth Drew, "A reporter at large (Zbigniew Brzezinski)," *New Yorker* (1 May 1978), pp. 116–17. Many others regarded the views of the "Vietnam generation" as the best hope for this nation's future. "What the country may have learned is that it should listen to its young. They never saw the cables. They read the handwriting on the wall. The Vietnam generation was 'the best and the brightest,' the term David Halberstam applies to the glittering Kennedyites who got us into the war in the first place." Mary McGrory, "The young people had it right," *Boston Globe* (1 May 1975).

15 An article on the African policy staff of the State Department described its leading members in this way; "The four are in the same age group—39–46—and they share a common experience of disillusionment with and then opposition to the Vietnam War. All remain highly skeptical about United States military involvement, direct and indirect, in areas where they feel the national interest is not obviously at stake." Graham Hovey, "Architects of U.S. African policy privately worried by Carter's attacks on Moscow," *New York Times* (4 June 1978), p. A3. See also, Steven V. Roberts, "A critical coterie on foreign policy," *New York Times* (5 April 1982), p. A20.

16 See, for example, comments by Samuel P. Huntington in Stanley Hoffmann et al., "Vietnam reappraised," *International Security*, 6 (Summer 1981), pp. 3–27; and Representative Thomas Downey's assertion that "The children of Vietnam are the adults of El Salvador." Steven V. Roberts, "The focus turns to foreign policy," *New York Times* (3 May 1983), p. D26.

17 Percentages recalculated from the data presented in Mandelbaum and Schneider, "The New Internationalisms," table 1.

18 Hazel Erskine, "The polls: is war a mistake?," *Public Opinion Quarterly*, 34 (1970),

pp. 134–50; Philip Converse and Howard Schuman, "Silent majorities and the Vietnam War," *Scientific American*, 222 (1970), pp. 17–25; John Mueller, *War, Presidents and Public Opinion* (New York: Wiley, 1973); and William Lunch and Peter W. Sperlich, "American public opinion and the war in Vietnam." *Western Political Quarterly*, 32 (1979), pp. 21–44.

19 Allison, "Cool it: the foreign policy of young America."

20 Neumann has defined a political generation as all those who underwent essentially similar historical experiences during the crucial formative years between 17 and 25. Sigmund Neumann, *Permanent Revolution: The Total State in a World at War* (New York: Harper & Bros, 1942), pp. 235–6. The importance of this period in the life cycle is emphasized by many others, for example James David Barber, *The Presidential Character* (Englewood Cliffs, NJ: Prentice-Hall, 1972).

21 The Connecticut Mutual Life Survey revealed significant generational differences on conscription and military preparedness, with the older respondents offering greater support to these policies. However, differences were slight on questions dealing with Vietnam, immigration policy for refugees, and protectionism. These were results from the public rather than the leadership part of the study. Unfortunately, results for the latter sample were not reported by age group. *Connecticut Mutual Life Report on American Values in the 80's.*

22 For example, Kirkpatrick and Regens report:

In fact, our examination of attitudinal content on an individual item basis suggests the absence of differences between veterans and non-veterans. Such commonalities tend to provide implicit support for the garrison state concept which implies the diffusion of shared attitudes supportive of the military's role in the polity throughout the mass public. Such a conclusion is limited, however, since those experiences do have an impact on the organization of foreign policy belief systems which is masked by analyses which merely focus attention on attitudinal content. Samuel A. Kirkpatrick and James L. Regens, "Military experience and foreign policy belief systems," *Journal of Political and Military Sociology*, 6 (Spring 1978), p. 44.

23 This seems a safer prediction about the Western democracies. It may even prove to be wrong about communist nations, only one of which has ever seen a woman rise to any important political position comparable, for example, to that achieved by Margaret Thatcher, Golda Meir, Indira Gandhi, Gro Harlem Bruntland, Vigdis Finnbogadottir, or Flora MacDonald. Aside from Milka Planinc of Yugoslavia, Chiang Ch'ing (Madame Mao) may be the closest exception to the rule, but her prominence derived solely from her position as the Chairman's wife, and it did not long outlast Mao's death.

A more detailed discussion of gender differences may be found in Ole R. Holsti and James N. Rosenau, "The foreign policy beliefs of women in leadership positions," *Journal of Politics*, 43 (May 1981), pp. 326–47.

24 Among the many controversies in the enormous literature on the development of sex differences is whether their source is primarily biological (e.g. hormonal) or social (e.g. learned sex-roles). The controversy lies outside the scope of this discussion. The use here of the term "sex-role" should not be regarded as a denial of any biological differences. Rather, it seems a more appropriate term to use in an analysis that deals not only with gender but also with occupation as key variables. For excellent discussions of the various positions on the issue, see Eleanor E. Maccoby (ed.), *The Development of Sex Differences* (Stanford: Stanford University Press, 1966). Especially helpful are the chapters by the editor, David A. Hamburg and Donald T. Lunde, and Walter Mischel. Other useful introductions to the literature on gender differences may be found in Arlie Russell Hochschild, "A Review of Sex Role Research," in Joan Huber (ed.), *Changing Women in a Changing Society* (Chicago: University of Chicago Press, 1973), pp. 249–67; Martin Gruberg, *Women in American Politics* (Oshkosh: Academia Press, 1968); Rita Mae Kelly and Mary A. Boutilier, *The Making of Political Women: A Study of Socialization and Role Conflict* (Chicago: Nelson Hall, 1978); Eli Ginzberg et al., *Life Styles*

of *Educated Women* (New York: Columbia University Press, 1966); and Kathleen Newland, *Women in Politics: A Global Review* (Washington: Worldwatch Institute, 1975).

25 An extensive classified and annotated bibliography on gender differences does not list a single study of foreign policy attitudes or beliefs, either among leaders or the public at large. Roberta M. Oetzel, "Annotated Bibliography," in Maccoby, *The Development of Sex Differences*, pp. 223–351. For an exception, see James N. Rosenau, *Citizenship Between Elections: An Inquiry into the Mobilizable American* (New York: The Free Press, 1974).

26 John E. Rielly (ed.), *American Public Opinion and Foreign Policy 1975* (Chicago: Chicago Council on Foreign Relations, 1975); and Rielly, (ed.), *American Public Opinion and Foreign Policy 1979* (Chicago: Chicago Council on Foreign Relations, 1979). However, two secondary analyses of the earlier survey have examined the impact of gender, whereas a third one failed to do so. Barbara Bardes and Robert Oldendick, "Beyond internationalism: a case for multiple dimensions in the structure of foreign policy attitudes," *Social Science Quarterly*, 59 (December 1978), pp. 496–508; Eugene R. Wittkopf, "The Structure of Foreign Policy Attitudes: An Alternative View," unpublished paper, 1979; and Mandelbaum and Schneider, "The New Internationalisms," in Kenneth Oye, Donald Rothchild and Robert Lieber (eds), *Eagle Entangled: U.S. Foreign Policy in a Complex World* (New York: Longman, 1979).

27 Gabriel Almond, *The American People and Foreign Policy* (New York: Harcourt, Brace & Co., 1950), p. 121; James N. Rosenau, *National Leadership and Foreign Policy* (Princeton, NJ: Princeton University Press, 1963), p. 181.

28 Lunch and Sperlich, "American public opinion and the war in Vietnam," *Western Political Quarterly*, 32 (March 1979), pp. 34–5.

29 Naomi Lynn, "Women in American Politics: An Overview," in Jo Freeman (ed.), *Women: A Feminist Perspective* (Palo Alto, Calif.: Mayfield Publishing Co., 1975), p. 369. However, the Maggiotto and Wittkopf study of public opinion found that "hardliners" were more likely to be women, whereas "accommodationists" were most likely to be men. They did not find any significant gender-based differences among "isolationists." Maggiotto and Wittkopf, "American attitudes toward foreign policy," *International Studies Quarterly*, 25 (December 1981), pp. 601–31. Contrary evidence emerges from a recent CBS–*New York Times* poll, which found that women of every regional, religious, and socio-economic bracket were substantially more fearful than men that "Reagan will get us into war." Albert R. Hunt, "Wider gulf indicated between the President and women voters," *Wall Street Journal* (6 May 1982), p. 1. Preliminary analyses of the 1982 election also appear to have uncovered a "gender gap" in voting.

30 Rosenau, *National Leadership and Foreign Policy*.

31 The previously cited Connecticut Mutual Life survey concluded that "gender does not seem to influence how Americans feel about any political issue." Moreover, whatever slight differences occurred did not fit into any significant pattern. For example, women were slightly more supportive of a strong military, but less favorably disposed toward conscription. They were less inclined to accept refugees into the United States, and slightly more protectionist. Their views on Vietnam were essentially the same as those of men. These results are drawn from the public part of the CML survey, as the leadership results were not reported according to gender. *The Connecticut Mutual Life Report on Values in the '80s*.

32 However, women were more inclined than men to attribute expansionist foreign policy goals to China.

33 Forty-nine of the 2,282 respondents failed to identify their sex. Return rates were approximately equal for women (54 percent) and men (53 percent).

34 Women's opportunities for political activity have more frequently been available at the local level (school boards, city councils, etc.) than at the international level. For example, during the half century ending in 1970, only ten American ambassadors and ministers were women, and as late as 1967, only three of the 103 chiefs of U.S. missions abroad were women. Lynn, "Women in American Politics," p. 380.

35 A multi-dimensional study of political involvement of adolescents in the 1970s revealed that gender plays almost no role. Roberta S. Sigel and Marilyn B. Hoskin, *The Political Involvement of Adolescents* (New Brunswick, NJ: Rutgers University Press, 1981). For further evidence that there is little difference between men and women in the level of political activity, see Rosenau, *National Leadership and Foreign Policy*, p. 181; and Sidney Verba and Norman Nie, *Participation in America* (New York: Harper & Row, 1972), p. 181.

36 The double classification scheme used in these analyses yielded at least eleven respondents in all groups except two: there were only four female labor leaders, and none of the clergy were women. Although it would clearly be desirable to have more adequate representation in these two groups, the findings reported here appear to have been affected only minimally by this deficiency.

6
End of the "Vietnam Syndrome?": Continuity and Change in American Leadership Beliefs, 1976–1980

Analyses in previous chapters have focused on leadership beliefs in 1976, within a year of the final American withdrawal from Vietnam. During the next several years different foreign policy leaders, other issues, and new crises came to dominate America's external relations. Have these, combined with the passing of time, eroded the impact of Vietnam on American thinking about foreign affairs? Have they served to forge a new consensus, as Vietnam receded into the past, and as Americans found their newspapers, evening news, and political debates centering on the price and availability of imported oil, trade balances and the declining value of the dollar, the Panama Canal, human rights abroad, Cubans in Angola and Ethiopia, hostages in Iran, Russians in Afghanistan, Syrians in Lebanon, turmoil in Central America, the Camp David accords, the intricacies of SALT, MX basing modes, yellow rain, and the deterioration of détente? As a consequence, have spokesmen for the Carter and Reagan administrations, who agree on little else, been correct in asserting that these events have erased the last traces of the "Vietnam syndrome," while bringing Americans together in a new, post-Vietnam consensus? In short, have the external features and internal structure of American leadership beliefs, circa 1976, been "overtaken by events?"

A second foreign policy leadership survey was conducted in 1980, within weeks of the Teheran embassy invasion that triggered the "hostage crisis" and the Soviet invasion of Afghanistan. At the time of the survey, the hostages were beginning their fourth month of captivity with no indication of imminent release. Soviet troops had been in Afghanistan for six weeks, a period that had witnessed substantial debate reappraising the entire spectrum of relations between Washington and Moscow. Two thousand five hundred and two American leaders took part in the second survey (a response rate of over 63 percent), providing a substantial body of evidence about foreign policy beliefs in the wake of turmoil in and near the Persian Gulf area. A comparison of the 1976 and 1980 data may provide answers to some of the foregoing questions.

Expectations about change and continuity in leadership beliefs may be linked to two quite different approaches to foreign policy analysis. The first, and probably most prominent, derives from the "realist" tradition. This approach has impressive intellectual roots in both Western (e.g. Machiavelli) and non-Western (e.g. Kautilya) thought and, although it has come under critical scrutiny in recent years, its status as the dominant descriptive and prescriptive theory persists. A full exploration of that perspective, including subtle nuances that may distinguish one from another of its most important advocates, is beyond the scope of this study. For present purposes it will suffice to identify several shared themes:

- The "operational environment" and the individual's subjective interpretation of it are essentially similar.
- Guiding concepts such as "the national interest" are clear, enduring, and thus should be widely shared among those who are properly informed about international affairs.
- Important changes in the operational environment will be reflected in the individual's diagnoses of the situation and prescriptions for how to cope with it. The national interest is enduring, but altered international conditions may call for new interpretations and flexibility of response. British Foreign Minister Palmerston's aphorism—"I say that it is a narrow policy to suppose that this country or that is to be marked out as the eternal ally or perpetual enemy of England. We have no eternal allies, and we have no perpetual enemies. Our interests are eternal and perpetual, and those interests it is our duty to follow."—effectively summarizes the realist ideal.[1]

A perspective that focuses primarily on the operational environment of American foreign policy during the 1976–80 period would, with little effort, uncover substantial evidence of conflict, trauma, and change. A not implausible inference is that such events would give rise to changing diagnoses of and prescriptions for foreign policy. It is perhaps not merely fortuitous that a foremost theorist and practitioner of the realist perspective, Henry Kissinger, has in fact changed from a leading proponent of détente to a hard-line critic of even the Reagan Administration.[2] Moreover, to the extent that changes in the operational environment may pose or heighten major challenges to the nation, some convergence toward a consensus about the nature of the situation and how to cope with it would be expected.

In contrast, a "cognitive" perspective emphasizes the beliefs, images, expectations, and preferences of the individual as important factors intervening in and mediating between the operational environment and subjective interpretations of it.

- Cognitive constraints on information processing make it impossible for individuals to meet the unrealistic criteria of objective rationality.

- Diagnoses of and prescriptions for dealing with developing situations are likely to reflect not only the operational environment, but also the "intellectual baggage"—the beliefs, perceptions, preferences, expectations, and information processing—of the individual.
- When the situation is ambiguous and complex, even well-informed persons who share core conceptions of the national interest (for example, preservation of the nation's territorial security, prosperity, peace) may differ sharply on diagnoses of the situation and prescriptions on how best to cope with it.
- Barring dramatic and unambiguous evidence about a situation and its implications (for example, the meaning of and intentions behind Japan's attack on Pearl Harbor, or Hitler's invasion of Poland), individuals are likely to interpret events in the light of pre-existing beliefs.
- The more those beliefs are structured into coherent, well-integrated "belief systems," the more likely they are to shape the interpretation of incoming information, and the more likely they are to persist.

These brief summaries inevitably fail to do full justice to either the realist or cognitive approach, but the purpose here has merely been to identify some differences that may be relevant to the data derived from the 1976 and 1980 foreign policy leadership surveys. Specifically, compared to the realist viewpoint, the cognitive perspective leads one to expect greater continuity and less change in leadership beliefs, owing to the very human tendency to interpret information in ways that tend to confirm rather than challenge basic beliefs. Although the four-year period in question was hardly free from conflict and change, a perspective that is sensitive to the tendency of beliefs to persist, even in the face of ambiguous or moderately challenging information, is more likely than others to predict continuity.[3] Barring a catastrophe, such as the outbreak of a major war, it is likely that pre-existing beliefs, expectations, and preferences will significantly shape the manner in which the operational environment is interpreted. A simple example will illustrate the point. Two equally informed observers of Soviet foreign policy may agree on the major facts (some 80–90,000 Soviet troops invaded Afghanistan in December 1979) and values (the Soviet action was a gross violation of international law). But if one believes that Soviet foreign policy motives derive from a strict reading of Marxist–Leninist ideology and its imperatives, whereas the other believes that they emerge from deep-seated (if not always realistic) fears for Russian security, their diagnoses of the situation and prescriptions for American responses are likely to diverge. Indeed, each analyst may confidently conclude that the invasion offers crucial corroborating evidence in support of a preferred theory about the roots of Soviet foreign policy.

Assessments of continuity and change of foreign policy beliefs in

1976 and 1980 will proceed in several stages. The first step is to compare responses of the two samples (2,282 respondents in 1976 and 2,502 in 1980) to ninety-five items that appeared in both questionnaires. Because the samples were drawn using the same criteria and the surveys were conducted with the same procedures, confidence in the utility of these comparisons is enhanced. However, because respondents to the two surveys differed in some respects (see Table 1.2), direct comparisons of aggregate results might be misleading. Thus, subsequent analyses examine the data in more detail, with a view to determining whether the internal structure of the results varied or remained relatively constant. For example, did various occupational and other groups respond to foreign policy issues as they did in 1976? Finally, a small group of leaders took part in both the 1976 and 1980 surveys, offering the possibility of assessing changes at the individual level.

Comparing Results of the 1976 and 1980 Surveys

Sources of Failure in Vietnam

When asked to diagnose the reasons for American failure in Vietnam, leaders participating in the 1976 survey tended to emphasize the role of other actors in the conflict, with special attention to North Vietnamese dedication to their cause, aid to Hanoi from the Soviet Union and China, and the absence of widespread popular support for the Saigon regime. They also judged American goals in Vietnam to be lacking in clarity and realism. Conversely, they were not inclined to attribute great significance to such explanations as lukewarm support from America's allies, insufficient American aid to Saigon after the Paris peace agreement of 1973, neglect of military advice, or the paralyzing effects of the Watergate crimes.

Table 6.1 summarizes and compares responses to several possible sources of failure that have received substantial attention in the post-Vietnam debates on the outcome of the conflict.[4] The pattern that emerges from the data is one of striking similarities and few startling changes during the four-year period. Once again the most frequently cited causes of failure included North Vietnamese dedication, Chinese and Soviet assistance, unpopular governments in Saigon, and American goals that were both unclear and unrealistic. Indeed, responses to only a single item yielded more than marginal changes; those rating Congressional interference in the foreign policy process as a "very important" source of failure in Vietnam declined from one leader in five to one in eight, with a consequent drop in rank for that item.

One other change is perhaps worth noting. On thirteen items the number of "not sure" responses increased—rather sharply on the importance of North Vietnamese violations of the 1973 Paris peace accord, and the adequacy of American aid to Saigon after that agreement. However, responses to most explanations of defeat remained virtually identical. Continuing debates about the Vietnam War have apparently not triggered basic revisions in diagnoses of the failed American undertaking.

Table 6.1   Diagnoses of the Sources of Failure in Vietnam: Comparing the Results of the 1976 and 1980 Surveys of American Leaders

Observers of American foreign policy identified several factors that may have prevented the United States from achieving its goals in the Vietnam undertaking. In your judgment, how important were the reasons listed below in America's inability to achieve all of its goals?	1976 survey (N=2,282)		1980 survey (N=2,502)	
	Rank*	Index	Rank*	Index
Americans underestimated the dedication of the North Vietnamese	1	.80	1	.80
The Soviets and Chinese provided aid to Northern Vietnam and the Vietcong	2	.78	2	.76
The regime in Saigon lacked popular support	3	.77	3	.74
America's goals in Vietnam were inherently unrealistic	4	.75	5	.73
The U.S. had no clear goals in the Vietnam undertaking	5	.72	4	.73
The U.S. lacked an understanding of nationalism in the "Third World"	6.5	.69	6	.69
Reporting by the mass media turned the public against the war	6.5	.69	8	.68
Americans were ignorant of Vietnamese history, culture, and society	8.5	.66	10	.64
Pressures from domestic dissidents cast doubt on American commitments	8.5	.66	9	.67
The United States fought with a "no win" approach	10	.65	7	.68
Much of world opinion opposed the U.S. goals and policies	11	.62	12	.57
Intelligence agencies failed to provide adequate information about the situation in Vietnam	12	.58	11	.61
North Vietnam violated the 1973 peace agreement	13	.57	14	.54
The use of American air power was restricted	14	.56	13	.55

Table 6.1 cont.

Observers of American foreign policy identified several factors that may have prevented the United States from achieving its goals in the Vietnam undertaking. In your judgment, how important were the reasons listed below in America's inability to achieve all of its goals?	1976 survey (N=2,282)		1980 survey (N=2,502)	
	Rank*	Index	Rank*	Index
Congressional involvement hampered the executive in the conduct of the war	15	.50	18	.43
America relied excessively on air power	16	.48	16	.46
Insufficient attention was paid to advice from the military	17.5	.46	15	.47
The Watergate scandal paralyzed the American government	17.5	.46	17	.45
America's allies failed to support us	19	.41	19	.41
U.S. military assistance to South Vietnam after the 1973 peace agreement was inadequate	20	.38	20	.40
The American case was unjust	**	**	—	.36

*   Ranks, based on index scores for each item, refer to relative position. For example, ranks of 1 were assigned to the item with the highest index score in 1976, as well as to that with the highest index score for 1980. Index scores were computed by scoring a response of "very important" as 1.00 "moderately important" as 0.67, "slightly important" as 0.33 and "not at all" important as 0.00, thereby creating a scale of 0 to 1.
** Item not included in 1976 survey.

An alternative method of measuring change, ranking responses to the twenty diagnoses of American failure in Vietnam, also reveals a pattern of consistency rather than change. This conclusion is confirmed by the correlation of 0.97 between the ranks in Table 6.1.

Consequences of the War in Vietnam

Leaders taking part in the 1976 survey predicted that the most important consequences of American participation in the Vietnam War would be both domestic (neglect of non-military threats to national security; loss of faith in American government), and international (the United States will adopt a more limited conception of the national interest; loss of American credibility in the eyes of allies). They were much less inclined to agree with some of the more apocalyptic predictions that the structure of the international system had been transformed by America's failure to prevent the collapse of the Saigon regime, and that, consequently, the "tide of influence has swung toward communism as a result of the Vietnam war."

A comparison of these results with responses to the 1980 leadership survey reveals a notable absence of change in the predicted consequences of American participation in the Vietnam conflict (Table 6.2). Despite heated debates throughout the late 1970s about America's standing relative to that of its adversaries, leaders in the more recent survey were no more disposed to accept alarmist assertions about the international system and a tide swinging toward communism; these two propositions garnered strong agreement from only 8 percent and 6 percent, respectively, of the respondents, and they ranked as the least plausible results of American participation in the Vietnam War. Moreover, the controversy surrounding the costs and benefits of détente did not give rise to any significant shifts among the two samples of leaders; those agreeing with the proposition that "The major assumptions of détente have been proven false by the war in Vietnam" remained at 35 percent. Concern for the nation's international credibility persisted among a great majority of leaders, and at the same time there was only slightly greater disagreement with the view that the United States would be unable to protect its interests abroad, with force if necessary. Nor were there notable changes concerning domestic consequences of the war. An increasing tendency to trace domestic economic ills to the war in Southeast Asia was balanced by reduced agreement with the proposition that long-term economic threats had been neglected as a result of Vietnam. Finally, the majority of leaders subscribing to the belief that "The American people have lost faith in the honesty of their government as a result of Vietnam" diminished only slightly.

The dominant pattern emerging from the findings, however, is that of constancy during the four-year interval between the two surveys. On a scale of 1.00 to −1.00, the largest change for any item is a less than dramatic decline (0.13) in agreement with the assertion that the real long-term threats to national security have been neglected as a result of Vietnam. When the predicted consequences of the war are ranked, the 1976 and 1980 results reveal only minor variations, and the correlation between ranks is 0.85.

Lessons of Vietnam

This project originated in the expectation that, long after the last American had been evacuated from Saigon, policy-makers, pundits, and others would be sifting through the record of the nation's longest war to find lessons that should guide the future conduct of American external relations, and that the breadth and diversity of such lessons would be more impressive than the level of agreement about what the future should learn from the past. These expectations were largely sustained by findings from the 1976 survey, which revealed substantial agreement on a few propositions (Soviet foreign policy goals are

Table 6.2 *Prognoses of the Consequences of the War in Vietnam. Comparing the Results of the 1976 and 1980 Surveys of American Leaders*

There has been quite a bit of discussion about the consequences of the Vietnam episode. Some of these are listed below. Please indicate your assessment of each statement.	1976 survey (N=2,282)		1980 survey (N=2,502)	
	Rank*	Index	Rank*	Index
The U.S. is likely to operate with a more limited conception of the national interest as a result of the outcome in Vietnam	1	.43	2	.40
The Vietnam episode has raised doubts about American credibility in the minds of our allies	2	.38	1	.44
The real long-term threats to national security—energy shortages, the environment, etc.—have been neglected as a result of our preoccupation with Vietnam	3	.36	6	.23
The American people have lost faith in the honesty of their government as a result of the Vietnam War	4	.33	5	.25
Communist nations have been encouraged to seek triumphs elsewhere as a result of Vietnam	5	.32	4	.30
The foundations of the American economy were seriously damaged by our involvement in Vietnam	6	.22	3	.31
The memory of Vietnam will prevent the U.S. from using force even when vital American interests abroad are threatened	7	−.05	7	−.14
The shape of the international system we have known since World War II has been irrevocably altered by America's inability to prevent the collapse of the Thieu regime in 1975	8	−.12	9	−.15
The major assumptions of détente have been proven false by the war in Vietnam	9	−.13	8	−.14
The tide of influence in world affairs has swung toward communism as a result of the Vietnam War	10	−.16	10	−.23
The consequences of Vietnam are likely to continue shaping American foreign policy despite recent events in Iran and Afghanistan	**	**	—	.45

Table 6.2 cont.

There has been quite a bit of discussion about the consequences of the Vietnam episode. Some of these are listed below. Please indicate your assessment of each statement.	1976 survey (N=2,282)		1980 survey (N=2,502)	
	Rank*	Index	Rank*	Index
The lessons of Vietnam have been superseded by events since the U.S. withdrawal from Southeast Asia in 1975	**	**	—	.07

* Ranks based on index scores for each item refer to relative position. For example, ranks of 1 were assigned to the item with the highest index score in 1976, as well as to that with the highest index score in 1980. Index scores were computed by scoring a response of "agree strongly" as 1.00, "agree somewhat" as 0.50, "no opinion" as 0.00, "disagree somewhat" as −.50 and "disagree strongly" as −1.00, thereby creating a scale 1 to −1.

** Items not included in 1976 survey.

expansionist rather than defensive; graduated escalation is a dubious policy; the costs of reneging on alliance commitments are high), and almost equal disagreement with others (on the desirability of military intervention in the Middle East in response to another oil embargo). On most issues, including several that had been accepted as almost axiomatic foundations of American foreign policy only a decade or two earlier, significant disagreement emerged within the leadership sample.

Table 6.3 lists some of the lessons most often cited in the debates about the implications of the war for the future conduct of American foreign policy, with a summary of responses by leaders participating in the 1976 and 1980 surveys. As was the case with other questions dealing with the Vietnam War, responses to the twenty-nine items that appeared in both questionnaires yielded far greater similarities than differences. Even the changes that did take place were almost uniformly of minor proportions. Reduced resistance to undertaking military action in the Middle East to protect oil supplies represents one shift during the four-year interval; however, opponents of such action continued to constitute a strong majority of two-thirds, as against a comparable figure of three-fourths in 1976. An increasingly benign interpretation of Chinese foreign policy goals stands in marked contrast to beliefs about the Kremlin's external motives and its uses of détente. The nation once described as the most dangerous long-term threat to the United States was, by 1980, characterized as "expansionist rather than defensive in its foreign policy goals" by less than one leader in five. Less notable changes occurred on several aspects of foreign policy decision-making: the role of the President in defining the national interest, the propensity of the government to tell the truth, and the role of military advice. In each case the changes reflected some softening of the critical attitudes that had been evident

Table 6.3 Prescriptions of the Lessons of Vietnam: Comparing the Results of the 1976 and 1980 Surveys of American Leaders

This question asks you to indicate your position on certain foreign policy issues that are sometimes described as "lessons" we should have learned from the American experience in Vietnam. Indicate how strongly you agree or disagree with each statement.	1976 survey (N=2,282)		1980 survey (N=2,502)	
	Rank*	Index	Rank*	Index
The Soviet Union is generally expansionist rather than defensive in its foreign policy goals	1	.59	1	.61
If foreign interventions are undertaken, the necessary force should be applied in a short period of time rather than through a policy of graduated escalation	2	.55	2	.57
A nation will pay a heavy price if it honors its alliance commitments only selectively	3	.49	3	.53
An effective foreign policy is impossible when the Executive and Congress are unable to cooperate	4	.47	4	.49
The American people lack the patience for foreign policy undertakings that offer little prospect of success in the short run	5	.39	6	.35
Americans lack an understanding of the role that power plays in world politics	6	.36	5	.43
The best way to encourage democratic development in the "Third World" is for the U.S. to solve its own problems	7	.27	8	.28
There is considerable validity in the "domino theory" that when one nation falls to communism, others nearby will soon follow a similar path	8	.24	12	.17
Limited war cannot be conducted successfully because of constraints imposed by the American political system	9	.23	9	.20
Americans have relied too much on Presidents to define the national interest	10	.22	13	.13
It is vital to enlist the cooperation of the U.N. in settling international disputes	11	.20	7	.31

Table 6.3 cont.

This question asks you to indicate your position on certain foreign policy issues that are sometimes described as "lessons" we should have learned from the American experience in Vietnam. Indicate how strongly you agree or disagree with each statement.	1976 survey (N=2,282)		1980 survey (N=2,502)	
	Rank*	Index	Rank*	Index
Revolutionary forces in "Third World" countries are usually nationalistic rather than controlled by the USSR or China	12	.19	14	.12
The efficiency of military power in foreign affairs is declining	13	.17	11	.19
Détente permits the USSR to pursue policies that promote rather than restrain conflict	15	.15	10	.20
Stationing American troops in other countries encourages them to let us do their fighting for those countries	15	.15	16	.06
The press is more likely than the government to report the truth about the conduct of foreign policy	15	.15	17	.04
Weak allies excessively influence U.S. foreign policy	17.5	.04	18	.02
America's conception of its leadership role in the world must be scaled down	17.5	.04	15	−.07
The conduct of American foreign affairs relies excessively on military advice	19	.02	21	−.12
Rather than simply countering our opponent's thrusts, it is necessary to strike at the heart of the opponent's power	20	.01	19	.00
Military aid programs will eventually draw the United States into unnecessary wars	21	−.11	24	−.27
Any communist victory is a defeat for America's national interest	22	−.14	20	−.06
Limited wars should be fought primarily with air power so as to avoid introducing American ground troops	23	−.17	22	−.20
Vital interests of the U.S. are largely confined to Western Europe, Japan and the Americas	24	−.19	28	−.43
When force is used, military rather than political goals should determine its application	25	−.21	25	−.28

Table 6.3 cont.

This question asks you to indicate your position on certain foreign policy issues that are sometimes described as "lessons" we should have learned from the American experience in Vietnam. Indicate how strongly you agree or disagree with each statement.	1976 survey (N=2,282)		1980 survey (N=2,502)	
	Rank*	Index	Rank*	Index
American foreign policy should be based on the premise that the Communist "bloc" is irreparably fragmented	26	−.25	23	−.26
China is generally expansionist rather than defensive in its foreign policy goals	27	−.27	27	−.38
The freedom to dissent at home inhibits the effective conduct of American foreign policy	28	−.43	29	−.46
The U.S. should undertake military intervention in the Middle East in case of another oil embargo	29	−.50	26	−.33
The U.S. should maintain its military commitment to South Korea	**	**	—	.41
Third World conflicts cannot jeopardize vital American interests	**	**	—	−.68

* Ranks, based on index scores for each item, refer to relative position. For example, ranks of 1 were assigned to the item with the highest index score in 1976, as well as to that with the highest index score in 1980. Index scores were computed by scoring a response of "agree strongly" as 1.00, "agree somewhat" as 0.50, "no opinion" as 0.00, "disagree somewhat" as −.50, and "disagree strongly" as −1.00, thereby creating a scale of 1 to −1.
** Items not included in 1976 survey.

earlier. Views on military issues reveal a mixed pattern. The proportion of leaders opposing graduated escalation increased very slightly, and resistance to military assistance programs declined, but there was also heightened opposition to permitting military rather than political goals to dictate the use of force, and skepticism about the efficacy of military power rose. Finally, the data indicate some increased support for employing the United Nations to resolve international disputes.

One other change is worth noting—a slight decline in support for several facets of isolationism. Leaders in the 1980 sample were less inclined to define vital American interests to include only Japan, the Americas, and Western Europe, as support for this key tenet of many isolationists fell from approximately two respondents in five to one in four. Agreement with the proposition that the United States should scale down its international role fell from a four-to-three margin in agreement to an even division. Evidence along these lines also emerges from two other items. Strong majorities agreed that the United States should maintain its commitment to South Korea (73 percent), and rejected the proposition that "Third World conflicts cannot jeopardize American interests" (89 percent, with 61 percent expressing strong disagreement). However, the latter two items did not appear in the 1976 questionnaire, and one should thus be cautious in drawing inferences about trends from responses to them.

Revisions on these issues notwithstanding, only minor variations marked responses to the great majority of them. That continuity between 1976 and 1980 outweighed change is evident in the high correlation—0.96—between the ranking of responses in Table 6.3. Extensive debates on the relevance of the conflict in Southeast Asia for contemporary American policy in the Middle East, Africa, and Central America appear to have solidified rather than transformed leadership beliefs about "the lessons of Vietnam."

Foreign Policy Goals

Comparisons of the 1976 and 1980 surveys have, to this point, been limited to interpretations of the Vietnam War. The data have revealed substantial persistence of leadership beliefs about Vietnam during the late 1970s. It remains to be determined, however, whether a similar pattern emerges on a broader spectrum of foreign policy issues.

Both leadership surveys included a cluster of questions on the importance of various foreign policy goals, responses to which are summarized in Table 6.4. The evidence once again points to a rather striking durability of leadership views, far outstripping indications of any fundamental transformations. More specifically, variations between the 1976 and 1980 results are uniformly confined to a narrow span of less than one-tenth of the scale ranging from 0 to 1.0.

Three closely related items focusing on American security responsibilities abroad—strengthening friendly countries, the security of allies, and maintaining a global balance of power—reveal a pattern in which each of the goals was accorded heightened importance. In 1976 these goals were rated as "very important" by 23 percent, 37 percent and 44 percent respectively, whereas the comparable figures four years later were 37 percent, 44 percent and 55 percent. These results would appear to be consistent with the observation that there may have been some diminution of isolationist sentiment during the interval between 1976 and 1980. However, in the absence of similar data from the mid-1950s, a period during which American alliance commitments expanded rapidly, it is only possible to speculate about the longer-term significance of these responses. It is a plausible guess that the 1976 survey took place at or near a post-1945 low point in support for global security commitments, and

Table 6.4 *Goals of American Foreign Policy: Comparing the Results of the 1976 and 1980 Surveys of American Leaders*

Turning to more general considerations, here is a list of possible foreign policy goals that the United States might have. Please indicate how much importance you think should be attached to each goal.	1976 survey (N=2,282)		1980 survey (N=2,502)	
	Rank*	Index	Rank*	Index
Promoting and defending our own security	1	.92	1	.95
Securing adequate supplies of energy	2.5	.85	2	.88
Keeping peace in the world	2.5	.85	3	.87
Fostering international cooperation to solve common problems, such as food, inflation and energy	4	.84	4	.86
Worldwide arms control	5	.82	6	.74
Combatting world hunger	6	.72	7	.73
Maintaining a balance of power among nations	7	.69	5	.76
Defending our allies' security	8	.67	8	.71
Helping to improve the standard of living in less developed countries	9	.65	9	.68
Containing communism	10	.63	11	.65
Protecting the jobs of American workers	11	.59	12	.58
Strengthening countries who are friendly toward us	12	.57	10	.67
Protecting weaker nations against foreign aggression	13	.53	13	.58
Strengthening the United Nations	14	.47	14	.53
Protecting the interests of American business abroad	15	.44	15	.50
Helping to bring a democratic form of government to other nations	16	.33	16	.38
Promoting the development of capitalism abroad	17	.24	17	.31
Keeping up the value of the dollar	**	**	—	.81
Protecting the global environment	**	**	—	.70
Worldwide population control	**	**	—	.67
Promoting and defending human rights in other countries	**	**	—	.52

 * Ranks, based on index scores for each item, refer to relative position. For example, ranks of 1 were assigned to the item with the highest index score in 1976, as well as to that with the highest index score in 1980. Index scores were computed by scoring a response of "very important" as 1.00, "somewhat important" as 0.50, and "not at all important" as 0.00, thereby creating a scale of 0 to 1.
 ** Items not included in 1976 survey.

that the 1980 data represent only a partial rebound that falls short of the support that a similar survey might have uncovered a quarter century earlier.

Three other small changes are worth noting. Those who described strengthening the United Nations as "very important" increased moderately, from approximately one leader in four (a very low baseline) to one in three. This is consistent with responses to another item cited earlier (Table 6.3)—"It is vital to enlist the cooperation of the U.N. in settling international disputes"—support for which increased from 63 percent to 70 percent. Evidently, strident attacks on the United Nations by some prominent politicians in both major political parties have not had an especially deep impact. The goal of promoting capitalism abroad did not gain many adherents, but those describing it as "not at all important" declined from 53 percent to 46 percent. Finally, the high level of importance ascribed to arms control in 1976—two-thirds of the leaders rated it as "very important"—eroded somewhat, but it remained at a relatively high level. The controversy surrounding SALT II, both before and after the Treaty had been withdrawn from the Senate in the wake of the Afghanistan invasion, an action that took place just a few weeks prior to the 1980 survey, was almost surely a contributing factor. Indeed, the persistence of concern for arms control, in the face of attacks on SALT and of the electoral successes in 1980 of its most vocal critics, may be more significant than the moderate erosion in importance accorded to the issue.

Infinitesimal shifts characterized the ratings of other foreign policy goals by the two samples of American leaders. That continuity is the predominant pattern in these data is also reflected by an analysis of the relative importance attributed to the goals. The most important goals (security, energy, peace, and international cooperation) were the same in both 1976 and 1980, as were the least important ones (strengthening the United Nations, promotion of business interests, democracy and capitalism abroad). The correlation between rankings of the seventeen issues common to both surveys—0.98—confirms that assessments of foreign policy goals remained quite constant during the four-year period between the two surveys.

Foreign Policy Performance

Leaders taking part in these surveys were also asked to appraise "the job that the United States is now doing" with respect to some of the foreign policy goals discussed above.[5] Data on other clusters of foreign policy issues have revealed a notable stability in leadership beliefs. The pattern that emerges from performance ratings is strikingly different. Respondents in the 1976 survey could not be described as having offered a ringing endorsement of the manner in which the United States was pursuing a variety of external undertakings, as "poor" ratings outnumbered "excellent" ones on every issue save one: "promoting and defending our own security." Despite this very low baseline against which to measure subsequent responses, appraisals of American foreign policy were even more dismal in 1980, as performance ratings declined on all ten items listed in Table 6.5, quite sharply in several cases. Leaders judging American performance as "excellent" on any issue were in a distinct minority; only 5 percent did so in connection with "promoting and defending our own security." Although that judgment represents a sharp decline from the comparable figure in 1976 (21 percent), Washington's conduct of foreign affairs on the other nine issues was rated even more negatively! Even if we assume that both "excellent" and "pretty good" assessments indicate approval, performance ratings on every single goal fell well short of achieving a favorable rating from a majority.

Table 6.5 *Assessments of Foreign Policy Performance: Comparing the Results of the 1976 and 1980 Surveys of American Leaders*

Now, please indicate how you would rate the job that the United States is now doing with respect to these goals.	1976 survey (N=2,282)		1980 survey (N=2,502)	
	Rank*	Index	Rank*	Index
Promoting and defending our own security	1	.23	1	−.12
Maintaining a balance of power among nations	2	.02	5	−.35
Defending our allies' security	3	.01	2	−.19
Protecting the interests of American business abroad	4	.00	3	−.23
Protecting the jobs of American workers	5	−.11	4	−.33
Fostering international cooperation to solve common problems, such as food, inflation, and energy	6	−.23	6	−.46
Helping to improve the standard of living in less developed countries	7	−.31	7	−.47
Worldwide arms control	8	−.39	10	−.73
Securing adequate supplies of energy	9	−.45	9	−.61
Containing communism	10	−.49	8	−.57
Promoting and defending human rights in other countries	**	**	—	−.41
Keeping up the value of the dollar	**	**	—	−.79

* Ranks, based on index scores for each item, refer to relative position. For example, ranks of 1 were assigned to the item with the highest index score in 1976, as well as to that with the highest index score in 1980. Index scores were computed by scoring a response of "excellent" as 1.00, "pretty good" as 0.50, "not sure" as 0.00, "fair" as −0.50, and "poor" as −1.00, thereby creating a scale of 1 to −1.
** Items not included in 1976 survey.

Conversely, over 80 percent of the respondents offered a negative judgment (either "poor" or "fair") on several issues: arms control, energy, containment, international cooperation, and protection of the dollar. It may be worth noting that these were not viewed as trivial issues, as four of them ranked among the seven most important foreign policy goals (Table 6.4). Moreover, on seven of the ten issues that appeared in both the 1976 and 1980 surveys, assessments declined by .20 or more on a scale of 1.0 to −1.0.

One should be wary about adducing broad generalizations from these findings. Caution is especially appropriate when searching for explanations of electoral outcomes in terms of foreign policy issues. The evidence that such issues rarely achieve primary rank among lists of causal factors in electoral behavior is voluminous, and it need not be reviewed here. However, the present findings may at least provide some fuel for speculation about the 1980 election, which not only brought an outspoken critic of American foreign policy into the White House, but it also resulted in the defeat of several Senators who had achieved some prominence in matters of external relations, including Frank Church and George McGovern. As a result, the victors and their supporters have not been reticent to claim a "mandate" in support of a thorough-going transformation of American foreign and national security policies.

The present data suggest that perhaps such claims are somewhat overdrawn, and that these results may be at least equally consistent with a somewhat more modest interpretation. The persistence of leadership beliefs on so many fundamental questions relating to this nation's goals, its relations with key nations and regions, and its general orientation toward international affairs has emerged from the evidence with a consistency that cannot be dismissed lightly. At the same time, the figures in Table 6.5 can only be read as an expression of deep and pervasive dissatisfaction with the formulation and execution of foreign policy, not only during the Carter years (as indexed by the 1980 data), but also during the previous administrations (as shown in the 1976 figures). Taken as a whole, the evidence can perhaps be summarized in this way: "Let us change directions incrementally rather than dramatically, but by all means let us be more competent in the conduct of foreign policy." The last two chapters will explore this interpretation in more detail.

America's Role in the World

Responses to a cluster of seven items about various American roles in the world reveal few changes during the four-year period (Table 6.6). The proposition that it is permissible to use the CIA to undermine hostile governments received strong agreement from 28 percent of the leaders in the 1980 sample, an increase of 7 percent and the balance between approval and disapproval of such action shifted from 51 percent–46 percent in 1976 to 56 percent–43 percent four years later.

Part of the explanation may be that the earlier survey took place at a time when Congressional inquiries into CIA activities gave the issue a currency that was absent in 1980.

Support for the thesis that "The United States has a moral obligation to prevent destruction of the state of Israel" was expressed by two respondents in five, whereas the comparable figure four years earlier was one in three. It should be noted, however, that on another question relating to the Middle East, "maintaining the security of Israel" was identified by only 7 percent as the goal that should guide Ameri-

Table 6.6 *America's Role in the World: Comparing the Results of the 1976 and 1980 Surveys of American Leader*

Somewhat more specifically, please indicate how strongly you agree or disagree with each of the following statements concerning America's role in the world	1976 survey (N=2,282)		1980 survey (N=2,502)	
	Ranks*	Index	Ranks*	Index
The U.S. has a moral obligation to prevent the destruction of the state of Israel	1	.31	1	.41
There is nothing wrong with using the CIA to try to undermine hostile governments	2	−.02	2	.08
The U.S. should give economic aid to poorer countries even if it means higher prices at home	3	−.05	3	.00
Even though it probably means higher food prices here at home, it is worth selling grain to the Soviet Union since it may improve our relations with Russia	4	−.23	7	−.44
We shouldn't think so much in international terms but concentrate more on our own national problems	5	−.24	5	−.24
The U.S. should take all steps including the use of force to prevent the spread of Communism	6	−.29	4	−.23
It is not in our interest to have better relations with the Soviet Union because we are getting less than we are giving to them	7	−.33	6	−.36

* Ranks, based on index scores for each item, refer to relative position. For example, ranks of 1 were assigned to the item with the highest index score in 1976, as well as to that with the highest index score in 1980. Index scores were computed by scoring a response of "agree strongly" as 1.00, "agree somewhat" as 0.50, "no opinion" as 0.00, "disagree somewhat" as 0.50, and "disagree strongly" as −1.00, thereby creating a scale of 1 to −1.

can policy in the region, well behind the majority (51 percent) who favored "maintaining an effective balance of power in the region." And, of course, these responses predate by over two years Israel's controversial invasion of Lebanon.

Despite the invasion of Afghanistan, dramatic changes were notably absent with respect to beliefs about Soviet–American relations. Disapproval of grain sales to the USSR increased from 28 percent to 39 percent. Two points are worth making in connection with this finding, however. The 1980 survey began just a few weeks after President Carter imposed an embargo on new grain sales to the Soviet Union in response to the invasion of Afghanistan, and the occupational group that expressed the greatest displeasure with that step— farmers—had very limited representation in either the 1976 or 1980 samples of leaders. The majority disapproving the use of all necessary means to prevent the spread of communism declined very slightly from 65 percent to 62 percent, but opposition to better relations between Moscow and Washington also decreased. Thus, despite a strong agreement that Soviet foreign policy goals are expansionist (Table 6.1), there appears to have been a notable lack of convergence in 1980 toward a hard-line approach to relations with the Kremlin.

On balance, however, the pattern of persistence in leadership beliefs is evident. The propositions receiving the strongest support in 1976—those relating to Israel, the CIA, and aid to poor countries— were the same four years later, and the correlation between rankings of the seven items is 0.75.

The 1976 and 1980 Surveys: Group Comparisons

Revealing as the comparison of the 1976 and 1980 surveys may be, and as much as they may tell us about continuity and change during the four-year period, it is necessary to probe more deeply into the data for several reasons.

● The two groups of leaders, although developed by similar sampling criteria in 1976 and 1980, nevertheless differ in some important respects. For example, access in 1980 to a higher level military school reduced the size of the military officer group, whereas higher return rates in the same survey resulted in stronger representation of labor leaders and clergy. (More details on the composition of the two groups of respondents may be found in Table 1.2.)
● Many of the most revealing findings that emerged from the 1976 survey resulted from analyses between groups of leaders classified in various ways. For example, the data indicated that the most potent predictor of foreign policy beliefs was the respondent's policy preferences on Vietnam during the early and late stages of the war in (Chapters 2 and 3). This was true not only with respect to interpretations of that conflict, but also on many other issues. Conversely other

analyses revealed that widespread speculation about generation and gender as sources of domestic cleavages on foreign policy were not sustained. Perhaps the pervasiveness of popular images describing men as more "hawkish" than women, and of members of the Vietnam generation as more "dovish" or isolationist than their elders, may be traced to beliefs that these relationships are so "obvious" as to reduce the need for empirical scrutiny. In any case, the 1976 data revealed that age and gender are among the weakest explanations of differences in foreign policy beliefs.

• A robust test of competing theories about continuity and change during the 1976–80 period requires examination not only of the aggregate results, but also of more complex relationships within the data. The findings discussed in the previous section are but one stage in a thorough analysis. The next step is to determine whether the same patterns of group differences that characterized the 1976 data also emerge from the survey undertaken four years later. For example, are the 1976 findings relating to the explanatory potency of Vietnam policy positions, generation, and gender also to be found in the 1980 data, or does the tendency toward continuity in the entire samples in fact mask important shifts that can only be uncovered through careful analyses of subgroups?

The purpose here is thus not to undertake a full-scale analysis of the 1980 data in the same detail that characterized Chapters 2 through 5. Rather, it is to determine whether there are internal differences in the 1976 and 1980 responses that would make it necessary to add important qualifications to the tentative conclusion that leadership beliefs remained exceptionally stable during the four-year period in question. Four types of analyses will be undertaken.

• Special attention will be paid to the relationship between "Vietnam policy positions" and other foreign policy beliefs, for two reasons: it proved to be a potent predictor of a wide range of foreign policy beliefs in the earlier analyses; moreover, as revealed in Chapter 1, current foreign policy debates continue to be dominated by the Vietnam analogy and by disagreements about the persistence and consequences of the "Vietnam syndrome."
• Other possible correlates of foreign policy beliefs—occupation, ideology, party, generation, and the like—will be examined with a view to assessing what significant shifts, if any, might have occurred during the 1976–80 period.
• Analyses in Chapter 4 revealed the existence of three quite distinct ways of thinking about foreign relations. Whether and to what extent these belief systems may have persisted will be explored in the 1980 data.
• A small group of ninety-five respondents took part in both surveys, making possible assessment of constancy and change at the individual level.

Vietnam Policy Position

An important reason for undertaking the 1980 survey was to gauge the continuing impact of the Vietnam experience on leadership views. For substantive and theoretical reasons, leaders' preferences about American policy in Vietnam played a central role in this examination of foreign policy beliefs. The question is not without policy implications as well. Observations that the hostage crisis and invasion of Afghanistan have—or should have—put an end to the "Vietnam syndrome" have been made regularly by proponents of a more assertive foreign policy. Because the 1980 survey was initiated less than three months after these events in Southwest Asia, the findings may be especially germane.

A classification scheme based on Vietnam policy preferences (Table 2.2) represents an effort to isolate the possible impact of Vietnam from such standard background characteristics as occupation, political party, ideology, gender, and the like. In the 1976 data it proved to be a powerful explanatory variable, one that withstood repeated efforts to undermine it by a series of multivariate analyses. Although not wholly independent from such factors as ideology or occupation, its potency remained even when other respondent attributes were held constant. The major conclusion can be summarized succinctly: the Vietnam experience compelled some American leaders to reassess their fundamental beliefs about foreign affairs; for others it confirmed previously held beliefs; the result was an American leadership divided by competing, internally-consistent, and largely mutually-exclusive belief systems that cannot be explained fully by reference to such standard background attributes as occupation.

The figures in Table 6.7 and 6.8 reveal a striking similarity of responses by leaders taking part in the 1976 and 1980 surveys. In both cases, majorities recall initially having supported the goal of victory in Vietnam, and later having advocated a complete withdrawal of American forces from Southeast Asia. Moreover, responses in both surveys yielded distributions of leaders across the seven groups— Supporters, Converted Supporters, Ambivalent Supporters, Ambivalents, Ambivalent Critics, Converted Critics, and Critics—that are virtually identical. But the more important question here is whether the pattern of responses by leaders in each group matched or varied from those of their counterparts four years earlier. The evidence offers a rather unambiguous answer: the seven groups continue to be characterized by sharply divergent views on virtually all aspects of foreign affairs, and cleavages within the 1980 sample are very similar to those recorded four years earlier. These conclusions may be documented in several ways.

• The ninety-five substantive items shared by the two surveys deal with interpretations of the Vietnam War, the nation's foreign policy

Table 6.7   Vietnam Policy Preferences: Comparing the Results of the 1976 and 1980 Surveys of American Leaders

Some people felt that we should have done everything possible to gain a complete military victory in Vietnam. Others felt that we should have withdrawn as soon as possible. Still others had opinions in between these two. Please indicate which position came closest to your own feelings—both when the war first became an issue (in the mid-1960s) and later toward the end of U.S. involvement (during the early 1970s).	(in percentages)			
	When the war first became an issue		Toward the end of U.S. involvement	
	1976 (N=2,282)	1980 (N=2,502)	1976 (N=2,282)	1980 (N=2,502)
I tended to favor a complete military victory	51	54	22	24
I tended to favor a complete withdrawal	22	21	57	54
I tended to feel in between these two	22	22	18	20
Not sure	5	3	3	2

goals and performance in achieving them, America's role in the world, and two domestic issues. Significant differences among the seven groups defined by Vietnam policy positions emerged on eighty-six of the ninety-five questions. Moreover, the pattern of significant and non-significant differences in the two surveys reveals impressive continuity, as only six of the ninety-five failed to yield similar results.

• Several earlier analyses of the 1976 data focused upon eight key issues because they reflect some important aspects of post-Vietnam foreign policy debates in the United States: the nature of the contemporary international system, Soviet foreign policy motives, détente, the Middle East, Third World revolutions, and the like. The 1976 and 1980 responses reveal very similar patterns, as disparities between Supporters and Critics persisted, whereas those within these groups but across the four-year time period did not (Table 6.9).

• A broader and more comprehensive way of reporting the results is to rank-order responses by leaders in each group to several clusters of questions that appeared in both surveys. Table 6.10 lists group diagnoses of the most important sources of failure in Vietnam, and compares them to rankings that emerged from the earlier survey. The results once again reveal sharp differences between groups, and strong similarities across time. As in the earlier survey, those on the Supporters end of the scale traced the lack of success in the Vietnam undertaking to self-imposed constraints and deficiencies, whereas leaders at the other end of the spectrum tended to assess the situation in Vietnam as one that offered little prospect of success, even had different strategies and tactics been employed. With only minor variations, moreover, those in each group tended to espouse the same diagnoses as their counterparts in the earlier study.

Table 6.8   The 2,282 1976 Respondents and 2,502 1980 Respondents Classified into Seven Groups by Positions in Vietnam During Early and Late Stages of the War*

Some people felt that we should have done everything possible to gain a complete military victory in Vietnam. Others felt that we should have withdrawn as soon as possible. Still others had opinions in between these two. Please indicate which position came closest to your own feelings—both when the war first became an issue (in the mid-1960s) and later toward the end of U.S. involvement (during the early 1970s).

TOWARD THE END OF U.S. INVOLVEMENT

WHEN THE WAR FIRST BECAME AN ISSUE	I tended to favor a complete military victory	I tended to feel in between these two	Not sure	I tended to favor a complete withdrawal
I tended to favor a complete military victory	SUPPORTERS 1976: 15.9% 1980: 18.4%	AMBIVALENT SUPPORTERS 1976: 15.2% 1980: 15.8%		CONVERTED CRITICS 1976: 38.0% 1980: 35.6%
I tended to feel in between these two	CONVERTED SUPPORTERS 1976: 5.6% 1980: 4.8%	AMBIVALENTS 1976: 5.6% 1980: 5.9%		
Not sure				
I tended to favor a complete withdrawal		AMBIVALENT CRITICS 1976: 2.8% 1980: 2.0%		CRITICS 1976: 16.6% 1980: 16.1%

* Nine 1976 respondents (0.4%) and thirty-three 1980 respondents (1.3%) did not indicate their position on Vietnam in either the early or late stages of the war.

● A similar analysis of the predicted consequences of American participation in the Vietnam conflict also reveals the persistence of substantial diversity between groups, and only minor ones across the two surveys (Table 6.11). As had been the case in 1976, leaders on the Supporter end of the scale once again foresaw the costs of Vietnam to be a marked deterioration of America's international position, with respect to both adversaries (who have been encouraged) and allies (who have come to doubt America's credibility). In contrast, the Critics tended to emphasize adverse domestic results, including neglect of non-military threats to security, damage to the economy, and loss of faith in the government.

● Table 6.12 identifies the most important lessons of Vietnam adduced by leaders in the seven groups. Significant disagreement between the seven groups are evident in the selection and ranking of lessons; for example, that regarded as most important by Supporters does not appear on the Critics' list, and vice versa. Not a single item appears on all seven lists. Thus, leaders in various groups appear to resemble the blind men who, grasping different parts of the elephant, drew quite different conclusions about the shape of the beast.

Although the two questionnaires shared twenty-nine possible lessons of Vietnam, group rankings of the most important ones in 1980 are quite similar, if not identical, to those emerging from the 1976 data.

Table 6.9 *Comparing Responses by "Supporters" and "Critics" to Selected Items in the 1976 and 1980 Surveys*

(in percentages)

		SUPPORTERS*		CRITICS**	
		Agree	Disagree	Agree	Disagree
	Survey	strongly	strongly	strongly	strongly
Any communist victory is a defeat for America's national interest	1976	42	5	2	51
	1980	40	7	5	48
There is considerable validity in the "domino theory" that when one nation falls to communism, others nearby will soon follow a similar path	1976	54	1	3	40
	1980	51	2	4	42
The U.S. should undertake military intervention in the Middle East in case of another oil embargo	1976	14	23	2	75
	1980	16	18	3	63
America's conception of its leadership role in the world must be scaled down	1976	5	44	32	8
	1980	4	50	29	11
Détente permits the USSR to pursue policies that promote rather than restrain conflict	1976	42	1	7	19
	1980	50	2	8	20
The Soviet Union is generally expansionist rather than defensive in its foreign policy goals	1976	70	1	25	6
	1980	81	1	27	8
The U.S. should take all steps including the use of force to prevent the spread of Communism	1976	32	8	1	68
	1980	30	8	3	60
Revolutionary forces in "Third World" countries are usually nationalistic rather than controlled by the USSR or China	1976	6	27	41	3
	1980	6	31	40	6

  * N=363 in 1976; 461 in 1980.
 ** N=378 in 1976; 402 in 1980.

Table 6.10 The Sources of Failure in Vietnam, Ranked in the 1976 and 1980 Surveys by Leaders Grouped According to Vietnam Policy Preferences During the Early and Late Stages of the War*

Sources of failure	Supporters 1976	Supporters 1980	Converted Supporters 1976	Converted Supporters 1980	Ambivalent Supporters 1976	Ambivalent Supporters 1980	Ambivalents 1976	Ambivalents 1980	Ambivalent Critics 1976	Ambivalent Critics 1980	Converted Critics 1976	Converted Critics 1980	Critics 1976	Critics 1980
The U.S. fought with a "no win" approach	1	1	1	1	2	2								
The use of air power was restricted	2	2	3	2										
Soviet and Chinese aid to North Vietnam	3	3	2	3	1	1	1	1						
Dissidents cast doubt on U.S. commitments					[5]	3	3	[4]						
N. Vietnamese dedication underestimated					3	[4]	2	2	[4]	1	1	1	3	3
Saigon regime lacked popular support							[5]	3	2	[4]	2	2	2	2
U.S. goals in Vietnam were unrealistic									1	2	3	3	1	1
U.S. misunderstood Third World nationalism									3	3				

* This table includes the three most important sources of failure for each group in 1976 and 1980. Ranks in brackets are not among the top three, but are included to facilitate comparison. The wording of some items is abbreviated. For the full text, see Table 6.1.

Table 6.11 Consequences of the War in Vietnam, Ranked in the 1976 and 1980 Surveys by Leaders Grouped According to Vietnam Policy Preferences During the Early and Late Stages of the War*

Consequences of Vietnam	Supporters		Converted Supporters		Ambivalent Supporters		Ambivalents		Ambivalent Critics		Converted Critics		Critics	
	1976	1980	1976	1980	1976	1980	1976	1980	1976	1980	1976	1980	1976	1980
Communist nations have been encouraged to seek other triumphs	1	1	1	2	1	2	2	3						
Vietnam has raised profound doubts about American credibility in the minds of allies	2	2	2	1	2	1					[5]	3		
The U.S. is likely to operate with a more limited conception of the national interest	3	3	3	3	3	3	3	2	[4]	1	2	1		
The foundations of the American economy were severely damaged							1	1	1	2	[4]	2	2	3
Real long-term threats to national security have been neglected									2	3	1	[4]	3	2
Americans lost faith in the honesty of their government									3	[4]	3	[5]	1	1

* This table includes the three most important consequences of the war in Vietnam for each group in 1976 and 1980. Ranks in brackets are not among the top three, but are included to facilitate comparison. The wording of some items is abbreviated. For the full text, see Table 6.2.

Table 6.12 The Lessons of Vietnam, Ranked in the 1976 and 1980 Surveys by Leaders Grouped According to Vietnam Policy Preferences During the Early and Late Stages of the War*

Lessons of Vietnam	Supporters 1976	Supporters 1980	Converted Supporters 1976	Converted Supporters 1980	Ambivalent Supporters 1976	Ambivalent Supporters 1980	Ambivalents 1976	Ambivalents 1980	Ambivalent Critics 1976	Ambivalent Critics 1980	Converted Critics 1976	Converted Critics 1980	Critics 1976	Critics 1980
In interventions, avoid graduated escalation	1	1	2	1	1	2					2	3		
Soviet foreign policy goals are expansionist	2	2	1	2	2	1	1	1	[5]	2	1	1		
Must honor all alliance commitments	3	3	3	3	[4]	3	2	2	[12]	3				
The "domino theory" is valid					3	[6]								
Executive–legislative cooperation is vital							3	[5]	2	1	3	2	[10]	3
Americans don't understand power							[7]	3						
American people lack patience									3	[7]				
Enlist U.N. cooperation to solve disputes													[5]	1
Third World revolutionaries are nationalistic													[4]	2
Too much reliance on Presidents to define the national interest									1	[5]			3	[9]
Excessive reliance on military advice													2	[4]
The press is more likely than government to tell the truth on foreign policy													1	[8]

* This table includes the three most important lessons of Vietnam for each group in 1976 and 1980. Ranks in brackets are not among the top three, but are included to facilitate comparison. Wording of some items is abbreviated. For the full text, see Table 6.3.

Thus, as did their counterparts four years earlier, leaders in the 1980 survey maintained quite different—internally consistent and mutually exclusive—interpretations of the Vietnam experience. If the so-called "Vietnam syndrome" derives in part from domestic divisions on the meaning of that conflict, then one must conclude that little changed between 1976 and 1980. Indeed, the evidence points to this conclusion: the impact of Vietnam persists as a source of dissensus rather than consensus.

• Further evidence that continuity between 1976 and 1980 is not confined to Vietnam-related issues emerges from respondents' assessments of seventeen foreign policy goals (Table 6.13). Although the list includes several goals that would seem to be relatively non-controversial—for example, maintaining American security, or world peace—leaders in the seven groups defined by Vietnam policy positions were no less divided than their 1976 counterparts on the importance they attributed to them. Supporters gave top priority to strategic and security concerns, whereas leaders at the Critic end of the scale emphasized non-military foreign policy goals. Equally striking is the close correspondence of the 1976 and 1980 goal rankings within the seven groups.

• Finally, the proposition that the United States has a moral obligation to prevent destruction of Israel represents a bridge across the seven groups (Table 6.14). Beyond that single common denominator, differences between groups outweigh the similarities in conceptions of America's role in the world, with notable divergences on the relative importance of strategic–military and other aspects of foreign affairs. With few exceptions, the priorities within each group remained stable during the four-year interval between the two surveys.

In view of the central role played by the Vietnam policy position variable in responses to the 1976 survey, the comparable 1980 results are of special importance for assessing competing theories of constancy and change in leadership beliefs about foreign affairs. It is not overstating the findings to conclude that response patterns characterizing the 1976 leadership sample have persisted into 1980, despite dramatic events during the intervening four-year period. An architectural metaphor may be used to emphasize this point. Analyses in the previous section established the existence of two structures with very similar external features, whereas those summarized here initiated the process of examining more closely the parts of which the structures are composed, and their interrelationships. They were found to be sufficiently similar that initial impressions, based solely on outward features of the structures, have received substantial confirmation.

Other Leader Attributes

The Vietnam policy position classification scheme played a central role in analyses of the 1976 survey, but interesting findings also

Table 6.13 The Goals of American Foreign Policy, Ranked in the 1976 and 1980 Surveys by Leaders Grouped According to Vietnam Policy Preferences During the Early and Late Stages of the War*

	Supporters		Converted Supporters		Ambivalent Supporters		Ambivalent Critics		Converted Critics		Critics	
	1976	1980	1976	1980	1976	1980	1976	1980	1976	1980	1976	1980
Promoting and defending our own security	1	1	1	1	1	1	3.5	1	1	1		
Securing adequate supplies of energy	2	2	2	2	[4.5]	2	2	[4]	3.5	[4]		
Containing communism	3	3										
Keeping peace in the world			3	[4]	2	3		2	3.5	2	3	2
Fostering international cooperation on economic issues			[4]	3	3	[4]	1	3	2	3	1	1
Worldwide arms control							3.5	[6]			2	3

* This table includes the three most important foreign policy goals for each group in 1976 and 1980. Ranks in brackets are not among the top three, but are included to facilitate comparison. The wording for some items is abbreviated. For the full text, see Table 6.4.

Table 6.14 America's Role in the World, Ranked in the 1976 and 1980 Surveys by Leaders Grouped According to Vietnam Policy Preferences During the Early and Late Stages of the War

U.S. role	Supporters		Converted Supporters		Ambivalent Supporters		Ambivalents		Ambivalent Critics		Converted Critics		Critics	
	1976	1980	1976	1980	1976	1980	1976	1980	1976	1980	1976	1980	1976	1980
There is nothing wrong with using the CIA to try to undermine hostile governments	1	1	1	1	1	2	3	2	[4]	3	3	3	1	1
The U.S. should take all steps, including the use of force, to prevent the spread of Communism	2	2	3	3	3	3								
The U.S. has a moral obligation to prevent destruction of the state of Israel	3	3	2	2	2	1								
We shouldn't think so much in international terms, but concentrate more on our own national problems							1	1	1	1	1	1	1	1
The U.S. should give economic aid to poorer countries even if it means higher prices here at home							2	3	3	[4]	[4]		[4]	3
Even though it probably means higher prices here at home, it is worth selling grain to the Soviet Union since it may improve our relations with Russia								3	2	2	2	2	2	2
											3		3	[4]

emerged from assessments in Chapter 5 of other group differences. These may be summarized briefly. Ideology shared with Vietnam policy position the top rank as the most potent predictor of foreign policy beliefs. Differences between occupations were also quite pronounced; for example, media leaders, clergy, and educators tended to adhere to views labelled as Post-Cold War Internationalism, military officers and business executives predominated among Cold War Internationalists, and labor leaders were substantially more pronounced in supporting semi-Isolationism than any other occupational group. Political party preferences were also related to foreign policy beliefs, but those relationships largely disappeared if ideology were held constant. Military service proved to be a rather weak predictor of foreign policy beliefs; it was especially weak after controlling for occupation, thereby permitting a distinction between career military officers and leaders who had experienced limited service in the armed forces. Finally, age and gender differences were especially weak explanatory factors; the most pronounced divisions cut within rather than across generations, and in most respects women and men responded very similarly to a broad range of foreign policy issues.

The question to be addressed here is whether responses to the 1980 survey yield a similar pattern of relationships. A detailed exposition of results for each respondent attribute would require a vast number of tables. As an alternative, Table 6.15 provides a compact summary of findings for the ninety-five items appearing in both questionnaires. The 1980 results bear a marked resemblance to those of the earlier survey, as summarized above. The relative potency of the several background attributes remains essentially unchanged and the pattern of group responses persists. For example, military officers and business executives consistently expressed views at one end of the scale, whereas media leaders, clergy, and educators tended to adopt a diametrically different position on a broad range of issues. These results provide further confirmation for the thesis of continuity rather than change in the foreign policy beliefs of American leaders.

Table 6.15 *Relationship of Seven Respondent Attributes and Ninety-five Issues in the 1980 Survey of 2,502 American Leaders*

	Numbers of items for which contingency coefficient (C) is:			
	.45 or more	.35–.44	.25–.34	.24 or less
Ideology	7	21	27	40
Vietnam policy position	7	19	28	41
Occupation	0	2	32	61
Political party	0	2	27	66
Generation	0	0	0	95
Military service	0	0	0	95
Gender	0	0	0	95

Three Foreign Policy Relief Systems

Chapter 4 described three quite distinct ways of thinking about foreign affairs, and patterns of responses to selected items indicated that the tripartite division could be found among leaders taking part in the 1976 survey. The data reveal that responses to the Cold War and Post-Cold War Internationalist items listed in Tables 4.1 and 4.2 remained virtually unchanged between 1976 and 1980, with the consequence that there was little change in either index. In contrast, support for the Semi-Isolationist perspective declined somewhat, as respondents in 1980 expressed less opposition to America's leadership role, military assistance, stationing troops abroad, and military advice in the conduct of foreign affairs. Whether responses in 1980 also conform to cleavages found in 1976 is the question to be addressed here.

Table 6.16 summarizes the correlations between questionnaire items representing the three belief systems, and it also indicates changes in correlations across the two surveys. The fifteen Cold War Internationalist items[6] yield a total of 105 correlation coefficients for each survey. In both 1976 and 1980 all correlations are positive, with a mean figure of .40, and several that exceed .50. Equally important, for present purposes, is the general lack of striking changes in correlations among each pair of items, indicating that the basic structure of the Cold War Internationalist belief system remained intact during the four-year interval between the two surveys. There are, to be sure, some changes, but they do not appear to form a consistent pattern that would warrant a major reinterpretation of this way of thinking about international affairs. For example, there is a general tendency for increasing correlations between an item on détente—"Détente permits the USSR to pursue policies that promote rather than restrain conflict"—a finding that conforms to the growing skepticism among most Cold War Internationalists about efforts to reach an accommodation with the Soviet Union. Conversely, correlations with items referring to "communism" tended to decline slightly. Perhaps this reflects the view, shared by at least some Cold War Internationalists, that it is the Soviet Union rather than communism that threatens the West; advocates of closer military ties between Washington and Beijing, for example, include some leaders who interpret foreign affairs from that perspective.[7]

Comparable figures for the Post-Cold War Internationalist belief system are also presented in Table 6.16. In both the 1976 and 1980 data, all correlations are positive, with mean figures of .30 and .32 respectively; moreover, few of them changed during the 1976–80 period. The most notable exception is the consistent increase in correlations relating to the importance of arms control as a foreign policy goal. The 1976 survey took place when the SALT process had the support of both the Republican Ford Administration and many leaders in the Democrat-controlled Congress. Four years later arms

Table 6.16   Correlations Among Items Presenting Three Foreign Policy Belief Systems: A Comparison of Results in the 1976 and 1980 Leadership Surveys

Correlation coefficients among items representing each belief system	N*	Mean correlation coefficient 1976	1980	Changes in correlation coefficients from 1976 to 1980 (% of items) ±.00–.05	±.06–.10	±.11–.15	±.16 or more
15 Cold War Internationalist items	105	.40	.40	78%	18%	4%	0%
8 Post-Cold War Internationalist items	28	.30	.32	68	32	0	0
7 Semi-Isolationist items	21	.22	.21	52	19	29	0
	154	.36	.36	73	21	6	0
Correlation coefficients among items representing different belief systems							
15 Cold War Internationalist vs 8 Post-Cold War Internationalist items	120	−.23	−.24	84%	16%	0%	0%
15 Cold War Internationalist vs 7 Semi-Isolationist items	105	−.19	−.14	61	24	8	8
8 Post-Cold War Internationalist vs 7 Semi-Isolationist items	56	.13	.13	70	23	4	4
	281	−.14	−.13	73	20	5	2

* N = Number of distinct pairs for which correlations calculated.

control had become the subject of acrimonious debates that might have killed the SALT II Treaty even without the Soviet invasion of Afghanistan. That perhaps explains the apparent tendency of the arms control issue to become a more central part of the Post-Cold War Internationalist belief system. On balance, however, the 1980 data are devoid of dramatic changes from those of the earlier survey. Rather, they indicate the persistence of Post-Cold War Internationalism as a moderately coherent way of thinking about foreign affairs, as it was in 1976.

Correlations among items representing the Semi-Isolationist belief system are also positive for all items in both surveys, albeit at a somewhat lower level than is the case for the other two perspectives.[8] The 1980 figures reveal a striking change in one respect—a significant decline in correlations relating to the proposition that "Americans have relied too much on Presidents to define the national interest." As revealed earlier (Table 6.3), leaders taking part in the 1980 survey were generally less inclined to agree with this item. The political context of the two surveys may offer a possible explanation. In early 1976 the Watergate crimes, the secretive style of the Nixon Administration, and a series of related issues that came to be identified as problems of the "imperial presidency" were still very much in the public's attention. By 1980, President Carter's support had declined precipitously, but for reasons that had little to do with conducting an imperial presidency. Rather, his detractors charged Carter with almost opposite failings: indecision, lack of forcefulness, excessive attention to trivial details, and general incompetence. That point aside, the Semi-Isolationist perspective persists, although linkages between its elements are somewhat looser than those of the other two belief systems.

The relationship between each cluster of beliefs and the other two, for both surveys, is also summarized in Table 6.16. Once more the predominant pattern is that of continuity, reflected in the fact that most of the correlation coefficients varied little between 1976 and 1980. All correlations between items that represent the two internationalist perspectives were negative in 1980, as they were in 1976. The data thus reveal no general convergence of these two ways of thinking about foreign affairs; the average negative correlation increased slightly during the four-year period, notably on two issues: arms control and the motivations of revolutionary forces in the Third World.

The pattern of relationships between the Cold War Internationalist and Semi-Isolationist items also persisted into 1980. Sharp differences on many items, very low positive and negative correlations on some others, and strong agreement on none characterized these two perspectives, which continued to differ on such central issues as the nation's proper leadership position, the role of military advice in foreign affairs, the likely consequences of military aid programs, and several others. The relationship between the Post-Cold War Internationalist and Semi-Isolationist viewpoints also remained stable. As was the case in the earlier survey, the 1980 data reveal mostly very low, positive correlations; half of them range between .12 and −.12. At the same time, these two perspectives tend to converge on some propositions; for example, that there has been an excessive military role in American diplomacy, a pattern that appears in both the 1976 and 1980 data.

Continuity and Change: A Panel Study

Although both aggregate and group results have indicated that continuity rather than change characterizes leadership foreign policy beliefs, it remains to be demonstrated that similar findings would result from analyses at the individual level. Mail surveys that honor the pledge of anonymity to respondents must normally forgo trend analyses at the individual level. However, 142 of the 1976 respondents signed their questionnaires despite instructions not to do so. These respondents were sent a 1980 questionnaire, along with a special cover letter asking for their participation in the survey. Not all of them could be delivered (owing to deaths and changes of address), but ninety-five leaders did complete and return the questionnaires.

This group of ninety-five thus provides a small panel whose responses to the two surveys can be matched and analyzed at the individual level. The results provide additional evidence supporting the thesis of continuity during the four-year interval. On each of the items discussed in this chapter, leaders who responded similarly outnumbered by a substantial margin those who expressed a change of opinion. The degree of continuity of course varied from issue to issue. For example, 14 percent of the leaders changed position on the proposition that "The Soviet Union is generally expansionist rather than defensive in its foreign policy goals"; conversely, 34 percent did so on the thesis that "Americans have relied too much on Presidents to define the national interest." These results are quite consistent with those reported earlier (see Table 6.3). Despite variations in responses across items, the overall pattern of continuity is pervasive.[9]

One might object, however, that a group of self-identifiers may well be highly unrepresentative. After all, respondents who differ with respect to one attribute (self-identification despite assurances of, and instructions for, preservation of anonymity), may well differ on others as well. However, an item-by-item comparison of all substantive responses and background information in the questionnaires revealed that the group of ninety-five differed from the larger 1980 sample in only one respect: they were somewhat older, as might be expected given the fact that they had also been picked up as leaders in the 1976 sample. Thus, it seems safe to conclude that the small panel group is not materially different, either in foreign policy beliefs or in background attributes other than age, from the larger sample of leaders.

Conclusion

Analyses in this chapter have undertaken various probes into responses to the 1976 and 1980 surveys with a view to assessing the degree of change in foreign policy beliefs during the intervening years. Each effort yielded similar and reinforcing results: changes are not wholly absent, but they represent a relatively minor theme in an overall pattern of striking continuity.

Against a background of domestic and international stability, these results might not seem especially noteworthy, but on any list of adjectives that might be used to describe the 1976–80 period, "tranquil" is among the least appropriate. The earlier survey was initiated with a recently-installed and popular Gerald Ford in the White House. Jimmy Carter was among the longer shots in a crowded list of Democratic presidential hopefuls, and Ronald Reagan's faltering campaign for the GOP nomination appeared to be the last hurrah in his political career. The Shah of Iran, a pillar of American security policy for the Persian Gulf region, was firmly on the Peacock throne and Afghanistan might as well have been located on the back side of the moon for all the interest or knowledge most Americans had of that obscure Southwest Asian nation.

Four years later, President Carter was waging a desperate battle to win his own party's presidential nomination, while Ronald Reagan, who would defeat Carter nine months later, was well on his way to an easy victory in the Rebublican primaries. The Shah had been expelled from Iran and was dying in exile. His successors in Teheran triggered a 444-day crisis by pillaging the American Embassy and taking hostage its personnel. Soon thereafter, Afghanistan was the victim of a brutal invasion by its northern neighbor, casting a distinct chill on relations between Washington and Moscow, if not an outright renewal of the Cold War. Even had the rest of the world remained free from conflict and change—evidence from virtually every region clearly proved that it had not—the period in question was undeniably characterized by tumult and turmoil. Against such a background, the major finding of the 1980 survey—the foreign policy beliefs of American leaders remained quite stable—is of more than passing interest, whether one's concern is with substantive, theoretical, or policy-oriented aspects of American foreign policy. The final two chapters will explore these issues in the light of evidence presented in this and previous chapters.

Notes to Chapter 6

1   Henry John Temple, Viscount Palmerston, Speech to the House of Commons on Charges Against Viscount Palmerston, 1 March 1848. Hansard, *Parliamentary Debates*, Series 3 Vol. 97, p. 122.
2   See, for example, Henry Kissinger, "Poland's lessons for Mr. Reagan," New York

Times (17 January 1982). p. 23; and Kissinger, "First, coherent policy," *New York Times* (18 January 1982). However, although his views on détente have changed, Kissinger has also called for ratification of the SALT II Treaty. Leslie H. Gelb, "Kissinger urges approval of 1979 arms pact," *New York Times* (13 May 1982). p. A17.

3 Predictions of persistence rather than change in leadership beliefs, derived from a cognitive model, appeared in a proposal to the National Science Foundation a year before the 1980 survey.

4 The 1976 questionnaire unfortunately omitted items that might have permitted respondents to assess the validity and success of the American undertaking in Vietnam. By a narrow margin of 52 percent–46 percent, the leaders taking part in the 1980 survey judged American intervention to be justified. These figures cannot reveal, however, the extent to which this judgment might have been colored by events subsequent to the North Vietnamese victory in 1975; for example, the general brutality of the Hanoi regime; the cruel plight of the "boat people" who were driven out of Vietnam, often for racial reasons; the invasion of Cambodia; and other manifestations of Vietnamese imperialism. The close division of views on the merits of the American policy did not, however, extend to appraisals of the outcome. Only 8 percent agreed that "it did achieve some important American foreign policy goals," whereas 90 percent asserted that the American undertaking "failed."

5 Performance ratings for some of the foreign policy goals listed in the previous table were dropped from the 1980 questionnaire at the last moment in order to include clusters of questions on the Iran and Afghanistan situations.

6 The Cold War Internationalism index used with the 1976 data included sixteen items, but one of them was dropped from the 1980 questionnaire.

7 Some Cold War Internationalists have lamented the decline of anti-communist fervor in American foreign policy; Norman Podhoretz is a prominent example. However, for many others the primary threat to the United States is Soviet expansionism, not communism. Evidence for this observation may be found in responses to an item on the desirability of an alliance between the United States and China. Support for the Sino–American alliance was strongest among leaders taking the "hardest line" on seven items dealing with the Soviet Union and its foreign policy: the Soviet Union abuses détente ($r=.23$), aims to gain control of the Persian Gulf ($r=.33$), is expansionist ($r=.19$), was involved in the Iran hostage situation ($r=.19$), and acted defensively in Afghanistan ($r=-.18$). Also, leaders favoring an alliance with Beijing opposed better relations with the USSR ($r=.17$), and reacted negatively to grain sales to Russia ($r=-.08$). The Cold War Internationalist case against playing the "China card" is presented in Daniel Patrick Moynihan, "A new American foreign policy," *New Republic*, 182 (9 February 1980), pp. 17–21.

8 The Isolationism index used with the 1976 data included eight items, but one of them (relating to Angola) was dropped from the 1980 questionnaire.

9 For more details, see Ole R. Holsti and James N. Rosenau, *Consensus and Change in Foreign Policy Opinions Among American Leaders*, Final Report for National Science Foundation Project SOC 79–13977 (1979–81).

7
Consensus Lost?
Consensus Regained?

American leaders are deeply divided on a wide range of foreign policy issues, hardly less so in 1980 than they had been four years earlier during the immediate aftermath of the Vietnam debacle. Reactions to these findings will depend on the value one attaches to a foreign policy consensus, as well as to beliefs about whether such a condition ever existed.

Complete agreement on all issues is likely to result in policies of great consistency, but at a high cost, for it is also likely to reduce the healthy processes of questioning basic assumptions, debating alternative courses of action, and adjusting to changing conditions abroad. Consistency may often be a desirable attribute of a nation's foreign policy, but it should not be confused with quality, as it may merely reflect a hardening of intellectual arteries and an ossification of premises and theories that have long outlived their utility. These caveats notwithstanding, a foreign policy that does not enjoy domestic "legitimacy" (which implies at least some degree of agreement on basic principles, ends, and means) is not likely to prove very effective over any extended period of time.[1]

The desirability of consensus is itself a part of the contemporary debate on foreign policy. Presumably, adherents of each belief system would prefer domestic agreement along the lines of the favored viewpoint. Failing that, however, they would tend to react rather differently to the prospect of conducting the nation's external relations in the absence of consensus. The Semi-Isolationists tend to assess such a condition with greater equanimity, for it would perhaps serve as a constraint against the types of international commitments and undertakings that they fear and oppose. The two groups of internationalists, on the other hand, view severe domestic dissensus as an impediment to the policies they regard as indispensable to shaping and maintaining a more congenial world order.

Consensus Lost?

A long view of American history suggests the possibility that consensus on foreign policy may be the exception rather than the normal state of affairs. Certainly the years leading up to World War II found

Americans deeply divided. Internationalists supported: American participation in the League of Nations and the World Court; efforts to contain the ambitions of the revisionist powers—Germany, Japan, and Italy; assistance to the victims of aggression; and military preparedness. These positions evoked powerful and often effective dissent from isolationists, who viewed each of them as a step leading inexorably into another war that they believed would have little connection with vital American interests and values. Not even the successes of the Nazi blitzkrieg, culminating in the rapid defeat of France in 1940, brought forth a consensus on America's proper response to the collapse of the world order that had emerged in the wake of World War I. Probably nothing less than the trauma of Pearl Harbor could have united Americans on questions of external relations.

The narrower issue of concern here is whether World War II and the onset of the Cold War served as the crucibles from which emerged a consensus on basic principles to guide American foreign policy. The weight attached to findings from the 1976 and 1980 surveys depends in part on the judgments about the extent that they represent a change from what comparable data (unfortunately, not available) from twenty, twenty-five, or thirty years ago would have revealed. Did the United States at any time after World War II enjoy a broad and effective domestic consensus on foreign affairs? Did domestic divisions over American involvement in Vietnam represent the loss of broad agreement on foreign policy, as is often asserted, or do we err in looking back, for example, to the 1950s through the rose-colored glasses of nostalgia? Would a systematic search through the evidence from the Truman, Eisenhower, and Kennedy years reveal that what has been called the "age of consensus" is a mirage, disappearing as one comes closer? Thomas L. Hughes advances this thesis, asserting that throughout the post-war period there have been persisting differences between the "security culture" and the "equity culture," positions that correspond roughly to Cold War and Post-Cold War Internationalism.[2] However, he asserts that for much of the time between World War II and Vietnam their adherents acted as an effective coalition, an observation that seems to reinforce rather than erode the consensus thesis.

A lack of directly comparable data from the two decades preceding the escalation of the Vietnam War during the mid-1960s rules out definitive comparisons between results of the 1976 and 1980 foreign policy leadership surveys and the degree of consensus prior to Vietnam.[3] However, it is possible to offer a few observations about consensus and its absence that may clarify the issue.

Unlike pregnancy, consensus is not a dichotomous condition. There are varying degrees of agreement, and there is no reason to believe that even during a given period there will be equal levels of unity on each of the many issues and undertakings that constitute a nation's foreign policy. Nor can one necessarily measure consensus by some arbitrary standard of percentage agreement in as much as most issues offer more than dichotomous choices. In a complex pluralistic society, moreover, consensus does not imply the absence of critics in legislatures, the media, the informed public and elsewhere, sometimes rather vocal or destructive ones. Even the most popular president since World War II, Dwight Eisenhower, was the target of scurrilous charges that he was the witting handmaiden of the "international communist conspiracy."

What, then, does it mean to assert that there existed a substantial foreign policy consensus during the two decades following the end of World War II? In the absence of a standard definition of the term, consensus as used here refers to broad agreement on some basic principles that define the nation's proper orientation toward the world. It does not necessarily mean full agreement on specific actions, some of which may indeed be quite controversial; for example, interventions by covert means, and the like. Given that definition of consensus, a plausible case can be developed for the thesis that there was a broad base of support for a number of fundamental propositions about the nature of the international system and America's appropriate international role within it, including but not necessarily limited to the following:

The United States has both the responsibility and capabilities to be actively involved in undertakings to create a just and stable world order. There were, to be sure, some prominent isolationists (for example, former President Herbert Hoover) who argued that such efforts would ultimately bankrupt the country. Moreover, even the internationalists might disagree on priorities (for example, whether primacy should be accorded to Europe or Asia), or on the most effective strategies and tactics of policy implementation. Nevertheless, a substantial majority of American leaders, including many confirmed isolationists of the interwar period, appear to have agreed with Senator Arthur Vandenberg that the 1930s had demonstrated the futility of isolationism.

Peace and security are indivisible. For many, among the most compelling lessons of the 1930s was the proposition that one cannot be selectively indifferent to the security of others, for one's own security ultimately depends on a just and stable world order in which aggression does not pay. It would therefore not do to dismiss, as did Neville Chamberlain in 1938, the security problem of "far away people of whom we know nothing." In 1954 President Eisenhower employed the metaphor of a falling row of dominoes to describe the likely consequences of successful aggression: "You have a row of dominoes set up, you knock over the first one, and what will happen to the last one is the certainty that it will go over very quickly. So you could have the beginning of a disintegration that would have the most profound influences."[4] American leaders were not in agreement about whether the United States should at that time intervene in Indo-China, but relatively few of them questioned the basic principle that peace and security are indivisible.

The primary threat to a stable world order stems from Soviet or Soviet-sponsored efforts to alter the status quo by force. Franklin Roosevelt's "grand design" for the post-war world assumed continued cooperation between the major World War II allies, including the United States and Soviet Union. Roosevelt's premises did not suddenly disappear with his death in 1945. Whereas some leaders, including George Kennan and Averill Harriman, were skeptical from the beginning about cooperation with the Soviet Union, for others the Czech coup, the Berlin blockade, or the invasion of Korea resulted in a more pessimistic view of the USSR. Moreover, even among those who agreed that Soviet foreign policy was expansionist, there were different theories about the sources of that policy: communist ideology, Russian nationalism, Stalin's paranoia, and various combinations of these and other factors. Such differences notwithstanding, within a half decade after the end of World War II, most Americans had come to believe that the Soviet Union was a primary source of international troubles.

Containment, rather than "roll back" or preventive war (or a retreat into isolation), represents the most effective means of meeting the challenge of Soviet expansion. Once again it is important to acknowledge that even within the majority supporting that policy there were differences of emphasis and detail. For example, George F. Kennan, "the intellectual father of containment," had serious reservations about the open-ended quality of President Truman's address to the Congress on 12 March 1947. John Foster Dulles engaged in rhetorical excesses in condemning containment as a static rather than dynamic policy during the 1952 campaign and, in a symbolic effort to demonstrate a break with past policies, he failed to assign Kennan to a diplomatic post in 1953, thereby forcing his retirement from the Foreign Service. That Dulles's policies were essentially a continuation of containment, however, became clear after Washington's responses to the East German uprising in 1953 and the Hungarian revolution three years later.

The United States should not only join, but it should take a lead in creating peacetime alliances. Formation of the North Atlantic Treaty Organization in 1949, followed by a flurry of alliance activity during the following decade, represented a sharp departure from the theory and practice of American diplomacy as it had developed over the previous century and a half. During the interwar period many Americans, fearing that the nation would be dragged into unnecessary wars by reckless allies, saw no reason to reject the advice of some Founding Fathers against "permanent entangling alliances." After World War II and the onset of the Cold War, however, most leaders accorded greater weight to the war-preventative functions of alliances—deterrence and collective security.

The United States should be actively involved in a broad range of international organizations. In part owing to President Roosevelt's ability to avoid the political mistakes that led to Senate rejection of the Versailles Treaty, American participation in the United Nations gained overwhelming public and Senate approval in 1945. The fact that some hoped and believed that the United Nations might be the forerunner of a stronger international authority, perhaps even of a world government (for example, the United World Federalists), whereas others were much more skeptical about the value of that organization (for example, Dean Acheson) does not undermine the proposition. Nor do the strident attacks on the United Nations by the John Birch Society and similar fringe groups.

Liberalization of foreign trade is necessary to avoid destructive trade wars that will damage all nations, while also contributing to political instability. Once again, the dominant view appears to have drawn significantly from the "lessons of the 1930s," which witnessed trade wars, competitive currency devaluations, a worldwide depression, and the subsequent collapse of democratic governments in Germany and elsewhere. The result was broad support for the Bretton Woods arrangements, GATT, and other institutions that were developed to promote the expansion of international trade.

Foreign aid programs, both economic and military, are not only an obligation for the richest nation, they are also a hard-headed expression of the national interest. Certainly there were critics opposing foreign aid as "international New Dealism" and "globaloney." Others may have opposed aid to this nation or that on the grounds that the assistance might sustain an authoritarian regime of the left or right. But the principle of foreign aid was generally accepted, and programs ranging from the successful Marshall Plan to the much less effective Alliance for Progress garnered strong support.

As a consequence of widespread agreement with these general principles, the Truman, Eisenhower, and Kennedy administrations could generally count upon a favorable response from the Congress, the media, other leaders, and the informed public when they pursued policies based on them. The point may be illustrated, but certainly not proved definitively, by an examination of Congressional voting on ten key issues from 1945 to 1964 (Table 7.1). These were selected not only because of their intrinsic importance, but also because many of them represented a sharp break from central aspects of American diplomacy prior to 1945. Thus, if there were deep domestic cleavages on fundamental principles of foreign policy during the years in question, these issues would have been more likely than others to have exposed them.

Although these figures do not answer all questions that might emerge from debates about the degree of agreement on foreign policy during the pre-Vietnam period, they do at least offer some circumstantial evidence on the issue. Certainly there were often vigorous congressional debates on these momentous issues and undertakings, and dissenting votes as well. Moreover, the Bricker Amendment, an effort to strengthen the role of Congress and to restrict the power of the President in treaty-making, generated substantial disagreement. But

Table 7.1 *Congressional Voting on Selected American Foreign Policy Issues, 1945–1964*

Issue	Date	Vote in	Vote	Majority (%)
United Nations	15 July 1945	Senate Committee	21–1	95
	28 July 1945	Senate	89–2	98
Truman Doctrine	23 April 1947	Senate	67–23	74
	10 May 1947	House	287–107	73
Marshall Plan, Interim	16 December 1947	Senate	Voice vote	—
	16 December 1947	House	313–8	98
Marshall Plan	18 February 1948	Senate Committee	13–0	100
	14 March 1948	Senate	69–17	80
	1 April 1948	House	329–74	82
North Atlantic Treaty Organization	22 July 1949	Senate	82–13	86
Japan Peace Treaty	21 March 1952	Senate	66–10	87
US–Korea Defense Pact	27 January 1954	Senate	81–6	93
Bricker Amendment defeated (George substitute)	26 February 1954	Senate	60–31	66
Eisenhower Doctrine	6 March 1957	Senate	72–19	79
Nuclear Test Ban Treaty	25 July 1963	Senate	80–19	81
Gulf of Tonkin Resolution	8 August 1964	Senate	88–2	98
	8 August 1964	House	416–0	100

in all cases except the Bricker Amendment, an issue that focused on the process rather than the substance of foreign policy, the debates culminated in impressive supporting majorities, usually in both major parties. It seems not altogether unreasonable to assume that these votes reflected substantial support, or at the very least, acquiescence, among wider leadership groups in the United States; would repeated votes in the 70 percent–100 percent range have been likely in a deeply divided society? Given the decided absence of agreement on foreign policy following the Vietnam War, it is hard to imagine similar Congressional votes on comparable issues. Contentious battles on the Panama Canal Treaties, the sale of AWACS aircraft to Saudi Arabia ,as well as the prospect of an even more bitter conflict over the SALT II Treaty had it not been withdrawn from the Senate in the wake of the Afghanistan invasion, offer a rather dramatic contrast to the experience of earlier administrations.

Thus, a tentative and impressionistic conclusion supports the consensus thesis. Despite the existence of such prominent and thoughtful critics as Walter Lippmann, George Kennan, Robert Taft, and Herbert Hoover (in contrast to destructive ones, notably Joseph McCarthy and his henchmen), the two decades following the end of World War II were marked by a substantial foreign policy agreement that supported internationalism over isolationism; containment rather than efforts to roll back the Soviet empire to its 1939 frontiers; the first peacetime alliances in American history; participation in a wide range of international organizations; liberalization of trade; and foreign aid on an unprecedented scale.

If in fact such a consensus existed prior to the Vietnam War, the data presented in previous chapters offer substantial evidence that, as a consequence of the conflict in Southeast Asia, it has diminished substantially, giving way to three rather distinct modes of thinking about foreign affairs. The eight general principles identified above have become the subjects of debate rather than "axioms" of American foreign policy. Moreover, the divisions found to exist in 1976 had not been effectively bridged four years later, frequent official proclamations to the contrary notwithstanding. The data may also offer some clues about the likely durability of the cleavages. Responses to both the 1976 and 1980 surveys indicate that Vietnam policy preferences, ideology, and occupation are most strongly associated with the three belief systems, whereas divisions corresponding to sex, age, and military service are much weaker. This array of findings, especially indications of hardening ideological cleavages on foreign policy issues, does not necessarily augur well for the expectation that a new consensus will emerge sooner rather than later.

However, instead of relying on these data alone, it may be useful to look beyond them for other evidence that might further illuminate the question of consensus. Specifically, it is worth considering the possibility that the preceding analyses have failed to take adequately into account: efforts by the Nixon, Ford, and Carter administrations to pursue consensus-creating policies; the impact of outrages by militants in Teheran or Soviet legions in Kabul during the closing weeks of 1979; and the results of the 1980 election and consequent claims that they reflect a broad mandate for a fundamental redirection of American foreign and defense policies.

Consensus Regained?[5]

Nixon, Ford, and Détente

Aware that severe domestic divisions on Vietnam had made possible the narrow Republican victory in the 1968 election, Richard Nixon and Henry Kissinger attempted to forge a foreign policy consensus around a modified definition of America's international role, most notably in its relationship with the USSR. The goal of détente was to persuade Moscow to enter into "constructive relations" with the United States by creating a complex network of incentives and penalties. The carrots involved economics (expanded trade and grain sales, credits to finance them, and access to American technology), security concerns (arms control negotiations, crisis-prevention and control measures), and status (recognition of the USSR as a superpower, legitimation of the status quo in Eastern Europe). The sticks included Washington's developing relationship with China, as well as continued efforts at deterrence and containment should the Soviet Union fail to act with restraint in the Third World; for example, during the invasion of Jordan in 1970, the India–Pakistan War in 1971, and the Angola conflict in 1974–5.

For various domestic and international reasons, détente did not prove to be the adhesive to bind a divided nation. Long before the invasion of Afghanistan, critics had accused Henry Kissinger, Richard Nixon, and their successors of naïveté or hyperbole, if not dishonesty, in proclaiming the end of the Cold War. The Cold War Internationalists challenged offers of carrots to a totalitarian state as neither desirable (unless linked to fundamental changes in the Soviet regime), nor as likely to be effective in containing Moscow. Those of other mind-sets were equally quick to attack when the Nixon and Ford administrations attempted to use the stick to restrain the USSR, describing such efforts as, at best, motivated largely by domestic politics (the American military alert in October 1973) and, at worst, as the first steps down the slippery slope into another Vietnam quagmire (the debates on the Angola issue).[6] Perhaps most importantly, the Soviets adhered to a narrow construction of détente as a relationship that was not intended to hamper support for "wars of national liberation" and other activities in the Third World. Consequently, the effort to create a post-Vietnam foreign policy consensus around the concept of détente was ultimately unsuccessful. By 1976, President Ford found it expedient to jettison the term from White House vocabulary as excessive baggage that he could ill afford to carry into his struggle to ward off Ronald Reagan's challenge for the 1976 Republican nomination. The meaning and value of that policy were also vigorously debated within the Democratic Party. Four years later, the harshest critics of détente rallied behind the successful Reagan campaign for the White House. Evidence to be presented below will assess whether that election marked the formation of an anti-détente consensus among American leaders.

Carter and Human Rights

A brief post-mortem on President Carter's human rights policy, an effort also calculated to find the basis for a revived domestic argument on foreign affairs, further illustrates difficulties in bridging post-Vietnam cleavages. Carter had based his campaign on downgrading the central position that Soviet–American relations had played during the preceding Administration, and on creating a "foreign policy that the American people can be proud of" by a heightened concern for human rights abroad. The effort to translate this theme into policy decisions, however, became more controversial, as the Carter Administration found itself under attack for a variety of failings with respect to human rights: naïveté, a double standard favoring governments of the right, a double standard favoring governments of the left, the needless meddling into matters that were none of its business. Cold War Internationalists, appalled by Gerald Ford's refusal to invite Alexander Solzhenitsyn to the White House, rejoiced during the early months of 1977, a period marked by some dramatic indications of White House concern for the fate of dissidents in the Soviet Union, notably the President's public letter to Andrei Sakharov. But when the Carter Administration turned its attention on Nicaragua, South Korea, or Rhodesia, the applause was quickly replaced by jeers and such critical observations as Henry Kissinger's: "The human rights campaign, as now conducted, is a weapon aimed primarily at allies and it tends to undermine their domestic structures."[7] Charges of a double standard—that the United States employed a high-powered microscope to examine and judge human rights policies of allies, while wearing blinders when it came to assessing those of adversaries—were not uncommon.

Conversely, the Post-Cold War Internationalists have shown much more acute sensitivity to the victims of repression in Santiago, Saigon, Seoul, Salisbury, South Africa, San Salvador or the Shah's Iran than to those in Pnom Penh, Pyongyang, Prague, Poland, post-unification Vietnam, or post-revolution Iran. Elections held in allied countries are often dismissed as fraudulent, whereas the absence of elections, even long after successful revolutions in Cuba, Nicaragua, and elsewhere, is rarely noted, much less the subject of adverse comment. Whereas the Cold War Internationalists regard Soviet performance in the realm of human rights as a valid index of their broader foreign policy motivations—and thus, for example, as a measure of their trustworthiness as partners to SALT and other agreements—the Post-Cold War Internationalists have generally been unprepared to sacrifice opportunities for expanded trade or arms control on the altar of vigilance for human rights in the USSR or elsewhere in the Soviet empire.[8] And the thesis that economic sanctions will not help the victims of repression is often invoked in connection with the USSR, but rarely with respect to South Africa.

While their internationalist brethren debate the appropriate targets for American attention, Semi-Isolationists take the position that the state of human rights abroad, an internal matter for the countries in question, lies beyond the proper or effective concern of the United States. Without condoning or justifying violations of fundamental rights wherever they may occur, the Isolationists disparage American efforts to rectify the situtation as basically counterproductive, whether the goal is to mitigate the obscene treatment of blacks in South Africa, Jews in the Soviet Union, or ethnic Chinese in Vietnam. The essence of the Semi-Isolationist position on human rights may be found in Kennan's observation:

> Fine, let us make sure that this country stands as a model for all humanity on human rights. But I do not think that any very useful purpose is served by pressing other governments in other parts of the world on this subject. I don't regard us as very good advisers to them. Very often we achieve just the opposite of what we wanted to achieve when we push them along this line.[9]

Thus, although the human rights issue may have commended itself to Jimmy Carter as useful, both to highlight the alleged amorality of the incumbents during the electoral campaign, and to re-establish a foreign policy consensus within the nation after the election, it would appear that, however helpful it may have been for achieving the former goal, it was less than a total success for the latter one. Ultimately Carter found himself the target of heavy fire from both ends of the political spectrum for alleged failings of American policy in Iran. Some attacked him for supporting the Shah, for even toasting him as a friend of human rights, and, later, for permitting the dying former monarch to come to New York for medical treatment of cancer. No less strident attacks emanated from the political right, which accused Carter of insufficient efforts to maintain the Shah's regime in Teheran.

The apparent decision of the Reagan Administation to recast American policy so as to emphasize violations by left-wing governments and groups, while muting its concern for those of the political right, has not ended debate on the issue. Rejection of the Ernest Lefever nomination to be Assistant Secretary of State for Human Rights by the Senate Foreign Relations Committee is perhaps indicative of continuing controversy. The Reagan policies reactivated the opposition of those who had criticized President Carter's early focus on suppression of dissidents in the Soviet Union, while bringing applause from those who are somewhat less sensitive to human rights violations by the political right. However, this approach may risk offending the substantial majority who rejected a selective international human rights policy; among leaders taking part in the 1980 leadership survey, only 3 percent indicated that the United States should "concern itself primarily with human rights in communist nations," whereas many more preferred a policy that promotes human rights "throughout the world" (54 percent) or in the United States only (29 percent). Thus, rather than serving as the tie that binds and brings America together after the divisive trauma of Vietnam, the question of human rights, when pursued as policy rather than merely stated as an abstract ideal, has once more exposed, if not widened, deep fissures on the American political landscape.

The Impact of Hostages in Iran and Russians in Afghanistan

However, perhaps external events have succeeded where détente and human rights did not. Specifically, did the Iran hostage episode or the Soviet invasion of Afghanistan serve as the catalysts for creation of a new foreign policy consensus, much as the attack on Pearl Harbor did four decades ago? As one senior Carter Administration official put it, soon after the invasion of the American Embassy in Teheran, "In terms of domestic politics, this [Iran] has put an end to the Vietnam syndrome."[10] It may be too early to pass final judgment on the lasting effects of these events in Southwest Asia. However, the immediate and familiar "rally 'round the president" reaction in times of external troubles was followed by a steady erosion of support for Carter by election time, as Administration policies failed either to bring home the hostages or to persuade the Soviets to withdraw from Afghanistan. But because one should always be cautious about interpreting election results in terms of foreign policy issues, perhaps a more important clue may be found in the reactions of various foreign policy analysts to the events in the Persian Gulf area. In brief, they appear to provide an almost classic example of the very human propensity to interpret new events in the light of previously-held beliefs, values, and expectations.

Thus, to the Cold War Internationalists, the events in Iran and Afghanistan served as further evidence of a catastrophic decay in American military strength and, even worse, of American will to use its power to preserve the nation's most vital interests, whether to protect long-time friends (the Shah) or geographically vital areas (the Persian Gulf) from the implacable enemies of the free world. The resulting prescription was fairly straightforward: beef up the military budget, replace the pusillanimous leaders responsible for creating the "present danger" with those who have the political acumen and backbone to stand up to the Russians, and unlearn "the false lessons of Vietnam," or as one columnist has put it, "No more 'no more

Vietnams.'"[11] This is, of course, the mandate that the Reagan Administration claims to have won in 1980.

The Post-Cold War Internationalists are not more inclined to applaud taking hostages or rolling across international frontiers as acceptable forms of international behavior. But whereas Cold War Internationalists perceive these events as a replay of 1939—the disastrous culmination of years of appeasement—many Post-Cold War Internationalists have taken both the Carter and Reagan administrations to task for a distorted definition of the situation (especially as it relates to Soviet motives), for overreaction and hysteria, and for rhetorical excesses that they believe have created a situation that is dangerously similar to that on the eve of World War I in 1914. Just as the Cold War Internationalist image of the USSR as inherently expansionist has shown substantial staying power, that of the Post-Cold War Internationalist has also resisted revision in the light of events that do not unambiguously support the theory of Soviet caution and conservatism in world affairs.[12] More specifically, they are inclined to argue that the Soviet Union acted only out of defensive motives in Afghanistan, while firmly rejecting the thesis that the invasion presages further actions to gain control over vital oil routes, or even the oil fields themselves, in the Persian Gulf region. Instead, many of them located the sources of that invasion in motives that are typical of major powers—ranging from "saving face" to a natural inclination to protect the southern regions of the USSR against potential infection should a fundamentalist Muslim regime achieve power in Kabul—rather than in expansionist ones. Some also blamed the United States on the grounds that it had failed to deliver on its side of the détente bargain. Moreover, citing the lack of any historical American interests in Afghanistan (in contrast to Russian ones that predate the Bolshevik revolution), they offered little more support to American policies on Afghanistan than did the Cold War Internationalists, characterizing such responses as the Olympic boycott or grain embargo as excessive. And whereas the latter typically castigated the Carter Administration for incompetence and reliance upon inadequate force in the effort to gain release of the hostages, many Post-Cold War Internationalists charged that the aborted rescue mission in April 1980, representing an unwise abandonment of diplomacy, should never have been launched in the first place.[13]

Finally, the Semi-Isolationists have also found in the Persian Gulf crises evidence to sustain the fundamental elements of their worldview. In a severe indictment of the Carter Administration for having acted immaturely, George Kennan argued that the events of 1979–80 did not warrant the conclusion that the Soviet Union had embarked upon an expansionist policy; moreover, the proper American response should not have been to augment its capability to deal militarily with events in that part of the world but, rather, to take serious steps through oil conservation to reduce the nation's dangerous dependence upon it.[14] Another articulate spokesman for a reduced American role in the world also found in these events sustenance for the thesis of disengagement:

> In this kind of world, we need more buffers between states, not more interdependence. War is the final form of interdependence in the strategic dimension, strangulation in the economic dimension.
>
> In his State of the Union Message in January [1980], President Carter looked out on the world and saw "turmoil, strife and change." There was nothing wrong with his eyesight, but there was something wrong with his vision. For he assumed that "the state of our Union depends on the state of the world." But with the world increasingly out of our control, it is time we made it less true.[15]

Thus, although there was no doubt broad agreement in deploring the invasions of the American Embassy in Teheran and Afghanistan, there is little evidence of consensus about the broader implications of these events for American foreign policy. On the contrary, they appear to have provided another occasion for exposing deep differences on fundamental aspects of the nation's proper conduct of international affairs, and for illustrating once more the propensity to interpret facts in the light of prior beliefs and expectations, in ways that will "save one's theory."

The 1980 Election: A Mandate and a New Consensus?

Efforts by the Reagan Administration to create a foreign policy consensus have also enjoyed only modest success. Reagan's campaign for the Republican nomination and during the general election posed a challenge not only to the premises of the incumbent Carter Administration, but also to those that had guided the policies of his own party's predecessors in the White House— Presidents Eisenhower, Nixon and Ford. Indeed, Reaganite rhetoric has described the 1970s as "the worst decade of the Cold War" and as a decade of "unilateral disarmament," even though the Republicans had controlled the White House during more than seven years of that period.[16] Thus, his foreign policy positions were not merely a typical partisan attack by a challenger against the incumbents. In proposing fundamental rather than marginal changes in American foreign and defense policies, Reagan and his supporters offered diagnoses and prescriptions that focused on several major themes:

- Soviet intentions and capabilities perpetuate a dangerous, bipolar, unstable international system, and pose unprecedented threats to the security and survival of Western civilization.
- The minimal American response to this situation must include: scuttling the obsession with détente; placing a higher priority on rebuilding neglected military forces than on arms control; and

reviving American willingness to play a more assertive role in protecting its vital interests abroad, while overcoming the debilitating grip of the "Vietnam syndrome."

Whether a new, post-Vietnam consensus has or can be developed around these propositions remains to be seen. Data from the 1980 leadership survey cannot provide definitive answers, but they may at least offer some preliminary clues.[17]

The International System and American Security

Table 7.2 summarizes responses to several questions dealing with the international system and the types of threats, challenges and opportunities that it poses for the United States. These findings support some facets of the Reaganite appraisal of the "present danger," but they offer much less for other aspects of it.

When confronted with a list of six possible threats to national security and instructed to select the two most important ones, leaders taking part in the 1980 survey selected: "a decline of American military strength relative to that of the USSR," and "an inability to solve such domestic problems as the decay of cities, unemployment and inflation, racial conflict and crime." Each of these options was selected by one half of the respondents. Fewer leaders checked Soviet expansion in the Third World and a growing gap between rich and poor nations as among the main sources of threat, and global population growth and excessive American interventions abroad clearly ranked at the bottom. These results are at least in part consistent with the Reagan diagnosis, but they also appear to pose a classic "guns versus butter" trade-off. The Reagan Administration has been highly sensitive to the former issue, with lavish spending authorizations for the Department of Defense, whereas its response to the latter issue has been quite different, with emphasis on budget cutting, decentralization of responsibility for remaining programs, and exhortations to the private sector to pick up the slack.

There is widespread agreement that Soviet foreign policy is expansionist—consensus on that point predates the invasion of Afghanistan—and that Soviet military strength, relative to that of the United States, poses a threat to national security. Although relatively few American leaders felt that Moscow was implicated in the hostage crisis, they were also more inclined to attribute the invasion of Afghanistan to aggressive rather than defensive motives. The strong consensus concerning the expansionist character of Soviet foreign policy goals did not, however, carry out into a view of a bipolar, communism-versus-free world international system. Most leaders distinguished between the Soviet Union and other communist nations; for example, China's foreign policy goals were viewed as more benign than those of the USSR (see Table 6.3). A majority expressed doubts about the permanency of divisions among communist nations.

Table 7.2 *Leadership Responses in 1976 and 1980 to Questions Concerning the International System and Threats to National Security*

	Reported response	1976 (n=2,282)	1980 (n=2,502)
		(percentage)	
Structure of the international system			
Revolutionary forces in "Third World" countries are usually nationalistic rather than controlled by the USSR or China	Agree	61	58
The shape of the international system we have known since World War II has been irrevocably altered by America's inability to prevent the collapse of the Thieu regime in 1975	Agree	40	38
The tide of influence in world affairs has swung toward communism as a result of the Vietnam War	Agree	40	35
American foreign policy should be based on the premise that the Communist "bloc" is irreparably fragmented	Agree	33	32
Third World conflicts cannot jeopardize vital American interest	Agree	*	10
Threats to national security			
During the last two decades of this century, which *two* of the following are likely to pose the greatest threat to American national security? (Check only two boxes)			
• a decline of American military strength relative to that of the USSR	Checked	*	50
• an inability to solve such domestic problems as the decay of cities, unemployment and inflation, racial conflict, and crime	Checked	*	50
• Soviet expansion into Third World areas	Checked	*	35
• a growing gap between rich nations and poor nations	Checked	*	25
• uncontrolled growth of the world's populations	Checked	*	13
• other	Checked	*	12
• American interventions in conflicts that are none of our business	Checked	*	8

Table 7.2 cont.

	Reported response (percentage)	1976 (n=2,282)	1980 (n=2,502)
The Soviet Union			
The Soviet Union is generally expansionist rather than defensive in its foreign policy goals	Agree	84	85
The Soviet invasion of Afghanistan is one step in a larger plan to control the Persian Gulf area	Agree	*	66
The Soviet Union was probably involved in instigating the takeover of the American Embassy in Teheran	Agree	*	35
The Soviet Union acted in Afghanistan largely to protect itself against having a hostile regime on its borders	Agree	*	30
Even though it probably means higher food prices here at home, it is worth selling grain to the Soviet Union since it may improve our relations with Russia	Agree	37	22
Communism			
Communist nations have been encouraged to seek triumphs elsewhere as a result of Vietnam	Agree	69	68
Any communist victory is a defeat for America's national interest	Agree	40	45
Containing communism (as a foreign policy goal)	Very important	39	41
The U.S. should take all steps including the use of force to prevent the spread of Communism	Agree	33	36
Coping with the international system			
A nation will pay a heavy price if it honors its alliance commitments only selectively	Agree	79	81
Fostering international cooperation to solve common problems, such as food, inflation and energy (as a foreign goal)	Very important	70	73
There is considerable validity in the "domino theory" that when one nation falls to communism, others nearby will soon follow a similar path	Agree	68	63

Table 7.2 cont.

	Reported response	1976 (n=2,282)	1980 (n=2,502)
		(percentage)	
It is vital to enlist the cooperation of the U.N. in settling international disputes	Agree	62	70
The efficiency of military power in foreign affairs is declining	Agree	62	63

* Item did not appear in the 1976 questionnaire.

Nevertheless, answers to a number of items revealed much less concern about "communist expansion" than about Soviet actions. Propositions concerning a zero-sum (your gain is my loss) view of international affairs, as well as containment, through force if necessary, of communism failed to generate support among a majority of leaders taking part in either the 1976 or 1980 surveys.

In many respects, however, the Reaganite definition of the contemporary international situation finds less support. American leaders were not inclined to accept the more pessimistic interpretations of a shift in global influence toward communism during the post-Vietnam era. General rules about adherence to alliance commitments and the domino theory gained strong support, but at the same time almost two-thirds of the leaders in both the 1976 and 1980 surveys agreed that "the efficiency of military power in foreign affairs is declining," and there was strong support for employing the United Nations to resolve international disputes.

Most importantly, however, many leaders were inclined to view the international system and threats to American security in multidimensional terms, thereby at least implicitly rejecting as at best incomplete the proposition that all of the nation's difficulties may ultimately be traced back to the Kremlin. The Soviet military build-up was widely viewed as having ominous implications, but it was by no means viewed as the only major threat to national security. Virtually all leaders rejected the view that "Third World conflicts cannot jeopardize vital American interests," but at the same time they were inclined to agree that even revolutionary forces in those parts of the world are likely to be acting out of motives that reflect national rather than Soviet or Chinese ambitions.

In summary, these data offer only partial support for the Reaganite assessment of the nation's current international problems. There is widespread concern about the nature and scope of Soviet international motives, but there appears to be substantial skepticism about any diagnosis that traces the ultimate source of all difficulties to machinations by the Kremlin.

Détente

Despite near unanimity about the expansionist character of the Soviet foreign policy goals, a far greater diversity of views emerges on the question of how best to deal with the USSR. Détente has been proclaimed by its advocates as marking the end of the Cold War and the beginning of a new epoch in Soviet–American relations, and denounced by its critics as appeasement on a scale comparable to the follies of Neville Chamberlain and Edouard Daladier on the eve of World War II.

A majority of American leaders agreed that the Soviets have employed détente to pursue conflict-creating rather than conflict-preventing policies, and there was rather limited enthusiasm for an early restoration of that relationship following the invasion of Afghanistan, even if Soviet troops did not move beyond that nation (Table 7.3). On the other hand, they rejected the apocalyptic assessments that characterized the rhetoric of its most vocal critics, as less than one-third of them felt that détente had contributed either to a decline of American global influence or jeopardized the nation's security. On the more general proposition about the desirability of improving relations with Moscow, only one leader in four agreed that it is "not in our interest" because "we are getting less than we are giving to them." However, a majority was dubious about the effectiveness of such strategies as grain sales to achieve that purpose.

This evidence reveals deep misgivings about Soviet policies, but there is much less support for the view that détente is a dangerous form of appeasement. For better or worse, most American leaders appear to favor efforts at stabilizing Soviet–American relations, and they seem substantially less critical than most top officials in the Reagan Administration of the efforts by Nixon, Kissinger, and others to do so during the 1970s. These findings would thus appear to suggest some difficulty in creating a foreign policy consensus around opposition to détente.

Defense Spending and Arms Control

A vast increase in defense spending lies at the heart of the Reagan prescription for American foreign and defense policy. A five-year spending program of $1.6 trillion (unofficially reported to have a real price tag that is almost 50 percent higher) has been offered as a means of coping with dangers arising from a dramatic increase in Soviet military capabilities during the preceding decade and a half. A corollary is opposition to arms control, at least as embodied in the SALT Treaties. Because acceptable arms limitations agreements cannot be negotiated from what Administration officials have consistently described as an American position of military inferiority, rebuilding the armed forces must be accorded a higher priority than arms control.[18]

Table 7.3 Leadership Responses in 1976 and 1980 to Questions Concerning Détente

	Reported response	1976 (n=2,282)	1980 (n=2,502)
		(percentage)	
Détente permits the USSR to pursue policies that promote rather than restrain conflict	Agree	57	60
The policy of détente as pursued by recent U.S. administrations has:			
• resulted in significant improvement in Soviet–American relations	Checked	*	4
• resulted in limited improvement in Soviet–American relation	Checked	*	44
• had little effect, one way or the other	Checked	*	20
• contributed to a decline of American influence in the world	Checked	*	14
• placed U.S. security in dangerous jeopardy	Checked	*	15
• not sure	Checked	*	3
If it seems clear that the Soviet Union does not intend to move beyond Afghanistan in Southwest Asia, the U.S. should be ready to restore a détente relationship with the Soviets	Agree	*	37
The major assumptions of détente have been proven false by the war in Vietnam	Agree	35	35
It is not in our interest to have better relations with the Soviet Union because we are getting less than we are giving to them	Agree	29	26

* Item did not appear in the 1976 questionnaire.

Evidence of leadership beliefs summarized in Table 7.4 provides modest support for the Reagan perspective on defense and arms control. Fears of a military imbalance between the superpowers led a majority of respondents to support increased defense spending; they outnumbered those preferring a reduced Pentagon budget by a substantial margin of three to one, with about one respondent in five expressing satisfaction with the spending levels proposed by the Carter Administration. But the data reveal a concomitant concern for arms control, cited as a "very important" foreign policy goal by a solid majority. Although during the late 1970s the SALT process had become a focal point of increasingly bitter attacks by critics (many of

Table 7.4 Leadership Responses in 1976 and 1980 to Questions Concerning Defense Spending and Arms Control

	Reported response	1976 (n=2,282) (percentage)	1980 (n=2,502)
Worldwide arms control (as a foreign policy goal)	Very important	66	55
If it can be resumed, the SALT process would:			
● make an important contribution toward a safer world	Checked	*	13
● be a useful but very limited step in the right direction	Checked	*	55
● be of little significance	Checked	*	15
● seriously jeopardize U.S. national security	Checked	*	15
● not sure	Checked	*	3
The United States defense budget should be:			
● increased, and taxes should be increased to pay for it	Checked	*	18
● increased, and domestic programs should be reduced to pay for it	Checked	*	40
● maintained at about the present level	Checked	*	21
● reduced, and spending on domestic programs should be increased	Checked	*	14
● reduced, and taxes should also be reduced	Checked	*	5
● not sure	Checked	*	3

* Item did not appear in the 1976 questionnaire.

whom hold important foreign and defense policy positions within the Reagan Administration), who often described it as "unilateral disarmament," that assessment gained very little support among leaders taking part in the 1980 foreign policy survey. Only 15 percent agreed that resumption of the SALT process would "seriously jeopardize U.S. national security," whereas more than four times that many leaders offered a moderately or strongly favorable judgment on the contribution of SALT toward a safer world.

Once more the findings suggest the absence of dramatic support on a key element of the Reagan program. It should be noted, moreover, that these responses reflect assessments in 1980. Debates two years later on the Reagan program, stimulated by the prospect of twelve-figure deficits for the foreseeable future, witnessed the defection of several prominent conservatives, including James Schlesinger, John

Connally, Gerald Ford, Mervin Laird, Senator John Quayle, and Representative John Rhodes, all of whom have in the past been strong advocates of defense spending. Schlesinger, a former acting budget director and Defense Secretary, for example, described the Reagan defense program as "a set of budget projections that knowledgeable people can only regard as preposterous . . . One scarcely knows what this budget does for waste—but it does seem to have left intact generalized fraud and abuse."[19] Impressionistic evidence suggests that even had President Reagan been correct in proclaiming that the 1980 election results provided him with a "defense mandate," a proposition that is not wholly beyond dispute, subsequent events have indicated that defense spending and arms control issues may be at least as likely to divide as to unify the country. Broad support for a nuclear freeze, some of it from such unexpected sources as former CIA Director William Colby, also suggests that concern for placing a ceiling on the arms race is not confined to fringe groups.

A More Assertive Foreign Policy

Revitalized military capabilities will serve not only to maintain an effective deterrent, according to the dominant view in the Reagan Administration, but they will also permit the United States to play a more vigorous and effective role in protecting its vital interests abroad. Defining interdependence in a bipolar world largely in geopolitical and strategic terms, the Reaganites find little practical merit in either the Semi-Isolationist prescription for redefining, reducing, and decoupling American security commitments, or in the Post-Cold War Internationalist thesis that interdependence is essentially limited to the economic realm.

The evidence summarized in Table 7.5 once more provides only partial support for the Reagan prescription, as not insubstantial numbers of American leaders are inclined toward at least selective skepticism about some aspects of foreign commitments. Doubts about America's ability to encourage democratic development abroad except through the power of example were widespread in 1976, and they increased rather than diminished four years later. Opposition to stationing American troops abroad and for scaling down the nation's leadership role declined somewhat during the same period, but to a point that reveals an almost even split rather than a consensus on either issue.

Although these propositions are consistent with an isolationist viewpoint, other evidence indicates less enthusiasm for general rather than selective reassessment of internationalism. Relatively few American leaders accept a narrowly circumscribed definition of the nation's global interests (for example, Western Europe, Japan, the Americas), even fewer believe that Third World conflicts are irrelevant to those interests (see Table 7.2), and opposition to military assistance programs has declined since the end of the Vietnam War. Responses to another group of questions further illustrate the mixed

Table 7.5 Leadership Responses in 1976 and 1980 to Questions Concerning America's Interests and Role Abroad

	Reported response	1976 (n=2,282)	1980 (n=2,502)
		(percentage)	
America's international role			
The best way to encourage democratic development in the "Third World" is for the U.S. to solve its own problems	Agree	65	67
America's conception of its leadership role in the world must be scaled down	Agree	57	49
Vital interests of the U.S. are largely confined to Western Europe, Japan, and the Americas	Agree	39	25
We shouldn't think so much in international terms but concentrate more on our own national problems	Agree	37	36
Military commitments and programs			
Stationing American troops in other countries encourages them to let us do their fighting for those countries	Agree	60	54
Military aid programs will eventually draw the United States into unnecessary wars	Agree	41	30
The U.S. should maintain its military commitment to South Korea	Agree	*	73
As a result of Afghanistan, the U.S. should conclude an alliance with China	Agree	*	36
General international obligations			
Maintaining a balance of power among nations (as a foreign policy goal)	Very important	44	55
Defending our allies' security (as a foreign policy goal)	Very important	37	44
Strengthening countries who are friendly toward us (as a foreign policy goal)	Very important	23	37
Protecting weaker nations against foreign aggression (as a foreign policy goal)	Very important	18	23

* Item did not appear in the 1976 questionnaire.

support for a more assertive American foreign policy. During his 1976 campaign for the presidency, Jimmy Carter announced that, if victorious, he would withdraw American troops from South Korea. Some reduction in forces there actually took place during the Carter years, despite almost unanimous advice to the contrary from the Pentagon and State Department. South Korea's less-than-spotless record on human rights made it a visible target for some critics, whereas others described that nation as having the potential for becoming "another Vietnam" should war break out again between the North and South. However, a strong majority of leaders favored maintaining a military commitment to South Korea. In contrast, only about one-third of them agreed on the desirability of an alliance with China. Efforts to maintain a global balance of power gained approval, but other propositions about protecting allies, friends and weaker nations elicited responses that fall somewhere between the expansive vision of President Kennedy's Inaugural Address and the program of the post-Vietnam Semi-Isolationists.

A similarly mixed pattern emerges in connection with American policy toward the Middle East (Table 7.6). Traditional support for Israeli security persisted, as three-fourths agreed that the United States has a moral obligation to prevent its destruction. But when asked to appraise a broader range of options for the Middle East, a majority (51 percent) preferred placing primary emphasis on "maintaining a balance of power in the region." No doubt in recognition of Western oil dependence upon that region, most leaders favored efforts to preserve the security of Saudi Arabia and Iran (despite the hostage crisis that had yet to be resolved), as well as acquisition of military bases in the region. The less-than-overwhelming majority favoring a commitment to preserve Saudi security perhaps presaged the divisive controversy on the AWACS issue eighteen months later. However, there are also indications that American leaders are more inclined to regard concern for the security of the oil-producing states as a necessary evil than as a wholly welcome obligation. An overwhelming majority, comprising almost 90 percent of the leaders in the 1980 survey, favored taking "all necessary steps, including gasoline rationing, to reduce dependence on oil from the Middle East." Moreover, less than a third of them were prepared to support military intervention in that volatile part of the world in case of another oil embargo.

The picture that emerges from these data is one that neither the Cold War Internationalists of the Reagan Administration nor adherents of other viewpoints will find wholly encouraging, as all of them can find evidence both for and against their preferred policy positions.

End of the "Vietnam Syndrome"?

If policies of the Reagan Administration depend on the nation having overcome what its spokesmen believe to be the dangerous and con-

Table 7.6 *Leadership Responses in 1976 and 1980 to Questions Concerning the Middle East and Persian Gulf Areas*

	Reported response	1976 (n=2,282)	1980 (n=2,502)
		(percentage)	
The U.S. should take all necessary steps, including gasoline rationing, to reduce dependence on oil from the Middle East	Agree	*	89
The U.S. should take all necessary steps to prevent Iran from falling within the Soviet sphere of influence	Agree	*	80
The U.S. has a moral obligation to prevent the destruction of the state of Israel	Agree	69	75
The U.S. should take whatever steps are necessary to sustain the present regime in Saudi Arabia	Agree	*	63
Afghanistan proves the need for American military bases in the Middle East	Agree	*	62
American policy in the Middle East should place *primary* emphasis on:			
• securing the friendship of the oil exporting nations of the area	Checked	*	10
• maintaining the security of Israel	Checked	*	7
• maintaining an effective balance of power in the region	Checked	*	51
• obtaining a national homeland for the Palestinians	Checked	*	6
• preventing the expansion of Soviet influence in the region	Checked	*	21
• not sure	Checked	*	5
In the light of the Afghanistan invasion, the U.S. should seek an accommodation with Iran	Agree	*	47
The U.S. should undertake military intervention in the Middle East in case of another oil embargo	Agree	22	29

* Item did not appear in the 1976 questionnaire.

stricting grip of the "Vietnam syndrome," the evidence summarized in Table 7.7 will not be completely comforting to advocates of that viewpoint. American leaders are sharply divided on the thesis that events in Iran and Afghanistan can be traced to American impotence arising from the Vietnam War. For better or worse, most leaders believe that it is wise to look to past events for guidance—as shown

Table 7.7 Leadership Responses in 1976 and 1980 to Questions Concerning Continued Impact of the Vietnam War

	Reported response	1976 (n=2,282)	1980 (n=2,502)
		(percentage)	
The consequences of Vietnam are likely to continue shaping American foreign policy despite recent events in Iran and Afghanistan	Agree	*	82
The lessons of Vietnam have been superseded by events since the U.S. withdrawal from Southeast Asia in 1975	Agree	*	54
Recent events in Afghanistan are a direct consequence of a decline in U.S. influence in the aftermath of the Vietnam War	Agree	*	54
Iran has brought an end to the "Vietnam syndrome" in which Americans were reluctant to use force abroad	Agree	*	51
Recent events in Iran are a direct consequence of a decline of U.S. influence in the aftermath of the Vietnam War	Agree	*	49
If officials would treat each new crisis on its own merits, rather than relying on past experience, they would usually make better foreign policy decisions	Agree	43	**
It is best to forget the foreign policy mistakes of the past as quickly as possible	Agree	17	**

* Item did not appear in the 1976 questionnaire.
** Item did not appear in the 1980 questionnaire.

repeatedly in previous chapters: however, they have not as readily agreed on what specific lessons we should learn—and there is no evidence of an epidemic of "Vietnam amnesia," a collective rush either to bury the past or to romanticize it.

Conclusion

It is not diminishing the magnitude of Ronald Reagan's impressive margin of victory in the Electoral College to suggest that the 1980 election results may have been less than a mandate for a revolution in

American foreign and defense policies. Foreign policy issues rarely play a decisive role in American elections. Any contribution they made to the outcome in 1980 may have been more a reflection of disillusionment with the performance of the Carter Administration than a massive yearning for thoroughgoing change. Evidence cited in Chapter 6 is at least consistent with that interpretation, as the data revealed relatively few changes in leadership beliefs during the four-year period prior to 1980. Moreover, at least some key elements of the Reagan perspective failed to elicit strong support, much less a consensus among American leaders. They appear united in their dissatisfaction with Washington's foreign policy performance. They are equally agreed in assessing Soviet foreign policy as aggressive and expansionist. But when asked about how to rectify the former or to cope with the latter problem, agreement is much harder to find. There was support for increased defense spending in 1980, but the data also indicate that American leaders were inclined to view many issues—arms control, human rights, détente, non-strategic problems, and others—in ways that deviate rather sharply from Reagan Administration positions.

There is not much evidence, moreover, that during its two years the Reagan Administration has been able to pursue its goals in a manner that has developed heightened support. On the contrary, an impressionistic assessment is that there has been an erosion rather than enhancement of support for at least several aspects of its policies, as the Administration has been relatively ineffective in eliciting support for its diagnoses or prescriptions, either at home or abroad.

• The Reagan program of lower taxes, higher defense spending, and a balanced budget—once described as "voodoo economics" by George Bush—had, by 1983, led to unprecedented budget deficits and prospects that they will become larger at least through the middle of the decade. Although there was apparently strong support in 1980 for increasing the Pentagon budget, it appears to have been declining, in part because the Reagan Administration has spelled out to neither the Congress nor the public a coherent strategic doctrine that underlies and informs priorities for vast defense expenditures. "More of everything" is not a particularly credible or persuasive way of approaching the task, especially for an administration that prides itself on wielding a sharp pencil when it approaches other parts of the federal budget. For example, goals such as "closing the window of vulnerability" created by the growing power and accuracy of Soviet missiles may evoke substantial support, but only as long as the Administration demonstrates that proposed weapons systems costing tens of billions of dollars are an effective means of coping with the threat. Yet the Administration's performance on the MX missile has been reminiscent of a Keystone Cops comedy, with frequent changes in basing modes that share only one attribute—they leave the missile vulnerable. By 1983, only residents of Utah and Nevada, whose states had been slated to house the Carter version of the MX, had been satisfied by the gyrations of the Administration. As demonstrated by the House vote against the MX in December 1982, not even all of those most convinced that a "window of vulnerability" actually existed had been persuaded that the "dense pack" or other basing modes for the MX announced in 1981 and 1982 would deal effectively with the problem.

More generally, loose talk and lack of effective reasoning about "limited nuclear war" and the prospects for "winning" such a conflict—capped by the stunning revelation by a high Pentagon official that an adequate supply of shovels would ensure survival in and rapid recovery from a nuclear war—have contributed to a growing anti-nuclear movement in the U.S. Unlike the Vietnam War protests, it appears to be solidly based in the "establishment" rather than in counter-culture groups. Even the Reverend Billy Graham, once a virtually automatic supporter of any assertive foreign policy undertaking, has joined the call for a radical change in defense policy. Reagan Administration officials are perhaps correct in describing a "nuclear freeze" and other such prescriptions as simplistic and dangerous, but they should recognize their own role in activating groups supporting such plans. In summary, whatever defense consensus may have existed in 1980—and the evidence indicates that it never fully supported Reaganite diagnoses or prescriptions—appears to have begun unravelling.

• Carelessness has also marked rhetoric and policy toward Western Europe; casual comments about "nuclear demonstration shots" in Europe are a case in point. The thesis for reviving NATO strength and deployment of new missiles in response to the Soviet SS-20 has been presented in a manner that has activated a substantial opposition which, despite claims to the contrary by the President, is by no means limited to the reflexive, anti-American left. Repeated assertions about the West's military inferiority have probably had the undesirable effect of generating more doubts about the credibility of deterrence. Washington's opposition to European purchases of Siberian natural gas is perhaps based on sound reasoning, but public lectures about allies' irresponsibility are hardly credible when the United States continues to sell grain to the USSR and to subsidize risky bank loans to Poland, even after the imposition of martial law there. Although the Reagan Administration backed off from sanctions on the pipeline— too late, however, to undo serious damage to such American firms as Caterpillar Tractor—this episode did little to erase post-Vietnam doubts about the quality of American political judgment and alliance leadership.

• American policies in much of the Third World have been dominated by the premise that turmoil there is merely another setting for the global Soviet–American conflict. However, Administration officials have not been consistently successful, within either the domestic or alliance arenas, in developing a persuasive case for this thesis.

There is little evidence, for example, that a Cold War perspective on Middle East conflicts has been presented in a manner that is compelling. Even the Saudis and others with whom the United States shares at least some interests have, rightly or wrongly, rejected the Reagan diagnosis of the major threats to that region.

Moreover, the Reagan Administration has been no more adept in efforts to gain domestic support for its program of increased military assistance and arms sales abroad, because it has failed to bargain effectively with some recipient nations. It risked and barely escaped an embarrassing defeat in the Senate on the sale of AWACS aircraft to Saudi Arabia, and yet there are few signs of reciprocal actions by Riyadh. Indeed, soon thereafter the Saudis re-established relations with Libya, boycotted Anwar Sadat's funeral, continued a hard-line policy against Egypt, Israel and the Camp David agreement, and initiated some friendly gestures to the Soviet Union. Washington has increased its assistance to Pakistan without any effort to obtain a quid pro quo, such as a pledge not to acquire nuclear weapons. Friendly overtures and arms sales to the tawdry military dictatorship in Argentina may have led Buenos Aires to believe that the United States would look the other way if the Falkland Islands were invaded.

Indeed, not only has the Administration failed to forge a new foreign policy consensus, but there are early-warning signs of divisions among the Cold War Internationalists. The "unilateralists" believe that most of America's allies, especially those in Europe who seek to perpetuate the follies of détente, have a totally inadequate appreciation of the threat from the Soviet Union. Consequently, they are unprepared to accept foreign and defense policies that are shaped in part by a desire to accommodate appeasement-minded allies. By mid-1982 there were visible signs that some of Reagan's erstwhile supporters were in open revolt against what they believed to be excessively "soft" policies, especially with respect to grain sales to the USSR, loans to Poland, resumption of arms control talks with the Soviets after KAL 007 "yellow rain," and various Cuban and Soviet activities in Latin America. George Will's observation that the Administration "loves commerce more than it loathes Communism" summarizes the conservative critique. "Reagan rolling over," "The new Rapallo," "Reagan's dim candle," "Revolt of the hawks," ". . . And what Ronald Reagan failed to say," are among the titles of articles and editorials by once confirmed Reaganites who were by 1982 castigating the President for almost precisely the same failings that they found in the preceding administration. "What single bold action has this administration taken in foreign affairs?" asks Irving Kristol. His answer is a deeply disappointed "None."[20] Perhaps only the departure of Alexander Haig, who had come to be viewed as hopelessly tainted with the sins of the Europeans and as an agent of the President's deviations from hard-line orthodoxy, has been of consolation to the unilateralists.

The "multilateralists" are no less skeptical of Soviet intentions, but they believe that the best deterrent to Soviet expansion remains a healthy alliance system which, in turn, requires some diplomatic sensitivity to the perceptions and domestic political needs of allied governments. Diplomacy and negotiation are therefore essential, for "Not a single problem in the Atlantic relationship—diplomatic, military, or economic—can be resolved by unilateral American action."[21] The unilateralists, in contrast, tend to be more ideological and their preferences are not free from isolationist implications. They would pursue assertive policies abroad, but do so unburdened by the doubts and equivocations of less zealous allies. Should the gap between the unilateralists and multilateralists widen, the future might well find American leaders divided into four groups, as depicted in Table 7.8, rather than three.[22]

Table 7.8   *Potential Divisions Among American Leaders*

	Liberal	Conservative
Internationalist	Post-Cold War Internationalists	Cold War Multilateralists
Isolationist	Semi-Isolationists	Cold War Unilateralists

Two years after the 1980 election and more than seven years after the last American was evacuated from Saigon, evidence of domestic divisions on foreign policy issues is much easier to find than are indications of fundamental accord. There are signs that the Reagan Administration has contributed to widening rather than narrowing cleavages that originated in the Vietnam experience and which have persisted through the past several administrations. Seemingly oblivious to the first part of Theodore Roosevelt's dictum, "speak softly and carry a big stick," it has managed to perpetuate and perhaps exacerbate divisions at home, and to heighten serious doubts among key allies about the quality of American leadership, without visibly impressing adversaries.

On the other hand, perhaps achievement of a consensus is at present beyond the reach of even the most skilled and inspired leadership, for the cleavages are by no means limited to foreign policy issues.[23] The Reagan Administration inherited a nation divided on most fundamental aspects of external relations. It may not have been very successful in creating a consensus, but the ability of the Democratic opposition to offer creative alternatives that promise to be more effective remains in doubt.[24]

The concluding chapter will consider some alternative strategies that might be employed to cope with this situation.

Notes to Chapter 7

1 For further discussions of "policy legitimacy," see Thomas Trout, "Rhetoric revisited: political legitimation and the Cold War," *International Studies Quarterly*, 19 (September 1975), pp. 251–84; Alexander L. George, "Domestic Constraints on Regime Change in U.S. Foreign Policy: The Need for Policy Legitimacy," in Ole R. Holsti, Randolph M. Siverson, and Alexander L. George (eds), *Change in the International System* (Boulder, Colorado: Westview Press, 1980), pp. 233–62; and George, "The Role of Cognitive Beliefs in the Legitimation of a Long-range Foreign Policy: The Case of F. D. Roosevelt's Plan for Post-War Cooperation with the Soviet Union," in Lawrence Falkowski (ed.), *Psychological Models in International Politics* (Boulder, Colorado: Westview Press, 1977).

2 Stanley Hoffmann, *Primacy or World Order* (New York: McGraw-Hill, 1978). See also, George Quester, "Consensus lost," *Foreign Policy*, no. 40 (Fall 1980), pp. 18–32; Paul Kattenburg, *The Vietnam Trauma in American Foreign Policy* (New Brunswick: Transaction Books, 1980), pp. 211–12, 258–9; Hugh Sidey, "Looking back to look ahead," *Time*, 116 (6 October 1980), p. 25; and Thomas Hughes, "The crack-up," *Foreign Policy*, no. 40 (Fall 1980), pp. 33–60. Hughes (p. 57) also suggests that when their expectations are not borne out by reality, persons in both of these "cultures" may "cop out." As a consequence, "this is a painless way to relearn isolationism imperceptibly without realizing it." His analysis thus identifies three groups that appear to correspond to those described in Chapters 4 and 5.

3 Although the issues and questions are not directly comparable, a study of leaders in the late 1950s revealed no hint of dissensus. James N. Rosenau, *National Leadership and Foreign Policy* (Princeton, NJ: Princeton University Press, 1963).

4 News Conference of 7 April 1954, reported in *New York Times* (8 April 1954), p. 18.

5 Parts of the next two sections are drawn from Ole R. Holsti, "Diplomacy and a Decade of Domestic Divisions?," paper delivered at the Foreign Service Institute of the Department of State, 27 May 1980; and Holsti, "Foreign policy issues and the 1980 election: context, hopes, and fears," *AEI Foreign Policy and Defense Review*, II, no. 5 (1980), pp. 15–18.

6 For an excellent and fuller discussion of détente and domestic constraints, see George, "Domestic Constraints on Regime Change in U.S. Foreign Policy."

7 Henry A. Kissinger, "Straight talk from Kissinger," *Newsweek*, 92 (11 December 1978), p. 62. See also, Ernest W. Lefever, "The trivialization of human rights," *Policy Review*, no. 3 (Winter 1978), pp. 11–26. Lefever's critique is of some interest in view of his appointment as Assistant Secretary of State for Human Rights in the Reagan Administration, even though it was withdrawn after its rejection by the Republican-controlled Senate Foreign Relations Committee.

8 There is no shortage of critical comment on President Carter's inclusion of the Soviet Union within American human rights concerns. See, for example, Samuel Pisar, "Let's put détente back on the rails," *New York Times Magazine* (25 September 1977), pp. 31–3 and 108–18; Stanley Hoffmann, "Muscle and brains," *Foreign Policy*, no. 37 (Winter 1979–80), pp. 3–27; Hoffmann, "Wrong on rights," *New York Times* (31 December 1980), p. A15; and Ronald Steel, "Motherhood, apple pie and human rights," *New Republic*, 176 (4 June 1977), pp. 14–15.

9 George F. Kennan, "An appeal for thought," *New York Times Magazine* (7 May 1978), p. 127.

10 Hedrick Smith, "Iran crisis helping U.S. shed fear of intervention abroad," *New York Times* (2 December 1979), p. A1. The same point has been made repeatedly by officials in the Reagan Administration, including the President.

11 James R. Schlesinger, "Some lessons of Iran," *New York Times* (6 May 1980); and George F. Will, "No More 'No More Vietnams,'" *Newsweek*, 93 (19 March 1979), p. 104. A typical Cold War Internationalist interpretation of the Soviet invasion of Afghanistan is Richard E. Pipes, "How real is the Soviet threat?," *U.S. News &*

World Report, 88 (10 March 1980), p. 33. Pipes emphasizes the theme that Afghanistan is a stepping stone to control the Straits of Hormuz, and an eventual victory over the United States without the need to resort to war.

12 An exception to this observation might be former President Carter's assertion that the invasion of Afghanistan caused him to change his mind about Soviet foreign policy, a confession that earned him widespread derision, both from those who agreed with his earlier, more benign viewpoint and from those whose views had long coincided with Carter's new, more malign interpretation.

13 See, for example, Robert Legvold, "Containment without confrontation," *Foreign Policy*, no. 40 (Fall 1980), pp. 74–98; Leslie H. Gelb and Richard H. Ullman, "Keeping cool at the Khyber Pass," *Foreign Policy*, no. 38 (Spring 1980), pp. 3–18; Fred Halliday, "Wrong moves on Afghanistan," *Nation*, 230 (26 January 1980), pp. 70–2; Ronald Steel, "Afghanistan doesn't matter," *New Republic*, 182 (16 February 1980), pp. 14–15; Stanley Hoffmann, "Reflections on the present danger," *New York Review of Books*, 27 (6 March 1980), pp. 18–24; Jerry Hough, "Why the Russians invaded," *Nation*, 230 (1 March 1980), pp. 225ff.; and Robert Lasch, "Lessons of Korea and Vietnam," *Newsweek*, 95 (18 February 1980), p. 23.

14 "Discussion in Washington has been dominated by talk of American military responses—of the acquisition of bases and facilities, of the creation of a rapid-deployment force, of the cultivation of military ties with other countries all along Russia's sensitive southern border. In these circumstances, anything can happen. But the fact is, this extravagant view of Soviet motivation rests, to date, exclusively on our own assumptions. I am not aware of any substantiation of it in anything the Soviet leaders themselves have said or done. On the contrary, Mr Brezhnev has specifically, publically and vigorously denied any such intention . . . We are now in a danger zone. I can think of no instance in modern history where such a breakdown of political communication and such a triumph of unrestrained military suspicions as now marks Soviet–American relations has not led, in the end, to armed conflict." George F. Kennan, "Washington's reaction to the Afghan crisis: 'Was this really mature statesmanship?,' " *New York Times* (1 February 1980), p. A27.

See also, Kennan, "How real is the Soviet threat?," *U.S. News & World Report*, 88 (10 March 1980), p. 33; and "George Kennan calls on the West to end sanctions against Soviet," *New York Times* (11 October 1982), p. A10. Kennan's thesis that democratic societies should undertake "modest" foreign policies because they do "very poorly in coping, philosophically, with the phenomenon of serious challenge and hostility to their values" is developed further in his "Cease this madness," *Atlantic*, 247 (January 1981), pp. 25–8.

15 Earl C. Ravenal, "Have Carter's critics taken real risks?," *New York Times* (30 April 1980). For an extended discussion of the defense implications of this position, see Ravenal, "Counterforce and alliance: the ultimate connection," *International Security*, 6 (Spring 1982), pp. 26–43.

16 For example, Reagan's address on commissioning the battleship New Jersey, reported in Lou Cannon, "Reagan defends arms boost," *Washington Post* (29 December 1982), p. 1.

17 As indicated in the previous chapter, there are some differences in the composition of the two leadership samples. Thus, direct comparison of aggregate results, as in Tables 7.2–7.7, must be undertaken with some caution. The data for 1980 are presented to offer some insight into the degree of leadership support for the Reaganite world-view. The 1976 figures are presented for approximate rather than precise comparisons, for which the reader should turn to Chapter 6. The thesis that Reagan won in 1980 *in spite of*, rather than because of his foreign policy stance, is developed in William Schneider, "Conservatism, Not Interventionism," in Kenneth A. Oye, Robert J. Lieber and Donald Rothchild (eds), *Eagle Defiant* (Boston: Little, Brown, 1983), pp. 33–64.

18 President Reagan has repeatedly asserted that the United States is militarily inferior to the Soviet Union. Even such traditional supporters of defense programs—for example, Senators Henry Jackson and Daniel Patrick Moynihan—

have strongly disputed the President's assessment. The question of the Soviet–American military balance is central not only to debates on the Reagan program for rebuilding the armed forces, but also to those on the federal budget deficit.

19 Quoted in Hodding Carter III, "Ronald Reagan's confederacy of inequality," *Wall Street Journal* (11 February 1982). See also, "Connally's outlook on gold and arms," *New York Times* (19 October 1981), p. D2.

A *Business Week* poll revealed that public backing for continued military increases fell from 71 percent in 1980 to 17 percent in the fall of 1982. Even business leaders appear to be worried by the effects of defense spending on budget deficits. A view that appears to be gaining increasing support is that of a prominent money manager: "The greatest danger [to the economy] I see would be the failure of the government to moderate its defense spending, which is grossly excessive, redundant, inflationary, doesn't create jobs and increases the federal deficit." Quoted in Gary Putka, "Forecasters as landscape gardeners: where the hedges go in '83 outlook," *Wall Street Journal* (3 January 1983), p. 47. See also Walter S. Mossberg and Rich Jaroslovsky, "Reagan's defense push draws increasing fire as big drain on budget," *Wall Street Journal* (27 December 1982), p. 1; Norman C. Miller, "The spreading panic over the Reagan budget," *Wall Street Journal* (13 January 1983), p. 30; and the double page ads, signed by business, government and academic leaders, on an "affordable multi-year defense buildup" and the "budget crisis," in *New York Times* (6 April 1983), pp.8–9, and (24 February 1983), pp. 36–7.

20 William Safire, "Reagan rolling over," *New York Times* (17 December 1981), p. A31; Safire, "The new Rapallo," *New York Times* (22 February 1982), p. A17; George F. Will, "Reagan's dim candle," *Newsweek* (18 January 1982), p. 100; William Safire, "Revolt of the hawks," *New York Times* (21 January 1982), p. A23; and Ben J. Wattenberg, ". . . And what Ronald Reagan failed to say," *Wall Street Journal* (23 April 1982), p. 26. Perhaps even more stridently critical comments have been aimed at the President by Irving Kristol, Normal Podhoretz, Midge Decter and the editorial writers of the *Wall Street Journal*, all of whom were enthusiastic Reagan supporters in 1980. See, for example, Irving Kristol, "The key question: who owns the future?," *Wall Street Journal* (11 January 1982), p. 27; Kristol, "Diplomacy vs. foreign policy in the U.S.," *Wall Street Journal* (15 April 1982), p. 26; Seymour Weiss, "The Reagan responses on Poland," *Wall Street Journal* (29 December 1981), p. 20; Norman Podhoretz, "The neo-Conservative anguish over Reagan's foreign policy," *New York Times Magazine* (2 May 1982), pp. 30–3ff.; and Suzanne Garment, "Intellectuals are abandoning Reagan foreign policy," *Wall Street Journal* (2 February 1982), p. 28. According to Ms Decter, "The Administration seems to be pursuing the same old policy of détente, and I think if Reagan were not in office now, he'd be leading the opposition." *New York Times* (21 January 1982), p. A20.

For examples of growing Cold War Internationalist impatience with allies, see Walter Laqueur, "Poland and the crisis of the alliance," *Wall Street Journal* (4 January 1982), p. 30; and Paul Seabury, "NATO: thinking about the unmentionable," *Wall Street Journal* (24 December 1981), p. 6. A broad plan for withdrawing American ground forces from abroad is developed in Jeffrey Record and Robert J. Hanks, *U.S. Strategy at the Crossroads: Two Views* (Cambridge, Mass.: Institute for Foreign Policy Analysis, 1982).

21 Secretary of State Haig, in a speech to the United States Chamber of Commerce, May 1982. At the same time he also asserted, "We can no more solve our problems by avoiding the negotiation table than by resting our hopes on it alone." This reference to American–Soviet relations garnered little applause from the unilateralists.

22 These categories are somewhat similar to those proposed in a study of public rather than leadership views: accommodationists, internationalists, isolationists, and hardliners. Michael A. Maggiotto and Eugene R. Wittkopf, "American attitudes toward foreign policy," *International Studies Quarterly*, 25 (December 1981), pp. 601–31.

23 See James N. Rosenau and Ole R. Holsti, "U.S. leadership in a shrinking world: the

breakdown of consensuses and the emergence of conflicting belief systems," *World Politics*, XXXV (April 1983), pp. 368–92.

24 Theodore Sorensen, "The absent opposition," *Foreign Policy*, (Summer 1982), pp. 66–81. See also, Harry McPherson and Richard Holbrooke, "A foreign policy for the Democrats," *New York Times Magazine* (10 April 1983), pp. 30–42.

8
Conclusion: Prospects for Consensus in the 1980s

American foreign policy is in disarray, and only the truest of true believers any longer believe that Reaganite nostalgia and nostrums will create order out of shambles. But the roots of disarray can be traced to the war in Vietnam, which long preceded Reagan's entry into the White House.

The Vietnam War abounds in ironies, not the least of which is that an American effort to prevent the unification by force of Vietnam ended in a unified Vietnam and in a disunited United States. It is too early for a final assessment of the war's full impact on the United States, its society and economy, but the profound and persisting impact of the Vietnam undertaking on the foreign policy beliefs of American leaders has emerged repeatedly from the evidence. The principle findings can be summarized briefly:

- American leaders are strikingly divided on a broad range of foreign policy questions; there is good reason to believe that dissensus far exceeds that of the period between Pearl Harbor and the mid-1960s; and these divisions appear to have congealed into several rather distinct, almost mutually-exclusive belief systems. The domestic cleavages appear to be at least as strong as those that characterized the United States during the years preceding World War II.

- The war in Vietnam represented a major landmark in American history, comparable to what students of domestic politics call "watershed elections," those that fundamentally alter voter alignments and loyalties. Among casualties of the longest war in American history are propositions that for two decades prior to Vietnam were regarded as virtually self-evident truths about international affairs. They are now among the most contentious points in discussions of American foreign policy.

- The effects of the Vietnam War have persisted beyond the immediate period following military defeat of the Saigon regime in 1975. Both survey and anecdotal evidence indicates that neither efforts of the past several administrations to develop a foreign policy consensus nor dramatic events since the evacuation of the last Americans from Saigon have successfully bridged the cleavages arising from the war in Vietnam.

As long as this condition exists, American administrations may be forced to rely upon shifting foreign policy coalitions, the composition of which will vary from issue to issue. *Ad hoc* coalitions might take several forms.

Cold War Internationalists (the dominant perspective within the Reagan Administration) and Post-Cold War Internationalists believe in the practical and moral necessity of an active American foreign policy; in international responsibilities arising from power and wealth; and in the potentially disastrous consequences of abdication, leaving it to others, or to no one at all, to create and sustain a more effective international order. What kinds of American undertakings would draw sufficiently upon these shared values is rather hard to predict because it would require muting the far greater differences between the two groups. They agree that American security is inextricably linked to the international system, but they share little in either their diagnoses of those links or in their prescriptions on how to deal most effectively with them (see Table 4.4).

Post-Cold War Internationalists and Semi-Isolationists generally agree more than they disagree in interpreting Soviet foreign policy actions and adducing their sources. They tend to describe the Soviet Union as a conservative nation beset with sufficient problems at home and abroad to render it at worst an uncooperative adversary, but one that is neither capable nor willing to pose a mortal threat to the United States or to the other industrial democracies. The Soviet Union, according to this perspective, is thus a typical great power with finite goals, rather than a revolutionary one with boundless global ambitions. Leaders in these two groups might thus join in supporting certain types of arms control agreements and other efforts at accommodation with the USSR but, of course, any prospects for such arrangements will also depend significantly on Soviet policies during the post-Brezhnev era. Such adventures as Afghanistan will virtually rule out any American consensus in favor of tension-reducing measures.

Finally, the Semi-Isolationists and Cold War Internationalists are united in a skeptical attitude about inflated definitions of economic interdependence; a denial of the thesis that Third World problems can be traced back to inequitable treatment at the hands of the Western industrial nations; and a rejection of the corollary that the United States has either special responsibilities or unique capabilities for assuring the material well-being of the less developed nations, especially of those that have demonstrated an unwillingness or inability to exercise the self-discipline for effective growth, or who remain wedded to values, ideologies and institutions that have demonstrably failed.[1] It is also not inconceivable that these two groups will also find a common cause in a significant redefinition of America's relationship to Western Europe and NATO, although probably for quite divergent reasons. Withdrawal of some or all American troops from Europe would be more consistent with the basic tenets of isolationism than with those of Cold War Internationalism. As indicated earlier, however, there are increasingly visible signs that some adhering to the latter viewpoint are more or less ready to write off Western Europe as hopelessly neutralist, if not defeatist, in its obsession for preserving détente, even in the face of Afghanistan, martial law in Poland, and other violations of the Helsinki accords. Some Cold War Internationalists who are troubled by the unprecedented magnitude of budget deficits also perceive that a reduction or total withdrawal of American forces for Europe offers the possibility of reducing the immense defense budgets proposed by the Reagan Administration.

Except in severe crises, persisting dissensus on foreign affairs would appear to rule out more enduring coalitions that might sustain long-term projects and ambitious American undertakings to cope with or to direct significant international changes. Bruising battles in the Congress—comparable to those marking the Panama Canal Treaties, the SALT II Treaty (before it was withdrawn), the sale of AWACS aircraft to Saudi Arabia and the MX missile—seem likely to emerge in the wake of many major foreign policy initiatives. To gain a victory on one issue an administration might well deplete its political resources in the Congress, consequently reducing its leverage on others. The Panama Canal Treaties were sufficiently divisive for both parties that President Carter was forced to invest virtually all of his political capital to ensure their acceptance by the Senate. It was widely believed that several key Senators (for example, Republican leader Howard Baker) would be forced, by virtue of their votes supporting the Administration on the Panama Canal, to oppose the President on the SALT II Treaty. Moreover, the absence of general agreement on guiding principles of foreign policy may enhance the prospects for success of single-issue political factions, be they ethnic groups determined to redress perceived grievances abroad (for example, Greek-Americans, who have been notably successful in shaping and constraining American policy toward Turkey), or any of a score of industry–labor coalitions determined to protect such fledgling industries as automobiles, steel, textiles, machine tools, dairy products, shoes, sugar, consumer electronics, and others against the ravages of international competition.

The preceding discussion may appear to have taken an excessively static view, writing off prematurely the ability of an administration, especially one that gained a substantial electoral victory, to forge a new foreign policy consensus. That Richard Nixon did not do so after his landslide victory in 1972 may perhaps be attributed to the Watergate scandal and its corrosive effects, as Nixon's energies and political resources were increasingly expended in a futile effort to stay in office. That Jimmy Carter failed to do so has been variously attributed to the narrowness of his electoral victory in 1976 and to a lack of political skill and acumen. Ronald Reagan suffers neither from the taint of major scandal nor from the ambiguities and constraints attending a close electoral victory. He has also demonstrated some political abilities in dealing with the public and the Congress that surpass those of his immediate predecessor. The 1981 tax bill is evidence of the latter point. However, as suggested in the previous chapter, his Administration has been less successful in gaining domestic support for his foreign and defense policies. What strategies might an administration then pursue for building a consensus? Several possibilities come to mind.

One approach to the problem is illustrated by a memorandum written by Secretary of State William Seward at a moment when the United States were becoming visibly disunited. To remedy what Seward perceived as the fact that "We are at the end of a month's administration, and yet without a policy, either domestic or foreign," he advised Abraham Lincoln:

> I would demand explanations from Spain and France, categorically, at once.
> I would seek explanations from Great Britain and Russia, and send agents to Canada, Mexico, and Central America to rouse a vigorous continental spirit of independence on this continent against European intervention.
> And, if satisfactory explanations are not received from Spain and France,
> Would convene Congress and declare war against them.[2]

Fortunately, Lincoln had the wisdom to reject Seward's mad suggestion—appropriately offered on April Fools Day, 1861—for dealing with domestic dissensus. War or external adventures may be perceived as tempting strategies for diverting attention away from seemingly intractable problems and domestic failures. Troubled dictatorships as varied as those in Argentina, Cuba, Libya, Iran, and Iraq have done so in recent years. It is, of course, a more dangerous strategy for major powers, but it may still be quite tempting to employ rhetorical fusillades against external adversaries as vehicles for creating national unity. At his confirmation hearing, Secretary of State Alexander Haig asserted that it is essential to "seek actively to shape events, and, in the process, attempt to force a consensus of like-minded people."[3] One cannot dismiss as totally implausible the hypothesis that repeated verbal clashes between Washington and Moscow during the initial months of the Reagan Administration were partly a consensus-building strategy.

Nor, of course, should one underestimate Moscow's ability to take precisely the actions that will sustain and add legitimacy to a hardline American policy toward the USSR. The Soviet invasion of Afghanistan may have been crucial to Reagan's nomination and election, both by offering vivid supporting evidence for his thesis of Soviet aggressiveness and by making the more optimistic Carter theory of Soviet behavior appear, in the eyes of many, to be naive and misguided. Soviet actions in and around Poland could have similar effects, although to date (1983) the situation in Poland appears to have had an impact very similar to that of events in Iran and Afghanistan: it has confirmed for many the validity of their prior foreign policy beliefs. Some examples will illustrate this point. Several Cold War Internationalists have asserted that neglect of American armed forces rendered the Administration impotent to deal effectively with the issue. They failed to note, however, that the Eisenhower Administration, which possessed clear military superiority, responded similarly to the East German and Hungarian uprisings. Many Post-Cold War Internationalists found in Poland's tragedy evidence of Soviet restraint. They therefore supported resumption of aid to Poland and of arms control negotiations with the USSR, and opposed efforts to establish linkages between issues. Finally, a leading Semi-Isolationist suggested that Poland was too vital to Soviet security to warrant demands that Moscow keep its hands out of affairs in that country, and warned against driving the USSR "to desperation by pressing it mercilessly against a closed door."[4]

The imposition of martial law on Poland thus illustrates once again the durability of belief systems and their impact on the interpretation of events. However, an outright Soviet military invasion of that unfortunate country, especially if it leads to large-scale resistance and heavy casualties, could well prove to be the catalyst for creating a hard-line anti-Soviet consensus. Some of Reagan's critics have gone beyond attacking him for a "do nothing" policy on Poland, suggesting that the erosion during recent years of anti-communist zeal lies at the root of the problem because it has eliminated the moral foundations of American foreign policy. Evidence presented here, however, indicates no overwhelming enthusiasm for anti-communist crusades. Indeed, even many of the staunchest Cold War Internationalists favor entering into an alliance with China as a means of containing Soviet expansion.[5]

A second road to consensus brings to mind the somewhat wistful comments of a Carter Administration official when the SALT II Treaty was about to be presented to the Senate for ratification: "If Eisenhower was [sic] President, all he'd have to do is say: 'I've read the treaty, and I think it's good,' and he'd get a tremendous number of people to follow him."[6] More generally, an administration might invoke all of the symbols and practices of the early post-World War II decades in an effort to gain public and congressional support for the main outlines of its external policies. Appeals to "the national interest," "bipartisanship," "politics stops at the water's edge," "national security requirements," and the like might be called into service. By themselves, however, they are more likely to prove effective for the short run, especially in times of genuine and acute crisis, than for the longer-range goal of building domestic support for major international undertakings.

Moreover, structural and other changes in the Congress during the past two decades have rendered the task more difficult. The premise that "the Executive knows best" on matters of foreign policy has not fared well in recent years; as one Congressman recently put it, "For us, it is conventional wisdom that the President of the United States lies. That was unthinkable before the 1960s."[7] The same period has also witnessed a significant decentralization of power in the Congress. During the Eisenhower era, if the President could gain the support of House Speaker Sam Rayburn and Senate Majority Leader Lyndon Johnson, that was usually sufficient to ensure Congressional support, but the power of legislative leaders and committee chairmen has since declined. In any case, it seems unlikely that, either by virtue of widely-perceived expertise or of overwhelming public popularity, Reagan and his top foreign policy advisers can come close to matching the Congressional and public support almost routinely accorded to Eisenhower.[8] Moreover, aside from anti-Soviet rhetoric, the Administration has been less than articulate in identifying the major conceptions that inform its foreign and defense policies, thus enhancing doubts about its competence to deal effectively with foreign affairs.

A third and far more modest approach is to follow the advice of the Semi-Isolationists, who propose that the United States should pursue external policies of retrenchment across a broad range of undertakings and commitments in part because such policies would not require a domestic consensus. That this approach would strike a responsive chord among a not insignificant minority of Americans seems clear from the evidence presented in previous chapters. This is not the place to debate the merits or demerits of the Semi-Isolationist prescription. Suffice it to say that, although the Reagan Administration may well adopt some isolationist measures (for example, despite rhetoric about the virtues of free trade, it has been somewhat protectionist in international trade), in most respects this approach to foreign policy appears to be too fundamentally at odds with the stated philosophies and goals of the President and his supporters to serve as the foundations of their foreign policies. However, future administrations might well find greater appeal in the isolationist approach.

There is at least one other approach to the task of consensus-building, but in many ways it is the most difficult of all to pursue effectively. Moreover, it offers no guarantee of success. It requires substantial political skills and perhaps more patience than one could reasonably expect, given the premium on short-run successes that arises from the frequency of elections and the ever-lengthening, virtually non-stop, electoral campaigns. This alternative requires a leadership capable of developing and articulating a vision of the world, of the American role within it, and of appropriate strategies and tactics that is persuasive in its diagnosis (what is the nature of the international system, what are the major trends, what are the primary threats and opportunities), its value component (what is desirable), and the assessment of the balance between available resources and existing constraints (what is feasible). It might stimulate an informed debate, not only to diagnose the threats from an international system that appears more firmly on the path to anarchy than to a "global village," but also to depict a vision of a preferred world order, of how the United States might best contribute toward its achievement, and of the means of doing so. According to this view, "The 'present danger' may be the failure to debate what it really is."[9] A short list of questions for discussion might include, but not necessarily be limited to, America's relations with each major sector of the international system.

What goals and strategies should govern American relations with the Soviet Union? Neither "détente" nor "human rights plus arms control," the dominant themes of the winning candidates in the 1972 and 1976 presidential elections proved especially effective, either for purposes of creating a post-Vietnam foreign policy consensus at home or for developing and sustaining more stable and cooperative relations with the USSR. It would be premature to pass final judgment on the Reagan approach to Soviet–American relations but, after two years, evidence of eroding domestic support for some of its key elements is not especially hard to find. Even some of Reagan's strongest supporters in 1980 have been critical of what they judge to be weak responses to the imposition of martial law in Poland and the KAL 007 incident whereas others fear that worsening relations between Moscow and Washington will lead, at best, to a costly and futile race and, at worst, to armed conflict. Farmers, who have welcomed the cancellation of the Carter grain embargo, may be a notable exception to this observation.

Recent years have witnessed a combination of rapidly increasing Soviet military strength and brutal interventions in both contiguous and non-contiguous areas, on the one hand, and, on the other, a growing list of seemingly intractable domestic problems, including but not confined to agriculture, economic growth, corruption, infant mortality rates, and rampant alcoholism. Even the nuclear "balance of terror," which could have been described as reasonably stable during the 1960s and 1970s, is becoming unstable owing to emerging technologies (especially those that are increasing the accuracy of missile guidance systems), the Lilliputian successes of SALT and other arms control negotiations, nuclear proliferation, and the deployment of weapons with clear "first strike" capabilities. If the land-based version of the powerful and highly accurate MX missile and its Soviet counterpart (the SS-18) represent the wave of the future in strategic deterrence, then that future is likely to be unstable, expensive, and unburdened by serious progress in arms control. And if the debates on the MX and its basing mode are indicative, the future will also be bankrupt in any creative ideas, for example, about strategies for enhancing crisis stability. This volatile combination hardly augurs well for Soviet–American relations during the 1980s. Moreover, the costs of a policy toward the Soviet Union that is all sticks and no carrots may be quite high, both at home (for example, among disaffected farmers if grain sales are once again cut off, and among the growing upper-middle class anti-nuclear movement), and among those allies who, wisely or otherwise, tend to prefer détente to a Cold War.

What kinds of arrangements should be established with the other industrial democracies for dealing not only with defense issues (for example, strengthening NATO, or the perpetual issue of defining a proper division of contributions and responsibilities within the alliance), but also with such common problems as inflation, unemployment, energy, and trade? During the period immediately following World War II, rapid and stable economic growth, fueled in part by cheap and ample oil, and supported by stable exchange rates and a strong American dollar, made possible a dramatic expansion of trade that was widely perceived as mutually beneficial. The "economic lessons of the 1930s" had seemingly been well learned. Today energy is scarce, expensive, and its availability is subject to political whim, in some cases of unstable and decidedly unattractive authoritarian regimes; high inflation and unemployment are the common lot of most industrial democracies; lack of confidence, not only in the dollar but also in other currencies, is reflected in the gyrating price of gold; and protectionist pressures have increased to the point that the danger of a trade war cannot be dismissed casually. Under these conditions, will the temptation to achieve a temporary advantage (that is, at least until the next election) by returning to the "beggar thy neighbor" economics of the 1930s prove too powerful? Or, can the industrial democracies establish new "regimes" for dealing creatively and cooperatively with these and other common problems? Can they establish the legitimacy of doing so among their respective domestic constituencies, or will they find that it is easier to mollify increasingly impatient electorates, first by placing the blame squarely on other nations, and then by taking actions that are consistent with such xenophobic diagnoses?

What relationships can be established with the less developed nations in order to cope with both the reality of a vast gap between the rich and poor nations, and the perception that the existing international order is structured so as to exacerbate rather than mitigate the problem? What kinds of risks should the United States be prepared to run for the luxury of being dependent for much of its oil on nations that have proven to be less than consistently sympathetic to American foreign policy, or with whom it has only a partial community of interest? What policies may be most effective in averting the economic collapse of one or more developing nations, or, should that occur, how can its results be contained so as to prevent a global economic collapse? How should the United States cope with what is certain to be a growing phenomenon: strident and reflexive anti-

Americanism generated by leaders who, unable or unwilling to deal with their own domestic problems, require an external scapegoat? Although the Soviet Union has made it clear that it feels no responsibility for bettering the lot of the poor nations, asserting that the source of those problems is "capitalist exploitation," there is every reason to expect that Washington rather than Moscow will be the target of choice. Finally, what role, if any, might the United States play in local and regional disputes in the Third World? What are the costs and benefits of a persistent tendency to define these conflicts as facets of the Cold War? Does the tendency to assert that disputes in the Middle East and elsewhere are linked to Soviet–American competition, without offering compelling evidence that this is so, risk offending all parties and so reducing American credibility as virtually to rule out any effective role in working out effective settlements? Conversely, what are the risks of a predisposition to "local-itis," the propensity to regard all turmoil as reflecting only unique local conditions, or of "Robin Hood-itis," the tendency to regard all revolutionaries as selfless democrats who seek power only to share it equitably?

Declining concern, if not disillusionment, with the less developed nations is fed and sustained by the growth there of authoritarian, sometimes totalitarian, rather than liberal institutions; by the murderous antics of the Khaddafis, Mengistus, Idi Amins, Castros, Bokassas, Khomeinis, Pinochets, Pol Pots, and Pham Van Dongs; by fears that some forms of assistance to the LDCs may be the first step into another Vietnam-like quagmire; and by the sentiment that, after all, charity begins at home. Plummeting public support for foreign aid may be found in poll after poll, but leadership views reveal a greater concern for the plight of poor nations, perhaps in recognition that benign neglect may be both a practically ineffective and morally inappropriate answer to the challenges posed abroad by responsible spokesmen for the "Group of 77" and in this country by former World Bank President Robert McNamara.[10]

A list of questions organized along geographical lines is bound to be a very incomplete one. Other issues that may merit serious discussion include these. *To what extent, and how, should the United States work cooperatively on problems that are international in both etiology and consequences: population control; population movements and refugees; pollution of the atmosphere, land, and oceans; proliferation of nuclear technologies and materials; periodic famines; protectionist pressures; and the like?*

It is naive to expect informed debate and clarification of such complex issues during election campaigns. The history of American elections does not offer a great deal of encouragement in this respect. In the best of times, they rarely provide a congenial setting for a "great debate" on monumental issues. Even less may be expected when there is a bull market in confusion, frustration, anger, and disillusionment about foreign affairs.[11] Recall the disgraceful tone of much campaigning during the 1950 and 1952 elections, when Americans were frustrated by the "loss" of China and the stalemated Korean War. Nor was the 1980 election especially illuminating.

A political campaign may preclude a high-quality discussion of foreign policy issues, but its end does not ensure that the discussion will take place in the less frenetic post-election atmosphere. The period since the 1980 election has certainly offered little to sustain the hopes of the optimists. Not only has the Reagan Administration failed almost completely to articulate a convincing set of fundamental principles that underlie its policies, but the Democratic opposition has not done much better. The content and tone of debates among spokesmen for various viewpoints does not augur well for informed discussion of these important issues. Perhaps some consolation may be found in the fact that most contestants have steered clear of the tactics espoused by Joseph McCarthy, Richard Nixon and other demagogues of an earlier generation.[12]

A century and a half ago, a sympathetic French observer of the American experiment wrote:

> As for myself, I do not hesitate to say that it is especially in the conduct of their foreign affairs that democracies appear to be decidedly inferior to other governments . . . [A] democracy can only with great difficulty regulate the details of an important undertaking, persevere in a fixed design, and work out its execution in spite of serious obstacles.[13]

In the face of the deep domestic cleavages described here, and an abundant agenda of critical international problems, the 1980s promise to provide an especially challenging decade for the United States to demonstrate that de Tocqueville's observation was fundamentally in error.

Notes to Chapter 8

1 See, for example, the similarities in diagnoses of Third World development in George F. Kennan, *The Cloud of Danger* (Boston: Little, Brown, 1977); and Michael Novak, *The Spirit of Democratic Development* (New York: Simon & Schuster), 1982.

2 J. G. Nicolay and John Hay, *Abraham Lincoln: A History*, Vol. III (New York: The Century Co., 1890), p. 446.

3 Haig continued: "Such a consensus will enable us to deal with the more fundamental tasks I have outlined; the management of Soviet power, the reestablishment of an orderly international economic climate, and economic and political maturation of developing nations to the benefit of their peoples and the achievement of a reasonable standard of international civility." *New York Times* (10 January 1981), p. 9.

4 See, for example, Seymour Weiss, "The Reagan response on Poland," *Wall Street Journal* (29 December 1981), p. 20; items cited in Chapter 7, note 20; Anthony Lewis, "Who lost Poland?," *New York Times* (7 January 1982), p. A27; Flora Lewis, "The gravest loss," *New York Times* (21 December 1981), p. A27; George F.

Kennan, "Jaruzelski's course," *New York Times* (5 January 1982), p. A15; and Kennan, "As the Kremlin sees it," *New York Times* (6 January 1982).

5   See, for example, Irving Kristol, "Consensus and Dissent in U.S. Foreign Policy," in Anthony Lake (ed.), *The Vietnam Legacy* (New York: New York University Press, 1976); and Norman Podhoretz, "Neo-conservative anguish over Reagan's foreign policy," *New York Times Magazine* (2 May 1982), pp. 30–3ff. Evidence on the issue of an alliance with China is summarized in Chapter 6, note 7.

6   Quoted in Steven V. Roberts, "Arms pact friends and foes rally for Senate battle," *New York Times* (13 April 1979). p. A2.

7   Representative Gerry E. Studds, quoted in Steven V. Roberts, "A critical coterie on foreign policy," *New York Times* (5 April 1982), p. A20.

8   Aside from Secretaries of State Alexander Haig and George Shultz, the total international experience of top leaders in the Reagan Administration (including the President, Secretary of State, Secretary of Defense, Director of the Central Intelligence Agency, and National Security Adviser) is very thin indeed. Casper Weinberger had been a domestic official throughout his previous public career, and CIA Director William Casey had only limited service in the OSS. Richard V. Allen served briefly in a minor role in the Nixon Administration, and William Clark had no demonstrable experience or expertise in foreign affairs. The latter two appointments also drew some unfavorable reaction because both Allen and Clark failed to earn the degrees they sought in post-graduate schools (University of Munich and Loyola Law School). Clark failed even to earn a BA degree. Following his confirmation hearing for the position of Undersecretary of State, Republican Senator Charles Percy warned: "Never again can we accept a man who professes no knowledge in the area for which he has been nominated." Clark later served until 1983 as National Security adviser, a position from which he apparently wielded very substantial power. *Wall Street Journal* (4 February 1981), p. 1.

9   James Reston, "The present danger," *New York Times* (17 November 1978), p. A29.

10   For a comparison of public and leadership views on foreign aid, see the figures in the 1975, 1979, and 1982 Chicago Council on Foreign Relations surveys. John E. Rielly, *American Public Opinion and Foreign Policy*, 1975; Rielly, *American Public Opinion and Foreign Policy*, 1979, both published by the CCFR; and Rielly, "American opinion: continuity, not Reaganism," *Foreign Policy*, no. 50 (Spring 1983), pp. 86–104. The data in Tables 3.1, 3.4, 6.4, and 6.6 above also indicate a comparatively favorable view toward foreign aid by leaders.

11   The data on performance ratings presented in Chapters 3 (Table 3.3) and 6 (Table 6.5) appear to justify this interpretation of leadership moods.

12   There are, however, exceptions. See, for example, the vitriolic attacks in Noam Chomsky, *Toward a New Cold War* (New York: Pantheon Books, 1982); and Irving Kristol, "What choice is there in Salvador?," *Wall Street Journal* (4 April 1983), p. 16. The latter writes that, "the very idea of fair play, like the idea of gentlemanly conduct, is part of a conservative political tradition, not of a liberal—and definitely not of a left–liberal tradition."

13   Alexis de Tocqueville, *Democracy in America* (ed. Phillips Bradley), Vol. 1 (New York: Knopf, 1945). p. 235.

Appendix A The 1976 and 1980 Leadership Samples

The ideal survey would be one in which the sample faithfully and precisely replicates the society's leadership structure. This study has proceeded on several assumptions: it is not possible to construct such a sample without expenditure of far greater resources than were available; no effort to do so would yield results that would satisfy all observers of American society; different return rates among sub-groups would almost certainly skew the resulting group of respondents in various ways; and, most importantly, the purposes of this study do not depend upon a construction of the ideal sample.

If the primary purpose here were to describe the foreign policy views of leaders in the aggregate, in a manner comparable to a public opinion poll, the failure to address more explicitly and precisely the structure of American leadership might pose serious problems of inference. However, the present goals are rather different, seeking to answer such questions as: What was the impact of the Vietnam War on foreign policy beliefs? Have these effects persisted? To what extent has the post-Vietnam era been characterized by the existence of fundamentally different foreign policy belief systems? What are the occupational, generational, ideological, and other correlates of foreign policy beliefs? The answers to these and related questions are to be found in the relationship of beliefs to each other, and of beliefs to respondent attributes.

As a consequence, the issues of whether media leaders should represent X percent or Y percent of the entire sample or whether it should include more business leaders than military officers—or vice versa—are not especially urgent. It is more important that the sample include representatives of many, if not all, major components of the nation's leadership structure and that there be enough respondents in occupational and other sub-categories to permit reliable comparisons among them. The sampling procedures were intended to satisfy these requirements.

Having eschewed the task of constructing a precise replica of America's leadership structure does not, however, imply that the sample is free of premises—some would call them biases—about American society. For example, the procedures summarized in Table A.1 clearly incorporate the pluralistic assumption that the foreign policy process in the United States is sensitive to a multiplicity of influences rather than merely to those of a narrow class or sector of society (e.g. business interests). However, because the data for various occupational and other groups are presented, readers who reject such premises may still find something of interest in the findings.

A search for a single source that identifies persons who occupy a variety of leadership roles, as well as those in sub-leadership positions who would have a high probability of occupying the top roles in the years ahead, proved fruitless. Thus, the 1976 and 1980 samples were constructed in ways that represented several types of compromises between the ideal and reality.

One part of each sample consists of almost 2,000 randomly drawn from the most recent edition of *Who's Who in America*, a useful source that includes biographical material about each person, as well as home addresses. The probability of a completed questionnaire being returned was assumed to be greater if it were received at home rather than at the office. In that case it was also less likely to be passed on to a colleague or subordinate for completion.

Who's Who in America is not without some significant drawbacks, however. Some groups are very heavily represented, especially business executives and educators. Conversely, military officers, labor leaders, the clergy, and several other important occupational groups are underrepresented. The age and sex distribution of its biographees may accurately mirror the leadership structure of American society, but the limited representation of women and younger persons rendered it less adequate for present purposes. A less serious problem is that *Who's Who in America*, which includes well over 70,000 persons, is silent about both the criteria of inclusion within its covers and the distribution of biographees according to attributes other than occupation.

The second part of the samples was constructed on the basis of quotas for leaders from each of eight groups that are inadequately represented in *Who's Who in America*: Foreign Service officers, military officers, labor officials, politicians, clergy, foreign affairs experts outside government, media leaders, and women. Names and addresses were drawn from various sources using random sampling procedures whenever feasible. In several cases the groups were sufficiently small that all members were included; for example, all chief editorial writers of newspapers with a circulation exceeding 100,000 were included in each sample, as were all presidents of state labor organizations.

The various sources were not equally valuable. In some cases (e.g. labor leaders and chief editorial writers) only office addresses were provided. Telephone directories were then used to trace home addresses, but it proved impossible to do so in all cases because of unlisted telephones or common names with multiple listings in directories. In other cases the sources were somewhat dated.

One of the largest occupational groups in the 1976 sample consisted of military personnel, including both senior officers (colonels and general officers, and their naval equivalents) then serving in the Pentagon, and junior and middle grade officers attending one of the service schools. These officers had already been identified by their branches of service as persons likely to achieve significant leadership positions during their military careers. The 1980 sample includes students at the National War College, a higher level service school

Table A.1 The 1976 and 1980 Leadership Samples and Sampling Sources

Group	Sub-group	1976 sample Sampling sources	N	1980 sample Sampling sources	N
General	—	Who's Who in America, 1974–1975	1,784	Who's Who in America, 1978–1979	1,845
Women	—	Who's Who of American Women, 1975–1976	233	Who's Who of American Women, 1979–1980	241
Media	Chief editorial writers	1975 Ayer Directory of Publications	104	1979 Ayer Directory of Publications	119
	Congressional press gallery	Congressional Directory 1975	60	Congressional Directory 1979	116
	Congressional radio–TV gallery	Congressional Directory 1975	76	Congressional Directory 1979	30
Foreign Service officers	—	Foreign Service List	226	Foreign Service List	224
Political leaders	—	Who's Who in American Politics, 1973–1974	224	Who's Who in American Politics, 1977–1978	243
Labor leaders	—	Directory of National Unions and Employee Associations	225	Directory of National Unions and Employee Associations	231
Military officers	Senior Pentagon officers	Congressional Directory, 1975	49	Congressional Directory, 1979	127
	Service school students	Roster, USNPGS, 1975–1976	843	Distributed to 1979–1980 class by National War College staff	160

		Source	N	Source	N
Clergy	Catholic	Official Catholic Directory	71	Official Catholic Directory	60
	Jewish	Who's Who in World Jewry, 1972	8	Membership List, The Rabbinical Assembly	20
	Protestant	Episcopal Church Annual, 1975 Christian Church Yearbook and Directory, 1974 Presbyterian Church in the United States: General Assembly Minutes, 1975 American Lutheran Church Yearbook, 1975 United Presbyterian Church in the U.S.A.: General Assembly, 1974 Southern Baptist Convention, 1973 Annual	152	Episcopal Church Annual, 1979 Christian Church Yearbook and Directory, 1978 Presbyterian Church in the United States: General Assembly Minutes, 1978 American Lutheran Church Yearbook, 1979 United Presbyterian Church in the U.S.A.: General Assembly, 1978	158
Foreign affairs experts outside government	—	Authors and editors, Foreign Affairs and Foreign Policy, 1973–1975	100	Authors and editors, Foreign Affairs and Foreign Policy, 1976–1979	90
		Biographical Directory, International Studies Association, 1975	135	Membership List, International Studies Association, 1979	150
Panel	—	1976 respondents who identified themselves (included in sources and Ns listed above)		1976 respondents who identified themselves	142

with smaller classes. For this reason, the 1980 survey includes fewer military officers.

As indicated at several points in the text, differences in the composition of the 1976 and 1980 samples, notably in the case of military officers, makes it necessary to use caution in comparing aggregate results of the two surveys. Comparison of results for occupational and other sub-groups are therefore a vital part of any effort to assess continuity and change during the four-year interval between the two surveys.

Return Rates

The first mailing in February 1976 yielded 1,899 completed questionnaires. In order to preserve their anonymity, respondents were asked to return the questionnaire to one address (a stamped, addressed envelope was provided for this purpose), and a postal card (also provided) acknowledging its completion to another. Names of those returning the postal card were removed from the list for a follow-up mailing sent out two months later which brought in another 383 completed questionnaires. Very limited research funds precluded a third mailing to the remaining non-respondents.[1]

Thus, 2,282 of the 4,290 questionnaire recipients (53 percent), completed and returned the survey instrument. The return rate may have been adversely affected by the length of the questionnaire and the atmosphere of distrust toward social science surveys prevalent in recent years.[2] A partial test of sample representativeness involved comparing reponses to the two mailings, assuming that those who had to be prodded a second time sufficiently resembled those who did not respond at all. If the 383 second-mailing respondents differed significantly from their 1,899 counterparts in the first mailing, concern that the sample was biased would have been heightened. In fact, significant response differences occurred on only two items; one of the two items concerned Angola, where the conflict was essentially resolved during the two-month period between the two mailings.

With one exception—the use of a third mailing—similar procedures were employed in 1980. The return rate reached 63 percent as there were 2,502 respondents among the 3,956 leaders who received the questionnaire. Of those responding, 80 percent did so to the first mailing, followed by 13 percent and 7 percent to the next two. This return rate compares favorably with comparable surveys.

Notes to Appendix A

1   As a further economy measure, non-responding officers at the military school were not included in the second mailing.
2   The Watergate scandal and revelations that illegal domestic surveillance activities by the FBI and CIA were not limited to the Nixon years have helped to create the atmosphere of distrust that has no doubt affected the return rate in all recent

surveys. Several cases of highly unethical surveys indicate that distrust is not wholly unjustified. An especially notorious example occurred when *Finance Magazine* sponsored an allegedly scholarly survey among international relations specialists, the result of which were then used to promote Richard Nixon for the Nobel Peace Prize. An episode revealing use of blatantly unethical techniques by commercial survey firms received wide publicity. On 10 November 1975, the *New York Times* summarized a longer report by Henry Gemmill, appearing in the *National Observer*, that was also picked up by a number of other major newspapers. For a further discussion, see John P. Dickson, Michael Casey, Daniel Wyckoff, and William Wind, "Invisible coding of questionnaires," *Public Opinion Quarterly*, 41 (Spring 1977), pp. 100–12.

Appendix B The 1976 and 1980 Questionnaires

Primary data for this study are drawn from responses to a twelve-page questionnaire used in 1976, and one of sixteen pages employed four years later.[1] A systematic review of articles, speeches, editorials, interviews, press conferences, and other materials from sources spanning a broad ideological spectrum served as the major source of questionnaire items relating to Vietnam. Three types of assertions were extracted from these materials: diagnoses of the sources of failure in Vietnam; predictions about the consequences of the American experience in Southeast Asia; and prescriptions or lessons of the conflict that should guide the future conduct of this nation's foreign policy. Several items in the questionnaire are verbatim quotations, but most of the original texts were paraphrased to reduce excessive wordiness or other problems. Pretesting the questionnaire provided an opportunity to identify ambiguities or other flaws in the wording of specific items.

In addition to asking respondents to assess the lessons of Vietnam and the sources and consequences of America's lack of success in the war, other items probed for general orientations toward foreign policy and some domestic issues, as well as for information about respondents' backgrounds. To permit comparisons with other surveys, several questions used in other recent studies of American leaders were included. One multi-part question on the goals and performance of American foreign policy was drawn from surveys conducted by the Chicago Council on Foreign Relations in 1975 and 1979. Several questions originally appeared in the Harvard–*Washington Post* and bicentennial survey, and other clusters of items were drawn from studies of American business executives and military officers, and of those heading major American interest groups.[2]

Just before the 1980 questionnaire went to press, mobs in Teheran invaded the American Embassy, triggering a fourteen-month long confrontation between Iran and the United States, and burying for the foreseeable future, if not forever, the premise that cooperation between these two nations would ensure stability in the Persian Gulf region. Several weeks later, Soviet armed forces invaded Afghanistan, touching off a major re-evaluation of American policy toward the USSR. Two clusters of items on the 1980 questionnaire asked respondents to assess the meaning of these events for the nation's external relations.

The 1976 and 1980 questionnaires are reproduced below. Numerical entries in the questionnaires depict the distribution of responses to each item.

Foreign Policy Leadership Project

sponsored by

Research Council, Duke University
Center for International Affairs, Harvard University
Institute for Transnational Studies, University of Southern California

February-March 1976

Foreign Policy Leadership Project

To what extent do you feel that the conduct of U.S. foreign policy has been affected by the American participation in the Vietnam War? (Check only one box)

To a very great extent	Quite Significantly	Somewhat	Slightly	Not at all
38	53	8	1	0

In your judgment, how long will the American experience in Vietnam continue to influence the conduct of U.S. foreign policy? (Check only one box)

As long as one can see into the future	14
Perhaps for a generation	40
Perhaps for about a decade	39
Through the next presidential campaign	6
It will have no impact on American policy	1

Some people felt that we should have done everything possible to gain a complete military victory in Vietnam. Others felt that we should have withdrawn as soon as possible. Still others had opinions in between these two. Please indicate which position came closest to your own feelings—both when the war first became an issue and later toward the end of U.S. involvement—by checking one box in each column.

	When the war first became an issue	Toward the end of U.S. involvement
I tended to favor a complete military victory	51	22
I tended to favor a complete withdrawal	22	57
I tended to feel in between these two	22	18
Not sure	5	3

Which of the following statements describes what your feelings were about the war in Vietnam? (Check one box in each column)

	When the war first became an issue	Toward the end of U.S. involvement
The war in Vietnam was one of my major worries and concerns at that time	28	58
I was concerned about the war, but it was not one of my major causes of worry	55	39
I was not very concerned about the war	16	2
Don't know	1	0

In retrospect, how would you assess the meaning of the Vietnam War for you personally? (Check only one box)

It was a profoundly important experience that is likely to influence my outlook for a long time	53
It had an important influence on me at the time, but this influence has now waned	30
It had no more effect on me than any other foreign policy issue	14
It did not influence my outlook in any significant way	4

NOTE:
Numbers indicate the percentage distribution of responses to each item, excluding non-responses and uncodable responses.

Turning to more general considerations, here is a list of possible foreign policy goals that the United States might have. Please indicate how much importance you think should be attached to each goal.

(Check only one box in each row on the right)

		Very Important	Somewhat Important	Not Important at all	Not Sure
2*	Containing communism	39	42	14	5
3	Helping to improve the standard of living in less developed countries	38	51	9	3
6	Keeping peace in the world	71	25	2	3
2	Worldwide arms control	66	26	5	3
8	Defending our allies' security	37	55	4	4
21	Promoting and defending our own security	85	13	1	1
8	Promoting the development of capitalism abroad	6	33	53	7
2	Securing adequate supplies of energy	72	25	2	1
1	Helping to bring a democratic form of government to other nations	7	44	39	9
12	Protecting the interests of American business abroad	14	56	25	5
4	Protecting the jobs of American workers	31	51	14	4
1	Protecting weaker nations against foreign aggression	18	60	12	9
8	Maintaining a balance of power among nations	44	41	9	7
5	Combatting world hunger	51	40	7	3
1	Helping solve world inflation	50	42	6	3
3	Strengthening the United Nations	25	37	30	8
4	Strengthening countries who are friendly toward us	23	64	9	5
4	Fostering international cooperation to solve common problems, such as food, inflation and energy	70	26	2	1

Now please indicate on these lines how you would rate the job the U.S. is now doing with respect to each goal. Put a 1 on the line if you think its performance is *excellent*, a 2 if it is *pretty good*, a 3 if it is *only fair*, a 4 if it is *poor*, and a 5 if you are *not sure*.

*Percent responding with a 1 (excellent).

Somewhat more specifically, please indicate how strongly you agree or disagree with each of the following statements concerning America's role in the world.

(Check only one box in each row on the right)

	Agree Strongly	Agree Somewhat	Disagree Somewhat	Disagree Strongly	No Opinion
The U.S. has a moral obligation to prevent the destruction of the State of Israel.	33	36	18	11	2
There is nothing wrong with using the C.I.A. to try to undermine hostile governments.	21	30	20	28	1
We shouldn't think so much in international terms but concentrate more on our own national problems.	11	26	29	33	1
The U.S. should give economic aid to poorer countries even if it means higher prices at home.	11	37	32	19	1
It is not in our interest to have better relations with the Soviet Union because we are getting less than we are giving to them.	9	20	35	34	2
The main goal of those who make American foreign policy is to protect the interests of U.S. business.	10	22	26	40	2
The U.S. should take all steps including the use of force to prevent the spread of Communism.	9	24	30	35	1
Even though it probably means higher food prices here at home, it is worth selling grain to the Soviet Union since it may improve our relations with Russia.	5	32	32	28	3

At the present time, and on average, how frequently do you engage in the following activities.

(Check only one box in each row on the right)

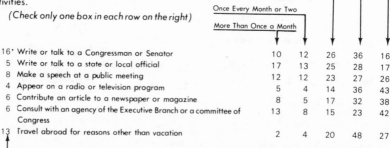

	More Than Once a Month	Once Every Month or Two	A Few Times in a Year	Once a Year, or Less	Never have Engaged in the Activity
16* Write or talk to a Congressman or Senator	10	12	26	36	16
5 Write or talk to a state or local official	17	13	25	28	17
8 Make a speech at a public meeting	12	12	23	27	26
4 Appear on a radio or television program	5	4	14	36	43
6 Contribute an article to a newspaper or magazine	8	5	17	32	38
6 Consult with an agency of the Executive Branch or a committee of Congress	13	8	15	23	42
13 Travel abroad for reasons other than vacation	2	4	20	48	27

Now please go back to these lines and indicate those activities in which Vietnam was a focus of your efforts during the late 1960s and early 1970s. Place a *1* on the line if you recall Vietnam to have been the **prime concern** of the activity, a 2 if it was only an **occasional basis** of the activity, and 3 if Vietnam was **never** the focus of the activity.

*Percent responding with a 1 (prime concern).

This question asks you to indicate your position on certain foreign policy issues, and to state the extent to which your position was shaped by the experience in Vietnam. First indicate how strongly you agree or disagree with each statement by *checking one box in each row on the right*. Then follow the instructions at the bottom of the page and go back through the statements by indicating on the line to the left the extent to which the lessons of Vietnam may underlie your present position.

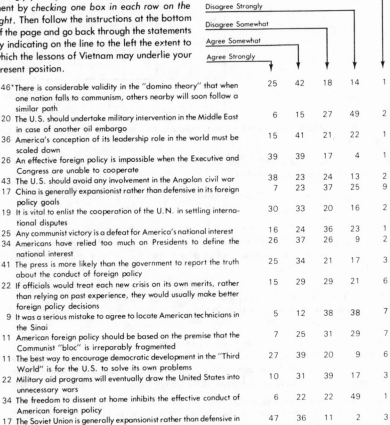

	Agree Strongly	Agree Somewhat	Disagree Somewhat	Disagree Strongly	No Opinion
46*There is considerable validity in the "domino theory" that when one nation falls to communism, others nearby will soon follow a similar path	25	42	18	14	1
20 The U.S. should undertake military intervention in the Middle East in case of another oil embargo	6	15	27	49	2
36 America's conception of its leadership role in the world must be scaled down	15	41	21	22	1
26 An effective foreign policy is impossible when the Executive and Congress are unable to cooperate	39	39	17	4	1
43 The U.S. should avoid any involvement in the Angolan civil war	38	23	24	13	2
17 China is generally expansionist rather than defensive in its foreign policy goals	7	23	37	25	9
19 It is vital to enlist the cooperation of the U.N. in settling international disputes	30	33	20	16	2
25 Any communist victory is a defeat for America's national interest	16	24	36	23	1
34 Americans have relied too much on Presidents to define the national interest	26	37	26	9	2
41 The press is more likely than the government to report the truth about the conduct of foreign policy	25	34	21	17	3
22 If officials would treat each new crisis on its own merits, rather than relying on past experience, they would usually make better foreign policy decisions	15	29	29	21	6
9 It was a serious mistake to agree to locate American technicians in the Sinai	5	12	38	38	7
11 American foreign policy should be based on the premise that the Communist "bloc" is irreparably fragmented	7	25	31	29	7
11 The best way to encourage democratic development in the "Third World" is for the U.S. to solve its own problems	27	39	20	9	6
22 Military aid programs will eventually draw the United States into unnecessary wars	10	31	39	17	3
34 The freedom to dissent at home inhibits the effective conduct of American foreign policy	6	22	22	49	1
17 The Soviet Union is generally expansionist rather than defensive in its foreign policy goals	47	36	11	2	3

Now please indicate on these lines the extent to which your position was influenced by the Vietnam conflict. Put a 1 on the line if you think it *greatly influenced* your judgment, a 2 if it *mildly influenced* you, a 3 if it had *no influence*, and a 4 if you are *not sure*.

*Percent responding with a 1 (greatly influenced judgment)

How would you describe your interest in international, national, and local politics?
(Circle one number on each scale)

	It is one of my major concerns ↓			Moderate concern ↓			I pay little attention ↓
International Politics	35	22	19	16	5	2	0
National Politics	37	32	19	11	2	0	0
Local Politics	16	13	14	22	14	12	9

Speaking of national and local politics, here are two issues on which we would like your views:

Generally speaking, do you think that racial integration is going too fast, not fast enough, or about right?   *(Check only one box)*

Too fast	Not fast enough	About right	No opinion
13	33	48	5

Some people say we must concentrate on fighting either inflation or unemployment because if we make an equal effort to fight them both we probably will solve neither problem. If you had to choose where to place the emphasis, which do you consider the more important problem to attack?   *(Check only one box)*

Emphasize fight against unemployment	Emphasize fight against inflation	Put equal emphasis on both, even at risk of solving neither	No opinion
24	47	27	1

Please indicate the relative importance you believe the U.S. should attach, in general, to the following policy objectives in its involvement with under-developed countries. If a choice must be made, which ones should be considered most important? *Use the numbers 1-7 with a 1 being the highest* rank. (Please do not assign equal ranks to objectives; assume there must be a choice):

34*	A stable government capable of preserving internal order
12	A government which is neutral or pro-American in its foreign policy
7	Rapid economic development
28	A government which maintains civil liberties
5	A government which retains the free enterprise system
25	A government which will not engage in unprovoked aggression against other nations
2	A government which allows broad opportunities for American business investment

*Percent responding with a 1 (highest rank).

Here is another question asking you to indicate your position on certain foreign policy questions and the extent to which your position was shaped by the experience in Vietnam. Again we request that first you indicate how strongly you agree or disagree with each statement by checking one box in each row on the right and then, following the instructions at the bottom of the page, indicate on the lines at the left the extent to which the lessons of Vietnam may underlie your present position.

	Agree Strongly	Agree Somewhat	Disagree Somewhat	Disagree Strongly	No Opinion
40*The American people lack the patience for foreign policy undertakings that offer little prospect of success in the short run	31	46	15	7	2
24 A nation will pay a heavy price if it honors its alliance commitments only selectively	37	43	15	3	3
38 Limited wars should be fought primarily with air power so as to avoid introducing American ground troops	9	24	26	25	16
26 Revolutionary forces in "Third World" countries are usually nationalistic rather than controlled by the USSR or China	21	39	22	12	5
37 The conduct of American foreign affairs relies excessively on military advice	20	29	30	18	3
48 The U.S. should never try to get by with half measures; we should apply necessary power if we have it	26	27	24	21	3
45 Limited war cannot be conducted successfully because of constraints imposed by the American political system	24	39	22	10	6
8 Détente permits the USSR to pursue policies that promote rather than restrain conflict	19	38	28	9	6
27 Stationing American troops in other countries encourages them to let us do their fighting for those countries	15	45	28	8	3
58 If foreign interventions are undertaken, the necessary force should be applied in a short period of time rather than through a policy of graduated escalation	49	29	8	5	10
44 It is best to forget the foreign policy mistakes of the past as quickly as possible	8	9	23	58	1
16 Vital interests of the U.S. are largely confined to Western Europe, Japan, and the Americas	13	26	29	30	2
18 Weak allies excessively influence U.S. foreign policy	10	39	31	10	10
33 Rather than simply countering our opponent's thrusts, it is necessary to strike at the heart of the opponent's power	21	25	23	22	9
30 The efficiency of military power in foreign affairs is declining	16	46	20	12	7
27 Americans lack an understanding of the role that power plays in world politics	29	43	18	6	4
42 When force is used, military rather than political goals should determine its application	16	20	24	34	5

Now please indicate on these lines the extent to which your position was influenced by the Vietnam conflict. Put a 1 in the box if you think it *greatly influenced* your judgment, a 2 if it *mildly influenced* you, a 3 if it had *no influence*, and a 4 if you are *not sure*.

*Percent responding with a 1 (greatly influenced judgment).

There has been quite a bit of discussion about the consequences of the Vietnam episode. Some of these are listed below. Please indicate your assessment of each statement by *checking only one box for each item.*

	Agree Strongly	Agree Somewhat	Disagree Somewhat	Disagree Strongly	No Opinion
As a result of the Vietnam experience, the U.S. is likely to keep military assistance to anti-Soviet factions in Angola to a minimum	65	28	4	1	1
The foundations of the American economy were seriously damaged by our involvement in Vietnam	33	30	21	15	1
The Vietnam episode has raised profound doubts about American credibility in the minds of our allies	33	40	19	7	2
Communist nations have been encouraged to seek triumphs elsewhere as a result of Vietnam	30	39	19	8	3
The major assumptions of détente have been proven false by the events in Vietnam	11	24	37	17	11
The American people have lost faith in the honesty of their government as a result of the Vietnam War	25	48	19	6	1
The memory of Vietnam will prevent the U.S. from using force even when vital American interests abroad are threatened	11	37	30	20	1
As a consequence of the Vietnam episode, American policies toward the "Third World" will emphasize humanitarian rather than military aid	9	45	29	9	9
The shape of the international system we have known since World War II has been irrevocably altered by America's inability to prevent the collapse of the Thieu regime in 1975	10	30	30	23	7
As a result of events in Vietnam, the U.S. is likely to engage in high risk ventures in order to re-establish its credibility	2	9	34	53	3
The tide of influence in world affairs has swung toward communism as a result of the Vietnam War	8	32	34	23	4
The U.S. is likely to operate with a more limited conception of the national interest as a result of the outcome in Vietnam	22	60	11	4	4
The real long term threats to national security—energy shortages, the environment, etc.—have been neglected as a result of our preoccupation with Vietnam	34	39	17	9	1

Other consequences of Vietnam? _____

Observers of American foreign policy have identified several factors that may have prevented the United States from achieving its goals in the Vietnam undertaking. In your judgment, how important were the reasons listed below in America's inability to achieve all of its goals? Please indicate your assessment by checking only one box in each row.

	Very Important	Moderately Important	Slightly Important	Not at all Important	Not Sure
Pressures from domestic dissidents cast doubt on American commitments	34	35	22	8	1
America's goals in Vietnam were inherently unrealistic	50	28	12	7	3
The regime in Saigon lacked popular support	51	27	14	4	4
Reporting by the mass media turned the public against the war	37	38	18	6	1
Congressional involvement hampered the executive in the conduct of the war	20	27	30	20	3
The Soviets and Chinese provided aid to North Vietnam and the Vietcong	55	27	14	3	1
The Watergate scandal paralyzed the American government	21	24	25	29	1
The United States fought with a "no win" approach	45	20	14	18	3
The U.S. lacked understanding of nationalism in the "Third World"	40	30	16	9	5
The use of American air power was restricted	33	21	20	23	4
Intelligence agencies failed to provide adequate information about the situation in Vietnam	24	32	20	13	10
The U.S. had no clear goals in the Vietnam undertaking	44	30	13	8	4
Insufficient attention was paid to advice from the military	22	21	19	30	9
America's allies failed to support us	14	23	29	30	4
U.S. military assistance to South Vietnam after the 1973 peace agreement was inadequate	14	18	24	35	8
North Vietnam violated the 1973 peace agreement	33	21	18	21	7
Much of world opinion opposed U.S. goals and policies	29	35	24	9	3
Americans underestimated the dedication of the North Vietnamese	57	27	10	4	1
America relied excessively on air power	19	25	25	22	9
The American people lost the spirit which led to greatness	19	18	16	37	10
Americans were ignorant of Vietnamese history, culture, and society	41	25	18	12	3

(Other factors?) ⸺⸺⸺⸺⸺⸺⸺⸺⸺⸺⸺⸺⸺⸺⸺⸺⸺⸺⸺⸺⸺

As you think about the steps that led to American involvement in Vietnam, how important a role do you believe the following events played?
  (Check only one box in each row)

	Very Important	Moderately Important	Slightly Important	Not at all Important	Not Sure
The policy of appeasement at Munich in 1938	12	15	18	38	17
The 1947 Truman Doctrine	15	26	25	16	18
The Marshall Plan of economic assistance to Europe	4	16	28	40	12
The Berlin airlift of 1948-49	7	22	30	30	10
The decision to send troops to Korea in 1950	38	40	15	4	4
The decision not to send troops to Indo-China in 1954	13	23	26	22	17
The 1956 decision not to intervene in Hungary	9	17	24	37	13
The dispatch of Marines to Lebanon in 1958	8	23	27	29	14
Support of the invasion of Cuba in 1961	14	27	24	26	9
Failure to contest erection of the Berlin Wall in 1961	10	19	25	35	11
The 1962 blockade to force removal of missiles from Cuba	23	35	19	17	7

Finally, we have a few questions for background information.

Male 90   Female 10   Year of birth _____

What is the highest level of education that you have completed?

Some High School	High School Graduate	Some College	College Graduate	Some Graduate Work	Graduate Degree	Type of Graduate Degree
0	1	6	10	22	60	

What is your primary occupation? *(Check only one)*

13 Business executive	22 Military officer	2 Physician
3 Labor official	9 Public official	0 Entertainer
25 Educator	9 Communications	7 Other (specify):
4 Clergy	5 Lawyer	_____

Roughly how many times since 1950 have you traveled to *(enter number of times in each box)*

Latin America	Africa	Eastern Europe and/or Russia	Western Europe	Middle East	Far East
47	25	26	78	34	46

Have you ever served in the armed forces?   Yes 67 No 33   If yes, what years? _____

Which of the following, if any, were your main sources of information about the course of events in Vietnam? *(Check as many boxes as are applicable)*

54	Time	42	New York Times	47	ABC News
43	Newsweek	27	Washington Post	74	CBS News
26	U.S. News & World Report	27	Wall Street Journal	63	NBC News
		7	Los Angeles Times	48	Other?_____

How would you describe your views in political matters?

1	Far left	26	Moderate	0	Far right
9	Very liberal	30	Somewhat conservative	2	Other
26	Somewhat liberal	6	Very conservative	0	Don't know

In 1976, what role do you expect to play in the various elections? *(Check as many as are appropriate)*

	National	State	Local
Make a financial contribution	55	30	24
Actively campaign for one or more candidates	17	14	12
Sign one or more ads on behalf of candidates	13	12	12
Write letters on behalf of candidates	10	11	9
Vote in the election	94	84	78
I do not plan to participate in the election	5	5	7

Generally speaking, do you think of yourself as a *Republican*, a *Democrat*, an *Independent*, or what?

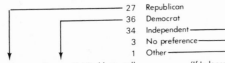

- 27 Republican
- 36 Democrat
- 34 Independent
- 3 No preference
- 1 Other

(If Republican or Democrat) Would you call yourself a strong (Republican/Democrat) or a not very strong (Republican/Democrat)?

- 18 Strong Republican
- 24 Not very strong Republican
- 26 Not very strong Democrat
- 30 Strong Democrat
- 1 Don't know

(If Independent, no preference, or other) Do you think of yourself as closer to the *Republican* or to the *Democratic* party?

- 38 Republican
- 27 Neither
- 35 Democratic

Did you have a child or children in college during the 1965-72 period?   Yes 38   No 62

How many?_____ Which colleges?_____

Were they *(Check one)*
- 5 active in the anti-Vietnam war movement
- 21 passively opposed to the war
- 5 passively supportive of the war effort
- 1 actively supportive of the war effort
- 2 other (briefly describe:_____)

Did you ever argue with any of them about Vietnam?	Yes	17	No	83
Was your relationship to any of them strained by the Vietnam issue?	Yes	3	No	97
Was your own position on Vietnam influenced by any of them?	Yes	11	No	89

Foreign Policy Leadership Project

sponsored by

Research Council, Duke University
Center for International Affairs, Harvard University
Institute for Transnational Studies, University of Southern California

March 1980

Foreign Policy Leadership Project

● Which of the following statements best describes the impact of the Vietnam War and the situations in Iran and Afghanistan on your beliefs about international affairs and America's role in the world? (Check **only one** box in **each** column)

	Vietnam	Iran	Afghanistan
It confirmed views that I had previously held	34	44	61
It caused me to question some of my views, and it confirmed some others	41	41	26
It caused a profound change in my views	22	11	7
Not sure	3	4	7

● Some people felt that we should have done everything possible to gain a complete military victory in Vietnam. Others felt that we should have withdrawn as soon as possible. Still others had opinions in between these two. Please indicate which position came closest to your own feelings — both when the war first became an issue (in the mid-1960s) and later toward the end of U.S. involvement (during the early 1970s) — by checking **only one** box in **each** column.

	When the war first became an issue	Toward the end of U.S. involvement
I tended to favor a complete military victory	54	24
I tended to favor a complete withdrawal	21	54
I tended to feel in between these two	22	20
Not sure	3	2

● In retrospect, how would you assess the American effort in the Vietnam War? (Check **only one** box)

4	The U.S. effort was justified, and it achieved some important foreign policy goals
48	The U.S. effort was justified, but it failed
4	The U.S. effort was unjustified, but it did achieve some important American foreign policy goals
42	The U.S. effort was unjustified and it failed
3	Not sure

NOTE:
Numbers indicate the percentage distribution of responses to each item, excluding non-responses and uncodable responses.

● Some people felt that the U.S. should have used all available military power to gain release of the hostages in the Embassy in Iran. Others favored bargaining with the regime in Iran to secure their release. Still others opposed bargaining prior to the release of the hostages, and favored the use of various strategies for effecting their release. Please indicate which position comes closest to your own feelings — both when the Embassy was first taken over and after the Soviet invasion of Afghanistan — by checking **only one** box in **each** column.

	When the Embassy was taken over	After the Soviet invasion of Afghanistan
I tended to favor immediate use of military power	17	8
I tended to favor bargaining with the regime in Iran	30	29
I tended to oppose bargaining prior to the release of the hostages and to favor using all means short of military power to secure their release	32	31
I tended to oppose bargaining prior to the release of the hostages and to support the use of military power if diplomatic and economic measures seemed unlikely to break the stalemate	20	26
Not sure	2	6

● Kindly estimate the impact on American prestige abroad of the Vietnam War, the hostage situation in Iran, and the invasion of Afghanistan.

 *(Check **only one** box in **each** column)*

	Vietnam	Iran	Afghanistan
Enhanced U.S. prestige significantly	0	2	3
Enhanced U.S. prestige somewhat	2	11	18
Did not affect U.S. prestige	2	9	29
Damaged U.S. prestige somewhat	22	34	25
Damaged U.S. prestige significantly	73	42	19
Not sure	1	3	7

● During the last two decades of this century, which *two* of the
following are likely to pose the greatest threat to American
national security? *(Check only two boxes)*

50 a decline of American military strength relative to that of the USSR

26 a growing gap between rich nations and poor nations

50 an inability to solve such domestic problems as the decay of cities,
unemployment and inflation, racial conflict, and crime

13 uncontrolled growth of the world's population

8   American interventions in conflicts that are none of our business

35 Soviet expansion into Third World areas

12 Other _____

● The statements below are drawn from debates about the
implications of the Afghanistan situation. Please indicate how
strongly you agree or disagree with each statement by checking *only one* box in *each* row.

	Agree Strongly	Agree Somewhat	Disagree Somewhat	Disagree Strongly	Not Sure
Soviet actions in Afghanistan do not affect vital American interests	6	18	32	42	1
The Afghanistan situation proves that the Cold War never ended	35	40	16	7	3
The Soviet Union acted in Afghanistan largely to protect itself against having a hostile regime on its borders	6	24	17	47	6
Recent events in Afghanistan are a direct consequence of a decline in U.S. influence in the aftermath of the Vietnam War	18	36	21	19	5
The Administration has overreacted to the situation in Afghanistan	10	20	26	42	3
As a result of Afghanistan, the U.S. should conclude an alliance with China	8	28	22	21	21
Restrictions on grain sales to the USSR will do nothing other than hurt American farmers	9	21	37	29	4
The Afghanistan situation has created the most dangerous international crisis since World War II	7	19	31	38	4
Afghanistan proves the need for American military bases in the Middle East	24	38	18	13	7
If it seems clear that the Soviet Union does not intend to move beyond Afghanistan in Southwest Asia, the U.S. should be ready to restore a détente relationship with the Soviets	10	28	26	29	8
The Soviet invasion of Afghanistan is one step in a larger plan to control the Persian Gulf area	32	34	14	6	14
It is proper for the U.S. to withdraw from the Olympic Games in Moscow	55	23	9	10	4

● This question asks you to indicate your position on certain foreign policy issues that are sometimes described as "lessons" that we should have learned from the American experience in Vietnam. Indicate how strongly you agree or disagree with each statement by checking **only one** box in **each** row.

	Agree Strongly	Agree Somewhat	Disagree Somewhat	Disagree Strongly	No Opinion
There is considerable validity in the "domino theory" that when one nation falls to communism, others nearby will soon follow a similar path	23	40	20	16	1
The U.S. should undertake military intervention in the Middle East in case of another oil embargo	7	22	30	36	4
America's conception of its leadership role in the world must be scaled down	12	37	24	26	2
An effective foreign policy is impossible when the Executive and Congress are unable to cooperate	40	41	13	5	1
China is generally expansionist rather than defensive in its foreign policy goals	3	16	43	28	11
It is vital to enlist the cooperation of the U.N. in settling international disputes	31	39	16	12	2
Any communist victory is a defeat for America's national interest	17	28	32	21	2
Americans have relied too much on Presidents to define the national interest	19	38	28	10	6
The press is more likely than the government to report the truth about the the conduct of foreign policy	17	35	23	19	5
American foreign policy should be based on the premise that the Communist "bloc" is irreparably fragmented	7	25	31	30	7
The best way to encourage democratic development in the "Third World" is for the U.S. to solve its own problems	25	42	19	9	6
Military aid programs will eventually draw the United States into unnecessary wars	7	23	40	26	4
The freedom to dissent at home inhibits the effective conduct of American foreign policy	5	22	20	52	1
The Soviet Union is generally expansionist rather than defensive in its foreign policy goals	53	32	9	4	3
Third World conflicts cannot jeopardize vital American interests	4	6	28	61	2
The U.S. should maintain its military commitment to South Korea	36	38	12	7	8

● How important, in your judgment, are each of the following reasons that have been used to explain American involvement in the Vietnam War?

(Check only one box in each row)

	Very Important	Moderately Important	Slightly Important	Not at all Important	Not Sure
To honor an alliance commitment	35	31	20	11	3
To protect American investments and markets in the area	11	21	32	34	2
To contain Chinese expansion	13	27	30	26	4
To prove that "wars of national liberation" could not succeed	9	15	17	51	8
To maintain a global balance of power	27	33	21	16	4
To forestall charges that the government was "soft on communism"	8	15	21	52	3

Other: _____

Here are two domestic issues on which we would like your views:

● Generally speaking, do you think that racial integration is going too fast, not fast enough, or about right?

(Check only one box)

Too fast	Not fast enough	About right	Not sure
10	37	48	5

● Some people say we must concentrate on fighting either inflation or unemployment because if we make an equal effort to fight them both we probably will solve neither problem. If you had to choose where to place the emphasis, which do you consider the more important problem to attack?

(Check only one box)

Emphasize fight against unemployment	Emphasize fight against inflation	Put equal emphasis on both, even at risk of solving neither	Not sure
8	72	18	2

Here are some questions on economic issues:

	Agree	Disagree	Not Sure
● U.S. economic policy has not been sufficiently responsive to the need for foreign market expansion and product competitiveness during the past decade	75	13	12
● U.S. industrial competitiveness is threatened by the most rapidly developing Third World Nations (South Korea, Taiwan, Singapore, Brazil, etc.)	45	44	11
● Efforts to protect weaker domestic industries from foreign competition are not a viable policy	62	26	13

● Here is another question asking you to indicate your position
on certain foreign policy questions that are sometimes described as "lessons" that we should have learned from the
American experience in Vietnam. Again we request that you
indicate how strongly you agree or disagree with each statement by checking **only one** box in **each** row on the right.

Statement	Agree Strongly	Agree Somewhat	Disagree Somewhat	Disagree Strongly	No Opinion
The American people lack the patience for foreign policy under-takings that offer little prospect of success in the short run.	26	49	15	9	2
A nation will pay a heavy price if it honors its alliance commit-ments only selectively	43	39	12	3	4
Limited wars should be fought primarily with air power so as to avoid introducing American ground troops	7	24	24	27	17
Revolutionary forces in "Third World" countries are usually nationalistic rather than controlled by the USSR or China	20	38	24	14	4
The conduct of American foreign affairs relies excessively on military advice	14	26	31	24	5
Limited war cannot be conducted successfully because of con-straints imposed by the American political system	18	44	22	9	6
Détente permits the USSR to pursue policies that promote rather than restrain conflict	23	37	26	8	6
Stationing American troops in other countries encourages them to let us do their fighting for those countries	11	44	31	10	4
If foreign interventions are undertaken, the necessary force should be applied in a short period of time rather than through a policy of graduated escalation	51	27	7	4	12
Vital interests of the U.S. are largely confined to Western Europe, Japan, and the Americas	8	17	26	47	2
Weak allies excessively influence U.S. foreign policy	10	39	29	13	8
Rather than simply countering our opponent's thrusts, it is necessary to strike at the heart of the opponent's power	20	25	21	22	11
The efficiency of military power in foreign affairs is declining	20	43	17	14	7
Americans lack an understanding of the role that power plays in world politics	34	43	13	6	3
When force is used, military rather than political goals should determine its application	14	18	25	38	6

● There has been quite a bit of discussion about the consequences of the Vietnam episode. Some of these are listed below. Please indicate your assessment of each statement by checking **only one** box for **each** item.

	Agree Strongly	Agree Somewhat	Disagree Somewhat	Disagree Strongly	No Opinion
The consequences of Vietnam are likely to continue shaping American foreign policy despite recent events in Iran and Afghanistan	27	56	14	3	1
The foundations of the American economy were seriously damaged by our involvement in Vietnam	34	34	19	11	3
The Vietnam episode has raised profound doubts about American credibility in the minds of our allies	35	44	16	4	2
Communist nations have been encouraged to seek triumphs elsewhere as a result of Vietnam	28	40	20	8	4
The major assumptions of détente have been proven false by the war in Vietnam	12	23	36	19	10
The American people have lost faith in the honesty of their government as a result of the Vietnam War	19	51	21	9	1
The memory of Vietnam will prevent the U.S. from using force even when vital American interests abroad are threatened	8	36	32	23	1
The shape of the international system we have known since World War II has been irrevocably altered by America's inability to prevent the collapse of the Thieu regime in 1975	8	30	29	24	9
The tide of influence in world affairs has swung toward communism as a result of the Vietnam War	6	28	35	26	4
The U.S. is likely to operate with a more limited conception of the national interest as a result of the outcome in Vietnam	20	61	11	4	4
The real long term threats to national security — energy shortages, the environment, etc. — have been neglected as a result of our preoccupation with Vietnam	26	39	21	12	2
The lessons of Vietnam have been superseded by events since the U.S. withdrawal from Southeast Asia in 1975	11	43	27	12	7

Other consequences of Vietnam? _____

● Observers of American foreign policy have identified several factors that may have prevented the United States from achieving its goals in the Vietnam undertaking. In your judgment, how important were the reasons listed below in America's inability to achieve all of its goals? Please indicate your assessment by checking **only one** box in **each** row.

	Very Important	Moderately Important	Slightly Important	Not at all Important	Not Sure
Pressures from domestic dissidents cast doubt on American commitments	36	35	20	7	2
America's goals in Vietnam were inherently unrealistic	47	28	14	8	4
The regime in Saigon lacked popular support	46	31	14	5	5
Reporting by the mass media turned the public against the war	36	35	21	6	2
Congressional involvement hampered the executive in the conduct of the war	13	25	30	26	6
The Soviets and Chinese provided aid to Northern Vietnam and the Vietcong	50	30	14	4	2
The Watergate scandal paralyzed the American government	21	24	22	31	1
The United States fought with a "no win" approach	48	19	14	16	4
The U.S. lacked understanding of nationalism in the "Third World"	41	30	17	9	4
The use of American air power was restricted	32	22	19	22	5
Intelligence agencies failed to provide adequate information about the situation in Vietnam	27	32	19	12	10
The U.S. had no clear goals in the Vietnam undertaking	48	26	13	9	4
Insufficent attention was paid to advice from the military	23	19	18	29	11
America's allies failed to support us	14	22	30	30	4
U.S. military assistance to South Vietnam after the 1973 peace agreement was inadequate	14	20	22	32	13
North Vietnam violated the 1973 peace agreement	27	22	18	20	13
Much of world opinion opposed the U.S. goals and policies	23	35	25	12	5
Americans underestimated the dedication of the North Vietnamese	56	28	9	4	2
America relied excessively on air power	15	26	23	23	12
The American case was unjust	18	14	16	41	11
Americans were ignorant of Vietnamese history, culture, and society	36	28	21	12	3

(Other factors?) _____

● This question asks you to indicate your position on certain foreign policy issues that are sometimes described as the "lessons" that we should learn from recent events in Iran. Indicate how strongly you agree or disagree with each statement by checking **only one** box in **each** row.

	Agree Strongly	Agree Somewhat	Disagree Somewhat	Disagree Strongly	Not Sure
The United States should have used its power to prevent the overthrow of the Shah's regime	16	19	18	43	4
The United States should not have permitted the Shah to enter a hospital in New York in 1979	33	16	15	35	2
Recent events in Iran are a direct consequence of a decline of U.S. influence in the aftermath of the Vietnam War	18	31	21	26	4
The U.S. should not become closely aligned with authoritarian regimes	21	32	28	15	3
The Soviet Union was probably involved in instigating the takeover of the American Embassy in Teheran	12	23	19	28	18
The U.S. should have returned the Shah to Iran in exchange for the release of the hostages	3	3	8	85	2
The U.S. should create a mobile strike force to operate in the Third World	40	28	10	15	6
The U.S. should take all necessary steps, including gasoline rationing, to reduce dependence on oil from the Middle East	68	20	6	4	1
The U.S. should have undertaken an air strike to destroy Iranian oil fields in response to the take-over of the U.S. Embassy in Teheran	5	9	14	67	5
The U.S. should take all necessary steps to prevent Iran from falling within the Soviet sphere of influence	45	35	10	6	4
In considering responses to the hostage situation, the U.S. should have been guided primarily by efforts to deter future attacks on U.S. diplomats	30	37	15	10	8
Iran has brought an end to the "Vietnam syndrome" in which Americans were reluctant to use force abroad	9	42	26	15	8
The hostage episode reveals the futility of economic sanctions	14	34	31	14	7
The U.S. should take whatever steps are necessary to sustain the present regime in Saudi Arabia	29	34	16	10	11
The hostage episode demonstrates that patience in foreign policy decision-making is a virtue	19	33	20	19	9
In the light of the Afghanistan invasion, the U.S. should seek an accommodation with Iran	9	38	23	20	10

● Here are some questions on current issues in American foreign relations. For each question, please check the statement that most closely expresses your own views. *(Check **only one** box for **each** item)*

If it can be resumed, the SALT process would:

13 make an important contribution toward a safer world
55 be a useful but very limited step in the right direction
15 be of little significance
15 seriously jeopardize U.S. national security
3   not sure

The United States defense budget should be:

18 increased, and taxes should be increased to pay for it
40 increased, and domestic programs should be reduced to pay for it
21 maintained at about the present level
14 reduced, and spending on domestic programs should be increased
5   reduced, and taxes should also be reduced
3   not sure

The United States government should:

54 actively promote human rights throughout the world
3   concern itself primarily with human rights in communist nations
7   concern itself primarily with human rights in nations that are allied to the U.S.
29 avoid concerning itself with human rights, except for those in the U.S.
7   not sure

The policy of détente as pursued by recent U.S. administrations has:

4   resulted in a significant improvement in Soviet-American relations
44 resulted in limited improvements in Soviet-American relations
20 had little effect, one way or the other
14 contributed to a decline of American influence in the world
15 placed U.S. security in dangerous jeopardy
3   not sure

American policy in the Middle East should place *primary* emphasis on:

10 securing the friendship of the oil exporting nations of the area
7   maintaining the security of Israel
51 maintaining an effective balance of power in the region
6   obtaining a national homeland for the Palestinians
21 preventing the expansion of Soviet influence in the region
5   not sure

● Turning to more general considerations, here is a list of possible foreign policy goals that the United States might have. Please indicate how much importance you think should be attached to each goal. *(Check only one box in each row)*

	Very Important	Somewhat Important	Not Important at All	Not Sure
Containing communism	41	46	11	2
Helping to improve the standard of living in less developed countries	44	49	7	1
Keeping peace in the world	76	21	3	1
Worldwide arms control	55	36	8	2
Keeping up the value of the dollar	63	34	2	1
Defending our allies' security	44	52	3	1
Promoting and defending our own security	90	9	1	0
Promoting the development of capitalism abroad	10	41	46	4
Securing adequate supplies of energy	78	21	1	0
Helping to bring a democratic form of government to other nations	10	54	33	3
Worldwide population control	45	39	13	3
Protecting the interests of American business abroad	19	60	19	2
Protecting the jobs of American workers	30	55	13	2
Protecting weaker nations against foreign aggression	23	65	8	3
Maintaining a balance of power among nations	55	38	5	2
Promoting and defending human rights in other countries	27	47	23	4
Combatting world hunger	51	43	5	1
Strengthening the United Nations	32	40	26	2
Protecting the global environment	47	42	9	2
Strengthening countries who are friendly toward us	37	57	4	2
Fostering international cooperation to solve common problems, such as food, inflation and energy	73	26	1	1

● Now, please indicate how you would rate the job that the United States is now doing with respect to these goals.
*(Check **only one** box in **each** row)*

	Excellent	Pretty Good	Fair	Poor	Not Sure
Containing communism	1	15	37	44	4
Helping to improve the standard of living in less developed countries	1	17	50	30	3
Worldwide arms control	0	6	34	58	2
Keeping up the value of the dollar	0	5	26	68	1
Defending our allies security	3	34	46	16	2
Promoting and defending our own security	6	39	35	20	1
Securing adequate supplies of energy	1	13	36	50	1
Protecting the interests of American business abroad	5	29	43	19	5
Protecting the jobs of American workers	2	25	47	23	3
Maintaining a balance of power among nations	1	23	51	22	3
Promoting and defending human rights in other countries	2	19	47	28	4
Fostering international cooperation to solve common problems, such as food, inflation and energy	2	16	47	33	2

● Somewhat more specifically, please indicate how strongly you agree or disagree with each of the following statements concerning America's role in the world.

*(Check **only one** box in **each** row)*

	Agree Strongly	Agree Somewhat	Disagree Somewhat	Disagree Strongly	No Opinion
The U.S. has a moral obligation to prevent the destruction of the state of Israel	40	35	13	10	2
There is nothing wrong with using the C.I.A. to try to undermine hostile governments.	28	28	20	23	1
We shouldn't think so much in international terms but concentrate more on our own national problems.	10	27	32	31	1
The U.S. should give economic aid to poorer countries even if it means higher prices at home.	10	43	30	16	2
It is not in our interest to have better relations with the Soviet Union because we are getting less than we are giving to them	8	18	38	34	2
The U.S. should take all steps including the use of force to prevent the spread of Communism	10	26	32	30	2
Even though it probably means higher food prices here at home, it is worth selling grain to the Soviet Union since it may improve our relations with Russia.	3	19	35	39	4

● **Finally, we have a few questions for background information.**

Male 88   Female 12   Year of Birth _____

● What is the highest level of education that you have completed?

Some High School	High School Graduate	Some College	College Graduate	Some Graduate Work	Graduate Degree	Type of Graduate Degree
0	2	6	12	14	67	_____

● What is your primary occupation?   *(Check **only** one)*

Business executive	18	Military officer	7	Communications	10
Labor official	4	Foreign Service	6	Lawyer	6
Educator	25	Public official (other than Foreign Service)	6	Health Care	5
Clergy	6			Other (specify):	6

● Check which of the following you have visited, other than as a casual tourist.

Latin America	Africa	Eastern Europe and/or Russia	Western Europe	Middle East	Far East	Iran	Vietnam	Afghanistan
41	26	28	85	34	50	12	16	3

● Have you ever served in the armed forces?

Yes 62   No 38

If yes, during:	World War II	Korean War	Vietnam War	Peacetime
More than one 13 period:	30	7	4	8

● Which of the following, if any, were your main sources of information about foreign affairs?

(Check as many boxes as are applicable)

46	Time	45	New York Times	45	ABC News
37	Newsweek	33	Washington Post	64	CBS News
27	U.S. News & World Report	42	Wall Street Journal	49	NBC News
67	Your local newspaper	6	Los Angeles Times	33	Other? _____

● How would you describe your views in political matters?

1 Far left	27 Moderate	0 Far right
6 Very liberal	32 Somewhat conservative	2 Other
25 Somewhat liberal	7 Very conservative	1 Not sure

● Generally speaking, do you think of yourself as a *Republican*, a *Democrat*, an *Independent*, or what?

30 Republican
38 Democrat
31 Independent
1 No preference
1 Other

(If Republican or Democrat) Would you call yourself a strong (Republican Democrat) or a not very strong (Republican Democrat)?

21 Strong Republican
23 Not very strong Republican
30 Not very strong Democrat
25 Strong Democrat
1 Not sure

(If Independent, no preference, or other) Do you think of yourself as closer to the Republican or to the Democratic party?

40 Republican
23 Neither
38 Democratic

● A number of foreign policy issues have resulted in a good deal of public debate. Please indicate whether you have engaged in the following activities in connection with each issue.

(Check each box for which the answer is "yes")

	SALT II Treaty	Iranian hostages	Panama Canal Treaty	Resettlement of "boat people"	Restrictions on imports	Energy proposals	The Vietnam War
Contacted a Congressman or Senator	18	10	18	5	8	26	25
Contacted a state or local official	2	2	2	3	3	15	6
Made a speech at a public meeting	8	6	5	4	4	14	16
Appeared on a radio or television program	3	3	2	1	2	6	7
Contributed an article to a newspaper or magazine	7	6	6	4	5	11	12
Consulted with an agency of the Executive Branch	11	8	7	4	7	15	11

Notes to Appendix B

1 There are a number of drawbacks to the use of mailed questionnaires. There is validity in the observation that elite interviews may provide more revealing information about attitudes and beliefs than questionnaires. This point is particularly relevant when the population of interest can be clearly defined, when it is quite limited in number, and when it is geographically concentrated rather than dispersed. These conditions would prevail, for example, in a study of members of a legislature or a foreign office. However, the present goal was to gain access to the occupants of a broad range of top leadership roles, and for this purpose interviews seemed out of the question. Given limited research resources, the trade-off is between a small number of interviews and much broader coverage by means of a mailed questionnaire.

2 John E. Rielly (ed.), *American Public Opinion and U.S. Foreign Policy 1975* (Chicago: Chicago Council on Foreign Relations, 1975); Rielly (ed.), *American Public Opinion and U.S. Foreign Policy, 1979* (Chicago: Chicago Council on Foreign Relations, 1979); Barry Sussman, *Elites in America* (Washington, DC: The Washington Post, 1976); Bruce M. Russett and Elizabeth Hanson, *Interest and Ideology* (San Francisco: W. H. Freeman, 1975); Allen H. Barton, "Consensus and conflict among American Leaders," *Public Opinion Quarterly*, 38 (Winter 1974–1975), pp. 507–530.

Index